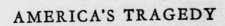

# AMERICA'S TRAGEDY

# America's Tragedy

By

## JAMES TRUSLOW ADAMS

Author of "The Epic of America,"
"The March of Democracy," etc.

CHARLES SCRIBNER'S SONS

NEW YORK          LONDON

1934

# PREFACE

THE story of the rise of the United States of America from a mere handful of settlers to a World Power is one of the great stories of history. For us it naturally has a peculiar interest but it is in itself peculiar. When the first pioneers ventured overseas to Virginia and next to Massachusetts, Europe was already old and made up of many nations of comparatively small geographic extent. The other new World Power, Japan, had a history of about twenty-five hundred years and a teeming population before she emerged from her obscurity. America alone of the great modern States started from nothing a little over three centuries ago, and had to people and subdue an entire continental expanse.

In this process two influences have been of prime importance,—that of the frontier and that of sectionalism. The present volume is chiefly a study of the latter. It is not a book about the negro or slavery, nor is it another "Civil War book." The author has attempted to trace from the beginning the rise of that unhappy sectionalism between North and South which incidentally involved us in the greatest war we have ever fought,—the first of modern wars,—and which it would be folly to say has yet disappeared.

Sectionalism, whether that of the North and the South, that of the East and the West, or others, is still a living force moulding our destiny. For that reason any work dealing with the history of sectional conflicts, social, psychological, military or economic, is likely to arouse in some readers emotions of controversy. A word may therefore be permitted as to the background of the author of this vol-

v

# PREFACE

ume. He is of both the North and the South, his father's family having been Virginian and his mother's from New York. His own memory begins in France. He has lived in several States and travelled on business through forty-five of our forty-eight, North and South. His relations fought in both the Union and the Confederate armies and navies. Residence in foreign countries is likely to bring out the inherent "Americanism" of the sojourner, and several such periods at intervals, added to his other experiences, have led him to feel himself neither a Northerner nor a Southerner but only an American. Unconscious, at least, of any bias, he has tried to tell the story sympathetically but impartially.

For various assistance his thanks are due, among others, to Dr. Will D. Howe of Messrs. Charles Scribner's Sons; to the staff of the Library of Congress, as always; and especially to Mr. Allen R. Boyd of that institution, who has kindly read the text and saved him from many errors.

J. T. A.

WASHINGTON, D. C.,
*April* 8, 1934.

# CONTENTS

AMERICA'S TRAGEDY

# Chapter I

## THE ROPE OF SAND

ON April 26, 1607, at four o'clock in the morning, anxious watchers on three small vessels which had left England on the 20th of the previous December descried the longed-for land of Virginia and soon found themselves sailing over the broad waters of Chesapeake Bay. A fortnight and more was spent in exploration before the unfortunate site of what was to become Jamestown was chosen for settlement. For nearly twoscore years the founders and their successors of this far-flung outpost of the English race in the New World were to suffer as happily no others were to be called upon to do. The loss of the fifty out of a hundred who later landed at Plymouth pales into insignificance against the more than four thousand out of fifty-six hundred or so who gave up their lives for the founding of Virginia between the first landing and 1625. Noxious insects, fever and other diseases, famine and the Indian, all—nature and savage man alike—seemed determined to keep this virgin land inviolate from the invader, as they had thus far succeeded in doing. But this time the battle was won, and the English race, as the Spanish had long been, was at last securely planted across the sea. Of all the noted vessels in our history the three of 1607, the *Constant,* the *Goodspeed,* and the *Discovery,* strangely symbolic in name, best deserve to be remembered, for they bore the first seed of the mighty harvest of a nation. Although not the oldest settlement within our borders, for St. Augustine had been settled in 1565, that at Jamestown was the earliest of the English, and it was the English who were to mould our destiny.

A dozen sickly, struggling years had gone by when three important events occurred. The end of April, 1619, a new governor arrived from England with instructions to set up representative government. Thus another seed, that of the power of the electorate, had been planted. A few weeks later, others were sown. "About the last of August," wrote John Rolfe, who married Pocahontas, "came in a Dutch man of warre that sold us twenty Negars." There had already been for a short time another "Negar," a colored woman named Angela, in the colony, but with the sinister arrival of the unnamed Dutch vessel we pick up the first end of the black thread which has run through our destiny. The following year, in December, the *Mayflower,* an English vessel bound for Virginia, landed her passengers instead on the bleak shore of Cape Cod Bay at Plymouth, and we pick up another thread in our story—the Puritanism of New England. Self-government, slavery, religious and social reform and fanaticism, a race-old system of labor, stirrings of new social ideas, all merely seeds in the ground, in 1620.

*　　*　　*

By 1700 the coast had been more or less sparsely settled by the English from Canada to Florida. Massachusetts, New Hampshire, Rhode Island, Connecticut, New York, the two Jerseys, Pennsylvania, Maryland, Virginia, and the Carolinas formed a string of English communities. The scenery varied greatly, although Northern poets who contrasted the lands of the palm and the pine were botanically and nationally ignorant. North Carolina had more pines than the Northern Colonies, but the coast did change as one went south from the rocky shore of Maine, with its balsams and pointed firs with comparatively few meadows and flowering shrubs, to the South where one encountered wide sandy beaches, and live oaks and cypresses, magnolias and roses, backed by limitless pine forests. Much of

2

the vegetation, in the far South, was also softened by the hanging gray moss which wove all things together in a half-melancholy, half-romantic background. In early days one difference which now exists was not noticeable, and the streams and rivers of the South were as pure and clear as those of the North. It was only as forests were cleared and the formerly tightly held soil came to be at the mercy of rains and freshets that the Southern waters became as they are today.

Nevertheless, in all the colonies the similarities were much greater than the differences; and the friendliness, against the outside world, much greater than the inevitable inter-colonial jealousies.

Considering the similarities first, we may note that, in spite of bodies of foreigners, such as the Dutch in New York and the Swedes in the lower counties of Pennsylvania, afterward to become Delaware, the population was not only preponderantly English but drawn from much the same social strata of the old country in most of the colonies. There was nothing, in the English sense, of an aristocracy anywhere. Probably there were more in the South who would have ranked with the "gentry" in England than in the North, and also more from the bottom of the English social and economic scales. For the most part, however, the population everywhere was a hard-working one, chiefly agricultural and owning or operating small farms, whether thus called in the North or dubbed "plantations" in the South. There were occasional large holdings in all the colonies, much the largest being in New York, where venal governors made grants ranging from 100,000 to, in one case, 2,000,000 acres to individuals or groups. Even the "baronies" of South Carolina, of 12,000 acres each, seem modest in comparison with that. In New England also, and notably in Connecticut where there was no Royal Governor and the godly were supposed to rule, there were scandalous land grants, one of which amounted to 100,000 acres.

At first the labor supply in all the colonies was much the same. As it was comparatively easy for an energetic man, out of debt, to acquire a freehold for himself, the colonial domestic supply of labor was small. The main reliance everywhere, therefore, was upon the indentured white "servant," who sold his services for a term of years to pay for his passage to the New World, or upon the slave, captured in Africa and sold for life in America. It has been frequently, though quite erroneously, asserted that the Body of Liberties passed in Massachusetts prohibited slavery. Slavery was quite as legal in that colony as in any other, and there were probably at least a thousand slaves there at about the end of the seventeenth century. In none of the colonies were they numerous until the eighteenth, and public opinion in all was about the same with respect to the institution. There were occasional protests against it, North and South, such as that of the Mennonites in Pennsylvania (1688), Keith's (1693), Sewall's much less vigorous one in Boston (1701), and Byrd's in Virginia (1736), but slavery was then part of the accepted civilization of the time, and such protests had no effect. Even the New England Puritan clergy were quite as anxious to own slaves as any one else, and the first law for the rendition of fugitive slaves was made in New England for the benefit of the Puritans in 1646.

At this period, there was little difference in the scale of living North and South. If New England was a land mostly of small yeoman farmers tilling their own farms with the help of an occasional servant or slave, so also was Virginia. The researches of such scholarly historians of their own State as Bruce and Wertenbaker have dispelled the fabled picture of seventeenth-century Virginia. It was at that time not a country of large estates and gay cavaliers but one peo-

4

pled almost wholly by sturdy small farmers. In 1700, slaves and servants combined averaged only a little over one to each land-owner, and probably two-thirds of the Virginians tilled their lands with no help except that of their own family. There were some rich men who knew how to make their way in the world in all the colonies, which, however, were in the main almost uniformly populated by small people, socially and economically, whose outlook on life was in many ways similar. As far as morals and legislation go the Blue Laws of Connecticut could be duplicated in Virginia, and one has only to study early New England court records with their interminable roll of slander, fornication, drunkenness, and so on to realize that even in that section laws represented ideals of social *mores* rather than the practice of them.

The same was largely true of education. The New England system was excellent in theory and laid the foundation for our modern one, but was frequently honored in the breach, and in 1700, taking all classes into consideration, I doubt if there was much to choose between the several colonies. At that time there were more public libraries in the South than in the North, and there seems to have been little difference in the private ones, collections such as the 3000 volumes of the Mathers in Boston, or, slightly later, of the 4000 volumes of Colonel Byrd in Virginia, being quite exceptional anywhere.

Nevertheless, in spite of this more or less similar background in the several colonies there were also marked differences to be noted. There was, first, the subtle and pervasive influence of climate. This factor has been greatly over-emphasized by many writers but because much nonsense has been talked about it there is no reason for wholly discarding its importance in cultural development and even mental outlook. The Southern climate is not tropical and exerts none of the extreme effects which a genuinely tropical one does on the so-called Nordic races. White men and women can do hard work in almost every part of our South. However, the climate has its effect. As Ellsworth Huntington has pointed out, most people like being warm rather than cold; and when they are too warm the easiest way to be comfortable is to do as little work as possible, whereas when they suffer from cold the way to get comfortable is to be energetically active. The reader has only to expand the inferences from that simple and sane observation to develop the differences in ways of living and thought that climate produces. It is not merely that a mild climate makes one less furiously energetic but that the greater ease of living also tempers one's philosophy. In warm sunshine one is more inclined to leave the universe to God, who made it, than to experience an irresistible urge to make it over and assume responsibility for it.

Allied to climate were various other geographic factors, such as soil and topography. All of these favored in the South the development of a staple crop agriculture, such as tobacco and later cotton, with a plantation economy as contrasted with the type of farming in the North, where the constant need was felt for developing other money-making enterprises, such as fishing, shipping, merchandising.

But apart from these various factors, the influence of which was to be notable in time, there were also others. If we look at the map of the colonies in 1700 we see them stretched along in a narrow line between the sea and the Appalachian Mountains, a strip much like Chili today. In the centre lies the pivotal colony of Virginia, most important of all, and throughout the colonial period to remain greatest in wealth, area, population, and influence, mother of States and Presidents to come in the early national period. At either end of the strip lie the two colonies of Massachusetts and South Carolina, the two protagonists in our tragedy. Later these two were to be the most separatist and least national of all the States, the most insistent always

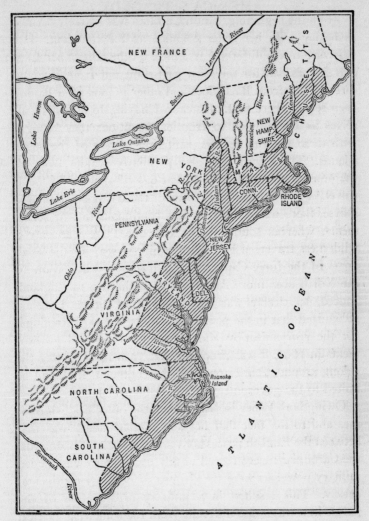

THE COLONIES ABOUT 1700

upon having their own way, leaders in fanning the flames of hatred, each certain of its own God-given mission and rightness. Even as early as 1700 the contrast between them deserves notice.

7

From the beginning, South Carolina was scarcely deemed to belong with her sister colonies on the continent. Her very origin was different, as, unlike all the others, her English settlers had for the most part come not from England directly, but from Barbadoes and other islands after having been settled there first. Instead of having to adjust themselves as Englishmen to frontier conditions they brought with them the full-fledged plantation system of the sugar islands. The colony was also peculiarly remote from all the other continental ones in that day of slow and difficult travel. From Virginia northward, though population was sparse, there was a more or less continuous line of settlements, whereas southward to Carolina there was only a wilderness traversed by Indian trail. At sea, for the small boats of the time, Cape Hatteras made the water route to the North even more dangerous than the trip to England. Indeed, so clearly was the isolation of South Carolina recognized that in the plan drawn up by Edward Randolph for the reorganization and grouping of colonial governments in 1694, it was proposed that, instead of linking the colony around Charleston with the continent, it should be united to the government of the Bahama Islands.

Owing both to her isolation from the other English colonies and to the fact that her southern boundary was that between the English possessions and the dreaded Spaniards, the Carolinians were forced to rely upon their own unaided military power as were the citizens of no other continental colony. This resulted in a military organization of the people in a way quite different from the somewhat farcical militia of the other colonies. The captains and colonels in this system were not mere holiday soldiers but continuously, during their terms of office, responsible for the maintenance of order in their appointed districts. Moreover, unlike the North, with its towns and counties, or the rest of the South with its plantations and parishes, South Carolina expanded from the one centre of Charleston, which gave a cast to Carolina society different from that elsewhere. Proud, cultured, in close touch with old England, isolated from her sister colonies, having to trust to herself for defence, South Carolina was thus from the start peculiarly aware of her own semi-independence and loyal to her own ways of life.

At the other extreme end of the line lay Massachusetts, then including Maine, almost equally aloof from the rest of the continent, except her smaller New England neighbors, but for psychological and not physical reasons.

The leaders in her settlement, who had kept firm control of the life of the colony, had been particularly strong English religious dissenters. Mostly of middle-class origin, perfectly convinced as religious enthusiasts that they, and they alone, knew the truth, and with no royal governor to act as balance wheel, they and their successors had for most of the century given free rein to fanatical and tyrannical tendencies. Not an argument can be used in favor of their course which is not equally valid to defend that of the Inquisition or any other tyranny, civil or religious, over men's minds and conduct. Her neighbors, Rhode Island, New Hampshire, and Connecticut, had each been founded by those for whom the oligarchy of the Bay Colony had proved unendurable.

In all the colonies there was strong local feeling. The citizen of one or another of them considered himself primarily as a New Yorker, a Virginian, or a Carolinian. In families, pride of wealth, of power, or of ancestry gradually developed. But these prides—politically separatist, or personally worthy, or snobbish—were innocuous as compared with the pride of considering one's self the elect of God and the sole judge of truth. It was this pride which grew up among the clergy and other leaders in seventeenth and eighteenth century Massachusetts. "God hath sifted a whole nation," wrote Stoughton, to found the colony. "We are as

a city set upon a hill," wrote Bulkeley. Leaders, lay and
clerical, like Winthrop and Cotton, disbelieved in and de-
tested democracy, "the meanest and worst of all forms of
government." A man who prides himself on being richer or
better born than his neighbors may become a bore, but a
man who believes that he is in sole possession of truth and
is a scourge of God, morally superior to those who may
differ from him, is not a bore but a flaming danger to all
about him. We must not interpret the events of earlier
periods by the intellectual standards of our own day, but
the moral or immoral isolation of Massachusetts from her
sister colonies is shown in the contrasted records. She stood
alone in her succession of banishments, such as those of
Mrs. Hutchinson and Roger Williams, in her persecution
of the Baptists and her bloody whippings in 1651, in her
judicial murdering of Quakers in 1659, in her wholesale
slaughter of witches in 1692, when nineteen were hanged,
one pressed to death, and a hundred and fifty imprisoned.
The reputation and character of the colony were such that
after 1640, when Cromwell and the Puritans came into
power in England, all immigration from the old country
practically ceased. Drawing a circle of assumed moral
superiority around herself, receiving no infusion of fresh
blood, educating her sons in what was then scarcely the
grammar school of Harvard instead of sending them
abroad, the mental horizon of the colony steadily contracted,
and the year 1700 marked perhaps the nadir of her intellectual life. For generations, however, before and after,
her people were to have driven into them the belief that
they formed a race apart, the chosen of God, the moral
censors of their neighbors.

Thus even at this early period which we have reached we
find the peculiar characteristics of the two colonies which
later as States were to play leading rôles in our tragedy,
South Carolina socially proud in her isolation and self-

sufficiency, Massachusetts self-wrapped in the assumed mantle of God's elect.

*     *     *

We need not dwell upon the minor separatism of the other colonies. I have told the oft-repeated story elsewhere, a story that has to be told of all colonies—Australia or anywhere—which begin as distinct entities and gradually grow together and to the need of union. The insuperable jealousies were clearly demonstrated in the French and Indian War in the mid-century, and led directly to the fatal efforts of the British Ministry to organize the continent better in matters of joint defence and taxation.

The Revolution, which resulted from these inept measures, did much to bring the separatist colonies together, as any outside pressure inevitably does. Strangely enough, the first note of union and nationality had been sounded, though not characteristically so, in South Carolina at the end of 1765 when Christopher Gadsden wrote privately to the agent of the colony in London that "there ought to be no New England men, no New Yorker, &c., known on the continent, but all of us Americans." It was a note that we find echoed publicly from the South, and not the North, at the first session of the Continental Congress in 1774, when Patrick Henry of Virginia thundered, "where are your landmarks, your boundaries of colonies? . . . I am not a Virginian, but an American." It was another Virginian who, without words but solely by force of character and example, held the discordant colonies together and made a nation—George Washington, Southern planter and slave-owner, great gentleman and incomparable patriot.

By that time, however, there had come to be another bond of union between the colonies, the frontier of the back country. We speak glibly of geographical sections as though each was uniform throughout its own extent, such as the South, North, and West. In reality there is no such unity. Even in so small an area as Connecticut, for example, there was a vast difference between the rich river meadows and the poor-soiled hill tops; and the hard-scrabble farmers on the latter differed both in culture and political views from the "Lords of the Valley." In all the colonies the richer and more successful had pre-empted the lands as far as they could along the seaboard and in the lowlands. The poorer classes of later generations and newcomers—not only English but Scotch-Irish, Germans, Swiss, and others—had gone into the uplands, notably in the great Shenandoah Valley of Virginia. This pioneer fringe ran along the back of almost all the colonies and formed a single area of united and similar public opinion. It is notable that Patrick Henry, who first gave voice in public to the belief in an American nationality, was a son of the back country and the pioneer belt.

But if, by the time of the Revolution, this connecting wire on which the thirteen jealous colonies were hung had come into being, in other respects the contrast between the North and South had become much greater than when we glanced at the colonies in 1700. There had been time for life to form itself into patterns, moulded by conditions, and these patterns were already diverging widely in the two sections.

Northern industrialism had not come into existence, with its beguiling dream of unlimited goods for all and its reality of fortunes for the few. Industry was everywhere as yet almost wholly confined to the household or practised on a small scale. The growing cleavage between North and South was rather that between the commercial and agrarian ways of life. In both sections the population was still, as it was long to remain, overwhelmingly agricultural, probably at least 90 per cent of all people being farmers. But in all human societies, from the most primitive to the most complex—not excluding even fraternally Communistic Russia—individuals or groups arise and by superior ability,

adroitness, opportunity, or what-not, obtain a dominant
position. To a great extent they will not only control the
sources of power in their communities but impress upon
others their own ideals, outlook, and type of ambition. We
shall discuss the contrasting forms of civilization in the
North and South more at length later when we come to the
crucial period in the nineteenth century, and need here merely note the differentiation which was already developing between them.

Wealth had greatly increased, and also concentrated, in
all the colonies since 1700, but the methods by which it was
gained and the life led by those who possessed it were very
different. Conditions in the North—soil, climate, markets—
were all against large scale agriculture, and the fortunes
which were being made there were chiefly from what we
may generically term "business." What was later to be the
"Empire State" was then comparatively unimportant and
had a population smaller than that of Connecticut. Although
the title deed to some miles along the Hudson might give
a certain distinction, money came from trade and not from
land. Northern riches, and with them social prestige and
political power, tended to concentrate in the seaboard
towns—New York, Bristol, Newport, Boston, Portsmouth.
War-trading and privateering had given a fillip to shipping
in the mid-century, and men like the Bostonian Charles
Apthorp could pass from their counting houses to the grave
leaving £50,000 or more. Land in the North was mainly
for the poor man to scratch a living from; or for the enter-
prising to speculate in, securing grants and sub-dividing and
selling; or, as in the case of Governor Wentworth of New
Hampshire, to plunder of its standing timber in a few
years. It has been said that his magnificent mansion contained fifty-two rooms, the badge of wealth gained by cash-
ing in, by sale or timbering, on 100,000 acres. The colonial
Northerner who wished to rise socially or economically

above the rank of a yeoman farmer had to become a clergy-man or to sharpen his wits to make money in all sorts of trading enterprises. The early theory of the relation of church to state in New England had made the form of set-tlement there one of compact towns. New York had little but its magnificent port and its wild hinterland of fur-trading. The conditions of the times tended to emphasize the town trend, and the North was already well on its way to become business and urban, as urban was then under-stood in a day when Philadelphia, the largest city on the continent, had about 29,000 inhabitants, followed by New York with 22,000 and Boston with 16,000.[1]

When we turn to the South on the eve of the Revolution we find a very different picture. Outside of what we may call the "city-state" of South Carolina, where approximate-ly 11,000 people formed a somewhat floating population in Charleston itself, there was not a town worthy of the name in the whole South. Although the population of Virginia was 450,000 as contrasted with 265,000 in Massachusetts, 160,000 in New York, and 250,000 in Pennsylvania, it could boast only of the attractive but comparatively hamlet-like urban centre of Williamsburg. Life in the South had already become dominated and shaped by the land. The staple crops raised—tobacco, rice, and indigo—fitted into the theory of empire which demanded that colonies should produce raw materials not to be procured in England and in exchange buy the manufactured products of the home country. Even when, as especially in the case of tobacco, the crop was soil-exhausting, its assured market and its general fitness to the scheme of things made its cultivation the line of least resistance. The innumerable bays, inlets, and streams made possible in the days of small vessels, the shipping of crops direct from the larger seaboard river plantations and the receipt of goods from England. The

[1] Approximate figures for 1771.

fortunate who rose to the top thus developed large and almost self-sustaining estates, and the "short circuit," as we might call it, of the direct plantation–London connection eliminated the necessity for towns as centres of trade and exchange.

Moreover it largely eliminated the need for the local merchant. When goods ordered from England or the North were delivered to the larger plantation owners at their own docks without the intervention of a middleman, a merchant class was prevented from arising on any considerable scale because those who in other communities would be its best customers had no need of its services. "Business" could not take on economic or social importance when limited to dealings with the poorest part of the white population or sometimes clandestinely with slaves. Only in South Carolina, unique in so many ways, did Charleston afford careers for other than planters.

As contrasted with a New York or Boston merchant in his counting house or a scheming Benning Wentworth in his mansion (which eclipsed any dwelling in the South), we may take "King" Carter as the typical grandee of this period in the staple colonies. When he died in 1732, having been fortunate in his own acquisitive instinct and that of his immediate ancestors, he left his children whole groups of plantations in a dozen or so counties, with dwellings, a hundred horses, a thousand each of swine and cattle, and seven hundred slaves. The Southern grandee was far from being stupid in business. Well before the mid-century William Byrd II had secured grants of the sites of both Richmond and Petersburg, foreseeing the future urban development, and building, as he said, "Citys in the Air." In the beginning, the fur trade, running a mill, and other "business" enterprises had helped along in the founding of the family fortunes, and the acquisition of lands and slaves, but the pattern of the socially good life soon became that of the landed gentleman who with his broad acres and family connections ruled socially and politically. We shall have more to say about this type of life and the character engendered later, and here need only note that it was well established by the time of the Revolution, when incidentally it has been stated that Southern planters were in debt to their London merchants to the amount of about £3,000,000 sterling.

The Southern planter had already begun to waste no love on the Massachusetts Puritan merchant. The feeling found expression with regard to the penchant for smuggling among the commercial colonies when William Byrd wrote in 1736 that "the Saints of New England . . . have a great dexterity at palliating a perjury so well as to leave no taste of it in the mouth, nor can any people like them slip through a penal statute."[2] The same great planter and liveliest writer of his time in the South is reported to have threatened to hang the next New Englander whom he found surreptitiously trying to sell Yankee gim-cracks to his slaves. These and a few other straws were already beginning to be tossed by the wind of dislike which a century later was to increase to devastating force.

Slavery was scarcely questioned even as yet except by an occasional individual idealist or reformer. There had been comparatively few slaves, as we have said, in any of the colonies before 1700, but in the eighteenth century the trade in "black ivory" became one of the most lucrative and important in the economic life of the whole world. Both old and New England obtained an increasing share in it, and the available supply for Americans at reasonable prices was thus greatly augmented. Owing partly to the form which economic life had taken in the North the demand there for slaves had become comparatively slight, except for house servants. The slave of our earlier period was

[2] Cited by A. M. Schlesinger, *Colonial Merchants and the American Revolution*, New York, 1918, p. 40.

very different from that of the later, a much larger proportion, of course, being savages newly imported from Africa. Such a man was of no use in commercial life and of comparatively little in the varied occupations of the small northern farm, apart from the greater difficulty of acclimatizing him there. Moreover, quarters were close in the North. The slave could not live comfortably in a somewhat draughty cabin as in the South. The rigors of the Northern winters called for huddling around the fire in a snug farmhouse, and in spite of the moral fervor in favor of the negro to be displayed later the Northerner has never understood the negro or been as kind to him as has the Southerner and has more greatly disliked close contact with him. The Northern farmer, if he could afford any assistance at all, came to prefer white "hired help."

In the South conditions were wholly different. The comparatively simple routine operations involved in the raising of the same staple crop year after year could be easily taught. The docile slave proved on the whole, or was thought to be, more efficient than the white indentured servant. The "servants" (so called merely because they had to *serve* their time out) were of all classes, including the criminal, a term which then meant little as compared with the same term today. Many were of excellent stock, either kidnapped in England or ambitious to rise and willing to give their time for a term of years in order to get passage to the New World. Not a few of the most noted families in America are descended from these ambiguously termed "servants," and two of the signers of the Declaration of Independence—George Taylor and Mathew Thornton—as well as the able Secretary of the Continental Congress, Charles Thompson, had been such "servants" themselves.

Under American conditions the labor supply was practically limited to a choice between these "servants," or redemptioners, and slaves. On the whole, the latter seemed preferable, and in the eighteenth century the numbers of them rapidly increased in the South. In that section, as in the North, there were occasional voices raised against both the safety and economy of the slave system and its morality. Indeed to Virginia belongs the honor of being the first political community to prohibit the slave trade, which she did in 1778, before any other American State and thirty years before Great Britain. But slavery as a labor system was in general unquestioningly accepted until after the Revolution. In the North, where the great Jonathan Edwards was a slave owner, a church congregation in Connecticut took up a collection of £20 towards helping its pastor to buy slaves; and in the South the distinguished Methodist leader, George Whitefield, pleaded with the trustees of Georgia in 1751 to allow the introduction of slave labor. In Massachusetts in his speech against the Writs of Assistance in 1761, James Otis made a strong plea against slavery, but John Adams, who was personally opposed to slavery, stated that he "shuddered" at Otis's doctrine and that "the best men" in Massachusetts thought the ownership of slaves "not inconsistent with their character." The claim that Massachusetts abolished slavery during the Revolution or in its Constitution and Bill of Rights of 1780 is as specious as is the claim for the Law of 1641. Strange as it may appear, it is impossible to say just when slavery was abolished in that State, but one has only to glance at the newspapers to see that it was not when it has been claimed. As samples of the advertisements after the passage of the Bill of Rights we may quote from *The Independent Chronicle* of December 28, 1780, and *The Continental Journal* of March 1, 1781:

"A Negro child, soon expected, of a good breed, may be owned by any person inclining to take it, and money with it."

"To be Sold, an extraordinary likely Negro Wench, 17 years old, she can be warranted to be strong, healthy and good-natured, has no notion of Freedom, has always been used to a Farmer's Kitchen and dairy, and is not known to have any failing, but being with Child, which is the only cause of her being sold."

In general we may say that the slave system was then accepted as part of the natural order just as the wage-system is today, or even more so. It is impossible to say accurately just how many slaves there were in the several colonies at the time of the Revolution, but in the first Federal Census taken afterward, 1790, there were over 32,000 in New York and New Jersey. It was in the South, however, that in this period of complete acquiescence the institution was most firmly and ineradicably entrenched. Maryland had 103,000, Virgina 292,000, North Carolina 101,000, and South Carolina 107,000. The assertion in the Declaration of Independence that "all men are created equal; that they are endowed by their Creator with certain inalienable rights; that among these are life, liberty, and the pursuit of happiness" made some people wonder how these statements were compatible with the presence of slaves, but, except for a brief period, they had little influence on contemporary opinion. The slave was simply out of the picture, as was the woman as voter for nearly a century and a half more. This was not true, however, of the man who penned the words. In 1779 Thomas Jefferson was on a committee to revise the laws of Virginia, and tried hard to have a system of gradual emancipation adopted. In his *Autobiography,* written over forty years later, in 1821, he commented that "it was found that the public mind would not bear the proposition, nor will it bear it even at this day. Yet the day is not far distant when it must bear it, or worse will follow. Nothing is more certainly written in the book of fate than that these people are to be free." If not emancipated in time, he added, "human nature must shudder at the prospect held."

The Revolution came, was won, passed, and the American colonies became free and independent States. Massachusetts and Virginia had led in the movement. Indeed without his persistent hatred of England and the years of preliminary work done by that ablest of agitators, Samuel Adams of Boston, there might have been no Revolution at all, as there would have been nothing more than a foiled insurrection and a series of hangings had it not been for the leadership of the Virginian Washington. Virginia, practically single-handed, had conquered the Northwest from the British, and a glance at the map will show the extraordinary size to which she had grown, even allowing for the claims, based on old sea-to-sea charters, of Massachusetts and Connecticut.

The war had been won by the former colonies acting in concert but with scarcely anything worthy the name of a central government. The Declaration of Independence had pronounced them to be "free and independent States," and as such they had co-operated through delegates to the Continental Congress, but the loose Articles of Confederation were not agreed to until the war was practically over, being signed March 1, 1781, the surrender of Cornwallis occurring October 19 of the same year. The wonder is not that Congress became so weak during the struggle as to become almost impotent but that it was able to carry on at all.

The problem of union appeared, indeed, well-nigh insoluble. The strong local pride and attachment of citizens to their particular colonies were naturally intensified by the rise in status of those colonies to independent sovereignties. An exhausting war had just been fought for the sole purpose of freeing themselves from the control and tyranny of a higher power having jurisdiction over them. To substitute for that power another superior one, though even of their own making, seemed fraught with heavy risk. The little States, such as Delaware with only 37,000 inhabitants, or Rhode Island with 52,000, feared that they might find themselves tyrannized over by the larger States such as Massachusetts with 307,000 or Virginia with 520,000.[3] States, such as Connecticut and New Jersey, chiefly dependent for their commerce on the ports of Newport, New York and Philadelphia in neighboring States, feared disastrous commercial regulation. It was expected that the sales of western lands would provide a large income to those States fortunate enough to possess them, and such States, like Maryland, as did not, feared that they might be ground down by taxation which would not be felt by the States with almost unlimited land resources, such as Virginia. These were some of the problems even if in a Confederacy every State should be given an equal voice. That, moreover, seemed unfair. It was asking too much of Virginia, with her 520,000 people and her truly imperial domain, to place herself on an equality with her little neighbor Delaware with only 37,000 people in a permanently restricted territory scarce the size of a county.

The Articles of Confederation as finally signed and adopted proved much too weak for their purpose but were nevertheless a great step forward. Maryland performed a public service by staunchly insisting upon cession to the central government as far as possible of the western lands, and early in 1780 New York, whose claims were rather insubstantial, offered to yield them. Connecticut did so also, though it was some years before she made the transfer. The turning point was the offer of Virginia to cede all her lands north and west of the Ohio, now including the States of Ohio, Indiana, Illinois, Michigan, Wisconsin and part of Minnesota.[4] It is not perhaps too much to say that the gift to the nation of this vast empire by the most powerful of the States rendered the making of the nation possible. To

[3] Approximate figures for 1780.      [4] See map on page 34.

the States mentioned we must add those of the present Virginia, West Virginia and Kentucky, as forming part of the Virginia of 1781, and recall that through ownership of both capes she controlled Chesapeake Bay and the commerce of the two ports of her own Norfolk and the Maryland Baltimore. Virginia could choose between union and an almost illimitable development as a separate power. No other State gave up so much to make a united nation. Other States also, however, relinquished to the Confederation lands and claims, and the vast western domain thus owned in common by all the States gave to the Confederacy a somewhat new complexion.

Nevertheless, the Federal Government was pitiably weak. Not only was its power almost stultified by the provision that practically every considerable decision had to receive the approval of nine of the equal votes of the thirteen States but the government was denied two important attributes, that of raising money and of regulating commerce. The "firm league of friendship" thus entered into in the "articles of Confederation and perpetual Union" so soon showed its inherent weakness and was in so few years to be replaced by our present Constitution that the original articles are seldom read. Leaving a fuller discussion of the thorny question of States' Rights to a later chapter, we may here note, however, that although it was provided in 1781 that each State should retain "its sovereignty, freedom and independence" and every power and right not conferred upon the Confederation, yet the States appear to have bound themselves to remain permanently within the Union. The term "perpetual" was several times used and the last clause of the instrument declares that the several articles of the Confederation "shall be inviolably observed by the States we [the signers] respectively represent, and that the Union shall be perpetual."

Again, although the Union was obviously intended to be

a Federal one of independent sovereignties there was no provision made, as in the League of Nations, for withdrawal. Indeed, on the contrary, Congress was declared to "be the last resort on appeal in all disputes and differences . . . concerning . . . any . . . cause whatever." Considering the jealousies subsisting between the States and the fears which all felt with regard to a central government, this absence of any provision for seceding from the Union, the insistence upon its perpetual character, and the provision for settling every sort of dispute within the Union itself, are certainly noteworthy.

The successive cessions of the western lands raised interesting questions. By these deeds from the original colonies, the central government came into possession of an area about as large as that of the States which had been wholly independent before joining the Union. It was provided that the territory owned in common should eventually be carved into new States which should have all the rights of the old. In spite of this provision, their origin would obviously be different from that of the original thirteen. It would need a deal of legal casuistry to prove that a State, erected upon soil belonging to others in common, and which owed its existence as a State to an Act of Congress, had ever been an independent sovereign entity before it became a member of the Union.

In connection with the contemplated erection of new States under the great Ordinance of 1787 we may note the emergence into our politics of a new factor,—the fear of the West as upsetting the old balance of powers in the East. Moreover, at the same time, slavery emerges into the political arena as an issue.

In the colonial period, although occasional voices might be raised in any colony, as they were, against slavery as an institution on either economic or humanitarian grounds, it was quite clear that no one colony could do anything about slavery in another. It was not only legal everywhere but the final arbiter in all legislation was England, and England was in favor of slavery on account of the slave trade. A good many laws passed in the South, with the object of diminishing or modifying the trade, had failed to receive approval by the Crown, though the old claim that these laws represented genuine desire to decrease or abolish the institution is for the most part not now accepted by Southern historians themselves. In the short time which had elapsed since the colonies had become independent States the problem had not arisen. No State dreamed of dictating to another, and in fact although Northern sentiment, especially in Massachusetts, had been becoming less favorable to slavery, it was not until some indeterminate date in the 1780's, that, as a result of successive court decisions and not any specific law, slavery may be considered as having become illegal even in the Bay State.

But with the coming into possession in common of the western lands the question arose as to the extension of slavery into the new States to be created. The experience of a hundred and fifty years had shown that, chiefly for economic reasons, slavery would never be important in the North. Outside of Massachusetts, where opposition was growing, there was no widespread dislike of the institution, though in all New England the fewness of slaves—Connecticut, the largest slave State of the section, having only about 2600 in a total population of 238,000[5]—made the slave status an anomalous one.

The problem of the political organization of the new territory had been under discussion for several years. In 1783 Thomas Jefferson drew up a plan according to which there should be no slavery in the western territory, South as well as North, after 1800, but this was not included in the Ordinance of 1784, which, however, never went into

[5] Census 1790.

effect. The provision that slavery should be excluded from what afterward became the States of Kentucky, Tennessee, Alabama, and Mississippi was lost by the vote of one State only, and Jefferson later wrote that "the voice of a single individual of the State which was divided, or one of those which were of the negative, would have prevented this abominable crime from spreading itself over the new country. Thus we see the fate of millions unborn hanging on the tongue of one man and Heaven was silent in that awful moment." When the later Ordinance of 1787 was under consideration, Rufus King and others again took up the slave clause, King claiming that, although any effort to disturb slavery where it existed until gradual emancipation could be arranged might bring worse evils than those meant to be cured, it could never be forgiven if slavery should be introduced into regions where it did not already exist. Jefferson was then in France but William Grayson and Richard Henry Lee of Virginia both worked for freedom in the Northwest, and when the clause was voted on, it was passed unanimously by the only States then present, Massachusetts, New York, New Jersey, Delaware, Virginia, both Carolinas and Georgia; South Carolina and Georgia probably consenting in the hope of obtaining slavery in the *South*west as a recompense. As finally passed the Ordinance provided that in the territory northwest of the Ohio there should be no slavery (except as punishment for crime), although fugitive slaves escaping into the district were to be returned to their lawful owners.[6]

It was Manifest Destiny that the Americans east of the Appalachians should cross into the great valley west of them, but with this destiny was intertwined that of our tragedy. Behind each of the thousands who trekked west-

---

[6] This Act of the expiring Continental Congress was confirmed in 1789 by the Congress of the United States, and in 1790 another, similar in most respects but without the anti-slavery clause, was passed for the territory *south* of the Ohio River.

ward to found States stalked a black shadow not of the sun's making. The land was not the domain of ancient and sovereign States but politically virgin soil and the property of the common citizenry of the *United* States. Given the trend of world opinion, the question, across the mountains, of slave or free could not be downed. The price of expansion would be the sowing of discord.

At first it seemed as though the West might be lost to us. The weak government of the Confederacy, hedged about as it was with every possible precaution to keep it from being strong enough to coerce a State, was unable to make itself respected. It was incapable of assuring the settlers of the Southwest against Spanish intrigues and threats of closing the Mississippi. In the Northwest the British had retained the military posts they had agreed to surrender, and John Adams found his complaints coolly disregarded as American Minister in London because the government behind him had no power. What with the British and Indians, settlement was slow north of the Ohio, and the British were in military possession. Time might prove to be on their side.

But the danger was not only in the West and in Europe. At home serious disorders arose due to hard times and the impotency of the governments, State and national. Mobs and rioting were the order of the day in many sections and by the fall of 1786 a considerable part of Massachusetts was in open and armed revolt against law and order. In all the States peace-loving citizens and men of property were alarmed, not least Washington himself, who watched the growing disorder in Massachusetts with deepest apprehension. Writing to Henry Lee of the latter's suggestion that Washington use his influence to appease the tumult in Massachusetts, he replied, "*Influence* is no *government*. Let us have one by which our lives, liberties, and property will be secured, or let us know the worst at once." The "firm league of friendship," perpetual as it had been stated to be, was becoming intolerable. It was unable to protect citizens at home or abroad. Foreign foes were intriguing to seize the West, and in the East, both in the North and South, the structure of society even in the oldest and most conservative States seemed crumbling into anarchy.

## CHAPTER II

## THE CHAIN OF IRON

DURING the month of May 1787 some of the most distinguished men from the several States began to arrive in Philadelphia. It had at last been agreed that a Convention should be held either to revise the Articles of Confederation or to draft a new constitution. Even Massachusetts, which like many other States had been opposed to such action, had consented. Shays's Rebellion had been the last straw for substantial men everywhere. Something had to be done or at least attempted. The ablest men in the country had long been revolving the almost insoluble problem of a form of union. None realized more clearly than Washington, from his experience during the Revolution, that there must be some central government which should have genuine power and not merely the ineffectual right to make recommendations. Bitter experience had taught him that pleading was no more "government" than was "influence." The brilliant young Alexander Hamilton had also been revolving in his mind how the Federal power could be strengthened, though his State was much opposed to it. Others too had been at work on the problem but above all James Madison of Virginia who was to become the "father of the Constitution" and who was the ablest thinker of the time in America on constitutional matters.

The fifty-five delegates assembled in the old red brick Independence Hall where only eleven years earlier another notable gathering had proclaimed the colonies to be free and independent, and there, behind locked doors, they struggled with their task through the heat of summer, Rhode Island alone remaining unrepresented. Madison, small, slender, unimposing in appearance, shy and readily blushing as he addressed the assembly, soon became the acknowledged leader of the debates by virtue of sheer intellectual power and knowledge. Like many Southerners of the time a graduate of Princeton, he had devoted himself since graduation to the study of the history and nature of government, and now the opportunity had come to the young man of thirty-six to mould the destinies of his country. Hamilton, six years younger, more brilliant and with a more magnetic personality, was to exert far less influence, owing in part to his hands being tied by the nature of the delegation New York had sent and in part to his insistence upon too extreme views as to the centralizing of powers in the new government. Among the others who shared in the labors and debates we may note George Mason and Edmund Randolph of Virginia, Rufus King and Elbridge Gerry of Massachusetts, John Rutledge and the two Pinckneys of South Carolina, Roger Sherman and Oliver Ellsworth of Connecticut, and Daniel Carroll and Luther Martin of Maryland, to name only some of the remarkable gathering. At times tempers as well as the weather grew hot but daily there sat at the table presiding over the meetings George Washington, always calm and just, above the disputes of the delegates by his acknowledged position, yet often influencing results and decisions by his infinite good sense and the universal respect in which he was held.

The first problem the Convention had to face was how to create a genuinely strong central government, clearly essential if the United States were (or was, depending upon how the name was interpreted) to remain a power among nations and not to disintegrate into a lot of little squabbling neighbors. The second problem was how to retain as much power in the separate States as each thought itself entitled to. It was a problem in Federal government on a scale and of a complexity never before attempted in history.

Madison had long been aware of the difficulties. "An individual independence of the States," he had written to Edmund Randolph, "is utterly irreconcilable with the idea of an aggregate sovereignty. I think, at the same time, that a consolidation of the States into one simple republic is not less unattainable than it would be inexpedient. Let it be tried, then, whether any middle ground can be taken, which will at once support a due supremacy of the national authority, and leave in force the local authorities so far as they can be subordinately useful." When the new Constitution had been agreed upon and was presented to the States for ratification, Washington, who had been throughout all of the proceedings a potent influence, expressed much the same idea in his general letter to them. "It is," he wrote, "obviously impracticable, in the Federal government of these States, to secure all rights of Independent Sovereignty to each, and yet provide for the interest and safety of all. Individuals entering into society must give up a share of liberty to preserve the rest. . . . It is at all times difficult to draw with precision the line between those rights which must be surrendered, and those which may be reserved." The differences between the States "as to their situation, extent, habits, and particular interests" made the problem, as Washington pointed out, peculiarly difficult.

One need not agree with Mr. Gladstone in his opinion that the Constitution as finally framed was "the most wonderful work ever struck off at a given time by the brain and purpose of man" to admit that it was one of the greatest steps taken in the advance of self-government. On the other hand, the very conditions of its production made it a veritable Pandora's Box of future emotional and constitutional disputes and honest differences of interpretation. In the course of the discussions in the Convention it became evident that our fundamental law would have to include a considerable number not only of compromises but even of evasions if there were to be any chance of its being accepted, the only alternative to acceptance being national disintegration and anarchy. We are here concerned with only a few of these, but the dilemma before the members was whether to leave possible disputes to later generations or admit shipwreck at once, and allow the efforts and hopes of the past to sink beneath the waves of anarchy.

The difficulty of reconciling the interests of the large and small States was got over, as far as it could be, by what is called the "great compromise," that is the provision that each State should have two representatives, and two only, in the Senate but that its number of representatives in the lower House should be based upon population. This compromise, however, at once raised the question as to whether slaves should be counted in estimating population, and caused a second compromise to be made. If slaves were "persons" like any others, then they would be entitled to the rights of persons. On the other hand, if they were not legally persons but merely "property," why should a Southerner who owned $5000 worth of slaves be entitled to a larger influence in Congress than a Northerner who owned a vessel worth $5000 or any other form of property? To save the situation, logic was thrown to the winds and it was provided that in estimating population three-fifths of the slaves should be added to the number of free whites. In other words two-fifths of a negro slave was property and three-fifths was a person for the sole purpose of determining the number of Congressmen (in the election of whom the slave could have no part). Few compromises on great political questions can ever have been more logically absurd or more practically essential.

Every effort was made to leave this delicate topic of slavery alone but it kept cropping up. For example, the discussion over general trade laws and the levying of import duties at once raised the specific question of the slave

31

trade. Ten of the States, including Maryland and Virginia, had already prohibited the further importation of slaves, but simply as States. South Carolina and Georgia believed that their economic future demanded an increase in this form of labor supply. If the new Federal Government were to be given power to control foreign trade, it might put a stop to that in slaves. At once the fat was in the fire. The Northern States, with their heavy stake in foreign trade, demanded that control over all trade should vest in the general government. The delegates from that section uttered a few protests as to the morality of slave trading, though that trade had built up the prosperity of Rhode Island, and both Connecticut and Massachusetts had been largely interested in it.

The strongest protests, however, came from the South. John Dickinson of Delaware demanded peremptorily the exclusion of any new slaves. Luther Martin of Maryland declared the trade to be "inconsistent with the principles of the Revolution, and dishonorable to the American character." Strongest of all in opposition was George Mason of Virginia, who called the traffic "infernal," and said that it would be in vain that Maryland and Virginia by law, and North Carolina in substance, should have prohibited the trade if South Carolina and Georgia were now to be allowed to carry it on. "The Western people," he said, "are already calling out for slaves for their new lands; and will fill that country with slaves if they can be got through South Carolina and Georgia. Slavery discourages arts and manufactures. The poor despise labor when performed by slaves. They prevent the emigration of whites, who really enrich and strengthen a country. They produce the most pernicious effect on manners. Every master of slaves is born a petty tyrant. They bring the judgment of Heaven on a country. As nations cannot be rewarded or punished in the next world, they must be in this. By an inevitable chain of causes and effects, Providence punishes National sins by National calamities." Few speeches have been more unhappily prophetic!

South Carolina, however, supported by Georgia and in part by North Carolina, was adamant. John Rutledge of Charleston bluntly said that religion and humanity had nothing to do with the question; it was a matter only of "interest." He, the Pinckneys and others asserted that they would never accept the Constitution if it stopped the slave trade. In history one must always keep the contemporary map in mind. At this time Georgia and the two Carolinas had not yet ceded their western claims. Their boundaries were not those of today but extended to the Mississippi River and their territory embraced well over a third of the United States, including the entire east bank of the great river from Kentucky to Spanish New Orleans at its mouth. Their population was about a fifth of the national total. For every reason it was felt necessary to keep them in the union. Besides, New England saw a chance for a profitable deal, though in the opinion of Virginia it was a compromise between money and morality. As a result of the first great log-rolling in our national annals, South Carolina agreed to let New England have its way in the granting of powers over trade to the Federal Government in exchange for a Constitutional guarantee that the slave trade should not be prohibited before 1808 and that meanwhile the duty on a slave should not be over ten dollars. South Carolina and Georgia thought that by that time they might have all the slaves they needed. New England knew it had got what *it* wanted. Like Rutledge it decided for "interest" rather than for morality, and agreed with Oliver Ellsworth of Connecticut when he said that after all "what enriches a part enriches the whole."

It was of little avail that the Virginians, Mason and Randolph, were so disgusted over the deal that they would

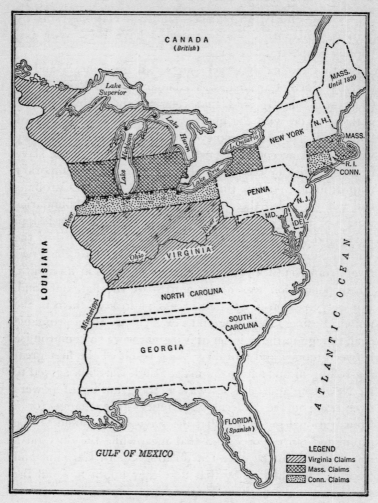

THE LAND CLAIMS OF THE THIRTEEN STATES

not sign the Constitution, though their disgust was largely
due to the complete power over commerce which had been
given to the new government. But as we turn from the
discussion in the Convention we cannot fail to hear the

steady footfalls of Fate. The effort of Jefferson to preclude slavery from all the new States had been lost by only one vote. At the time the Convention was sitting, not only had ten States already forbidden the further importation of slaves but opinion in them was steadily moving against the institution. In no Northern State were the leading men more opposed to it than in Virginia. We have already heard Mason and Randolph. Richard Henry Lee had thundered in the House of Burgesses against the slave trade. Patrick Henry, a slave-owner like others because of the difficulty under the circumstances of using other forms of labor, insisted on the evil of slavery and hoped for its extinction. Washington wrote that "there is not a man living who wishes more sincerely than I to see a plan adopted for the abolition of it." John Tyler thought "nothing could justify" the trade, and wished it "handed down to posterity that he had opposed this wicked cause." Jefferson, whose efforts to limit slavery have been noted, was its steady opponent, and speaking of it said that "I tremble for my country when I reflect that God is just," and that "I can say with conscious truth that there is not a man on earth who would sacrifice more than I would to relieve us from this reproach in any practicable way." Other leading Virginians, and men in Delaware, Maryland, and North Carolina expressed themselves in the same way.

Climate and other conditions in the North, not moral repugnance, had relieved that section of the burden. Down the coast to South Carolina leading men were now struggling with the problem of how to rid themselves of it. Many, like Washington in his will, or Robert Carter of "Nomini Hall" in his lifetime, emancipated their slaves, but the problem, legally and socially, was exceedingly difficult. Carter's neighbors, moreover, complained that his freedmen were indolent and thievish and were demoralizing the other negroes. It was hoped by all that the institution would disappear in time. Cotton, machinery, the ingenuity of the New England inventor Eli Whitney, were all in the unknown future. Slavery had become unimportant in the North. It seemed tending to extinction in Maryland, Virginia, and perhaps North Carolina. New England was purely selfish in its desire to have the Federal Government control commerce, but it would have been a great evil and source of weakness as the world developed had it been unable to do so. The far Southern States did simply what New England did in having something written into the Constitution which was for *their* interest, but it proved evil and not good. Who was to blame? No one, but Fate dogged our footsteps as we tried to rise.

Without discussing the entire Constitution at length we must note here that as finally passed and ratified it fairly bristled with vaguenesses, ambiguities, and disputable points. The proceedings of the Convention had been secret. No records were supposed to have been kept of the discussions. The words of the document were intended to stand by themselves, but words and phrases even when meant to be of the clearest are capable of different interpretations. If there were not frequent need of such interpretation for wills, contracts, laws, and other efforts of man to express his meaning to others without ambiguity, the civil courts would lose half their business and more. How much more liable to various interpretations would be an entire Constitution of a novel sort!

The very name chosen for the nation was ambiguous, the *United States,* and the opening words of the document equally so, "We the People of the United States," which had read in the discarded first draft "We, the people of the States of New Hampshire, Massachusetts," etc. In spite of the attempt to make the division of powers clear as between the Federal Government and the individual component States, endless dispute could be honestly carried on as to just how "sovereignty," with all its disputable eighteenth-century metaphysical implications, had been divided between them. Just how completely sovereign was a State and how were the States united? Was there a new "people of the United States" as distinguished from the peoples of the several States?

The ratifications of the Constitution by a number of them were intended to clarify the instrument, yet how capable of fine-spun legal quibbling are the words of even the ratification by Virginia, for example, when taken simply by themselves. It reads, "we, the delegates of the *people of Virginia* . . . do, in the name and in behalf of the *people of Virginia,* declare and make known, that the powers granted under the Constitution, being derived from the *people of the United States,* may be resumed by them whensoever the same shall be perverted to their injury or oppression." The axiom that power was derived from the people and could be resumed by them when wrongly used by those to whom it was delegated, was a fundamental doctrine of eighteenth-century Liberalism and of our own Revolution, but who were "the people" in this case? If the Virginia delegates had said that the powers being derived from the *peoples* of the *several States* could be resumed by them in any one State when wrongly used, the statement would have been clear. But if the change of term from the "people of Virginia" to the "people of the United States" meant that there was a people of the United States as distinguished from the combined peoples of the several States, then the powers could be resumed only by the people as a whole and not by the people of any one State. In the Constitution itself there was no provision made for secession, but one could, if he wished, assume that such right was implicit in the sovereignty left to the States, and until the question of the practicality of peaceful secession was settled by the force of arms but never of logic, the practical point was one on which honest men might differ, as they still can on the logical and theoretical. An intellectual puzzle cannot be solved by brute force.

The actual wording of the new instrument of common government was, as we have said, full of ambiguities. In interpretation, the reasoner might well try to arrive at the intentions of the framers and such opinions held by them as might elucidate the document they framed. But here again there is a wilderness of conflicting thought and expression forming an arsenal from which, like the Bible, texts can be drawn to suit all tastes. Probably no one understood the problem better than the great Virginian, Madison, who is reported as saying in debate that "some gentlemen are afraid that the plan is not sufficiently national, while others apprehend that it is too much so. . . . Some contend that the States are sovereign, when in fact they are only political societies. There is a gradation of power in all societies, from the lowest corporation to the highest sovereign. The States never possessed the essential rights of sovereignty. These were always vested in Congress. Their voting by States in Congress is no evidence of sovereignty. The State of Maryland voted by counties. Did this make the counties sovereign?" In answering Hamilton, who had asked if New York could ratify the Constitution on condition of certain amendments being made, Madison replied emphatically that New York could not be received on such a basis, that "the Constitution requires an adoption, *in toto* and forever."

I wish here merely to emphasize the vast possibilities of honest and lasting difference of opinion as to the meaning of many parts of the new instrument of government adopted in 1787. The instrument itself has to be interpreted. The letters, speeches, debates of those who framed it and ratified it have to be interpreted. At the end there is no truth such as a mathematical demonstration to be arrived at,—only opinions, and the instrument itself provided for no supreme arbiter in differences of opinion.

Its ambiguities, compromises, illogicalities, and evasions were the price paid for creating a nation. Given the world trend of both thought and action in the next century the price was one which would have to be paid eventually in blood and bitterness.

If however a document has to be interpreted, it must also be remembered that a Constitution is a living thing. Nothing rigid in this world can survive. The fundamental law of any people must be capable of adaptation to changing conditions or when the strain between rigid law and altered outlook and custom shall have become sufficient, it is bound to be overthrown. A Constitution is not necessarily rigid because it is written. It may be altered by the mere acquiescence of the people at large in new ideas or ways of doing things until they have become so firmly intrenched as to have become *de facto* part of the Constitution even though there have been no verbal changes made. An instance of such a case is the development of the Supreme Court. No one would say today that it is *unconstitutional,* though he might think it hampering to progress, for that Court to pass on the constitutionality of laws enacted by Congress. Yet nothing in the original Constitution and no formal amendment has given it that power.

Again, the fundamental law may be altered by formal amendments (which are now becoming fairly frequent), arrived at as the result of peaceful discussion or armed force. The point is that although the wording of an original document may remain the same, it must at every stage be interpreted in such a way as to meet the changing conditions of the people. Though its words may be carved in granite, it becomes itself a living, changing thing or settles into the rigidity of death. All these necessary changes in interpretation may cause honest differences of opinion, but at the end of a lapse of time the same words must come to have a different meaning as reflected in the practices, customs, and court decisions of a people. A Constitution avails only when it serves the needs of the living, not when it is merely a verbal monument to the dead. If a people can on the whole agree on interpretations which will serve their needs, new or old, then there will be harmonious growth; if they cannot, then no amount of antiquarian research into the original meaning of the phrases, or chopping of logic, will avail to save them from the horrors of a decision by force.

\*     \*     \*

Growth and change in the Constitution began almost at once. Jefferson had not been in America at the time of its drafting but on his return from France he became Secretary of State in Washington's Cabinet. Hamilton occupied the post of the Treasury. Jefferson, who wished for a central government which should exercise as little power as possible as against the States, was for a "strict construction" of every clause granting powers to the Federal Government, whereas Hamilton wished to stretch every such clause to its limit of meaning. The classic contest between them came over the bill passed by Congress for the creation of a national bank as desired by Hamilton. Both submitted their written opinions to Washington at his request.

Briefly, Jefferson claimed the tenth amendment to the Constitution provided that all "powers not delegated to the United States by the Constitution, nor prohibited by it to the States, are reserved to the States respectively, or to the people"; and that the power to create a bank was not given to the United States. Hamilton rejoined that there were "implied" powers as well as "expressed," and that just what powers were given to the Federal and what reserved to the State governments had to be decided by fair reasoning. Not only, did Hamilton argue, was the Federal the supreme sovereign power but that in the general clause in the Constitution authorizing Congress "to make all laws necessary and proper for carrying into execution the enumerated powers," the word "necessary" should be construed as it was customarily used, that is, as meaning needful, requisite, incidental or conducive to. Washington was convinced by the reasoning of Hamilton rather than that of Jefferson, and signed the bill which Congress had passed. The doctrine of implied powers, so potent in our whole history, thus began its profound influence upon the interpretation of the Constitution.

Soon there was to be another alteration in that document. As the result of a compromise between those in the Convention who had wished for a President chosen simply by Congress, in which case he would have had but little power, and those who wished a strong executive elected by the people, it had been provided that electors should be chosen in the several States and that these electors, who were expected to be leading and wise citizens, should elect the President. It was thus hoped to avoid making him merely the creature of Congress on the one hand or the choice of the mistrusted people at large on the other. As early as 1796, however, not only were the peoples of six States voting direct for electors but the electors were practically pledged to vote for certain candidates. By 1800 the plan of the Fathers had completely crumbled and we have practically ever since been electing our Presidents in a way never intended by the framers of the Constitution, which has been twisted in such a way as to be more consonant with the political habits of the people.

The Hamiltonian theory of the implied powers, with all that it presaged as to the direction of growth of the central government, had deeply disturbed Jefferson and many who thought as he did. But when it was a question of meanings of words and interpretations of expressions who was to decide? Did the final decision, in case of conflict, rest with the Federal Government, the State legislatures, or the vote of the people at large? The Constitution was silent on that point. In June and July, 1798, Congress, John Adams then being President, passed the group of acts known as the Alien and Sedition Laws, and further alarmed those who watched with fear the increasing assumption of power by the Federal Government. The administration had become unduly frightened by the French Revolution and its slight repercussions in America. The acts passed were repressive in character, involving particularly the freedom of speech and of the press, guaranteed in the Constitution. Both Jefferson and Madison evidently thought that an opportunity was ripe to halt the actions of the broad constructionists, and chiefly through the manipulation of Jefferson the resolutions known as the Kentucky and Virginia Resolves were passed by the legislatures of those States, the former being written by himself and the latter by Madison.

These Resolves, together with the answers which they drew from the legislatures of the other States, are chiefly of interest as marking the first collision, though a peaceful one, between the States over the interpretation to be given to two of the most fundamentally important but most ambiguous points in the Constitution, namely the nature of the Federal tie and the question as to who should decide in case of dispute about it.

In the Kentucky Resolves Jefferson claimed that the Constitution was merely a compact between independent and sovereign States which retained all their rights as such, and that as "in all other cases of compact among parties having no common Judge, each party has an equal right to judge for itself as well of infractions as of the mode and measure of redress." The Resolution proceeded specifically to declare the Alien and Sedition Acts as "altogether void and of no force." In the Virginia Resolves Madison was somewhat more guarded in language but also declared for the compact theory of the Constitution and made the States the judges of what might or might not be constitutional in the legislation of Congress.

Of course the Constitution itself, whatever it might mean, was in no way altered by these two papers. They were mere expressions of opinion of the two great men who drafted them and of the majority of the members of the two legislatures which passed them. Beyond that they had no validity whatever. Certainly if such a pronouncement by a State legislature should have to be considered as a final and valid interpretation of the Federal Constitution, then such a pronouncement by any one State was as final as that by any other. As, in reply to requests from Virginia and Kentucky, all the other States, except Georgia and the two Carolinas, did make such pronouncements, we are left in no doubt as to what was the majority of opinion at that time. All the other States denounced the theories of the Resolves. Delaware considered them "very unjustifiable"; Rhode Island "unwarrantable" and full of "evil and fatal consequences"; Massachusetts that they led to anarchy; Pennsylvania that they threatened the very existence of government; and other States were equally strong in their denunciation of the doctrines. Several pointed out that if the State legislatures were to be the judges of the Constitution and there should be difference of opinion, each would "have no resort for vindicating its own opinions but the strength of its own arm." Four of the States advanced the theory that the Supreme Court must be the ultimate arbiter while Pennsylvania declared that Congress was the body which must interpret the Constitution, and the Supreme Court the one which must pass on the constitutionality of Congressional Acts.

It is an odd fact that although the first attempt to decide

in what body lay the right to interpret the Constitution had thus brought out the fact that nine States were opposed to the theory of State interpretation against two in favor, and that although according to that theory the decision of each of the nine was as valid as that of either of the two, nevertheless among the States' Rights advocates, in any section of the country, the Kentucky and Virginia Resolves came to be considered almost in the light of part of the Constitution itself, and little or nothing was ever heard of the other nine. Virginia herself had been divided, a minority of the legislature bringing a report opposed to the Resolve.

So far from any interpretation of the nature of the Federal Government being possible of irrefragable logical demonstration, almost every State in the Union down to 1860 was to endorse or reject the States' Rights theory as one or the other interpretation suited its political needs of the moment, and this applies to the North as well as to the South. In 1798, however, several of the States had the vision to point out, as we have noted, that if the individual States were to be the interpreters of the Constitution and the arbiters of Congressional action, not only would there be constant bickering and a paralysis at any moment, however critical, of the central government but that when disputes became sufficiently bitter they could end only in war.

Virginia at that time was unquestionably the intellectual leader of the union in matters of state, and the question of how to avoid anarchy and create some final arbiter in constitutional disputes had been occupying the attention of another great Virginian, John Marshall, who had been made Chief Justice of the Supreme Court by John Adams. Born in a log cabin on the Virginia frontier but with good blood in his veins and of intelligent and ambitious parents, Marshall had acquired an education without going to college. This son of the frontier had been hard put to it, like Lincoln in his youth, to find books in his neighborhood to read, yet was to become the most eminent jurist America has produced and in a very real sense a "second maker of the Constitution." In the oft-quoted words of Lord Bryce, "the Constitution seemed not so much to rise under his hands to its full stature, as to be gradually unveiled by him till it stood revealed in the harmonious perfection of form which its designers had framed."[1] Perhaps, as the original framers had differed among themselves as to what the form should really be, it would be more correct to say that Marshall seized upon that line of development which the somewhat vague and uncertain phrasing of the document would have to take if it were to become the fundamental law of a strong, permanent, and indissoluble nation.

He was now, with equal caution and courage, to undertake to resolve one of the most difficult of the open questions left by the framers. As we have seen, in the Alien and Sedition Act controversy eleven States had expressed their opinions as to where ultimate judgment on the Constitution lay, and they could not agree. Two were in favor of the State legislatures and nine opposed, but these nine did not all agree among themselves. The majority, however, were in favor of the Supreme Court, and that also had become Marshall's choice. In 1801, in the celebrated case of *Marbury vs. Madison* he boldly stated his opinion that "it is emphatically the province and duty of the judicial department to say what the law is," and that a law repugnant to the Constitution is not law. Thus the Court assumed the duty of constitutional interpretation. There was nothing in the Constitution which gave it such right and the solution of the dispute over the meaning of words could become permanent only with the acquiescence of the people. Meanwhile Fate had given us a glimpse into the bloody abyss.

[1] James Bryce, *The American Commonwealth*, New York, 1891, vol. I, p. 375.

The relations between politics and the Constitution in the next dozen years or so were filled with sardonic humor. In 1800 Jefferson, the author of the Kentucky Resolves, was elected President, to the utter dismay of the Federalist party and all who had been working for a broad construction of the Constitution. When he entered the White House, the western boundary of the United States was the Mississippi River, and beyond it, for its whole extent, lay the territory of the declining though intriguing power of Spain, which also owned both sides of the River's outlet into the Gulf. The grave danger of losing our western States unless some amicable and permanent arrangement could be made with Spain for their use of the River had been well understood by Jefferson before he suddenly got wind of the fact that there had been a secret cession of all Spain's vast possessions, known as "Louisiana," to France.

Aggressive, Napoleonic France would be a very different neighbor from Spain. If our own West were to be saved to us something would have to be done at once to settle the Mississippi navigation question. Even Jefferson, lover of republican France and hater of monarchical England, considered that the day France took possession of New Orleans we might have to "marry ourselves to the British fleet and nation." He tried diplomacy, however, and in 1803 decided to offer the French up to 50,000,000 francs for New Orleans and the Floridas, and other lesser terms down to the purchase of a mere guarantee of the right of navigation and deposit. Meanwhile for reasons of his own, Napoleon had decided to make a quick sale of the entire recently acquired French empire in North America. Our envoys, to their own intense astonishment, were able to purchase the whole of "Louisiana," for about $12,000,000.

The Constitution was silent as to any additions to our national domain and the creation of new States out of such land as we did not own in 1787. Louisiana would double or treble the size of the United States, depending on what boundaries might eventually be determined as correct. The chance to control the Mississippi and perhaps save our West to the nation had to be seized immediately or possibly be let slip forever. Napoleon and Napoleon's fortunes were not matters to linger over. The opportunity was a gift of the gods but even those who believed in the broadest construction of the Constitution had never dreamed of buying and incorporating with the first United States a second one for $12,000,000! Yet faced by destiny and not by legal theory, the strictest of constructionists made the plunge. Louisiana became ours, though Jefferson acknowledged that there was nothing in the Constitution which permitted his action. He hoped for an Amendment which would validate his act,— and theory,—but the people swallowed Louisiana at a gulp and never bothered about the Constitution, which thus was again altered without formal amendment simply in answer to the living need of the people for whose welfare, wishes, and happiness it had been designed. Louisiana, which had never been a sovereign State but merely *real estate,* passed from the ownership of Spain to that of France and then to that of the United States; and our way was open for indefinite constitutional expansion. The footfall of Fate was particularly heavy the day the treaty was signed. As the historian Edward Channing has said, "had there been no Louisiana Purchase there would have been no Missouri Compromise, no Texas annexation, no Mexican War, no Oregon boundary! The Kansas-Nebraska Act would never have been passed and there would have been no struggle for Kansas! Indeed there would have been no War for Secession with its attendant orgies of Reconstruction." At least, we may say, had war come between the old States it would have been wholly different in nature and in consequences. Yet the destiny of the nation was thus thrown into the hands of Fate by the man who only six years before had asserted it as a final Constitutional axiom that "whensoever the general government assumes undelegated powers, its acts are unauthoritative, void, and of no force." Fate in her steady stride had brushed away the meshes of cob-web logic.

But the humor of these years was not limited to Jefferson's having to turn himself at one of the most fateful moments in our history into the broadest of constructionists. The leaders of the ousted Federal party, who had been playing that rôle until Jefferson's election, now found themselves, as he had, forced to change sides. In Congress the New England Federalists voted practically solidly against the purchase, partly because it was a Democratic measure but also because, as Uriah Tracy of Connecticut bluntly said, "the relative strength which [the addition of Louisiana] gives to a Southern and Western interest is contradictory to the principles of the original Union."

This, of course, was largely true, and with every addition of territory the balance of power in the nation would become more heavily weighted against New England. However, in the New England States, which only five years before had given scathing replies denouncing the theory of the Constitution as set forth by Kentucky and Virginia, a group of prominent men now determined on breaking up the union and forming a separate nation in the North, to be composed of the New England States, New York, and New Jersey.

In a letter written in December 1803, the Federalist Timothy Pickering of Massachusetts struck a note of social dislike which was to be heard in New England again and again and of which we shall have more to say later. He did not yet despair, he wrote, for he anticipated "a *new confederacy* exempt from the corrupting influence and oppression of the *aristocratic democrats* of the South." Roger Griswold made a report on the financial condition of the possible "Northern Confederacy." George Cabot feared the time was not ripe as people were too prosperous at the moment. He was sure, however, that "the separation will be unavoidable when our loyalty is perceived to be the instrument of impoverishment," and he was in the counsels of the plotters. We need not go into the detailed story of the plot, which failed disastrously, leaving a stain on the names of many leading men in the section. Its mere existence is enough for our purpose here, and, like the action of Jefferson, illustrates the truth that throughout our history the Constitution has been interpreted and used, not like a proposition in Euclid, which has been impossible, but as seemed best to serve the needs of parties, sections, and groups, North, South, and West, at different times. To assert that fact, based on human nature, is far from denying the sincerity of the interpreters. There is, for example, not the slightest doubt in my mind of Jefferson's complete honesty when the good of the nation seemed to force him to drive the Louisiana coach and horses through his Constitutional theory. By doing so, he proved himself to be a statesman and not a doctrinaire. Had he refused to do so our expansion might have been blocked by a strong and hostile power. Not only that but we might have lost a considerable part of the "West" we then owned. It is interesting to observe, however, that the author of the Kentucky Resolves preferred to save the Union and its future rather than to remain a strict constructionist.

A few years later, in 1809, there was a case of conflict between the authority of the Federal Government and that of Pennsylvania; and the legislature of that State again brought up the question of where the supreme right to decide might rest. Pointing out in its Resolves that "in a government like the United States, where there are powers granted to the general government, and rights reserved to the States, it is impossible, from the imperfections of language, so to define the limits of each" that disputes should not arise, the legislature proceeded to suggest that the Constitution might be so amended as to create some body which would have the ultimate voice in deciding. Eleven States, in reply, denounced the plan, the legislature of Virginia in especial elaborately defending the Supreme Court as being such a body already in existence The position of the two States as expressed by their legislatures had thus been almost completely reversed from a decade before.

The conflict of interests between sections in the War of 1812 again brought out clearly how inevitably Constitutional interpretation was colored by political desires. The war had been brought on by the South and West against the wishes of the shipping North, and we need not repeat the well-known story of the obstructionism and disloyalty of New England throughout the struggle, punctuated by constant talk of secession and culminating in the notorious Hartford Convention. A contrast, however, between the pro-Administration newspaper constitutional interpretation in the South and anti-Administration in the North is interesting. In a series of articles *The Columbian Centinel* of Boston asserted that "we are a divided people," that no "two hostile nations on earth" could have more diverse views of government than the North and the South, and that *"the States are separated in fact* when one section assumes an *imposing Attitude,* and with a high hand perseveres in measures fatal to the interests and repugnant to the opinions of another section." . . . On the other hand, in Virginia, *The Richmond Enquirer* was thundering that "no man, no association of men, no State, or set of States, has a right to withdraw itself from this Union on its own account. . . . The majority of States which formed the Union must consent to the withdrawal of any branch of it. Until that consent has been obtained, any attempt to dissolve the Union, or distract the efficacy of its laws, is Treason."

\* \* \*

On June 3, 1808, there had been born to Samuel Davis, a tobacco planter of Kentucky, a son who was named Jefferson. Some months later, February 12, 1809, only about a hundred miles distant in the same State, there was born to a backwoods pioneer, Thomas Lincoln, a son whom his parents called Abraham.

\* \* \*

However practically obstructive New England had been in the carrying on of the war, and however politicians might talk about secession, *The Independent Chronicle* was probably not far from right when it said that 999 New Englanders out of a thousand would probably vote against it. In spite of temporary bickerings, rationalized as always by appeals to the Constitution, the war, with its final victory at New Orleans, had greatly added to the emotion of nationalism in the rank and file of citizens. We had beaten the British again, if somewhat dubiously; were free from the broils of Europe; and were realizing more and more the possible riches of our own development. The West was ours, and the race began.

The fear on the part of New England of the creation of new States over the mountains was based on the clear view that a third section was bound to grow rapidly and disturb the equilibrium of the older two. It might prove that the new one would merely hold the balance of power between the seaboard North and South, or that Northern or Southern influence might become preponderant in it and so make one of the older sections permanently the dominant factor in the Union. For a far-sighted statesman, in view of the growing cleavage between the old North and South, the question was of transcendent importance. The North was investing its money in shipping, banking, and nascent manufactures; the South in western lands. The future seemed with the South, and the first State to be created west of the Mississippi was that of Louisiana in 1812, an event which had so raised the ire of New England as to cause Josiah Quincy to say in Congress that if the bill passed it would virtually dissolve the Union, freeing the older States from their moral obligations, and that "as it will be the right of all, so it will be the duty of some, to prepare definitely for a separation; amicably if they can, violently if they must."

We shall comment on the life of the three sections in the critical years from 1820 to 1860 somewhat in detail in the next chapter, but may note here that the West had no wish to be made the pawn of either section in the East, and that the two eastern sections had diverged rapidly from each other by the earlier year. The European wars at the end of the eighteenth century had thrown a large part of the carrying trade into American hands, our re-exports of foreign products rising from only about $500,000 in 1790 to over $45,500,000 by 1800. The North, as the section interested in shipping, had accumulated a large aggregate of liquid capital which found outlet in business. On the other hand, the development of the cotton industry, due to the invention of spinning machinery in England and Eli Whitney's cotton gin in America, had been prodigious, so that by 1803 cotton had out-distanced tobacco and become the leading staple of the South. Cotton raising fitted in to the agrarian life of the South, and the profits seemed illimitable. The South went in for more and ever more land; the North for factories. The foundations of the "Cotton Kingdom" of the lower South were already being laid, and the transference of leadership from Virginia to South Carolina and the Gulf was imminent. With the exception of the un-

52

happy term of the able and honest John Adams, elected by
a majority of only one vote, every President, from the founding of the nation to 1824, had been a Virginian, but the
days of Virginian leadership were rapidly drawing to a
close.

In spite of the fact that by 1820 the Chief Executive
had been a Virginian for twenty-six out of thirty years the

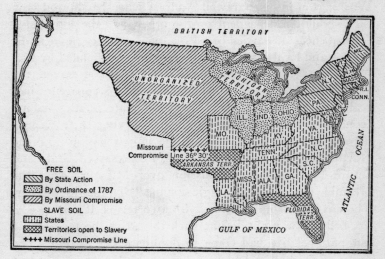

two sections were equally represented in the Senate; and
the North, from increasing population, had 105 members of the House as compared with only 81 from the
South. However, the almost simultaneous desire of Maine
to become a separate State and the demand for statehood
by the slave-holding territory of Missouri aroused the fears
of both North and South owing to the growing differences
between them. In 1820 the problem, thus become acute in
the minds of the voters, was temporarily settled by what has
ever since been called the Missouri Compromise. Maine was
admitted as free, Missouri the next year as slave, and it was
agreed that thereafter slavery should be prohibited in the

remainder of the Louisiana Purchase north of the parallel of thirty-six degrees thirty minutes, practically the southern boundary of Missouri.

The nation found itself at last definitely ranged in two geographical and cultural sections, contending against each other and also for the control of the new one arising in the West. These three had been clearly envisaged by Washington in his Farewell Address when he showed how each should be dependent on the other, and the intolerable consequences of parties based on supposed geographical divisions and local interests. The danger apprehended by him had in less than a quarter of a century confronted the American people with a suddenness more apparent than real. Step by step Fate had led us on, climate, politics, habits,  economics, discovery, invention—all driving their wedges between the great sections of the united nation. To the Northerner, John Quincy Adams, Secretary of State and future President, the discussion over Missouri was "the preamble to a great and tragic volume." To the Southerner, Thomas Jefferson, President for two terms, it came as "a fire-bell in the night." The dark thread in the tapestry of our national life had come to dominate the pattern. The unity of the nation had been broken by the avowal at last that the hopes, institutions, and culture of the two distinct geographical halves of the country were in opposition to one another. Henceforth the Union was not to be knit close with the strength of affection and common interest but to be the precarious resultant of carefully balanced economic and political forces. In a rapidly changing world only a miracle could keep such a balance; and at last the ambiguous words of a paper Constitution would be scattered before the tempestuous winds of ambition, self-interest, and passion untempered by understanding or love. To keep the balance even in 1820, we had to stretch an imaginary line of division between the sections across our entire land.

# THE CHAIN OF IRON

Invisible but potent with a thousand evils, it was symbol of inevitable conflict. As the fathers of the Constitution had been forced to compromise and evade, so we should continue to compromise and evade for another forty years, but our evil Fate marched on. With *that* there could be neither compromise nor evasion.

CHAPTER III

THE BACKGROUND, 1820–1860

THE background, economic, intellectual, and emotional,
of the three sections in the fateful years from 1820 to
1860, can obviously be sketched only in broadest outlines
within the limits of a single chapter. Not only was each
section in itself enormously complex, but American life,
then as always, was in flux. It has not been the advent of
the cheap car which has made us a nation of migrants. The
car has simply made our habitual migration easier albeit
of a new type. Incessant change of place, like the shifts of
a multiple shuttle, has always been weaving the sections together in a little realized intricacy of family relationships.
Let us take at random a few men who will appear in our
story. Of Abraham Lincoln's seven American ancestors
not one died in the house where he was born or even in the
same town, and only one in the same State. From Massachusetts, through Pennsylvania, Virginia, and Kentucky,
they passed to Illinois. Jefferson Davis's Welsh grandfather emigrated to Philadelphia, drifted along the mountain foot-hills to Georgia, his son moving to Kentucky, and
the future President himself to Mississippi. The grandfather of Henry Hitchcock, an officer on Sherman's staff,
was Attorney General of Vermont, his son Chief Justice of
Alabama, and Henry himself, after residence in Connecticut,
was living in St. Louis when the war broke. The grandfather of Alexander Stephens, Vice-President of the Confederacy, was a Pennsylvanian. The father of A. S. John-

ston, the distinguished Confederate general, moved from Connecticut to Kentucky, which was then filling up with families from Maryland and Virginia. The General's mother was from Massachusetts. He himself moved on to Texas. John C. Calhoun's grandfather settled first in Pennsylvania, then in Virginia, and finally in South Carolina, and it is interesting to speculate on what Calhoun's own views on States' Rights might have been had the family remained in the North.

Such instances of family migration could be repeated indefinitely. Although there was much of it between the old North and South, it was the West which felt the full effect of this mixture of peoples. In general, the migrant assumed the outlook of the section to which he went, and there were no stronger defenders of slavery in the South than those Northerners who had gone thither. The Western migrant was no exception, but the West was as yet more of a state of mind than a settled society with well-defined patterns. The rapidly moving pioneer frontier, the "settled frontier," the established town, followed each other with such amazing swiftness across the same land that occupations, habits, and social organization might change three or four times within a decade or two. To have lived for a generation on the same spot was to have seen vast changes and to have become one of "the old families."

There were, indeed, two Wests, the slave West south of the line of the Missouri Compromise, and the free West north of it. The indentured servant of old had long since disappeared as potential labor supply, and for obvious reasons in the free West there was practically no agricultural labor to be obtained. It was therefore a land first of small clearings, then small farms, backed farther east by the steadily rising cities with their jobbing and manufacturing enterprises following the markets and produce of the pioneers. Until the advent, in the latter part of the period, of the foreign immigrant and of farming machinery, the pioneer could not think in terms of thousands of cultivated acres. He himself labored to make a home. The emigrant to the Southwest often did the same but his dream was of a great plantation. When the future General A. S. Johnston took up his 1300 acres or so, clearing but a small part with his own hands and the help of a single slave family, he hoped, as he sat in his log cabin, to be able some day to buy more slaves and to develop a great estate.

But these two portions of the West were bound together by the River, down which the produce of the Northwest was floated to serve the needs of the Southern Cotton Kingdom. Even if the Northwest was composed of free States and believed with extreme literalness in the words of the Declaration of Independence, it was dependent for decades on the institution of slavery for an outlet for its crops, though by 1860 the new railroads to the East were rapidly lessening this vassalage to the South. Both North and South were fighting for economic and political control while the West believed in its own star of destiny. Southern emigration had washed up into it north of the Ohio River, but still farther north, within nearly the precise bounds of the old Massachusetts and Connecticut claims,[1] was a broad band which was almost pure New England. Economically the whole Mississippi Valley was destined to be a unit, however the two eastern sections, reaching out westward, might struggle for mastery of portions. Thinking in terms of its huge purchases of Northwestern foodstuffs, the South believed that in any final decision that section would have to cling to it. It never dreamed that the Northwest might decide for the eastern North and yet insist upon the unity of the whole Mississippi Valley. Meanwhile the West was intent on its own development, intensely democratic, steadily stretching out wider and wider over

[1] See map, p. 34.

plain and prairie, little given to books or culture or social forms but proudly conscious of its future.

\* \* \*

When we come to consider the North, generalization, always dangerous, is peculiarly difficult, for not only were there many sorts of people but the period was one of unusual ferment. How describe in a few words a society which included small farmers on lonely hillsides; shipping magnates in the great ports; every conceivable kind of reformer and crank; clerks; mill hands; scholars; inventors; poverty-stricken immigrants; Astors, Vanderbilts; to suggest a few types of which a Whitmanesque listing could fill a page?

On the whole, however, in spite of the overwhelming number of farmers, we may say that the dominating type had become that of the rich and successful business man, whatever his origin, whether he had a pedigree leading back to a Dutch patroon or a New England clergyman of early vintage, or had arrived as an ignorant immigrant, like Astor, or "climbed through the hawse hole" like some of the "merchant princes" of New York and Boston. Riches were the easiest road to social influence; and business of one sort or another was the surest if not the only road to riches. The professions, except that of the church in New England, ranked lower, although lip service was paid to outstanding success in literature or at the bar, even if not accompanied by great wealth. There were, of course, many "old families" who were as socially charming as any anywhere at any time. There were teachers, authors, scientists, and others devoted to the intellectual life. There were the reformers of all brands. But it was not they who gave the tone to the North but the business man, who was almost invariably a town or city-dweller.

In spite of severe panics, the opportunities for business

in the North had been staggering. Foreign trade; the quick growth of cities; the rise of manufacturing to supply the growing South and West; railroads and other new inventions; all seemed to hang Aladdin's lamp on every tree. It is human to wish to control power and to enjoy prestige. The ambitious man turned to business, and left politics to his hired politicians, city, State, and national. When money was power, and might be acquired quickly, why toil through twenty years in Congress to become a Senator? Even a great Northern statesman such as Daniel Webster allowed himself to be in part supported by the loans or gifts of rich business men among his constituents. Speaking generally (as, of course, I am doing throughout this chapter), the North sent inferior men to Washington, which was the chief meeting place of North and South. Even James Russell Lowell, who hated the South, could write during the war that "we doubt if the Slave States have sent many men to the Capitol who could be bought, while it is notorious that from the North of Mason and Dixon's line many an M. C. has cleared, like a ship, for Washington and a market." In general the Northerner thought of political affairs only as they affected business, and it occurred to few to consider that a life spent in the service of the country was itself a career and a distinction.

As a rule, the important Northern business man was against any agitation of the slavery question. The South was one of his most important markets, if not the most so; and for the great textile trade, it was the sole source of raw material. Any agitation is "bad for business," and moreover an employer of labor, free or slave, does not like too much reform. With the first rise of industrialism in the North, most of the labor had been American, living in the vicinity of their work. Conditions were good, as they then went, and some employers, notably at Lowell, Massachusetts, took great interest in the welfare of their employees.

But the peopling of the Western empire was a strain on the North, as we shall see it was, in a different way, on the South. In fact, the western drag on the East and South and the struggle for western control by the two sections are the keys to the whole period. Fate, like the pioneer, was tramping toward the setting sun.

Between the first census in 1790 and that of 1840 the population of New England, at the natural rate of increase, should have risen to about 3,500,000 instead of which it was only 2,212,000. This difference, to which must be added the number of immigrants from Europe, roughly indicates what it was costing the East in numbers to build up the West. Conditions in Europe, however, particularly in Ireland and Germany, were starting the huge flood of emigration which was to bring millions to our shores in the next few years. Owing partly to climate, partly to dislike of slave competition, and partly to other reasons, this flood was chiefly directed to the North, and helped not only to people the Northwest but to make up what would otherwise have been a disastrous, indeed a catastrophic, loss to the labor supply in the Northeast.

Both the poverty and numbers of the newcomers enabled the manufacturers and other employers to exploit the laborers, who in many cases were shamefully treated. Self-respecting American labor largely refused to compete except from sheer necessity, and in many instances the slave in the South was better off, except for a doubtful "freedom," than was the hand in a New England mill, worked at top speed for from twelve to fourteen hours a day for a pittance under bad conditions. In Rhode Island in 1831 there were almost 3500 children under twelve worked in the mills for usually fourteen hours a day, six days a week, for $1.50 a week, the manager of one mill proudly pointing to the fact that they were allowed to go to school on Sundays! No Southern planter would have treated his small slaves that

way, even if for no more humane reason than that a
"prime" slave of older age was much too valuable to ruin
young. The Northern employer on the other hand too frequently thought of his workers in the same terms as of his
machines—something to be used and thrown away when
worn out, getting the utmost profit from them both meanwhile.

If the North was humming with business, there was
nevertheless a great intellectual ferment also going on in it,
as there was in Europe. Across the water the first half
and more of the nineteenth century was a period of intense
faith in the future of Man and in the capacities of the individual man. On the continent, revolutions toppled over
autocracies and strove for democracy. In England the great
Reform Bill of 1830 promised a new era. Invention and
science seemed to open illimitable vistas of prosperity and
control over nature. Reforms of every sort were in the air—
anti-slavery, women's rights, education for the masses,
temperance, and a host of others. Almost every ill of man or
supposed ill had its ardent conquering heroes. The Victorian
era may have got stuffy at its end but in its beginning, and
in the few decades preceding it, there was a renascence in
many ways comparable only to the years of Elizabeth. The
rationalism of the eighteenth century gave place to a flowering of romance, humanitarianism, and emotionalism, of
faith, hope, and charity.

Although after the War of 1812 we happily turned away
from the political complications of Europe, we continued to
receive the westward flow of all its intellectual currents, and
to reflect them all in our own. That is, in the North. The
socialist and communistic doctrines of an Owen in England or a Fourier in France received almost immediate
translation into formation of Northern experimental communities—Brook Farm, Fruitlands, New Lanark, Hopedale,
and others—though practical men might wisely look askance.

The anti-slavery crusade in England, launched by Wilber-
force and others, found its prompt echo, as did the other
movements and "isms" of the time. Many of the leaders of
them were pure cranks, some fanatics, and almost all of
them utterly impractical, but life was fluid, flowing fast and
furiously, and almost any idea got a hearing.

Literature received its impulse here as abroad, and indeed may almost be said to have been born. Excluding
political discussion and a few speeches, there is scarce a
book written in America before 1830 which now is read
for other than local, historical, or antiquarian interest. But
in the first half of the nineteenth century appeared Irving,
Emerson, Thoreau, Lowell, Whittier, Longfellow, Cooper,
Herman Melville, Prescott, Parkman, Bancroft, and a host
of lesser writers in the North. There was a demand for
their books which might well make a modern novelist, historian, or poet envious. The greater publishing houses
were started and did a thriving business. Mass education
was then probably better in the North than anywhere else
in the world. The colleges of the section, though they
could not compete with the old foundations of Europe,
were rapidly going ahead, and attracting scholars from both
the other sections, Calhoun, though perhaps the most
nationally known of all the graduates of Yale, being only
one of a host of Southerners who came North to study.

It was a period, as I have said, of vast optimism, of
which Emerson was the prophet. The whole world was
spinning swiftly up the first spiral of the new economic
order. The North was wholly in tune with the age, which
demanded democracy, machinery, industrialism, change,
*laissez-faire*. The vast mass of the people overlooked the
grievous evils of the system; the small minority of reformers, each almost insanely possessed by his own "ism,"
whatever it might be, and all as sure of themselves as was
ever an Endicott or a Cotton of colonial Massachusetts, be-

lieved in their own ability to save the world. As Wendell
Phillips proclaimed in one of his eternally egotistical addresses, "In God's world there are no majorities, no minori-
ties; one, on God's side, is a majority," and of course every
reformer, like Phillips himself, believed that he was that one,
whatever the reform or cult. So what with the ordinary
man ignoring the evils and the reformer sure of curing
them between himself and God, optimism and ferment were
rampant. It was noted by several, Miss Martineau among
them, that the Abolitionists, calling down death and destruction on the Union and their neighbors, were all "happy
people" with "bright faces"!

The Northern civilization was, as we have noted, largely
one of towns and cities. It is where men are gathered together that new ideas have their most fertile soil. The talk
of an evening gathering after a day's work calls for what is
new and stimulating rather than what may be true but old,
whether the new be gossip or the accepted intellectualism
of the day. Either to praise or curse it, the North felt no
hesitation about the freest discussion of the new. The
world was fluid, hopeful, convinced that it was on the right
road, though we are far from as sure of that now as were
our ancestors of that time. The North felt itself floating
along the main stream. Like any society, it ignored or soft-
pedalled discussion about what might affect its economic
interests. The Indian was still an important landowner to
be dispossessed, and practically nothing was heard of *him*.
Labor had its place, and its place was to make money for
the employers. Little was heard of *it*, except from its own
ranks. When most of the Northern States had been beaten
down to a ten-hour day, Massachusetts mill owners could
still claim that if a fourteen-hour one were not preserved
"the morals of the operatives will necessarily suffer if longer
absent from the wholesome discipline of factory life."

Yet below the surface of all this coarseness of venial

politics, ruthless business, often hypocritical social doctrine, egotistic reform, there was a healthy stirring of new life, a belief in freedom, even though freedom might mean economic serfdom, and a devotion to the Union little dreamed of by most people, and least of all by the fanatical Abolitionists who denounced it with vitriolic curses. There was also in many communities and in countless homes a charm of social life. In our varied American scene there are few more perfectly satisfying things than a New England village with its wide elm-shaded streets, its common, and its white "colonial" houses. Whether in such homes or in town residences or country estates, throughout the North, there dwelt people who like the best in all ages and lands have learned the true values of the "good life," equally at ease with their neighbors of similar sort in the North or those in the South and Europe. And in countless homes which could not boast ancestral portraits or wealth, there was the energy, intellectual honesty, idealism, and patriotism which Jefferson had envisaged in his dream of the ordinary man. The North was infinitely far from being all speculators and ranting fanatics. The real North did not find its voice either on Abolition platforms, within the walls of the Stock Exchange, or even in the halls of Congress.

* * *

When we come to the South, we encounter fresh difficulties of interpretation in a few pages. Although on the whole its agrarian civilization was less complex than the agrarian-industrial-commercial one of the North, it was far more complex than the tradition has made most people believe. We are assured, for example, by one Southern writer that there was no such thing in ante-bellum Virginia as a "middle class," the only two classes being the "lords of the soil," all descended from the "gentry" of old England, and their negro slaves—nobody else. In this smug ignoring of all the others one is reminded of a society woman's leaving a city of toiling millions in the heat of summer with the remark that "there is simply *nobody* in town." But the real complexity of the South is only one of the difficulties. The Southern plantation life of before the war, like the cowboy West, has become simplified into a stereotype. The truth has been largely sacrificed to the hunger of a nation which craves, like all peoples, for a golden age of color and romance in its past.

In addition, in the South itself, we must reckon with the psychological effect of the overwhelming disaster of the downfall of the Confederacy and all that followed. In those terrible days, the past, for those who had been prosperous and happy in it, was almost all that was left. It was natural that they, to a great extent, particularly the women, should live in it, idealize it, sanctify it, until it came to seem, as one wrote of the old South, that it was "the fairest land, the purest social circle, the noblest race of men, and the happiest people, on the earth."

In that period also, even for historians, the ordinary man was of little interest. Writers busied themselves with the doing of those at the top, with the ladies and gentlemen, the rulers, statesmen, diplomats, generals. But with the new interests of history and the rise of historical research in the South itself, such Southern historians as J. S. Bassett, U. B. Phillips, Avery Craven, W. E. Dodd, W. G. Brown, R. B. Vance, and others have been enabling us to understand better what the old South really was. If it was wholly different from the caricatures of it in hostile Northern writing of the last century, it was equally so from the over-simplified Southern picture of it as every Southern man a cavalier and every woman a queen in a dream-land of great white houses and troops of happy and devoted black slaves. It was not that, though at its best its life was the most charming which our country has known.

# THE BACKGROUND, 1820–1860

No more than the North was the South a geographical unity. The "solid South" was the product of historical, not natural conditions. We have to contrast not only the tidewater South with the upland; the almost northern climate and appearance of a large part of Virginia with those of the lower portions of the Gulf States; the huge peculiar territory of the Appalachian Highlands (covering 100,000 square miles and forming considerable parts of eight States) with the rest of the South, but also innumerable and more local differences of soil and topography, all inducing variations in social and economic life. As has been well said, "there was a South of the plantation, and of the upland farm; of the Coastal Plains and of the mountains; the South with lands almost incredibly fertile and the barren South where living was hard; the civilized South, and nearby the South ignorant and rude; the austere Calvinist South, and the South of romance; the haughty, aristocratic South and the Democratic South."[2]

With all these differences, however, arising largely from geographical conditions, there were certain major simplifications. The first of these was the fact that the entire South, in all sections, was overwhelmingly agricultural. The life of the mountain white, who disliked slavery, was as firmly based on the land as was that of the cotton magnate in the "Black Belt." In that, Southern society was a unit as contrasted with the industrialism and commercialism of the North. The other great unifying factor was the presence of the negro. Although the proportion in different States and sections of those who owned slaves to those who owned none varied greatly, a very large proportion of the Southern people were numbered among the latter. In Virginia, for example, in 1860 there were only 52,128 slave owners in a white population of 1,047,299. If we consider each slave

[2] Quoted by R. B. Vance, *Human Geography of the South*, University of North Carolina Press, 1932, p. 22.

owner as head of a family, which he or she certainly was not, and estimate a family as consisting of five persons, then only about 50,000 white families out of 200,000 owned negroes.

The unifying influence of the negro, however, was felt in two ways. From the foundation of the government down to 1860 the ratio of whites to blacks throughout the South was kept steadily at about two to one. In other words, two races, which could not be merged, occupied the same territory, each in sufficient numbers to create in the dominant race that sense of solidarity which always develops under such conditions. Moreover, the white man who was at all ambitious socially, economically, or politically, was forced to dream of buying slaves if he had none. There was a definite limit to the size of a farm which could be cultivated by himself alone or his family. To enlarge one's operations one had to use other labor and for the most part the only Southern labor practically available was that of the slave. Just as in the North the badge of distinction had come to be success in business, so in the South the same badge was the ownership of a large plantation. Governor J. H. Hammond of South Carolina wrote that he had endured every sacrifice to make his sons not only educated and well-bred but also "*independent* South Carolina *country gentlemen,* the nearest to *noblemen* of any possible class in America." Even a distinguished lawyer, like James L. Petigru, who ruined himself in the effort, felt it necessary, for social reasons, to expend $35,000 in buying a plantation near Savannah and $41,000 more for slaves to work it. Thus, though there were many who disbelieved in slavery and who did not buy slaves or who emancipated those they had held, yet for the South as a whole the slave-holding and non-slave-holding whites were welded together through the negro by both personal ambition and racial solidarity.

Before considering the white society we must examine the slave on whom it largely rested. We now look back on slavery as a curse but that is because the opinions and conditions of society have passed beyond it. Originally it probably marked a great advance over the previous wholesale slaughters of those captured in savage wars. Old as recorded human history, few voices were raised even individually against it until the eighteenth century. As we have seen, the Puritans of New England believed in it; important New England commerce thrived on it; New England clergymen made use of it. The chance of geographical location alone saddled the South and not the North with the problem of how to get rid of it, or what to do with it, when world opinion at last and rather suddenly changed with regard to it.

Except by inconceivable economic sacrifice, the slaves could never have been emancipated as a whole. When the rising tide of humanitarianism finally forced England to abolish slavery in her island colonies she compensated the owners to the extent of $100,000,000, but after the suggestion of the Virginian, James Madison, that the money to be derived from the sale of public lands, estimated at $600,000,000, should be used for the gradual emancipation of our own infinitely larger number of slaves, nothing was heard of compensation until in the midst of war, yet as we have just seen in the case of Petigru, the value of the slaves was usually in excess of all the land and improvements. With little liquid capital in the South, how could a planter carry on if he sacrificed more than half his fixed capital to start a system of free wage labor? The North had no answer. Moreover, the experience of the South with the free negro had not been conducive to the belief, to say the least, that the emancipated slave would be happy, industrious, or qualified for citizenship. With notable exceptions, the presence of the free negro everywhere created difficult problems, and to free them all suddenly seemed to invite a collapse of society.

The negro, slave or free, was present to the extent of more than one-third of the entire population, and there was no possibility of replacing him by white labor. Concentrated in the South there was no other place for him to go, and so long as he was there, white labor would not come in. He was treated worse in the North than in the South, and there was so much opposition to his presence that some States would not allow his entry. Had there been interstate migration of emancipated slaves on any large scale, the alarmed free States would have certainly taken means to prevent it. For a while, many influential people, South and North, experimented with colonization in Africa as a solution but this, after some years, was realized to be a failure. It was not only costly and impractical but the nineteenth-century negro himself, who had no knowledge of any land but America, had usually as little wish to be shipped off to the African coast as would an Irishman in New York or a Swede in Minnesota. As the century advanced, the demand for labor increased. Practically the only labor obtainable was that of the negro. His presence was ineradicable. Fate had determined that. The problem was that of his status, and however undesirable many might consider slavery, there appeared to be no practical alternative, whatever the future might hold.

Meanwhile, what of his condition? The question bristles with difficulties. For white America, I believe there is no question that slavery and all that has flowed from it has been an unmitigated curse. The misunderstanding of the sections, war, hatred, a black South, arrested development, the negro problem, and other ills make our national tragedy. But the balance sheet for the former slave is not so easy to figure.

No one can minimize the horrors of the old slave trade. At first the traders in Africa secured only those negroes who were already in slavery there or captives taken in native wars, but as the demand increased wars were waged for the purpose of making captives for sale at the "castles" of the traders on the coast, to which would be brought the coffles of blacks from the interior to be exchanged for rum and goods. Then came the "Middle Passage," the ships packed to capacity with slaves laid in layers, like sardines, often between decks where the space did not even permit of sitting upright, and the slaves slept "spoon-wise," sometimes dead and living wedged together. Foul air, sickness, the wallowing in filth, took a heavy toll. The sharks well knew this as they followed in the ship's wake ravenous for their meal of human flesh as corpse after corpse and sometimes even diseased living bodies were thrown to them. There is no need to dwell on the sickening details, which have often been described. The South having little shipping of its own, this traffic was in the hands of the Spanish, French, English, and of our North. Still carried on clandestinely, though to a much lesser extent, after its legal abolition in 1808, conditions on the slavers when the trade became "boot-leg" were worse even than before. It is impossible to estimate accurately the extent of an illicit trade, but, carried on largely in New York and New England ships, it was heavy, particularly after 1840 and even more so in the decade of 1850–1860. In the nineteenth century, however, the great mass of slaves were native born in the South.

Horrible as the traffic was, and disastrous as it proved for us, it is yet an open question whether, for those who were brought here and their descendants, it did not prove good. Unlike the immigration of all other peoples who have come to us, that of the black was involuntary. Had he not been brought as a slave he would never have come at all, and his situation should not be compared with that of the voluntary immigrant from other lands but with what would have been his fate had he been left in Africa. The condition of the portion of that continent from which he came was one not only of savagery but of chronic warfare, quite irrespective of the activities of the slave traders. A negro in his native land was liable at any moment to be attacked, captured, enslaved by other blacks, torn from his family, or killed and in some cases eaten. Would the 12,000,000 of negroes in the United States today prefer that their ancestors had never been enslaved and that therefore they themselves, if alive, should at this moment be living as savages or barbarians in the African jungle? Would a Du Bois prefer to be head man to an African chief instead of a Harvard graduate, scholar and writer? Would a Robeson prefer beating a tom tom to thrilling audiences throughout the world with his beautiful voice? Would the colored washerwoman I had in the North give up her comfortable house and her car, in which she motored her family to Virginia each summer, for the ancestral grass hut in the jungle?

But what of the negro as a slave? To answer this we must first consider both the individual nature of slave and master and then the general condition of slavery itself.

We speak of the "negro" but in fact the black slaves were of many types with markedly different characteristics and temperaments. There were the proud Coromantees, the easy-going Whydahs, Pawpaws, and Nagoes, the Eboes, the Gaboons, good for almost nothing, the talented Mandingoes and Foulahs with Arab blood, and others. Mrs. Lovell tells an interesting story of the slaves on the Spalding plantation on one of the Georgia islands when there was a threatened attack by the British in 1813. The 400 slaves were under the charge of a Mohammedan black, who prayed to Allah each morning. When Spalding armed the slaves to resist the attack, Bu Allah remarked that "I will answer for every negro of the true faith but not for the Christian dogs"! There were also those, after a time, with large infusion of white blood, the mulattoes, quadroons, octoroons, and so on. The word negro, with a small letter, came to mean something different from Negro with a capital and signifying pure or preponderant racial character. A slave might be three-quarters or even seven-eighths Caucasian and only the smaller fraction Negro, and yet be considered both slave and a "negro." The reaction of the slaves to slavery, and all it entailed, would evidently differ largely according to their own individual and varying characteristics.

There were also good masters and bad, extremely kind ones and occasionally cruel ones, though it would seem that the really cruel or hard master was a marked exception, condemned by public opinion. This is confirmed by the conduct of the slaves in the war. It was not true, as sometimes claimed, that *every* slave was loyal to his owner, but it was practically so, and this almost universal loyalty of a subject race to their masters when attacked by others with the intention, after the Emancipation Proclamation, of freeing them is one of the most extraordinary incidents in history. That the white master could go into the army, leaving his often lonely and remote farm or plantation, his wife and children, frequently even money and jewels, in the care of the slave for whose liberty his opponent was fighting, not only speaks volumes for the qualities of the black race but indicates at least that there could have been no widespread hatred of the masters or resentment against them.

We may try to balance the account from the standpoint of the slave, given a good master. On the credit side he, or she, could count on being clothed, housed, fed, and medically attended to, from birth to death. Unemployment, sickness, old age, too many children, were not spectres which stood at his side as they did at that of the Northern factory hand, or any free laborer without capital. Much was made of this point by pro-slavery advocates, and in the light which the experience of a few more generations has shed on the workings of the *laissez-faire* system of capitalism and "free" labor it is almost beginning to appear that possibly Edmund Ruffin of Virginia saw the future more clearly than any one else. That system, he held, although then dominant in much of the world, could be only a sort of "half-way house" and not a permanent adjustment of the problem. Labor would at last come to demand the same economic protection which the slave had, that is, support in bad times, sickness and old age. Such provision, he held, could be made for every one only in some form of socialistic State. The choice in his opinion was not between slavery and free labor but between slavery, with its high individualistic development in a dominant class, and inevitable future Socialism with its deadening level for all.

The house servants on a good plantation were almost members of the family, and their work was light. The mechanics, field-hands, and others, who lived in their row of cabins not far distant from the "big house" of the large estates, had long hours of work at certain seasons, but no longer than a New England textile worker and under much healthier conditions. They usually had garden plots of their own and were allowed to make money for themselves by the sale of produce, and in other ways. On amply stocked plantations or where slaves were redundant, they were frequently allowed to hire themselves out, retaining a considerable proportion of their earnings for themselves. They usually identified themselves with the family, and, if it were a well-known one, they took great pride in their relationship to it. Naturally philosophic, of a sunny disposition, unambitious, lazy, living for the moment, the average slave, when well treated, was probably the least worried and the happiest person we have ever had in America.

There were other aspects of the institution, however, which stand on the other side of the account. The slave might have a bad master or a bad overseer. Usually the relationship between slave and master was a personal one and there was none of that impersonality which has done much to brutalize relations in industrialism. But if the plantation was of unusual size or if the master owned several of them in different places and was thus an absentee, this personal relationship might be lost, and the slave's life could be made a hell on earth. The overseer's lash in cruel hands might cease to be chiefly a symbol of authority and be plied unmercifully on bare backs. The slave codes were severe and although in ordinary times they were as much mitigated in practice as were the almost unbelievable criminal laws of early New England, nevertheless in the main the slave's chief reliance for protection was on the public opinion of his master's white neighbors. Where there were old families, this was usually as humane as the fundamental exigencies of the institution permitted, but there were also isolated farms and lonely plantations, petty tyrants and hard new-rich magnates.

Moreover, even when a slave was most happily placed, there was always the danger of his being sold. The best families prided themselves on not selling their slaves and on not breaking up slave families, but even the best of such owners might themselves be subject to accidents of death, debt, or other calamities which would necessitate disposal of the slaves. This was especially true with the development of the Cotton Belt and the West, with their insistent demand for labor, at a time when the demand had fallen off in the seaboard South. We have already spoken of the heavy drag which the West exerted on the North, but there, as we have pointed out, the loss was to a considerable extent made up by white immigration from Europe to fill the vacuum in population. The seaboard South had to stand the full brunt of its own westward movement with no outside help. The difference is startling. In 1850 the foreign-born residents in the seaboard North, above the Potomac River, numbered about 1,220,000 whereas those south of that river numbered only 43,000. This practically unanimous refusal of immigrants to enter slave territory must be contrasted with the enormous efflux of seaboard Southerners to settle the States of Georgia, Alabama, Mississippi, Louisiana, and Texas. By 1860, 193,000, or more than two-fifths of the entire living native-born whites of South Carolina, had emigrated from that State. In Virginia, the soil, almost completely worn out by tobacco, was ceasing to support the population. By 1833 Fairfax County was described as a ruin, and through much of both tide-water and eastern Piedmont the landscape was one of deserted fields yielding to cedar thickets and of plantations so run down that they could scarcely support the slaves, much less the masters. In 1847 a Virginian, Henry Ruffner, stated that Norfolk had lost half its commerce in twenty-five years.

These shifts in economic conditions, and the drag of the Gulf States and the Southwest, had its effect on the slave. When the master or one of his sons, no longer able to maintain himself in the old home, moved to a new State, it meant as a rule breaking up of slave families to an extent never known before. Washington had foreseen the future, though conditions temporarily improved a bit after his death. In 1794 he had written that "were it not that I am principled against selling negroes, as you would cattle at a market, I would not in twelve months hence, be possessed of a single one as a slave. I shall be happily mistaken if they are not found to be a very troublesome species of property ere many years are passed." Unhappily his prophecy was true. The Virginian was to find himself, however kind-hearted, utterly unable to maintain his slaves and their natural increase on his own lands. The situation was made worse by the rapid rise in the price of slaves, caused by the great profits and need for labor in the rich lands westward, which made their labor even less profitable in the east.

Slavery in Virginia had been kinder and easier than in any other State. It was at its worst in the newer Gulf States, where the plantations were larger, the work harder, the overseer more frequent, and the owner too often a hard self-made man, from either North or South, bent only on reaping riches as quickly as possible. There were, of course, innumerable exceptions to this. Many of the best old sea-board families were represented, and there were good masters among the newer men, the plantation of Jefferson Davis in Mississippi being a model, with an almost complete system of self-government devised by him and carried on by the slaves themselves. But in general the statement is true, and the negroes had a horror of being "sold South."

For the reasons noted, the inter-state slave trade came to assume large proportions, with attendant misery as masters became impoverished in spite of improvement in agriculture, largely due to the teaching of Ruffin. The taunt was thrown at Virginia that she had become a "breeder of slaves." She never did in the sense intended, but she did sell the surplus slaves which she could not sustain. It is difficult to see what else, under the system, could have been done, and it is one of the strongest indictments to be brought against it. It was suggested that Virginia sell *all* her slaves South, turn to white labor and invest the proceeds in manufacturing and business. To any one who realizes the relation which for the most part existed between a Virginian and his slaves, this was an impossible solution. It was hard enough to sell some without selling all, even aside from the impracticality of a completely agrarian civilization turning itself into an industrial one overnight. We shall recur to the effort of Virginia to free herself from slavery in the next chapter, and will only add here that the domestic slave trade was in some ways an even greater evil than the African slave trade, for it dealt to a large extent in human beings of much higher grade.

Another indictment brought by the antislavery people both in England and the North is an unpleasant topic but must be noticed—that of the sexual relations between a slave-owner and his female slaves. Prostitution and fornication are universal in time and place, and there was unquestionably much illicit relation between white men and negro or mulatto girls. An ardent Southerner, defending his section against the attacks of Miss Martineau, wrote in *The Southern Literary Messenger* in 1837 that it had to be admitted that on this topic her statements had all too much truth in them, but he put the situation in its right relations which she did not.

Throughout North and South there was the double standard. A woman was ruined if she was not chaste, whereas men, especially the young and unmarried ones, could do much as they chose. In the North a man who wished could choose among white mill hands, servant girls, and others who might be willing, or among professional prostitutes, of whom there were said to be 10,000 in New York City in 1850. As the Southerner upheld the honor of white women at all points, his relations were limited to the blacks and mixed bloods, many of whom when young might be of quite extraordinary beauty. This was due to the presence of the negroes as an inferior race socially and not to slavery. The cases in which a man, as owner, forced a girl against her will were probably extremely rare. The passionate nature and lax morals of the negro are well known. During youth the sexes of the blacks mingled among themselves fairly freely, and it was considered a comparatively venial offence in a young negress, carrying practically no penalties of conscience or social relation.

As to the frequency of the inter-racial illicit connection, there are, of course, no statistics. There is no question that married men sometimes had young black or mulatto mistresses in the South, as they had white ones in the North, but nothing to indicate that any larger proportion did. Probably a large number of the young men indulged themselves, as everywhere. A mulatto or other mixed blood was mute evidence of such a relation having taken place sometime, but as a mulatto married to a black would perpetuate mulattoes the number of mulattoes would greatly exceed the number of births from white and black connections. The most careful study which has yet been made of the problem[3] throws much unexpected light on it. In the Federal Census of 1850, nearly one-half of the negroes in the North were of mixed blood as against only one-ninth in the South. Moreover, if, as the Northern Abolitionists claimed, slavery were responsible for the racial mixture, we should expect to find the largest proportion of mulattoes in the rural districts, where on farm or plantation opportunity, power, lack of diversion, might all seem to point to a high ratio as compared with the towns and cities. In fact this was not so, for the South. Taking the proportion of mulattoes to the total negro population, we find, in 1860, that it was in

|  | per cent |
|---|---|
| Savannah | 18.1 |
| Rest of Georgia | 8.2 |
| New Orleans | 48.9 |
| Rest of Louisiana | 11.0 |
| Charleston | 25.2 |
| Rest of South Carolina | 5.5 |

[3] *The Mulatto in the United States. A Dissertation for the Degree of Ph.D.*, Edward B. Reuter. Boston, 1918.

The fact seems to be that in the South, by far the highest percentage of concubinage was not between slave owners and their slaves, but between free mulatto women, plying their age-old profession, and men without slaves. As far as the slaves were concerned, such relationships, all things considered, may be regarded as the least of their troubles, though there were undoubtedly occasional cases of force and brutality. It has been said that slavery was more demoralizing for the white than for the black, and it certainly was in this instance. As the child of a slave mother was itself a slave, there must have been a good many cases in which the sons and daughters of the master in the slave quarters were half brothers and sisters of the children in the "big house." Admitted but seldom mentioned, this was one of the blackest shadows cast by an institution which, in spite of idealizing, cast many.

Taking the slave system as a whole and balancing the good and bad in it for the slave himself, the chief indictment would seem to be that of the very concept of slavery itself, that is, the complete control over the whole life of one man or woman by another. Given a good slave and a good master, the relationship undoubtedly brought out certain fine qualities in each,—loyalty in the slave, a sense of responsibility to others in the master,—each a quality we sadly need today. Nevertheless, the system was demoralizing to both, and the better human being the slave became, the more anomalous was the relationship. Without accepting all the sentimentalism of the "old black Mammy" school one may yet admit that the relation was frequently a beautiful one, but the final comment may be, is there a negro today who would willingly go back to slavery, or a thinking Southern white who would wish to see the system restored?

The social class next above the slaves was that of the free negroes, not numerous but constituting a problem. Their legal and what we may call their "opportunity" status varied from time to time and State to State. In North Carolina at one period they were even allowed to vote. Depending largely perhaps on the mixture of tribal bloods, to say nothing of often first-class white, they themselves varied from shiftless, lazy good-for-nothings to able and ambitious men. In Georgia, for example, there was a negro who became a prominent merchant and was followed to his grave by a procession of the white merchants of his town. Another became a skilful physician and the partner of a white doctor. Others in the South owned plantations, hotels, and other enterprises, sometimes, though rarely, valued at $100,000. As a rule when a negro prospered he himself became a slave owner, some owning as many as twenty-five or more. Not infrequently slaves were allowed to make enough money to buy their own freedom and even that of their families. Although this was almost invariably done by men there was one odd case, in Norfolk, of a negro woman who owned and worked her husband, the latter when offered freedom by the Yankee soldiers in 1861 declining to accept it! On the whole the free negro got better treatment in the South than in the North. The Southerner understood and liked the black. The Northerners, except the professional negrophiles, did not like him, and it is more than questionable if his staunchest defenders among them ever understood him. The position of the free negro, however, was a difficult one. Looked down upon even by the slaves of the "best families," disliked by the free whites of their own economic scale, with whom they came into competition; regarded with suspicion when fears of slave uprisings were abroad; cumbered with legal restrictions; the only wonder is that some were able to rise in the scale. By 1860 there were about 250,000 of them in the South.

The next social class, although in spite of their white skins almost below the free negro and slave, were the "poor whites" despised by all. They were scattered through practically the entire South, living in the pine barrens and on other poor soils, often in close proximity to better soils and rich neighbors. Licentious, frequently drunkards, aimless, probably suffering from hook-worm, they formed an incredibly poor and miserable population, not unlike, in some respects, those of a southern portion of New Jersey today. Their numbers, like their origin, is vague but they probably made up five per cent of the total white population, Governor Hammond stating in 1850 that there were at least 50,000 whites in South Carolina unable to make enough to live on. Unable to compete with slave labor and with little opportunity of becoming industrial workers, they sank steadily lower until their condition, economical, physical, and moral, was abject.

They must be sharply distinguished from the "mountain whites," who, although also poor, frequently lazy, and idle from want of incentive on their rough and isolated patches of farms among the valleys and coves of the highlands, were nevertheless virile, respected, and far above the poor whites of the lowlands. They owned practically no slaves and were largely anti-slavery in sentiment. They lived a pioneer life, with their log houses, spinning wheels, and primitive economy, but were well-mannered, intelligent, and a fine stock, forming perhaps at least another five per cent of the total population.

There was also a considerable class of whites who were employed as laborers. If we take the figures for the Census of 1850 for *free* persons over fifteen years of age gainfully employed in the States of Virginia, the two Carolinas, Georgia, Alabama, Mississippi, and Louisiana, we find that over 452,000 were engaged in agriculture, although there were only about 305,000 farms and plantations. If we consider that there was one owner "engaged in agriculture" on each, that would leave a little over 157,000 "laborers" but, of course, many of these were probably sons of the smaller farmers. In addition, however, 125,568 were noted as being employed as non-agricultural laborers, though the Census suggests that many were connected with farming. As no distinction was made between free whites and blacks we may deduct most of the free male blacks. There were more than 54,000 of these in the States named but if we assume two-thirds of these to have been over fifteen, we still have a white laboring class of well over 100,000 even allowing most of the "farm laborers" to have been members of the farmer's family.

Out of a total working free population in the States named, there were also over 44,000 connected with law, medicine, divinity, or other pursuits requiring education, and about 169,000 engaged in commerce, trade, and other non-agricultural pursuits.

When we consider the 452,000 agriculturists out of the 790,000 total we must again make distinctions. There was first the important class of yeoman farmers bridging the gulf between the mountain whites and the planter classes. The yeoman farmer stemmed back most frequently to an able indentured servant who had risen or to the streams of German and Scotch-Irish immigration. Independent, self-respecting, democratic, religious, often Puritanical, condemning cards, dancing, drinking, and other "sins," they formed a large and valuable portion of Southern society in its wider sense. In economic position they ranged upward from the possession of a small farm without slaves to one of a thousand acres or more with a few score blacks. Some were wealthy, but all were likely to be different from the planter classes in their life and outlook. They were more practical, homespun and with no ancestor worship, though as they engaged largely in diversified farming instead of the single plantation crop they were frequently more comfortable than the smaller planter or decaying aristocrat.

The planter classes were complex, though they all depended on a single crop, mostly cotton as the century advanced, and were bound to the plantation economy, including reliance on credit. At the bottom was "the rabble of small planters," as one Southern historian has described them—men with few slaves, ignorant, thriftless, and often worse off for comfort and money than a Northern working family. Above these were the middle-class planters, who formed, perhaps, the backbone of the South. Often self-made, and without the social graces of the aristocrats, they were sound citizens and not lacking in the refinements of life. Usually running their plantations without overseers, both they and their wives worked hard in their appointed spheres. Without luxury or ostentation their homes were comfortable, when they were not allowed to be run down into slovenliness.

When we come to the upper-class planter we can here merely differentiate between the plutocratic and the aristocratic, noting in passing that there was much to distinguish those of different sections, such as Virginia, the Charleston district, the Black Belt, Creole Louisiana, and Blue Grass Kentucky. The plutocratic planter was mostly in evidence in the newer Gulf States and after the great speculative period of 1837. Like booms and bonanzas everywhere, the sudden rise of the Cotton Kingdom brought together a motley crowd,—sons of old families from the seaboard South, ambitious young Northerners with blue blood, gamblers, ne'er-do-wells, and hard-headed men with a knack for turning opportunity to profit. One contemporary word picture of an emigrant shows him in the shafts pulling a cart with a few belongings, his wife walking, carrying a rifle and leading a cow. Another shows an almost Abrahamic change of residence,—the seaboard planter at the head in a gig, the family following in a huge carriage, numerous wagons carrying goods and sick or old negroes, all materials for camping, numerous cooks, and a train of other slaves behind. As always, it was far from being the case that the cultivated man of gentle family won the highest prizes and became in a few years the lord of the widest acres and the most slaves. For a time it was a wild struggle for quick riches under almost frontier conditions, and it might prove that the man in the shafts would beat the man in the gig. Indeed, the whole South was rapidly changing from the days of old Virginia and South Carolina, and leadership was passing into new hands. Comparatively poor men, risen from the non-slave-holding class, had attained to power,—Clay, Jackson, McDuffie, Calhoun, and others— until it came to be said that only poor boys make great men. It was as true of multitudes of others in the nation as of the protagonists Lincoln and Davis; and political control in the South was to follow economic success and largely to centre in the new-rich Cotton Belt.

But if the aristocratic planter class was losing control it gave the tone to the South. The plutocratic planter copied its way of life, and often with little distinction between the two types, it has been that way of life which has set the stereotype for romance. All else is made to fade from the picture of the Old South.

In speaking of aristocracy it may be pointed out that although the aristocratic planter-group formed the nearest approach to an aristocracy in the generally accepted Old World sense which the United States has seen, it was one which was not transplanted but which grew up from the conditions of the new land. It was American not English. To compare it with the feudal aristocracy of the Middle Ages is much like comparing a comfortable but simple though charming mansion on the James River with Warwick Castle.

Genealogy is a peculiarly American passion. Perhaps it stems from an unconscious nostalgia for the homeland which sent us forth; perhaps in a land of incessant change from a thwarted desire for some continuity with the past. For whatever reason, the making of genealogies and the easy gliding over of weak links in them is a marked American trait. Most of us like to prove descent from a lord, a *Mayflower* passenger, a soldier in the Revolution, or whatnot, even though the real or mythical ancestor may have been a cad or a wastrel. A *Mayflower* immigrant, though only one-third of the number were "Pilgrims," is considered *ipso facto* as a saint and a hero; and a Royalist refugee as a member of the English aristocracy, although, as regards the latter, William Byrd of Virginia pointed out early in the eighteenth century, when the "aristocracy" of his colony was beginning to take shape, that "these people were no more all earls and dukes than the royal army was composed of earls and dukes."

Modern scholarly Southern historians now take a reasonable view of the origins of the most great Southern families. "Did the Carters, Burwells, and Randolphs," writes one with regard to Virginia, "the Pages, Nelsons, and Braxtons, the Fitzhughs, Wythes, Washingtons, and Lees derive from noble English houses through gentlefolk always living in elegance and maintaining lofty standards? If so, the records of the seventeenth century are at fault."[4] The genealogical link with England is always one hard to cross if not a *pons asinorum,* and we read in the work of another Virginian historian that the origin of the Harrisons is to be "inferred"; that of the Carters "unknown" but to "be conjectured as"; that of the Pages "supposed on reliable evidence to be"; that of the Fitzhughs "probable" and "some reason to think"; that of the Masons "unconfirmed tradition" asserts; and so on.[5] Of that very "aristocratic" State, South Carolina, its own son and most distinguished

4 U. B. Phillips, *Life and Labor in the Old South,* Boston, 1929, p. 26.
5 P. A. Bruce, *Social Life of Virginia in the 17th Century.* Richmond, 1907. *Passim.*

historian, in his day President of the South Carolina Historical Society and Vice-President of the American Historical Association, wrote of the Cavaliers that in the sense in which that word is generally understood "there were none among the early settlers and but few came afterward," and "any tradition that connects the provincial aristocracies of the Southern States with the Old World patrician origin is pure sentimental fiction; that is, not only contrary to common sense and to all evidence, but is in defiance of colonial history itself. The social order of South Carolina has been the outgrowth of her peculiar circumstances."[6]

Judging from all the evidence, the fact seems to be that there was a large sprinkling of blood of what in England are called "gentle-folk" in the earlier seaboard Southern colonies, derived chiefly through those who had fallen on evil times, found themselves on the wrong side in politics, or younger sons without scope in England, all from the middle class, for it must be remembered, despite blood, that cousins near or distant, even younger sons, of an English titled nobleman are no more members of the English "aristocracy" than are knights or baronets. The immigrants were mostly from the squirearchy, the smaller landed proprietors and merchants, often with good blood and well-connected in "the county," but not at all great people in the English social scale. A "Lord of the Manor" in England, for example, is a quite unimportant person, who might frequently, as in the case of Washington's ancestor at Sulgrave, be an iron merchant who had made money and bought himself a modest country place, in accordance with English social tradition.

It was precisely that tradition, however, which was maintained in the South and nowhere else. The very fact that the Southerners wished to maintain it indicates that a much larger proportion of them were of that society and

[6] McCrady, *History of South Carolina, op. cit.*, vol. I, p. 317.

tradition in England than was the case in other colonies. Moreover, perhaps equally important, their new surroundings helped to mould them. The Bostonian, and indeed other New Englanders, might pride themselves on family portraits (of which there were perhaps as many in the North as in the South), on their clerical or other early ancestry, on their moral and mental attainments, but there is not the slightest indication that even the most undemocratic of them thought of himself as wanting to live in the tradition of the English landed hierarchy reaching down from aristocracy to county family. It is difficult to imagine a Bostonian as preferring to think of himself above all else as a "country gentleman."

The ideal which took root in the South was distinctly that of English country life in which the owners of broad acres should also constitute the dominant class in government, though this was steadily disputed by the back counties where democracy reigned. In many ways, particularly in that of educating the boys in England, the South was in much closer social contact with the upper classes in England than was any part of the North in the early period. The peaceful Southern planter played no such part as had the feudal lord of the past, but his large plantation, remote from others and on which he exercised a lavish hospitality, was nearer to the English country estate of the upper middle class than anything else in America, and in England a country estate was a badge of social distinction without which a merchant or professional man could not be wholly accepted. Families inter-married and built up cliques which ruled socially and politically. The aristocratic Southerner laid far more stress on family, land, agreeable manners, and political power than he did on mere wealth; and the long days on the plantation led him to cherish social life as an art. His house was no bigger or better than the rich Northerner's, for the best of the Southern houses, such as "Westover," were merely comfortable, moderate-sized country houses, which could easily be duplicated in New England and elsewhere in the North. Nor was there more luxury in the South in spite of the romantic tradition. The silver plate gleamed as lavishly on Northern mahogany as on Southern.

The difference lay in the hundreds or thousands of acres which surrounded the Southerners' houses, and made of their owners something quite different from merely rich men. It lay in the scores to hundreds of slaves which made of their owners something likewise quite different from the employer of casual labor in the North. It lay in the ideal of public life and participation in it as part of one's social status, and in the presence of a subordinate race, all of which gave the Southerner the sense of belonging to a genuinely governing class. It was not by accident that the South sent her ablest men to Washington until 1860; that they occupied such a number of high national offices as was out of all proportion to her white population; or that most of the best of society in Washington was Southern until that city became practically the social centre of the South rather than of the nation.

The English social distinction between the land-owner and the business man, which is only beginning to pass, was based on something more than mere snobbery. Each type has its good and its bad qualities, but they are different. In the city, where everything changes quickly, where there can be no thought of living for generations in the same house, where one is forever "moving on," actually and metaphorically, where the upstart of yesterday may be the leader of tomorrow, where all is in flux, a whole set of values which govern life in the more stable and unchanging country come to be more or less discarded. Psychological qualities become different. Where success means money, and one spends one's time largely in thinking of making money, certain qualities are strengthened and others weakened. A successful town money-maker has to develop shrewdness and some hardness, as well as mere knowledge of his trade. On a big plantation no amount of shrewdness avails against the weather though knowledge may help toward a big crop. In town, where social life is largely, for men at least, the fag end of a day during which they have been in contact with all sorts of other men, it has not the same charm in and for itself that it has in the country where visits of days or even weeks break the monotony of otherwise lonely and unchanging life. In town one has little chance to study or dwell on the things and thoughts of the past. The new idea of the moment is too insistent. The town is radical; the country conservative. We need not insist on the differences further but perhaps it may be accepted that the able and important man who draws his wealth from the soil on which he lives, where his family has lived for generations and where he expects them to continue to live, whose social position and political power stem largely from his long association with a particular estate, is quite different in make-up and outlook from the man who draws *his* wealth and power from an office in a busy commercial life where he has no roots. Even when there is no marked social line drawn between such classes, as there was in England, they will usually dislike and not understand each other.

The aristocratic Southerner was frequently highly educated, but in this also he differed from the Northerner of equal standing. From the manner of his life, new ideas were less insistent for him. He was essentially a classicist. The many winds of doctrine, of which we have spoken in the North, did not blow around him. Rather, he steeped himself in history and classical literature, when he was intellectual, and in works on government, as befitted a man of a ruling class. At its best this type of culture produced a Jefferson, a Madison, and a Marshall. In the formative period of the nation, the intellect of the South, as far as the great and pressing problems of the day were concerned, was certainly superior to that of the North, the only Northerner to compare with the great Virginians being Hamilton, who, in fact, was not a New Yorker but a brilliant young immigrant from the West Indies.

After about 1830, however, there was a great change. While the North forged rapidly ahead, the South fell behind. This was notable in every direction, although the South was far from being the intellectual desert sometimes pictured. Nevertheless, the new leaders of the South—the Rhetts, Yanceys, Calhouns, Dews, Davises, Stephenses, and others—quite apart from the accident of their leading a cause that was to fail, cannot be compared with the Southern leaders of a generation or two earlier in sheer ability. Nor, if we accept almost any standard,—that of the place they hold in modern literary criticism, in public interest, in world repute—can the writers of the South in pure literature of this period compare with those of the North. It is true that Edward Coote Pinkney's lyric, "A Health," beginning

"I fill this cup to one made up of loveliness alone"

is one of the best in the English language and of more exquisite perfection than any Northern poem I know. Poe, although born in Boston of a Maryland father and an English mother, can be claimed by the South as he lived most of his life in Baltimore. William Gilmore Simms, who wrote in 1847 that "the South don't care a damn for Literature or Art," is a close second to Cooper, but although the novelist and poet exaggerated in his statement, the plain fact remains that the South was producing more cotton and riches but less mental ability, in spite of occasional men like Maury in science. In fact the columns of *The Southern Literary Messenger* and other magazines and newspapers were filled with complaints to that effect, lamenting that there were no publishing houses in the section and that even the most ordinary school text books had to be imported from the North and were all written by Northerners.

Many reasons have been suggested for the decline in intellectual ability but most of them are unsatisfactory. It was not the plantation system in itself, for that had produced some of the ablest men and thinkers in the nation. It was not slavery *per se,* for the earlier Southern leaders had been slave owners, and in the past brilliant intellectual civilizations have rested upon slavery, such as the Greek. The real cause was the change of world opinion as to slavery. From 1830 onward the world was to enter upon a period of broad humanitarianism such as it had never known before. European in origin, the North shared in it, as already stated. The South, however, was caught in a way that it did not realize.

Not only was the South classical and extremely conservative in its culture, little given to the taking up of new movements, but the thinking of all of us is likely to be colored by our economic interests. Slavery nowhere else in the world formed the apparently indispensable economic base for a great and civilized society that it did in the South. The abolition of it in the West Indies by England in 1833 was a comparatively simple matter, it being so localized as to affect only slightly the interests of the Empire, and so limited as to allow of compensation to the slave owners. In the South the situation was wholly different, and as we shall see later, the year of the Hayne-Webster debate, 1830, may be taken as approximately the turning point in Southern attitude toward the institution. Not only did the Nat Turner slave insurrection in Virginia do much to destroy antislavery sentiment but the extraordinarily rapid rise of the Cotton Kingdom, which dates from about 1830, seemed to prove both the profitableness of slavery and the impossibility of getting rid of it without tearing down the foundation of a great and growing economic order.

The South was in a desperately cruel position. Its system of labor had only a few decades earlier been universally accepted in America and in the world at large. In the enlightened opposition to it which slowly formed, the South had taken an honorable share. But almost at the very moment when that movement, in common with the general humanitarianism of the age, was to flood the world in one vast tide of feeling, the South was swung outward on an equally vast economic development which apparently could be based on nothing else except the peculiar form of labor which the South had inherited and could not replace. The bitter and vindictive attacks of the Abolitionists in the North aroused equal bitterness in the hearts of Southerners, but the tragedy of the Southern situation lay essentially in the fact that the South seemed to be offered no alternative between cutting itself off from and opposing the whole trend of world thought and cutting its own economic throat and plunging headlong into economic bankruptcy and social chaos.

Its spiritual isolation was recognized after 1830. In the South Carolina Convention of 1833, Robert Barnwell Rhett, one of the group of Southern "Fire Eaters" who share with the Northern Abolitionists much of the responsibility for the growing hatred of the two sections for each other, asserted that a slave-owning people were mad who did not control their own destinies, for it is not "our Northern brethren alone,—the whole world are in arms against your institutions." This note continued down to the War. In an article in *The Southern Literary Messenger* on "The Duty of Southern Authors" in 1856 they were implored to instruct the world in the blessings of slavery, for "the rest of Christendom stands united against us, and are almost unanimous in pronouncing a verdict of condemnation." For a whole generation the best brains of the South, in press, pulpit, and public life, had to bend themselves to the task of defending that section against world opinion on what the world considered a great moral question. Such a position entails heavy intellectual penalties. Slavery and conservatism were held to be synonymous, and the felt need for fighting the world on one front of its advance led, to a considerable extent, to the need of fighting it on others. Every new idea had to be tested as to what its effect might be on the defence of slavery.

Even one who loves the South cannot fail to find something pathological in the intellectual life between 1830 and 1860. In the North the fresh winds of new ideas carried many voices on them, of which the often lying screeches of the Abolitionists were but one. In the South there seem to be no winds, and only the refrain of slavery as against the world. In almost everything the South was aligned against the general movement of the times. In spite of occasional efforts to establish manufactures, the slave economy was essentially agrarian, whereas the world trend was toward industrialism. Southern churches, having to defend what those of the rest of the world mostly condemned, were forced to separate themselves. Authors had to engage largely in painting in the most attractive colors what the rest of the world considered wrong. Statesmen had continually to fight for an institution which was doomed by world judgment. Every political act, every constitutional question, had to be considered in the light of slavery. But this situation was fraught heavily with danger for the healthy spiritual life of both individuals and the people.

Modern psychology has taught us much of the hidden springs in the sub-conscious. It may seem absurd to speak of the proud, haughty, charming South suffering from an inferiority complex; yet it did precisely what a person or people so suffering always does. It not only withdrew itself into something of a dream world of its own, but having its standards and moral values attacked by the rest of the world it set up a defence mechanism by assuming other virtues superior to those of its attackers. There was magnificent human material in the South. If any proof were needed, the war was to show the splendid courage and virility of both men and women. At their best they had a finer humane culture and greater social charm than any other Americans. But as they felt the world more and more against them, this was not enough. Walter Scott provided the escape. As they devoured his novels of feudal life they came to think of themselves as knights with arms at rest against peoples who did not understand the laws of chivalry, as an aristocracy forced to defend themselves against plebeians. The theory of every Southerner a lord and every Southern woman a queen of love and beauty was born. The rôle scarcely fitted the practical hard-working yeoman farmer or the "cotton snob" of the newer rich, nor their wives. The finest women of the South, used to the saddle from childhood, ready at marriage to undertake the arduous work, calling for great efficiency, of acting as mistress of slaves and acres, were far removed from the languid heroines of the Waverley novels. They were as capable and effective women as this nation has ever seen, with the added charm of the Southland and of a social life which they made an art. But the mechanism of defence did not stop with the setting of the South off in a world of romance. When the pressure became greater, as we shall see in the next chapter, the Southerners evolved the theory that they belonged to a superior race. The extent to which this was carried in the leading journals of the section is only an indication of the degree of mental warping resulting from the necessity, for such it was, of standing out against world opinion with regard to what that opinion had come to consider a morally anachronistic type of civilization.

So far as I know, no other people in history has been forced by sheer compulsion of circumstances to undergo such a test. The South had not been responsible for the presence of slavery. It could not rid itself of it. As Lincoln said, "if all earthly power were given me, I should not know what to do with the existing institution." The South had suddenly, due to inventions of the North and of England, found itself one of the richest and most important economic sections of the earth. To a great extent the prosperity of France, England, and our North and West depended on its slave-grown cotton. Yet the world which had created the demand for cotton increasingly demanded that the South should rid itself of slavery, though it could offer no suggestion as to how to do so. The South was forced into a position of defence, which meant expansion as well as mere maintenance of the institution, which itself, on the other hand, was forcing the South more and more out of the main currents of the modern world.

# Chapter IV

# THE FOOTSTEPS OF FATE

As in the preceding chapter we sketched lightly the general background of the sections in the period from 1820 to 1860, so in this one we shall narrate as briefly the events which led to the central action of the tragedy, seeking for their inevitable sequence rather than describing them in detail.

In 1831 there occurred in Southampton County, Virginia, one of the only four serious negro insurrections which took place in the whole history of American slavery. Even this would seem to have been rather a racial than a slave revolt, as Nat Turner, the leader, had received a good education and one of his lieutenants was a free negro. Before the uprising was quelled over fifty whites had been murdered. The great demand for slaves from the South and West was only just beginning, and antislavery feeling had been strong in the State, manumission having been so constantly practised that there were over 47,000 free blacks within its borders. The year following Turner's revolt, however, was to be one of the most fateful in our drama.

The fear, always lurking in the minds of the whites, of the presence in large numbers of the negro, free or slave, had been intensified by the brutal horrors of the massacre; and the legislature of 1832 set itself to solve the problem of how to make Virginia both a white and a free State. After a debate marked by surprising freedom of speech it was voted in the House, 79 to 41, that a system be adopted for the gradual transportation and colonization of the then free negroes and any freed thereafter, it being felt that if the

State could be saved from the menace of the free negroes and if the master who freed his slaves could also be saved from the additional cost of getting rid of them, emancipation would proceed far more swiftly. Unhappily the measure so pregnant with possibilities was lost in the Senate by only one vote.

Various plans for gradual emancipation of the slaves were also proposed but no practical one could in that session be agreed upon, and the momentous opportunity passed, although the Richmond newspapers had come out boldly for antislavery, *The Whig* calling the institution "an evil which all men confess to be the sorest which ever a nation groaned under," and *The Enquirer* endorsing the speech of Mr. Moore when he spoke of it as "the heaviest calamity which has ever befallen any portion of the human race" with an "irresistible tendency . . . to undermine and destroy everything like virtue and morality in the community." The fear of the free negro had been strengthened by the insurrection. Failure to agree on a plan appeared to make a solution impossible. The rise of the radical Abolitionists in the North, scandalously attacking the morality of all slave owners alike, threw Virginia into a position of self-defence. Moreover, the now quickening demand from the new sections for slaves, with the attendant rise in price, seemed to solve at once the economic and deportation problems. Thus the inter-State slave trade instead of emancipation was the disappointing resultant of the great opportunity of 1832. The slightest tipping of the scales in that year's session of the legislature would have set the great State of Virginia on the road to freedom and white labor, to be followed almost certainly by North Carolina, and probably by some of the border States. The desire was present but the ability to solve the problem was not; and the result was a wholly different alignment of States in 1860 from what might otherwise have come to pass. The pattern of our history was again being woven by Fate and not by the will of man.

Meanwhile other events were happening which were likewise to set the new pattern of the next thirty years, and add to the inevitability of the final conflict. History is disappointing to those who naïvely believe in an "absolute" truth. We have already seen Northern and Southern States completely reversing themselves on fundamental interpretations of the Constitution within a decade; we have seen the strict constructionist, Jefferson, become in an instant the broadest constructionist we have perhaps ever had; we have seen the broad-construction Massachusetts Federalists close up, like sensitive plants, at the touch of Jefferson's policy, into the sect of the strict. We have now again to watch the same very human process at work.

In the second decade of the century there were three sections of the country, the North which was rapidly becoming industrial, though the shipping interest of Massachusetts stood out stoutly for transporting goods instead of making them at home; the West, agricultural but flirting with nascent manufactures and demanding transportation facilities; and the South, agricultural but also trying manufactures in South Carolina and elsewhere, without much success. There were likewise in public life three young men, Daniel Webster of Massachusetts, Henry Clay of Kentucky, and John C. Calhoun of South Carolina, each representing one of the three sections. Each was to aspire passionately to the Presidency and each to miss it. All three were remarkable men, though Clay was perhaps the weakest of the triumvirate. Less impressive in personal appearance than either of the others, he neverthless invariably won audiences with his oratory and had the more loyal following among the ordinary people of his State. Possibly this was in part because his knowledge was less profound than Webster's and his mind less subtly logical than Calhoun's. In spite of decisions to quit public life he was continually returned to it, and when he nearly lost his beloved home in Kentucky on account of his debts, unknown admirers throughout the country raised a fund of $50,000 to save it. All three were highly self-conscious. Great orators, like actors, are apt to be, but we are less aware of the trait in Clay, even when using his snuff box to produce a graceful effect, than we are in the shock of hair and glowering eyes of Calhoun embodying the type of the "profound thinker" or in Webster with his huge head and frame and his "Olympian" greatness and majesty, the finished "Senator."

In the second decade of the century, Webster, thinking of the shipping interests of his State, and therefore opposed to a protective tariff, doubted its constitutionality. Calhoun, then strongly nationalistic, favoring internal improvements, and the building up of Southern manufactures, was in favor of protection and expounded the Constitution by the light of that interest. Those who know only the later Calhoun, the strict constructionist who with subtlest of hair-splitting logic tortured the ambiguous words of the Constitution to make them indubitably yield the doctrine of secession, will not recognize him in his earlier Congressional days. In 1817, defending the use of Federal money for roads and canals, he could say: "I am no advocate for refined arguments on the Constitution. The instrument was not intended as a thesis for the logician to exercise his ingenuity on. It ought to be construed with plain good sense. . . . Why should we be confined in the application of money to the enumerated powers? . . . The uniform sense of Congress and the country . . . surely furnish better evidence of the true interpretation of the Constitution than the most refined and subtle arguments." For the ardent nationalist Calhoun of that day, the Constitution was evidently not a legalistic formula but a living thing changing to meet the needs of a growing nation.

The nation was indeed growing fast and furiously, and altering. In the 1820's the manufacturing interest in Massachusetts was to win over the shipping. Webster was to turn a complete somersault on the tariff, and to declare (in the interests of his own particular State) that the Federal Government could be maintained only by "administering it on principles as wide and broad as the country over which it extends!"

In South Carolina, where profound changes were also taking place, Calhoun was to perform a similar somersault, so that both men found themselves still facing each other but from precisely the opposite positions from which each had made his leap. For some years after 1818 the country was generally in the throes of one of our periodical depressions. In South Carolina this was heavily accentuated by the drag of the new cotton States just west of her. From 1800 to 1830 the increase in her white population was only one-quarter of that of the nation at large, and was practically stationary between 1830 and 1840. Between 1823 and 1828 the imports at Charleston decreased fifty per cent. The Cotton Kingdom was beginning its expansion, and the exodus to the new and rich but low-priced lands threatened almost the very life of South Carolina. In addition, the great increase in the supply of cotton combined with depression abroad and at home had lowered the price of the State's staple to disastrous figures. These facts were recognized by some of the intelligent Carolinians but a scape-goat was called for. It proved to be the tariff.

To help themselves through the hard times, the manufacturing interests of the great Middle States had demanded and received a higher scale of duties in 1820. South Carolina objected, and murmurings were heard of States' Rights, but the House of Representatives of that State passed a Resolution which, while opposing protection, insisted that they must protest against "the practice, unfortunately become too common, of arraying upon questions of national policy, the States as *distinct and independent sovereignties* in opposition to, or . . . with a view to exercise a control over the general government." In these words we catch the faint murmuring in the air of the hurricane to come.

In the midst of the distress Henry Clay proposed his "American System," strongly advocating protection as essential to making the nation self-supporting, using all the arguments for a protective tariff which have been used since. On the theory, advanced by Oliver Ellsworth when consenting to the extension of the slave trade in 1787, that what "enriches a part enriches the whole" Clay now asked the South to put up with some loss for the sake of all. On the other hand, he bound the agricultural West to the industrial North by proposing that the excess revenues derived from a high tariff should be used in internal improvements, affording the Western farmer better access to Eastern markets. Appealing strongly to those who would benefit by it, the argument had the weak link of being able to offer little to the Southern States.

Almost coincident with the devastating rise of Garrison and the other Abolitionists in Massachusetts, of whom we shall speak later, there now appeared on the scene in South Carolina one of the equally devastating "Fire Eaters" of the South, Robert Barnwell Rhett. A distant cousin of John Quincy Adams, Rhett's temperament and course were strangely like those of another distant relation of Adams but not of his own, Samuel Adams of Revolutionary Massachusetts. Each burned with undying hatred of the general government under which he lived; each strove unceasingly to arouse the people against it, using every device of persuasion, argument, and invective until his purpose was attained; each was a born revolutionist, destructive, not constructive; and each, when the independence of his State had been proclaimed, found himself set aside for abler and saner men, and himself openly opposed to the new government which he had helped to bring into being.

Rhett, in his speeches at this time, tried to arouse the South Carolinians by parallels with the American Revolution. He echoed Adams's phrases about liberty and "insatiable oppressors." When the "Tariff of Abominations" was passed in 1828 as a result of strange political intrigues which cannot be detailed here, and Webster and Calhoun turned their respective somersaults, Rhett wrote an address to the people warning them that the Constitution if it were to survive must be brought back to its original principles; that although he wished for union it could be maintained only by force; and that faced with the choice of liberty or union none could hesitate. "If you are not prepared to follow up your principles wherever they may lead, to their very last consequences—if you love life better than honor —prefer ease to perilous liberty and glory, awake not! stir not! Impotent resistance will add vengeance to your ruin."[1]

Whether he made his succeeding issues a tariff, slavery, or what-not, Rhett himself added little to that statement throughout his long life of agitation, and when the time came, he was to be in almost as strong opposition to the government of the Confederate States as he had been to that of the United States. Through both his family control of one of the most influential papers in the South, *The Charleston Mercury,* and his own writings and speeches, he shares with Yancey and other Fire Eaters of the South and the Abolitionists of the North, the responsibility, not merely for the war, but for the steadily mounting and ever more disastrous misunderstanding and hatred between the sections.

If Rhett and others, in the period now under review,

[1] Quoted by Laura E. White. *Robert Barnwell Rhett* (New York, American Historical Association, 1931), p. 15.

played the part which Samuel Adams had done in arousing hatred in the earlier one, there was also as before the need that far abler men should rationalize the position to which the virulent denunciations of the Fire Eaters would lead. It is impossible in a few words to explain the causes of the remarkable change of mind in South Carolina at this time—the exigencies of local politics in a peculiarly mixed party situation, the business distress falsely attributed to the tariff, the fear of the rising tide against slavery, and Carolinian localism and fiery pride. Nor could we give a true picture of the period without discussing the writings of men like Judge William Smith, Robert J. Turnbull, Henry L. Pinckney, Thomas Cooper, and others who all stirred the smouldering fire to flames. There was little talk of slavery, only of the tariff and of the tyranny of the Federal Congress in imposing it, but secession and its right began to be freely bruited about. In some cases men changed their fundamental opinions almost overnight, like George McDuffie, who at first proclaimed that most of the talk about "prostrate State sovereignties" came from "ambitious men of inferior talents, who, finding that they have no hope to be distinguished in the councils of the national government, naturally wished to increase the power and consequence of the state governments," where they could shine.[2] Soon he was comparing the tariff of 1828 to the Stamp Act of 1765 and warning the North to remember that the Carolinians were of "noble ancestry."

The most marked change, however, was that of Calhoun, who was now to evolve and fix the form of the Carolina doctrine of States' Rights. So completely and suddenly did he shift from the opinions which he had been expressing in Congress that in the *Life* of himself which he wrote anonymously he completely suppressed all references to them. It

[2] Quoted by Frederic Bancroft, *Calhoun and the South Carolina Nullification Movement* (Baltimore, 1928), p. 51.

is natural that a man should change some of his opinions as he becomes older and more experienced. Perpetual consistency is a sign of stubborn lack of thinking rather than of intellectual virtue. It is impossible to reach down and grasp the motives of most men, far less a politician who has been stung by the desire for the Presidency. One cannot but ponder, however, when one finds two such strong minds as those of Webster and Calhoun, in the tariff debate, changing their fundamental views of the Constitution to fit the needs of their constituents and their own political fortunes. Calhoun saw that if he did not join the radical wing of his party and remain a power in his State, he could never remain one in the nation and become President. Moreover, although we talk of reason as something absolute, our reasons are often strangely moulded by our circumstances. There is perhaps no cause to consider either of the two great exponents of their sections as consciously changing sides from personal ambition; but the fact that both could change and did do so certainly indicates that there was a genuine question as to what the Constitution really meant.

In his famous "Exposition" of 1828, Calhoun, the nationalist, now came out strongly for the "compact" theory of the Federal Government, and claimed that each individual State, as sovereign, had the right to nullify any Act of Congress within its borders, if deemed "unconstitutional" by it. Curiously enough he leaned heavily in his argument on the Virginia and Kentucky Resolves, although they were no part of the Constitution, whereas he said nothing of the Resolves of the nine opposing States in 1798. Nor did he explain how such a construction of the Constitution would permit the Federal Government to function at all. Four years later he carried his argument to its logical conclusion by asserting that every State had the right to secede from the Union.

Although the temptation is great, there is nothing to be

gained by here entering upon a discussion of the possible abstract "rights" of nullification or secession. If we consider the Constitution, which Calhoun had earlier said it was *not*, as "a thesis for the logician to exercise his ingenuity on," the ablest of logicians can, did, and may always differ. In our short narrative we have already seen the keenest minds taking views opposed to one another; we have seen the same man taking opposed views at different stages of his career; we have seen State legislatures differing from each other and also reversing their own positions. If, on the other hand, we consider society as a growing organism to which the interpretation of the Constitution will have to adapt itself, opinions again can honestly differ, and men's opinions are, quite honestly, largely formed by their interests, even though we do not rate ourselves as cheap as he of whom old Samuel Butler wrote:

> "What makes all doctrines plain and clear?
> About two hundred pounds a year.
> And that which was proved true before,
> Prove false again? Two hundred more."

Without taking sides on the question in its logical abstractness we may, nevertheless, point to some of the difficulties, considering the nation as a growing and developing organism. At first that organism was simple, as a jelly fish is simple. A part might have been cut off without much injury, mental or physical, to the whole. But as the nation became more complex, so its parts became more essential. A theory or practice of lopping off parts which may suit a jelly fish may not so readily be applied to a human being or other highly complicated organic creation.

When the Union was formed, every State had fronted on the Atlantic seaboard. With the small vessels of that time, each, although some better than others, could carry on over-seas trade. As the size of vessels increased, the States

with good harbors received an advantage. As the size of
the country grew, many States were formed with no access
to the sea. In 1787 a State might have seceded with less
damage to the whole than the division of Germany by
thrusting the Polish Corridor between east and west Prus-
sia. The thrusting of a wedge between portions of the
Union would have been a nuisance but not fatal to it. The
situation became wholly different when the commerce of the
entire nation was concentrated through a few ports. The
States which were formed in the additions made to the
United States, almost wholly by those who believed in the
States' Rights doctrine, were guaranteed equal rights with
the original States. As a practical matter could the great
interior today allow the States possessing the ports of New
York, Philadelphia, New Orleans, Galveston, and San Fran-
cisco to secede and leave the other States throttled?

We need not stress the obvious fact that if at any moment
any State or group of States could nullify an Act of Congress on grounds of its unconstitutionality, then the powers
of the central government would be voided. South Carolina claimed that a protective tariff was unconstitutional,
yet the Constitution provided that Congress shall have the
"power to lay and collect Taxes, Duties, Imposts, and Ex-
cises . . . for the common Defence and general Welfare of
the United States." The North and West decided that the
duties laid in 1828 were for the "general Welfare." South
Carolina denied it. According to another clause no vessel
bound from one State to another should pay duty on its cargo. If South Carolina decided that a duty levied under the
first clause was unconstitutional but its own shipment under the second was not so, it could theoretically have made
its own city of Charleston the only free port in the United
States, have drawn all the commerce of the country to itself,
and deprived the nation of any revenue from customs.

Again we may note that logically the rights of nullification and secession, if they inhered anywhere, inhered only in *each State*. Nevertheless, in spite of talk from time to time, it was early recognized that as a practical matter the only possible successful secession would be that of a *section*, such as New England in 1814 and the South in 1860. There was a marked but recognized difference between theory and practicality. Both however depended on the logical demonstration that a *State* had the right. In 1861 each State seceded before the Confederate States were formed. They were contiguous, with an extensive coastline. But if the mere logical theory is correct why should not the States around the entire rim of the United States—the Atlantic seaboard, the Gulf, Mexico, the Pacific, Canada—be allowed to secede, leaving the nineteen interior States, comprising by far the larger part of the nation, completely shut off from the world? That a vast *section* of the country should break off from the rest because of divergent interests is both understandable and possible, but there is something curious about a theory which gives a single *State* the right to do so and yet recognizes that it will not do so except as part, or a prospective part, of a *contiguous section*.

There is, however, as we have said, no use in spinning out logic on the question. Logic cannot answer it, and if, as Calhoun said in his earlier period, the Constitution should be "construed with plain good sense," it is the sense of the ordinary man which will count at last. During the next thirty years the South was to rely on logic whereas the North and West were to be motivated by "sense," whatever that means, each section basing its views on its own self interests. The outcome of such a situation, there being no umpire superior to each, was inevitable. After Clay's exposition of the tariff nothing was henceforth to our own day to be added to the theory of protection; after Calhoun's exposition of the States' Rights doctrine of secession nothing was to be added to that; after the Fire Eaters demanded secession, first on the tariff and next on slavery, nothing was to be added to them; after the Abolitionists started, nothing was to be added to antislavery. The rest of the fateful decades was compulsion, emotion, and Fate. The resultant events must be run through briefly.

The slavery agitation which preceded the Compromise of 1820 had clearly brought out the underlying and increasing antagonism of the sections to each other on that ground, but the question having been temporarily more or less quiescent as a sectional one slavery did not form one of the leading topics in the rancorous discussions of the 1830's. The tariff, as we have noted, was admirably adapted to creating a maximum of ill-feeling. The South Carolina Fire Eaters continued to insist that protection for the North was not merely the cause but the only cause of the woes of their State. Manufacturing had not gained much of a foothold in the South, less because it could not be made profitable than because the whole temper and training of the people were agrarian, and because they also believed that they could invest their money more profitably in land and slaves than in factories and mills. The consequence was that almost every manufactured article the Southerners bought came from the North. Long lists of such were frequently declaimed to show how everything they used, from getting out of bed to going back to it, came from the increasingly disliked section of the North.

With all the compelling eloquence of which the Southerner was a master, it was driven home to people already disliking the North socially, feeling for it also that instinctive mistrust of the agrarian for the industrialist, and beginning to fear the North's antislavery views, that if the North combined with the West could succeed in its protective policy, it would mean not only the economic ruin of the South but its political vassalage. The emotional material was of the most combustible sort, but it was only in South

Carolina that the fire blazed dangerously. The vassalage was in reality more to the slave system and the pure agrarian ideal of life than to Northern manufacturers, for the South was rich in resources, as in the then neglected Birmingham District and elsewhere. It had some of the finest water-power on the continent. It had ample industrial opportunity. If it insisted on *using* the products of an industrial age and yet would not *make* them itself, the reason was in the social system and ideals, not in any reliance upon others forced by geographical conditions. But this naturally was not seen, whereas the really sectional nature of a tariff as the sections were constituted was easily apparent. The rest of the South, though far from being willing to go the full length of the South Carolinians, agreed largely with their theories. The agrarian but partly industrialized West, hungry for money to be spent on improvements, held the balance. As it felt and voted, the nation would be Protectionist or Free Trade, slave or free, agrarian or industrial. Both North and South held out baits to win the third section to their views.

As one of the many moves in this delicate game, in January, 1830, Senator Hayne of South Carolina made a strong attack on New England as threatening the growth of the West by its protective policy and urged the West to join the South in opposition. When Webster rose to reply he skilfully retorted that other Southerners had complained, contrary to Hayne's view, that the North was in fact building up the West, and then drew the Southern senator into an exposition of States' Rights, nullification, and secession. From that point he went on to make the famous "Reply to Hayne" which was, however, really a reply to Calhoun and the whole secessionist school. All three, oddly enough, had changed sides within a few years, and assuredly could not claim that they were consistent or that logic was absolute. Webster was not a great constitutional lawyer; Calhoun was a hair-splitter; and Hayne on this occasion was a pawn.

They were all great figures, however, in the Senate when the Senate was really great, and were powerful orators in a day when oratory swayed men's souls.

The importance of the occasion was that Webster, who never afterward rose to the height of his speech of January 26, 1830, gave voice to that entire portion of the American people which believed in the Union above all else, and which looked upon the Constitution, as Calhoun had declared it to be a few years before, as something which, however it might be construed logically at one moment or another, was living and growing with the nation's needs. Calhoun in his new phase had given the South its fine-spun logic for the doctrine of secession; now Webster gave the rest of the nation the basis for its national and Unionist emotions. As we have pointed out many times, there was no Absolute Truth, no Ultimate Judge, but two men had set the cords of the nation's mind and heart vibrating in disharmony, a disharmony so strong that it was certain in time to make the national structure quiver more and more until the final crash. These were the giants of the mind; it was left to lesser men to cause the bitterness and hatred that mere battles would not have brought.

Always in politics or business the actual events which can readily be recorded are the resultants of the intricate inter-play of personalities, with their ideas, ambitions, emotions, much as the pattern of a Persian rug is the result of the fast-moving fingers which ply the shuttle and tie the knots from behind the design. In a brief narrative one cannot, even if it were possible, recite in detail all the sub-surface motives, wire-pullings, ambitions, other emotions, which caused the events in the obvious pattern. Moreover, even the events have to be selected in such small numbers as to give a false impression of simplicity to that pattern. Although, looking back, the main lines of the design are now fairly clear, we must recall that during the three decades after 1830 events, big or small, in connection with our tragedy were almost constant, yielding a growing sense of confusion to those of that day; and that behind those events human passions, individual, crowd, and sectional, were steadily rising like waves of the sea when the storm-winds lash them. There were occasional lulls, but in general the intensity grew until the cone of the storm swept into South Carolina in 1861.

Andrew Jackson was President in 1830 when Webster replied to Hayne while Calhoun as Vice-President presided over the debate, his deep-set eyes glowing like coals from the sallow, sickly face under its great shock of hair. Although a Southerner, the President had expressed himself clearly enough as to his disbelief in the Vice-President's secession doctrine. It is odd that there should have been any doubt as to where Jackson stood, though the South Carolina leaders appear to have believed that he was with them. The Tariff of 1832 was a compromise measure, unsatisfactory to everybody. Nevertheless the Carolina Nullifiers decided to act, and at a convention assembled for the purpose the State formally declared the Act null and void, and provided for armed protection of the people should the Federal Government attempt to enforce it. Unfortunately for the belief in absolute logic, this does not mean that the State was a unit in its opinions. Although outnumbered, there was at this time a strong Union party among leading men, such as J. L. Petigru, J. R. Poinsett, William Drayton, Alfred Huger, Langdon Cheves, and others. These were called "slaves," "sneaks," "renegades," and other such names by the Nullifiers, whereas the latter in turn were dubbed "Jacobins," "madmen," "conspirators," and such by the Unionists. There were even armed conflicts between the parties. Speaking of the election in Charleston, Petigru wrote on October 29—that its "turbulence . . . far outdid anything you ever saw here. We [the Unionists] were beset at Seyle's night after night by a disorderly mob and obliged to arm ourselves with bludgeons and march out in files."[3]

The simple registering of the State as in favor of Nullification fails to make us realize the discussion, disagreement, tumult, ferment, and anger behind that decision. However, the decision was taken, although the rest of the South was lukewarm. Practically the whole section, including both parties in South Carolina, was opposed to a protective tariff, but many believed, as did Petigru, that the only problem lay in the choice of means to defeat it, and that "resistance by nullification is the fatal source of bitterness and discord." Petigru, like many other prominent men, thought of emigrating. "If the Union is severed my mind is made up to quit the negro country," he wrote to a friend, "but where to go? Aye, there is the rub." So many did leave that the *Sumter Whig,* for example, noted that if the volume of emigration continued Sumter would soon be a howling wilderness, and other newspapers recorded the same conclusion as to their localities elsewhere. Poinsett wrote that there was scarcely a family not divided in opinion.[4]

In his inaugural address as Governor of South Carolina in December, former Senator Hayne announced that his State had been obliged to "put herself upon her sovereignty . . . assert her just rights or sink into a state of colonial vassalage," and threatened to repel by armed force any attempt by the Federal Government to enforce the Tariff Act.

President Jackson at once sent General Winfield Scott to Charleston and took various military precautions. On

[3] James Petigru Carson, *Life, Letters, and Speeches of James Louis Petigru* (Washington, 1920), p. 103.
[4] *Vide* C. S. Boucher, *The Nullification Controversy in South Carolina* (Univ. of Chicago Press, 1916), pp. 269 ff.; and Carson, *Petigru, op. cit.,* p. 127.

December 10 he also issued a proclamation to the people of South Carolina utterly repudiating the doctrine of nullification and secession. In words strangely prophetic of Lincoln's a generation later, this Southern President, who always considered himself a son of South Carolina, warned his "native State" that "disunion by armed force is *treason* . . . the Government of your country . . . cannot accede to the mad project of disunion, of which you would be the first victims. Its First Magistrate cannot, if he would, avoid the performance of his duty." South Carolina then began to arm, and the situation was critical. Although, as Petigru wrote to H. S. Legare, "the war and revolutionary party are a decided minority" they had got an ascendancy over the minds of many and "the idea of 'going for my own State' is a stumbling block."

The flow of oratory and incendiary writing continued unabated, although the other States of the Cotton Belt showed no intention of following South Carolina out of the Union, and Virginia suggested that her hot-headed sister take time to consider. Jackson, though a Southerner, was, as many others were also at this period, a passionate lover of the Union. During the celebration of Jefferson's birthday on April 13, 1830, at the end of many toasts in favor of States' Rights, he had proposed his celebrated one of "our Federal Union—it *must* be preserved." He had also written to a relation that "when a faction in a State attempts to nullify a constitutional law of Congress . . . the balance of the people composing this Union have a perfect right to coerce them to obedience." Writing to Martin Van Buren, the doughty old President pointed out what he believed to be the absurdity of the secession doctrine. "Congress," he said, "have the right to admit new States. When territories they are subject to the laws of the Union; the day after admission they have the right to secede and dissolve it. We have paid five millions for Louisiana. We admitted her into the Union. She too has the right to secede, close the commerce of six States, and levy contributions both upon exports and imports. A State cannot come into the Union without the consent of Congress, but it can go out when it pleases." Such a Union, he added, could not last a month. At the end of 1832 he wrote to the Unionist J. R. Poinsett, in Charleston, that he could send 100,000 men to maintain the Federal Government in less than three months, and that "we will strike at the head and demolish the monster, Nullification and secession, at the threshold."

Jackson, however, although his blood was up, was also a low-tariff man, and in March, 1833, Congress passed two Acts, which he signed, one giving him authority to collect the duties in South Carolina by force and the other lowering the tariff. The result of the Force and Compromise Tariff Bills was thus a drawn battle. The Federal Government could assert that it had maintained its authority; and the Nullifiers that they had forced that same government to yield to their wishes. Nothing was settled. Merely another compromise had been made and the ultimate decision by arms had come nearer. The quarrel between the sections had been over the tariff. But, as Petigru wrote, nullification had "done its work; it has prepared the minds of men for a separation of the States, and when the question is mooted again it will be distinctly union or disunion." Jackson said that this time the demand for secession had come from the tariff; that the next time it would come from slavery. Southern nationalism was beginning to take shape, with the dream of a great Southern Confederacy, though this was as yet largely limited to the Fire Eaters of South Carolina. Economic and political sectionalism had become strongly marked between 1820 and 1830. It was for the extremists on both sides in the next decade to color the conflict of interests with extraordinary bitterness, and to make any further compromises more and more insecure.

In the North the Abolitionists began their campaign of immediate, universal, and unrecompensed emancipation which was marked far more by an almost insane vilification of all who differed from them than by humanitarian sentiment. Perhaps the first "immediatist" was the Rev. George Bourne in 1816, but the movement did not emerge well into public view until the fanatical genius of William Lloyd Garrison began to lead the crusade about 1829. Although "the Abolitionists" differed much among themselves in personality and at times in policy, it was the early Massachusetts witch-burning temper, megalomania, unwillingness to "compromise with truth," combined with the burning belief that they alone knew what was "truth," on the part of certain leaders which stamped the movement and created the havoc. Garrison, at the head, was as convinced of his own God-given mission to end slavery at whatever cost as Sam Adams had been to break up the British Empire or a man like Rhett was to carry the South out of the Union. Such men change history but are likely to leave behind them a fiery legacy of hatreds even when successful.

Another characteristic of the Abolitionists was their utter unwillingness to consider anything but their own point of view, any historical causes, any practical consequences. In his demand for immediate emancipation of all slave property—quite as much property under the Constitution as was Garrison's own investments, property lawfully owned and the confiscation of which would ruin a large proportion of the honest citizens of the nation—Garrison could only declaim that to reimburse the slave-owner would be "paying a thief for giving up stolen property." The measure of the man, like that of many of his followers, may be found in his statement that "passion is reason." In 1831 he founded his newspaper, *The Liberator,* devoted to the Abolitionist cause, though like most professional reformers of that period he took up every "cause,"—temperance, Anti-Mason, women s rights, world peace, and others. Such men were what Roosevelt was later to call "the lunatic fringe" of all great movements.

It is impossible without reading the Abolitionist literature to realize the amazing bitterness, vituperativeness, exaggeration, narrowness, and lack of practicality of the Abolitionists themselves. For thirty years they steadily failed in their object of immediate emancipation but they did so stir sectional hatreds into flame that even now the fires are easily blown again among the embers. The spirit of these men was that of old John Endicott of early Massachusetts. What they believed was what the world must believe, and they were willing to spread it by fire and sword. They cursed the Constitution, the churches, and all that stood in the way of their immediate object. "I say, my Curse be on the Constitution," shouted Wendell Phillips, and Garrison called it "a covenant with death and an agreement with hell." Because the Methodist Episcopal Church would not adopt his views, another agitator, S. S. Foster, went up and down the country denouncing it as "worse than any brothel in the city of New York." For such men, as for the old Puritans of Massachusetts Bay, truth, as Phillips said, was "one forever, absolute"; and they believed that they themselves alone possessed it. They made no allowance for their own error, no allowance for the historic process which had fastened slavery on the South, no allowance for the economic and social problems involved in emancipation, no allowance for the hundreds of thousands of honorable, kindly white masters who found themselves caught in the nexus of a type of civilization which the world was only suddenly beginning to denounce. As is the way of reforming zealots always, they struck out venomously at the morality of all who differed with them.

The anger and resentment they aroused was Northern as well as Southern. The period was, as we have already noted, one of intense intellectual ferment and confusion. There were racial riots and mobbings in the North against Irish and other foreigners. There was religious strife, with burnings of Catholic churches and convents. As the Abolitionists added their voices to the growing hubbub, those who were opposed to their mad course used the same terroristic methods against them. We cannot here detail the innumerable cases of stormy public gatherings, of such mobs as the Boston one of 1835 when Garrison had to be rescued and put in jail to save his life, of the murder of the editor Lovejoy in 1837. Cases of the forced rendition from the North of fugitive slaves served to exacerbate public opinion on the question. If the utterances and publications of the Abolitionists aroused anger among a large part of the Northern people, they also raised the question of free speech which seemed to be threatened by the necessity of not discussing slavery. The confusion grew.

In the South the reaction to the attacks on slavery took several forms until, as the distinguished Southerner who is now our Ambassador to Germany has pointed out, the revolution in Southern thought became comparable only to that in Germany after Bismarck.[5] The earlier South of Jefferson, Madison, Washington, and others had largely looked upon slavery as an evil which might in time be eradicated, but the new school of Southern prophets now arising, Thomas Cooper, Thomas R. Dew, W. L. Yancey, Chancellor Harper, and many more, preached to willing ears the doctrine that slavery was a positive *good*, not merely morally and scripturally defensible, but an ideal system for both races.[6]

As a preliminary, the political philosophy of Jefferson was repudiated, with its belief in human equality before the

[5] William E. Dodd, *The Cotton Kingdom* (Yale University Press, 1919), p. 59.
[6] See the writings gathered in *The Pro-Slavery Argument,* Charleston, 1852; and *Cotton Is King,* Augusta, 1860.

law and its doctrine of inalienable rights. The Declaration of Independence was scrapped and in its place was set up the Prussian doctrine of inherent inequality and the right of a superior race to rule. The lower race, according to Harper, was to be kept in subjection to do the lowest and hardest forms of labor. They were to be left uneducated, as there was to be no chance of their ever rising in the scale, and their moral and sexual standards were also to be kept at a lower level than those of their rulers. The slave, he said with approval, "has no character to establish or lose," and "has no hope that by a course of integrity, he can materially elevate his position in society." Such might seem to be a damning indictment of a social system but one after another, Calhoun, Jefferson Davis, and other Southern leaders went over to the new doctrine of slavery as a positive good, with all that such a doctrine implied. Although in part due to the supposed economic necessity of slavery and the impossibility of supplanting it by any other labor system in a rapidly developing section, this change in thought was also largely due to the attacks of the Abolitionists on the morality of slave owners. These had to be answered, and the fiercer the denunciations became, the more violently did the Southerner defend his institution.

The new theory of basic inequality involved several corollaries of a similar Prussian sort. The idea of a permanent class of serfs, with a class of rather unimportant whites and at the top a ruling class of magnates, easily led to a revival of the feudal system in the new Southern thought. If Carlyle greatly influenced the belief in the right of the strong to rule, another new author, Walter Scott, provided the romantic setting for a sort of neo-feudalism in social outlook, and it was said that his books were shipped South in car-load lots. From the fourth decade of the century, Southern books, letters, and diaries become glutted with talk about cavaliers and knights. The dream world was being rapidly built up. If the rabid Abolitionist believed that he alone possessed truth, no less did the Southerner come to believe, encircled by almost universal hostility to his "peculiar institution," that the rest of mankind was wrong, and that he himself was the developer of a superior type of civilization which the rest of the world would have to adopt. Justly he pointed to the great abuses of labor under the industrial civilization of the North and of England, and contrasted them with the more or less general contentment and comfort of the slaves. Moreover, during the ensuing decades the doctrine of the superior race came to be extended to the white Southerner as compared with the Northerner until, as we shall note later, in the 1850's the theory assumed such a fantastic form as we of our day have witnessed nowhere except in Germany. It is against this background, and not the earlier one, that we must place the events of 1830 to 1860. The South was right, in its own opinion, and the world was wrong. Slavery was not an evil but a good. The white Southerner was a superior being, superior to both the negro and the Northern white. The extension of slavery was a necessity, not only within the Union but anywhere else where slave territory could be added, Cuba, Texas, Mexico. Dreams of a great slave empire grew in vividness.

Meanwhile incident followed incident in swift succession, only a few of which can be noted. Secession was frequently mentioned both North and South, and the dislike between the sections grew apace. The legislature of Georgia in 1831 offered $5,000 reward to any one who would arrest and convict Garrison or any one circulating his paper *The Liberator*. This and other antislavery literature was finally practically excluded from the mails in the South with the consent of the Postmaster General, Amos Kendall, dividing the country into two sections, in one of which it was lawful to circulate the literature and in the other it was not. The

Abolitionists being a small minority, this met with the approval of most Northerners but served to indicate the widening chasm between the sections. Most antislavery men in the North, including Lincoln, were themselves opposed to the Abolitionists, but the South took no note of this, and the legend of different races grew. The Northerners and Southerners, wrote Chevalier in 1834, "are the same men who cut each other's throats in England, under the name of Roundheads and Cavaliers." As yet, however, neither section was willing to follow the extremists. In the North the mobbing of Abolitionists continued and in the South, when Rhett demanded an amendment to the Constitution or immediate secession his demand fell flat, though Senator Johnston wrote to his brother Albert, the future Confederate general, that he had better prepare for a "Civil War."

However, in the North the sensibilities of people who were far from being rabid Abolitionists were often being lacerated by the spectacle of runaway slaves, frequently nearly white in color, being captured and returned to slavery. Such cases occasionally attracted wide attention, with much resentment that the governmental machinery of free States should have to be used to condemn men to slavery. The Fugitive Slave clause of the Constitution unquestionably provided for this but South Carolina chose to go beyond the Constitution. In 1835 the legislature of that State had passed an Act providing that any colored person found on a vessel entering her ports should, at the expense of its owner, be kept in jail until the vessel again sailed.

As so often, the Palmetto and the Bay States were the protagonists of the drama, and Massachusetts finally decided to test the constitutionality of the law, sending the well-known Samuel Hoar south for the purpose. A case was to be opened which should eventually reach the Federal Supreme Court, as provided by the Constitution in disputes between States, and so little did Hoar think that there would be any difficulty that he took his daughter with him. The upshot was that, after threats of personal violence, Hoar was deported from the State, and the legislature passed a new Act declaring that any one who came with any commission from another State to "disturb, counteract, or hinder" any Act South Carolina should choose to pass regarding either slave or free blacks should be guilty, with heavy penalties, of a "high misdemeanor." When Hoar left he pointed out that, inconsistent with the Constitution, South Carolina refused the rights granted to other States and their citizens, by mobs and by her legislature; and asked if the other States were henceforth to be regarded as the conquered provinces of South Carolina. In refusing to allow the case to take its regular course up to the Supreme Court, that State unquestionably put itself beyond the pale of the Constitution, and it could not well complain thereafter if some Northern States did not enforce the Fugitive Slave clause.

A few months after this episode came the annexation of Texas, a territory large enough to have six or eight States carved out of it, and the absorption of which was regarded by many Northerners as a Southern trick to increase the power of the slavocracy in the national government. Following filibustering expeditions to Cuba and Central America, the proposed annexation seriously disturbed many Northern States. While on the one hand South Carolina was calling for annexation of Texas or the dissolution of the Federal Union, on the other the legislature of Maine passed a resolution declaring that the annexation was unconstitutional and if persisted in would "tend to drive the States into a dissolution of the Union." The legislators of Massachusetts voted that they would never consent to the annexation of more territory except as free, and after the fact was accomplished declared that it was not legally binding. Lowell, then probably the most popular poet in Amer-

ica, wrote, in his widely circulated *Biglow Papers,* of the
North and South,

> "Man hed ough' to put asunder
> Them thet God has noways jined;
> An' I shouldn't greatly wonder
> Ef there's thousands o' my mind."

The annexation of Texas had practically coincided with
the settlement with England of the Oregon boundary dispute, and followed by the War with Mexico and the Gadsden
Purchase rounded out the present continental area of the
United States. What States should be created out of the
vast addition to the national domain, and whether slave or
free, brought the slavery controversy into its final phase.
The "Wilmot Proviso" that slavery should never exist in
any of the territory acquired from Mexico, many times introduced into Congress but never passed, was an indication
of the new fears aroused in the North and of the then inevitable political aspect of the problem. One last effort was
to be made to compromise a question which in fact was becoming too fundamental to be compromised.

In 1848 the "Free Soil" party appeared in the elections
but the crucial year was 1850. Economic conditions although by no means all determinative in history do greatly
affect its course, and the South was especially embittered at
this time because of several years of unusually low prices
for cotton. Insisting that it had the right to take its slave
property into the newly acquired territory, it failed to recognize the equal right of the North to develop that territory
in accordance with its own type of free civilization, and the
fact that free white settlers and labor would not settle where
they had to compete with slaves. In the session of Congress
of 1850 Webster, Clay, and Calhoun met for the last time,
and as a final effort at compromise they succeeded in securing the passage of five Resolutions, which taken together

have been known as "the Compromise of 1850." Briefly,
California was to be admitted as a free State; the slave
trade was to be ended in the District of Columbia; the
status of what was then called New Mexico was to be left
open; some minor adjustments were made as to the boundaries and public debt of Texas; and a drastic Fugitive Slave
Law was enacted. In his famous speech of the 7th of
March, Webster pleaded with all the rhetorical oratory of
that day for the preservation of the Union, but he himself
was damned by the antislavery people of the North, and
although the Compromise did hold the bonds of union for
another decade it could not permanently satisfy either
section.

In the North public opinion had become so strong against
slavery that whereas only the more radical wished to disturb
it in the States where it already existed, most men did not
wish to see it extended farther and could not bring themselves to enforce the Act for the return to servitude of
escaped slaves. Not only did the Act become almost as
completely nullified, even when legislatures did not pass
resolutions against it, as had the tariff of 1832 in South
Carolina, but the so-called Underground Railroad came into
being which was organized to help fleeing slaves to escape
from the South to Canada. It was not that the North cared
for the negro. It did not, most emphatically, as is amply
proved by all the evidence. It did, however, care for freedom, the difference between the two sections being well
summed up by Carlyle when he remarked that "the South
says to the nagur, 'God bless you! and be a slave,' and the
North says, 'God damn you! and be free.'" Nevertheless,
the insistence of the South upon the return of its escaped
human property probably did more to solidify Northern
feeling against slavery among common-place conservative
people than had all the ranting of the Abolitionists for the
previous twenty years. It is true that legally the South was

entitled to what it claimed. A slave was as indubitably "property" as was stock in a railway, but in the modern world it had become an anachronistic form of property, as obsolete outside the South as marriage by capture, and no amount of legal reasoning could alter the changed sentiment of the world.

While the Compromise was being debated in Congress, the first session of a convention of nine Southern States was in session at Nashville to consider the interests and possible action of the South. Representatives from South Carolina and Mississippi were for extreme measures, and resolutions advocating immediate secession were introduced as the only remedy for the "aggravated wrongs" and the future "enormous evils," which that section was suffering from, or threatened with.

On the whole, however, the South was not yet ready to cast the die, and although in Mississippi John A. Quitman and other political leaders were in favor of seceding, a State Convention held in the same year passed a resolution declaring that secession was not sanctioned by the Federal Constitution! Rhett and other Fire Eaters of South Carolina, with Yancey of Alabama, had planned that Georgia should secede first, to be immediately seconded by South Carolina, and within a year and a half to be followed not only by the entire South but also by New Mexico, California, and Utah, after which Mexico was to be conquered. However, the more important Georgia leaders, Toombs, Stephens, and Cobb, were against extreme measures, and favored the Compromise.

This in no way deterred Rhett from his course, and he now came out for immediate disunion, even if South Carolina had to move alone. "Let it be that I am a Traitor," he declaimed in one of his speeches. "The word has no terrors for me . . . I have been born of Traitors . . . in the great cause of liberty. . . . Instead of shrinking, we might pant for the trial which shall isolate South Carolina in this great conflict." In speeches throughout the State he proclaimed the glories of an independent South Carolina, though he never believed that the State would have to stand alone. He looked forward always to a Southern Confederacy, and believed the rest of the Gulf States at least would have to follow. The results, however, were disappointing, and although he was elected United States Senator in 1851 South Carolina became for a while torpid on the subject of secession, and refused to rally to Rhett's rhetoric.

Nevertheless, to an extent that cannot be realized by the few incidents given above, the South had become used to considering secession as a possible move, and the Union sentiment of an earlier generation had become greatly weakened. What one continually talks about as a possible remedy begins to lose its terrors, if it held any. In this work William L. Yancey of Alabama now took the lead of Rhett. Although little is heard of him in the briefer histories written by Northerners, there is good reason to believe that, as a Southern historian has said, he was one of the half dozen men who had most to do with the shaping of our destiny in the nineteenth century. He was one of the supreme orators of the South, swaying a power which no Northerner did by speech, in a section in which oratory far surpassed the printed word in influence. From the Mexican War he was whole-heartedly for secession as the only means of maintaining slavery. Rhett and many other Southerners might send their sons to Harvard and other Northern universities but the real university of the South for the great mass of the people was the public platform at political meetings, barbecues, court days, and camp meetings; and the influence of Yancey, who the Chief Justice of Alabama said was the greatest orator he had ever heard, cannot be overrated in leading the South on its path.

It is impossible to recite all the various events which were increasing the tension between the sections. For years old

John Quincy Adams had been fighting in Congress for the right of petition in connection with antislavery petitions from many bodies in the North, although not himself an Abolitionist; and Southern feeling had been exacerbated. In connection with the Wilmot Proviso and slavery in the territories both Virginia and North Carolina had threatened secession. Vermont had declared slavery a crime and that it could not be permitted to exist any longer in any territory under the jurisdiction of the United States. Jefferson Davis, with Quitman and William Walker as aides, was planning for the acquisition of Cuba and Mexico for the creation of more slave States. There was ferment on every side.

In 1852, although in the Presidential campaign of that year slavery was stated to be a dead issue after the Compromise of two years before, a book was published in the North which proved to be one of the leading factors in bringing on the final war. Harriet Beecher Stowe, the wife of a poor clergyman, trying to make money for her household, wrote *Uncle Tom's Cabin.* Unfair in the extreme to the South as a whole, its public success was immediate and prodigious. Selling 300,000 copies in the first twelve months in America, it was translated into twenty different languages and circled the globe. Painting the evils of slavery in the most lurid colors there was no single incident in it which could not have been duplicated in real life, but sweeping all the possible horrors into one gripping story the impression was profoundly misleading. The effect was to indict an entire people for the crimes and cruelty of a small minority, and the South went up in a flame of passion. In the North the recital was taken as a true picture of slavery as it existed in daily life in all the slave States, and tens of thousands of people who had turned deaf ears to the radical Abolitionists or mere antislavery advocates, were now cursing not only slavery but the Southerner as pictured in the book. At the same time other New England authors, notably Lowell and Longfellow, had become bitter haters of everything Southern and were spreading the feeling. Even after the war was over both the latter would have nothing to do with charming Southern people who were staying in Cambridge, merely because they were Southern.

On the other hand, in the South the misunderstanding of the North, and the new theory of "race," were rapidly making any compromise impossible. Thanks perhaps to the Abolitionists, the whole "North" had come to be considered as merely a hated New England writ large. *The Southern Literary Messenger,* the best literary magazine in the South, teemed with articles against Northern character as the war approached. One author claimed that New England was settled by descendants of the ancient British and Saxons whereas the South had been peopled by those of the Normans, and that the Northerners required to be governed and would never realize their incapacity to govern until taught "by the light of their burning cities." The Southerners, he went on, "come of that race, who today sit upon all the thrones of enlightened Europe and give law to the million." Admitting certain good qualities in Northerners he added that "they still require *control,* and the Southern people of this country possess the capacity, the position, and power to do so (*sic*)."[7]

In another article on "Northern Mind and Character," we read that the Northern "priesthood prostitutes itself to a level with the blackguard, and enters the field of secular politics, in the spirit of a beer-house bully," while the women of the North, "deserting their nurseries, stroll over the country as politico-moral reformers, delivering lewd lectures upon the beauties of free-love and spiritualism, or writing yellow back literature, so degraded in taste, so

[7] "The Difference of Race Between the Northern and Southern People," *Southern Literary Messenger,* June, 1860, *passim.*

prurient in passion, so false in fact, so wretched in execution, and so vitiating to the morals of mothers in the land,
as almost to force them to bring up daughters without virtue
and sons without bravery." The author admitted as a fact
that "the legislation of the country for the past ten years
has been in the hands of Southern leaders, yet, with singular
fatality, nearly every important move has redounded against
the South." Nevertheless he claims that it is "the mission of the Norman blood of this country—assisted in its
efforts by the institution of African slavery"—to control the
North where "private life [is] stained by every extreme
known in the annals of lust and crime." "Not a breeze that
blows from the Northern hills but bears upon its wings
taints of crime and vice, to reek and stink, and stink and
reek upon our Southern plains.[8]

*De Bow's Review* took up the same strain, claiming that
the South was all "Cavalier" and the North "Puritan" and
that the Northerners "hate us, because their fathers hated
ours." It speaks of the irreligion of Northern women, of
their degradation, of the substitution of "brutal lust" for
love and protection. In another issue it stated that "the
Cavaliers, Jacobites, and Huguenots, who settled the South,
naturally hate, condemn, and despise the Puritans who
settled the North. The former are master races; the latter,
a slave race, descendants of the Saxon serfs." It is unfair
to blame such arrogant and utter nonsense all on Walter
Scott, but he had much to answer for in the South. We shall
have to quote later from newspaper articles during the war,
but they may be considered as propaganda in the madness of
deadly conflict. These articles were published before the
war in the best two monthly magazines in the South, and
taking similar outpourings in the North, we can realize how
swiftly the sections were hastening to the brink.

Trouble over the Fugitive Slave Act continued. Not only

[8] *Ibid.*, November, 1860.

did some of the Northern States, as noted, pass resolutions against both it and slavery but these also poured into the South from innumerable Northern towns and villages. One from Massachusetts to South Carolina was returned by the governor of the latter, who in commenting on it in his message to the legislature said that he considered it "as an insult and an outrage upon every member of the Confederacy. . . . A State whose Legislature deliberately and unblushingly, impiously violates her constitutional obligations, and whose people resist the execution of law, even to the shedding of blood, is not entitled to comity from us. . . . The interchange of civilities with a people who feel it to be no dishonor to prevent the recovery of stolen property . . . is incompatible with the respect which honesty owes to itself. . . . Civil war is a direful calamity but its scourges are to be endured in preference to degradation and ruin."[9]

Of course, the fundamental difficulty was not the question of honesty with regard to stolen property but the changed moral sense of the world outside the South with respect to property in human beings. What had come to be the Northern idea was never better expressed than by Lowell in writing of the election of 1860. "When a man invests money in any species of property," he wrote, "he assumes the risks to which it is liable. If he buy a house, it may be burned; if a ship, it may be wrecked; if a horse or an ox, it may die. Now the disadvantage of the Southern kind of property is—how shall we say it so as not to violate our Constitutional obligations?—that it is exceptional. When it leaves Virginia, it is a thing; when it arrives in Boston, it becomes a man, speaks the human language, appeals to the justice of the same God whom we all acknowledge, weeps at the memory of wife and children left behind—in short hath the same organs and dimensions that a Christian

[9] H. D. Capers, *The Life and Times of C. G. Memminger* (Richmond, 1893), p. 235 *f*.

THE FOOTSTEPS OF FATE

hath. . . . There are people at the North who believe that, beside *meum* and *tuum* there is also such a thing as *suum*— who are old-fashioned enough, or weak enough, to have their feelings touched by these things, to think that human nature is older and more sacred than any claim of property whatever. . . . This, no doubt, makes it hard to recover a fugitive chattel."

Between that humanitarian view of a human being and the strict Constitutional view of the rights of property, there could be no compromise. There was simply no common ground whatever possible. Moreover it may be noted that the language now held by South Carolina with regard to the practical nullication of the Fugitive Slave Act could in no way be reconciled with its own theory of nullification as to tariff or other Acts. If the majority was not to rule and if the Supreme Court was not to be the body ultimately to pass on the Constitutionality of Acts of Congress but the legislature of each State was to be allowed to do so, and nullify, then why could not the legislature of a Northern State, however bad its Constitutional reasoning might be, pass on a Fugitive Slave Law as readily as South Carolina on a Tariff Act? There would appear to be no logical reason against it, and South Carolina's new stand was merely another example of the constant shift on the part of every individual and every section in interpreting the original Constitution to suit the exigencies of the moment.

In spite of the Compromise of 1850, freedom or slavery in the territories continued to be a burning question. In 1854 Senator Douglas, after proposing his doctrine of "squatter sovereignty," *i.e.,* the theory that the inhabitants of each territory should elect for themselves whether it should be free or slave, managed to get through Congress the Kansas-Nebraska Bill which provided that two Territories should be created, Kansas and Nebraska, and that the old Missouri Compromise of 1820 should be declared void. This opened the country north of the line of 36° 30' to slavery, and alarmed the North as much as it delighted the South. Both sections hastened to secure control of Kansas, but by means of the Emigrant Aid Societies the North poured settlers into it much faster than did the South. It was the period of "bleeding Kansas" as peaceful voting gave place to violence between the "border ruffians" who poured at intervals over the Missouri border to fight or vote against the Kansans from the North. Murders, forays, false voting, attempts to make free and slave constitutions, were the order of the day, and the violence threw up to the country the name of a certain John Brown, connected with murders at Pottawatomie. Just before the election of 1856, Theodore Parker wrote to a friend, "If Buchanan is President, I think the Union does not hold out his four years; it must end in civil war, which I have been preparing for these six months past. I buy no books except for pressing need. Last year I bought fifteen hundred dollars' worth; this year I shall not order two hundred dollars' worth. I may want money for cannon. . . . God save the United States of America."

The South began to talk of reopening the slave trade which had been prohibited in 1808, in order to restore to the South "its equality of power in the central government," as the Governor of South Carolina said. A bill to import 2500 slaves to be indentured for fifteen years failed of only two votes in passing the Louisiana legislature. "It takes people to make States," said Alexander H. Stephens of Georgia, "and it requires people of the African race to make slave States." In the North the Republican Party was formed on a "national" basis in 1856 and adopted a platform which opposed the repeal of the Missouri Compromise, demanding the admission of Kansas as a free State; declared that slavery could not exist in any Territory; and denounced the Ostend Manifesto, which had had for its object the acquisition of Cuba with or without the consent of Spain. Although a national party it was a sectional platform, and only four slave States, and those border ones, were even partially represented in the Convention. Had its ill-chosen candidate, Frémont, been elected the South might have seceded then and possibly have been allowed to go in peace, but Buchanan secured the Presidency and when secession came four years later the North was aroused to an extent of which the South little dreamed.

Nevertheless the bitterness and misunderstanding between the sections steadily increased. The scenes in Kansas were accustoming the people to violence. Law and order there were thoroughly disregarded by Southern raiders while the cool direction of a series of murders by the Northern fanatic John Brown sent a thrill of horror through the land. Even the Senate chamber itself, the most august meeting place in the nation, was not free from violent acts, and in May, 1856, Preston Brooks of South Carolina, suddenly and without warning, attacked Senator Sumner of Massachusetts, beating him so ferociously about the head as nearly to kill him. Sumner had two days before made an unjustifiably bitter speech against Brooks's uncle, Senator Butler, but the cowardliness and brutality of such an assault against an unarmed man of national distinction and in such a place, sent a wave of anger through the North, even among those who had no liking for the pompous and conceited Sumner. Although the distinguished Southern banker and ship-owner, G. B. Lamar, wrote to Howell Cobb that the assault was "unjustifiable, unmanly, ill-timed . . . and totally indefensible as to time, place and manner," this was not the general Southern opinion. Both the action itself and Southern comment on it served to increase the bitterness of those who already misunderstood and disliked Southerners and who sneered at that section's pretensions to chivalry.

In 1857 a young North Carolinian, Hinton R. Helper, twenty-seven years old, belonging to the smaller slave-holding class, published a violent attack on slavery in a volume which has been said to have sold or been given away to the extent of about a million copies in the next four years, having been used as a Republican campaign document in 1860. At first *The Impending Crisis,* as the book was called, did not appear to disturb the South but when it was seriously taken up and discussed in the North Southern anger knew no bounds. Although the author's argument was based primarily on statistics which he claimed showed that slavery was economically unprofitable, the volume was in reality a violent attack not only on slavery but on the larger planter class, and was occasionally vitriolic in its abuse of what Helper called the "haughty cavaliers of shackles and handcuffs" or the "lords of the lash." What the South needed in that respect was a satirist like Thackeray to picture its new cotton snobs, or humor like that of Cervantes to clear its brain of the obsession of being knights and cavaliers. Breeding, courtesy, chivalrous feeling, all that goes to make the gentleman or gentlewoman, and which the best in the South possessed in abundance, were not out of date, but the whole social machinery of a novelist's views of a feudalism which never even existed in reality was.

Helper, with a pen dipped in gall, attacked the South at all its dearest points, its prosperity, its peculiar institution, its dream of romantic plumed knighthood, its theory of superior race, its assumption that the whole of the South which counted was a charming, high-bred society, though such in fact constituted but a small part of the population. Helper's criticism was of the wrong sort, and in any case the South was in no mood to listen to criticism of any sort. Freedom of speech had mostly disappeared. Whereas in the preceding generation the question of slavery could be freely discussed from every standpoint, those opposed to the institution were now likely to get short shrift. In 1860 a man in Caroline County, Virginia, suspected of holding Abolitionist views was told to leave the county, and when two Virginians undertook to defend him, they were also told to leave their homes within ten days.[10]

In the same year in which Helper's book first appeared, 1857, came the Dred Scott decision, which aroused the North as had almost nothing else as yet. Taney, the Chief Justice, and a majority of the Court were Southerners, and in the decisions handed down by them it was declared not only that under the Constitution a negro was not, and could not become, a citizen of the United States but that Congress was utterly powerless to legislate as to slavery in any State or Territory, thus indicating that not only was the Missouri Compromise unconstitutional but even the great Ordinance of 1787 for the Northwest. Congress had to protect slavery, because the slave was property, but it was powerless to hinder slavery; and the result would be that all the vast unorganized territory of the nation, and all future acquisitions, would be thrown open to slave exploitation with the consequent hindrance to white immigration and free labor. The North had never assumed that it could interfere with slavery in those States where it had existed, or, of late, even in such as the inhabitants might elect to come in as slave, but it had no intention of being overwhelmed by a colossal expansion of the system. A wave of anger swept over the section and the inevitable conflict drew one step nearer.

In fact two wholly incompatible civilizations had grown up on the continent, bound together by a "scrap of paper" of dubious meaning, and they had come to hate each other. We might say three, for there was the commercial and industrial North, and the free agricultural North and West and the slave agricultural South. Although about once each generation we have had an agrarian revolt, the war now coming was far more than that and different, for the agrarian

[10] *Richmond Enquirer*, August 31, 1860.

West was divided from the agrarian South. It was the clash of two completely different civilizations which under the conditions of the world of 1860 could no longer live peacefully together.

In the most famous State election in all our history, that of Illinois in 1858, all the issues of the time were gathered together and debated by the well-known Senator Douglas and the as yet little-known Lincoln. In one of his speeches the latter, who had never been an Abolitionist, put the situation as clearly as it has ever been put. " 'A house divided against itself cannot stand,' " he said. "I believe this government cannot endure permanently half slave and half free. I do not expect the Union to be dissolved—I do not expect the house to fall—but I do expect it will cease to be divided. It will become all one thing or all the other. Either the opponents of slavery will arrest the further spread of it and place it where the public mind shall rest in the belief that it is in course of ultimate extinction, or its advocates will push it forward, till it shall become lawful in all the States, old as well as new—North as well as South."

Just as the North did not do justice to the finer qualities of much of Southern civilization, qualities which it has been a large part of our tragedy to have lost to some extent, so the South did not do justice to the moral basis of Northern dislike of slavery, one of the strong winds that was blowing through almost the whole civilized world at that time with the exception of the secluded South. A Southern historian has estimated that between 1856 and 1860, when the South was agitating for the reopening of the slave trade, at least 50,000 slaves were imported clandestinely direct from the jungle.[11] Lincoln himself had a full realization of the difficulties of the Southerner and no hatred. Speaking somewhat earlier of slavery he had said "I surely will not blame them for not doing what I should not know how to

11 W. E. Dodd, *Jefferson Davis* (Philadelphia, 1907), p. 176.

do myself." But his vision was clear as to the inability of the two types of civilization to continue to exist in separate compartments of the same nation, given the trend of world opinion.

Thus far, as was truly stated in the article quoted a short space back from *The Southern Literary Messenger,* the control of the Federal Government had been in the hands of the South with its Northern allies—and they were many, particularly among business men—from the start. Most of the Presidents had been Southern or of Southern sympathies; the South had almost invariably controlled one or both houses of Congress; and continuously a majority of the Supreme Court had been Southern. Nevertheless, the population of the North and West far outnumbered the South, and with the rise of a purely sectional party opposed to any further extension of slavery the South felt itself menaced as never before. That the radicals of both sections, one in control of offices and the other of votes, should both have been declaiming for a decade and more against the insufferable "tyranny" exerted by the other, was merely a symptom of the innate incompatibility of the two civilizations, and of their growing distrust and dislike of one another. Not only the older political parties but the very Union itself was beginning to melt in this crucible of hatred.

When Congress met in 1858 it was clear that it contained many of the extremists from both sides. War was in the air. Representative Reuben Davis meeting General Quitman asked him if his group had any definite policy, to which the General replied: "We have, and its aim and end is disunion."[12] The incident was only one of too many to be recounted. By this time Rhett and Yancey were working in harmony, each doing what he could to prepare the public mind for the secession which they felt must be forced by

[12] Reuben Davis, *Recollections of Mississippi and Mississippians* (Boston, 1889), p. 370.

1860. The temper of the members of Congress may be illustrated by another episode given by the Mississippi member. When the Republican Grow from Pennsylvania moved over to the Democratic side of the House, Keitt of South Carolina demanded what he was doing, adding, "Damn you, go back to your own seat." Grow answering, "You can't crack your negro whip over me, Sir," a fight ensued which quickly developed into four or five free-for-all fights on the floor of the House at once. Congressmen began to carry arms, and the air of the Capitol was tense.

Yet even now the great majority of people of all sections perhaps did not wish to destroy the Union. In the North the Abolitionists might declaim against the Constitution and burn it publicly. In the South, Rhett and Yancey, now out-and-out secessionists, could not build up their League of United Southerners or create their Committees of Safety. Yet the slavery question would not down, and passions rose even though most people were more anxious to recover from the depression following the panic of 1857 than to discuss Constitutional problems. Thousands were sick of the slavery question, yet they could not get away from it. It had come to color the whole of the national life. Like a poison gas it flooded every nook and cranny. North and South the politicians were busy with it. Society, even families, were being divided by it. A business man had to take it into consideration in making a transaction for the future. In Washington hostesses had to be careful how they seated or even invited guests, depending on their slavery views. Mrs. Senator Clay's discussion with her husband on driving to dinner at the British Ambassador's as to what would happen if she were to be taken in to the dining room by a Republican and her hot reply that she would refuse to accept her escort were merely symptomatic of the feelings and difficulties of that last season of the old régime.

In the midst of this nervous tension there occurred on October 16, 1859, an event which rang out through the entire nation like a pistol shot in the night. Old John Brown, of Kansas fame, crossed the Potomac with a small band of followers and seized the Federal Arsenal at Harper's Ferry. Few actions in our history are more veiled in mystery and none has been the subject of more varying interpretations. Brown was one of the type of fanatical Puritans who felt himself obliged to do the Lord's work as he saw it, and that for him was the complete extirpation of negro slavery. Whether he was sane or insane can never be known. He himself denied the latter and in many ways he was sane enough. His plan, however, vague as it was; the constitution he drew up for his new free State to be erected in the heart of the South; and other aspects of his thought indicate something akin to madness. Surrounded in the Arsenal by State troops and United States Marines, under command of Colonel Robert E. Lee, Brown and his band were captured after desperate fighting, and after a quick trial the leader was condemned and hanged. His dignity and evident simplicity and sincerity impressed even his Southern judges, while his patriarchal bearing lent itself magnificently to creating popular sympathy. Lincoln, the following year in his famous Cooper Union speech, said of the affair that it merely corresponded "with the many attempts related in history at the assassination of Kings and Emperors. An enthusiast broods over the oppression of a people till he fancies himself commissioned by Heaven to liberate them. He ventures the attempt, which ends in little else than his own execution."

While that explains Brown fairly well, it is much more difficult to understand the attitude of leading men in the North toward him and his enterprise. There was no possibility of his success, and the arming of the slaves and inciting them to leave their masters and follow him might have had the most awful consequences for the whites, women and children as well as men, on isolated plantations, had it not been for either the apathy or the loyalty of the negroes. To risk one's own life in a cause in which one believes is noble, but Brown's enterprise was criminal folly which might have entailed the most frightful sufferings on thousands of innocent people. Yet he was backed in it by men of standing and supposed sense, such as Frank B. Sanborn and Thomas Wentworth Higginson, while others, such as Emerson and Thoreau, likened him to Christ, and he at once became a popular martyr.

Had the Virginian authorities sent him to jail or an insane asylum, the episode would have had far less effect. As it was, the hanging, though thoroughly deserved if he was sane, made him such a hero as to render the whole mad affair one of the greatest blows struck against slavery so far as popular sentiment in the North was concerned. The feeling in the South, following news that armed men from the North had crossed the border to rouse the slaves, had naturally been one of frenzied terror and blazing anger. The attitude of the slaves themselves, however, and the quick and complete failure of what was practically a madman's effort would have made the episode less important had it not been for the applause which the attempt won among prominent Northerners. The South became convinced that not only their institution and property but their very lives were now endangered by the antislavery elements in the North. Brown freed no slaves but his act probably created tens of thousands of Republicans in the North and tens of thousands of secessionists in the South.

The Congress of the winter and spring of 1860 was in a constant turmoil, though the spring itself was one of the loveliest Washington has ever known. On January 6, in the course of the debate over the choice of a speaker, Representative W. P. Miles of South Carolina said "to gentle-

men of the other side, that they greatly underrate, altogether underrate, the profound state of excitement now
existing in the South. We are in a state of convulsion. It
matters not to argue whether we ought or ought not to be;
whether we be so with much or little reason. I am speaking of
*facts.*" Rehearsing the Southern doctrine of States' Rights,
he added: "Sir, there are those, even at the South, who
deny the right of peaceable secession, and contend that there
is no remedy for intolerable ills arising in this voluntary
Confederation of sovereign States short of forcible revolution. . . . Call it then revolution. Practically, it will be that.
If we cannot agree on the constitutional right of secession,
we can on the inalienable right of revolution." The South,
he further declared, was impregnable and if necessary could
face the entire world in arms. About a fortnight later, on
the 25th, Representative Keitt of the same State, also after
reviewing the Southern doctrine, said that if the Union attempted to restrict slavery secession would follow, and the
Southern seceded States would form a new Confederation.
"What would such a confederacy have to fear? Absolutely
nothing. Foreign powers would court her alliance, and no
Government on this continent would dare to invade her."
The South, he added, was "now more imperial than Rome
ever was." The West and North could be obliterated but
not the South unless "the advance of nations would be
arrested, and every throne in Europe would be reduced to
dust and ashes."[13]

It is true that there were voices raised for union, and the
Unionist paper, *The Daily True Delta* of New Orleans, for
example, suggested that if any States were suffering from
the non-enforcement of the Fugitive Slave Act and other
Northern policies it was the border States and not those
leading in the secession movement. In an editorial it quoted
with approval the Resolution passed by the legislature of

[13] *The Charleston Mercury,* January 14, February 2, 1860.

Tennessee which read "that in the opinion of this general assembly, all the evils growing out of the present intense slavery agitation—all the discord, alienation and bitter hatred now growing up and extending between the North and South—are the legitimate fruit, not of any necessary and 'irrepressible conflict' between free and slave labor, but of a conflict between rival aspirants in the race of ambition, north and south, urged on by an inordinate greed of official power and plunder."[14]

This, however, was after the election later in the fall. The politics of the year, always vastly more complex than appear on the surface or than can be described briefly in any history, were unusually so in this fateful year of 1860. The old Whig Party was dead. Several minor ones were of no importance. When the Democratic convention met to choose candidates and a platform in Charleston in April, discord was apparent from the start. After days of discussion, Yancey of Alabama threatened that the Northern Democrats would not take the one ground needful, namely, that slavery was right and must be protected. Senator Pugh of Ohio in reply declared that in his opinion the party was being weakened in the North by the policies which had been forced upon it by the South. The North could not be forced to cover its mouth and not say what it thought. "Gentlemen of the South, you mistake us—you mistake us —we will not do it." The deadlock was complete and a few days later, the delegates from Alabama, South Carolina, Mississippi, Florida, Texas, and Arkansas, withdrew, leaving the Northern rump to ballot day after day unsuccessfully and then to adjourn to Baltimore. From the confusion three principal parties emerged, nominating respectively Stephen A. Douglas of Illinois, John C. Breckenridge of Kentucky, and John Bell of Tennessee for the Presidency.

[14] Issue December 15, 1860.

The comparatively new Republican Party, which held its convention in Chicago in May, was also far from a unit. A large part of it came from the Democrats, and there were also the interests of the West and East to reconcile, of Abolitionists who climbed on the band-wagon and of conservatives, and others. Thus the platform adopted called for both tariffs and internal improvements; branded the reopening of the slave trade as "a crime against humanity"; came out strongly for the Union "to which this nation owes its happiness at home, and its honor abroad"; declared that the party held "in abhorrence all schemes for disunion," that the "normal condition of all the territory of the United States is that of freedom," that the "new dogma" that the Constitution of itself carried slavery into any Territory was a "dangerous political heresy," although the right of each State was inviolate to maintain its own domestic institutions as it saw fit.

In other words, there was to be no extension of slavery into unorganized territory but no interference with it in States which might proclaim it or already possess it. To the great disappointment of the East, Abraham Lincoln was nominated for President, and in the ensuing election was overwhelmingly elected in the Electoral College, receiving 180 votes to 123 divided among the other three candidates. Of the popular vote he received only 1,866,452 as against 2,815,617 scattered between the fragments of the broken Democracy, and none in ten of the Southern States. The North and West had elected a President on the pledge that "the union of the States must and shall be preserved." The South had threatened that if he were elected, the Union would be broken. The colonies which had stood shoulder to shoulder to win their independence, the States which had hopefully formed a more perfect and perpetual Union, now faced each other from their two sections with sorrow, anger, or burning hatred. The long road from the day when the "twenty Negars" were landed at Jamestown in 1619, leading down through common trials and struggles, compromises, Northern inventions, Southern tobacco and cotton, the industrial revolution in Europe, a changed world outlook on democracy and slavery, had come to its final turn. Fate had led us to the field of bood.

# CHAPTER V

## THE HOUSE DIVIDES

BEFORE the war, many wealthy Southerners frequently spent their summers in the North. There was a considerable Charlestonian summer colony in Rhode Island at times, and Mrs. Williams Middleton and Mrs. Alston Pringle used as girls to spend the hot months at Newport. The Richard Middletons summered at Bristol, sometimes joined by Hugers and Ravenels, or the Marstons from New Orleans. Other parts of the South were represented there and elsewhere, and Saratoga abounded with Southern planters and beauties. Some went to the Maine coast, such as the Montgomery Blairs and others. In 1858 Jefferson Davis in search of health had gone to Portland, where Mrs. Davis reported she found the people were "as kind as our own could have been," and where they met many Southern acquaintances. Even after the terrible struggle Mrs. Davis could recall the extreme kindness with which in Boston she and her husband had been met by strangers, like Mrs. Harrison Gray Otis, when their baby suddenly fell ill; reminiscences, she wrote long afterward, which "soften all the asperities developed by our bloody war."

But the great summering place of the South was White Sulphur Springs, Virginia, where leading Southerners met by the hundreds and discussed politics and indulged in delightful summer social life. From there, on September 5, 1860, James Petigru, the leading and much-respected Unionist of South Carolina, could write that even if Lincoln were elected "I don't think South Carolina will secede. If such a thing, however, shall take place, we may spare our regrets, for it will prove that disruption was inevitable. No possible issue could be more untenable than to make his bare election a *causus belli,* without any overt act against the Constitution or even, the Dred Scott decision. If our planters were in debt, or cotton was 5 cents, as I have seen it, such a thing might be likely; but our magnanimous countrymen are too comfortable for such exercise. Therefore I don't believe they are going to set fire to the Union."[1]

In spite, however, of much intercouse between North and South, the sections had long since ceased to understand each other. The South, particularly South Carolina, had talked secession for so long that the North can hardly be blamed for not believing in it if such a well-posted Carolinian as Petigru himself did not. As for the South, it had thoroughly convinced itself that secession could be peaceful, and it had come to believe that "Black Republicanism" meant the end of slavery, and the beginning of Abolitionist rule, in spite of what Lincoln had said. *The Richmond Examiner* soon after election could say that it made little difference perhaps whether the nation was ruled by "a gentleman or ruled by a baboon . . . but with Lincoln comes something worse than slang, rowdysim, brutality and all moral filth . . . with all those comes the daring and reckless leader of Abolitionists," though Lincoln had condemned the Abolitionists, and they formed but a very small section of the party.

South Carolina had been making her preparations and both her members of the United States Senate resigned their seats. On December 20, a convention of her people, assembled for the purpose, unanimously passed an Ordinance of Secession. The joy and excitement in Charleston knew no bounds. Church bells rang, cannon were fired, the Palmetto flag seemed to break out spontaneously from buildings, men and women cheered and felicitated one another

[1] *Life, Letters, and Speeches, op. cit.,* p. 356.

on the streets. "Thank God they have put her out at last," said one, as another answered, "I breathe free now." "Do you feel giddy?" said one of the members of the Convention to Miss Middleton. "We are afloat!" Ignorant of all its horrors, she wrote, "we were full of eager interest in the possibility of *war*."

That evening, in Washington, old President Buchanan was attending a wedding at the home of a Mr. Parker, and after the ceremony was seated in the drawing room when a commotion began in the hall. Mrs. Roger Pryor hastened out to see what it was and found Lawrence Keitt, Representative in Congress from South Carolina, "leaping in the air, shaking a paper over his head, and exclaiming, 'Thank God! Oh, thank God! . . . South Carolina has seceded! Here's the telegram. I feel like a boy let out from school.' " The news was immediately communicated to the President, who called for his carriage and drove to the White House. "This was the event," Mrs. Pryor adds, "which was to change all our lives—to give us poverty for riches, mutilation and wounds for strength and health, obscurity and degradation for honor and distinction, exile and loneliness for inherited homes and friends."[2]

For a few weeks after the election, confusion had reigned in the North. Seventeen Southern law students at Harvard promptly left and scattered to the South. A hundred and fifty medical students in New York met to discuss the same problem, and amid both applause and much hissing finally passed resolutions to do the same.[3] Northern opinion was much mixed as to the prospect. Three days after the election Horace Greeley wrote in *The Tribune* advising that if the Southern States should secede, although the movement would be a revolutionary one, they should be allowed to go in peace. "We hope never to live in a republic, where-

[2] Mrs. Roger A. Pryor, *Reminiscences in Peace and War* (New York, 1908), pp. III *f*.
[3] *Charleston Mercury*, November 15, 1860.

of one section is pinned to the residue by bayonets." Henry Ward Beecher preached much the same doctrine, and when the enormous influence of both of these men is allowed for the strength of the profound devotion to the Union as it existed deep in the subconsciousness of the North can be realized. Nevertheless, there was deep anxiety. "Confusion and alarm are the order of the day," wrote Charles Eliot Norton to A. H. Clough in Europe. "The movement for breaking up the Union has acquired a most unexpected force. No one could have supposed beforehand that the South would be so blind to its own interests . . . as to take such a course as it has done since the elections a month ago. This course if followed out must bring ruin to the Southern States, and prolonged distress to the North. . . . At present there is universal alarm; general financial pressure, great commercial embarrassment. [The North] feels that this is but the crisis of a quarrel which is not one of parties but of principles."[4]

As Southern anger was much concentrated against Massachusetts, so we get glimpses of the same Northern feeling against South Carolina. "As for that bullying State," wrote Miss Sedgwick in the same month, "one would not care. As C. says, 'let the damned little thing go!' or as C. B. (two of the most humane men I know) says, 'Plow them under, plow them under! It has been a little wasp from the beginning.' "[5] In New Orleans Miss Le Grand wrote later in her diary, "we can never forgive the Massachusetts Puritans for what they have done." Mrs. Chesnut reported in her journal, after a conversation with some leading Southerners, "these men are not sanguine—I can't say without hope, exactly. They are agreed in one thing: it is worth while to try a while, if only to get away from New

[4] *Letters of Charles Eliot Norton*, ed. Sara Norton and M. A. DeW. Howe (Boston, 1913), vol. I, pp. 211 *ff*.
[5] *Life and Letters of Catharine M. Sedgwick*, ed. M. E. Dewey (New York, 1872), p. 387.

# THE HOUSE DIVIDES

England." The notes, North and South, are constant, Massachusetts, or New England, and South Carolina.

Looking back it may seem strange that the people at large had not heard the steady foot-falls of Fate. Here and there men did realize that a crisis must occur some day that would threaten the very life of the nation, but even at the end of 1860 most people in the North believed that some compromise would yet be found, and that the South was not wholly in earnest; whereas in the South few believed that if they seceded war would follow. They dreamed merely of a happy independence and of a possible wide extension of empire. Lowell could write of the Presidential campaign in *The Atlantic Monthly* that "we are persuaded that the election of Mr. Lincoln will do more than anything else to appease the excitement of the country"; while the leaders of secession in the South, except a few like Jefferson Davis, declared that the North would never lift a finger against a seceding State. War always seems impossible in the midst of peace; and the misunderstanding of each section for the other was now utter and complete.

Events, however, began to move swiftly. By the end of February six other States had seceded—Georgia, Florida, Alabama, Mississippi, Louisiana, and Texas. To a reader used to the necessary but over-simplification of the ordinary brief historical narrative, it would seem as though there must have been some single and all-powerful motive to account for such momentous decisions, but this ignores the extreme complexity of life and human nature. In fact, there was at the time a surprising lack of unanimity not only as to the decisions taken but as to the reasons for taking them. Even after the war had begun so keen a psychologist as Hawthorne could write of the country that "we seem to have little, or at least a very misty idea of what we are fighting for. It depends upon the speaker; and that, again, depends upon the section of the country in which his sympathies are enlisted. The Southern man will say, 'We fight for States' Rights, liberty, and independence.' The Middle-Western man will avow he fights for the Union; while our Northern and Eastern man will swear that from the beginning his only idea was liberty to the blacks and the annihilation of slavery."[6]

Even this national analysis was much too simple. Leaving out of the question the *right* of secession, which we have tried to show is an insoluble problem, just why did the South secede? In the Ordinance of Secession passed by South Carolina stress was laid on the failure of the North to obey the Fugitive Slave Law, on the antislavery agitation, and on Lincoln's election, as a result of which it was claimed that "the South will no longer have the power of self-government or self-protection." Thomas R. R. Cobb of Georgia declared in the Legislature that the voice of the ballot box in the North had declared that he should be a slave. On the other hand some leading Southern papers, such as *The New Orleans Bee,* asserted that the election afforded "no possible excuse for hasty and precipitate action." Reuben Davis, of Mississippi, wrote later that whatever the abstract rights of either side might have been, the contest was one for or against slavery. Yet Alexander H. Stephens wrote that it was due solely to abstract questions of the form of government, and slavery happened to be merely the question on which these principles were brought into conflict. On the other hand, the State of Mississippi in giving its reasons for secession declared that they were "thoroughly identified with the institution of slavery," that a blow at slavery was a blow against civilization, and that the State had no choice between secession and bowing to Abolition.

*The Richmond Enquirer,* which like *The Charleston Mercury* was one of the hottest of secessionist journals, took

[6] Julian Hawthorne, *Nathaniel Hawthorne and His Wife* (Boston, 1884), vol. II, p. 290.

the stand soon after Lincoln's election that the election of a President by a section of the people was both a "declaration of war" and an "act of war," and that the South must choose between subjection and resistance if the North would not give adequate guarantees of the rights of the South. What these must be it then explained. "Let each Northern State, through her legislature, or in convention assembled, promptly repeal all nullifying laws passed for the injury of the constitutional rights of the South, pass laws to secure the easy and prompt execution of the Fugitive Slave Law; pass other laws imposing adequate penalties on all malefactors who shall hereafter assist or encourage the escape of fugitive slaves; pass other laws declaring and protecting the right of slaveholders to travel and sojourn in Northern States, accompanied by their slaves; instruct their senators and representatives in Congress to repeal the law prohibiting the sale of slaves in the District of Columbia, and to pass laws sufficient for the full protection of slave property in all the territories of the Union. . . . This, and nothing short of this, will suffice to prevent *revolution*."[7]

It is little wonder if even those men in the North who had the least desire to disturb slavery where it already existed felt that the South was becoming unbearably arrogant in tone. Nothing would seem to suit *The Enquirer* except that the 19,000,000 of whites in the free States should bow in complete submission to the 8,000,000 in the slave States of whom perhaps at most 300,000 were heads of slave-owning families. Nothing less was demanded than that the North should yield its own moral feelings, which had become those of the world at large, its own interpretation of the Constitution, its own rights in the Federal Capital and the territories, and its own desire for the perpetuation of the Union to the demands of the South as the price of avoiding war.

[7] *Richmond Enquirer,* issue of November 19, 1860.

The influence of popular leaders was very great, such as Rhett in South Carolina, Yancey in Alabama, Jefferson Davis in Mississippi, and Toombs in Georgia. In the latter most important State the fight for secession was the hardest fought. As we have already mentioned there were only about 1900 planters there in 1850 as against 81,000 farmers and the State was very prosperous, as was all the South, in 1860. When the question of secession came up in the legislature after Lincoln's election, Cobb, Toombs, and others pleaded with passion for taking the State out of the Union immediately, but Stephens, who, although like almost all Southerners believing in the *right* of secession, had been a strong Union man, urged that it was inexpedient. He pointed out that the mere election of Lincoln could do the South no harm as the Senate and House were against him, and added that the tariff policy was no excuse for secession as South Carolina had voted in favor of it with Massachusetts, and "the lion and the lamb" had lain down together. The only real grievance was the practical nullification of the Fugitive Slave Law, and redress for that should be found inside the Union.[8]

The conservative views of the future Vice-President of the Confederacy, however, did not prevail. As in other States a convention was elected to consider action, and in the whirlwind campaign, carried on, as everything was in those times, in tense excitement, the secessionist leaders were the more powerful. In his autobiography, the Georgian, Herschel V. Johnson, wrote of it that "my opinion now is, and always has been, that a fair and energetic canvass would have showed a large majority of the people against the policy . . . there was no time allowed for discussing the subject upon the hustings, and what speaking there was, was confined almost entirely to the secessionists.

[8] Quoted by J. F. Rhodes, *History of the United States* (New York, 1907), vol. III, p. 210.

They were more than zealous—they were frenzied. They did not, in my judgment, present the issue fairly. . . . They insisted that it would be peaceable—that it would not bring war—that if it should the Yankees were cowards and would not fight—and that, at the worst it would be a short war in which the South would achieve an easy victory and that we should then have a Southern Confederacy, with a homogeneous population and interests, which would enjoy the friendship of all nations and the admiration of all mankind."[9] As it was, the vote has been estimated as 50,243 in favor of secession and 37,123 against. In view of the universal belief in the right of secession, and the great bitterness felt against the North at the moment, these figures are significant.

There had long been two schools of secessionists, those who believed in the secession of the separate States and the "co-operationists" who believed that the States should take united action. The first having won there was much bitterness in the border slave States, which felt that they had been left to be the battle-field while the lower South had suited its own wishes of the moment without thought of them. The border press was almost unanimous in condemning the action taken by the seceders. *The Nashville Patriot* struck the popular note when it declared that "of all coercion that we ever heard of, this is the most arrogant, the most despotic, the most unnatural, ungrateful, and monstrous."[10]

Aside from what we may call the professional secessionists of the South, like the professional Abolitionists of the North, the strength of the secession movement lay in the aristocratic and plutocratic planter class who saw the world from their own point of view as any great capitalist class always does. Once in the war, however, the entire South was a unit. The psychology of war always unifies a people,

[9] Percy S. Flippin, *Herschel V. Johnson* (Richmond, 1931), p. 170.
[10] Quoted by D. L. Dumond, *Southern Editorials on Secession* (New York, 1931), p. xix.

united in a supreme effort against a common enemy. But there was more to the unity of the South than that. There was intense unity of life and thought. It may be, as has been stated, that eighty per cent of the men who were to fight in the ranks of the Confederate army were non-slaveholders but, as we have tried to show, slavery had created a strong bond among all Southerners, and had set their society off not only from that of the North and West but increasingly from that of the rest of the world. Under outside pressure, the Southerners had grown together. Their reaction had been the doctrine of the superior race and a romanticizing of their in many ways charming type of civilization. Their ultimate safety was felt to lie in an interpretation of the Constitution which made peaceful secession a fundamental of their constitutional creed. No Southerner doubted it. It had become axiomatic. Any other theory of government seemed to them not only to belie history and logic but to be essentially tyrannical, so firmly had this one interpretation been established among them.

But no people goes to war for a logical abstraction. Their lives must have in some way been deeply affected by it. Those who say that the war was caused by slavery and those who say it was not are both of them right and both wrong. Yet, had there never been a black or a slave on the continent, it is unlikely that the war would ever have occurred. Had the South, like the North, been built up on free white labor there would have been no such conflict of sectional interests. *IFS* in history are not worth pursuing far, but I think the fact remains that if there had been no slavery, there would not only have been no Missouri Compromise, no Abolitionism, no Fugitive Slave Law, no fight over Kansas, none of the many causes of bitter feeling, but the types of civilization in the two sections would have necessarily more nearly approximated one another. One has only to think of a white South, with no three-fifths representation of slaves, open to manufacturing and banking, without a dominant planter class based on slave labor, to realize the enormous differences which slavery made. There is nothing in a parallel of latitude to change the interpretation of the Constitution. If the South were all for States' Rights and secession and the North for Union, the difference was not one of climate. The different interpretations stemmed from the different needs, and they in turn from the different conditions and institutions.

Every political question between North and South had had its immediate origin in either slavery or the tariff, mostly in slavery. A large part of the South did not secede or go to war merely to protect slave property. After the secession of his State but before his own election as President of the Confederacy, Jefferson Davis, his wife reports, said one day in despondent mood, "In any case, I think, our slave property will be lost eventually," and then went on to speak of the "immense standing army that would be necessary if the slaves were to be kept forever in bondage." Speaking to one of his slaves after Fort Sumter had been fired on, Senator Chesnut of South Carolina said, "Let the war end either way and you will be free. We will have to free you before we get out of this thing."[11] Old Sam Houston, the Unionist Governor of Texas, declared that the South was going to war for slavery but the first shot fired would sound its knell. Others likewise felt that the outcome of war would mean freedom to the slaves whichever way the fortunes of the struggle might turn. It is interesting also to note in this connection that whereas among the distinguished generals who were to serve on the Southern side Fitzhugh Lee, A. P. Hill, and Joseph E. Johnston, among others, had never owned slaves, while Robert E. Lee had emancipated his own slaves before the war began and also carried out the instructions in the will of his father-in-law,

[11] *A Diary from Dixie* (New York, 1929), p. 45.

Mr. Custis, that the slaves left to Mrs. Lee should be emancipated within five years after his death, which occurred in 1857. All of these Southern generals disapproved of the institution, yet Grant, the great Northern leader, did own some, or at least his wife did, and the family were slave owners until the Emancipation Proclamation!

However, in the South, what with slavery and the plantation type of life as an actuality and an ideal, there had grown up an entire civilization totally different from that of the North, and increasingly antagonistic to it. With the scarcity of labor of all sorts except slave in America, as in all new countries where opportunity to rise is great, the South, without the slave, would have had to be content to be a land of farmers or like the North and West adopt other means of making money. No more than in the other two sections, before the introduction of farm machinery, would there have been the development of the plantation economy on a large scale, with all its economic, political, and social consequences. Owsley makes the remarkable statement that "without slavery the economic and social life of the South would not have been radically different," that it would still have been much the same "as it still is after sixty-five years of 'freedom'!"[12] But in the sixty-five years of freedom the ample labor supply was there. Where would the labor supply have come from in the South without slavery any more than in the West? In the same essay he speaks of the slaves in the war "some of whom could still remember the taste of human flesh and the bulk of them hardly three generations removed from cannibalism." Allowing for the violence of language, would these "cannibals" have voluntarily emigrated to the South, or if captured would they have been brought home on a wage basis? And if the negro had not been present, would the Irish, English, Scotch, Ger-

[12] *I'll Take My Stand*, by Twelve Southerners (New York, 1930), p. 76.

man, or other European immigrant have been more content in, the South than elsewhere to remain a laborer or tenant to build up ancestral estates, to be field-hand or devoted household servant for generations? The free immigrant and the indentured servant had long since given the answer to that question.

As was often said by Southern statesmen, slavery was the cornerstone of their civilization, and with the constant menace to slavery the Southerners had felt their entire way of life menaced. The economic motive of property bulked large, but above and beyond that was the fear for all they held dear, and their hatred of possible Yankee domination on the theory of majority rule.

Before the horrors of war had greatly intensified the latter feeling perhaps not many felt as bitterly as did old Edmund Ruffin, who fired the first gun against Fort Sumter and committed suicide when Lee surrendered. The last words he penned before he shot himself were: "With my latest writing and utterance, and with what will be near my latest breath, I here repeat and would willingly proclaim my unmitigated hatred to Yankee rule—to all political, social, and business connections with Yankees, and the perfidious, malignant, and vile Yankee race."[13] Nevertheless, fear and dislike of the Northerners had taken deep hold in the South. As Mrs. James Chesnut, the wife of the senator, said, "we separated North from South because of incompatibility of temper. We are divorced because we have hated each other so."[14] Even counting three-fifths of the negroes in Congressional representation, majority rule, owing to the more rapid development of the North, was clearly going to mean more and more in the future the curbing of Southern power, and in 1864 Jefferson Davis said that the South had really seceded to rid itself of the rule of the majority.

[13] Craven, *Edmund Ruffin, op. cit.*, p. 259.  [14] *Ibid.*, p. 20.

The dominant class in the South, at least, was prosperous and happy, and like all such everywhere it asked only to keep things as they were, to be let alone. They did not realize that in any case their way of life was even more certainly doomed than that of the English landed aristocrat which they so much admired. The war and reconstruction were to bring untold suffering on the South, but even without them the old ante-bellum society could not have projected itself far into the future. The forces of the modern world would have been too much for it. It was becoming as anachronistic as feudalism itself which lived only in the Waverley Novels. Slavery might have ended peacefully or gone down in a whirlwind flame of horror of which we shudder to think. It is impossible to conceive of its lasting indefinitely.

But to those who voted for secession the future was rose-colored. Secession not only promised to get rid of the disliked Northerner and to settle all vexed questions in favor of the South, which thereafter should guide her own destiny, but that destiny seemed of the fairest. The world was to stand still and the old delightful life go on forever in a new and glorious empire which might be greatly extended. There was no realization that the North was as devotedly attached to the Union and its own interpretation of the Constitution as the South was to her opinions. Most believed that there could be no war because according to their constitutional views a war would be wholly unwarranted. As Jefferson Davis said, "very few in the South at that time agreed with me," although for "my part, while believing that secession was a right, and, properly, a peaceable remedy, I had never believed that it would be permitted to be peaceably exercised." The South envisaged at most a short and glorious struggle ending quickly in her triumph and independence. Only here and there a far-sighted man realized the full nature of the step she was taking. Secession seemed a clear way either to wringing permanent concessions from the North or independence and a great future.

Moreover, the King Cotton theory had not illogically taken deep hold of the South, which in 1860 was enormously prosperous. Many of the gloomy statistics in Helper's book had been discredited in the three years since it had been written. The South was making money hand over fist. *The Richmond Enquirer* merely mentioned a typical case when it chronicled that a Mr. Burnside had just bought another sugar plantation in Louisiana for $500,000, that three years before he had bought one for $1,000,000 and made twenty per cent the first year, and that this individual who had been a clerk in a dry-goods store twenty-five years earlier was then worth $6,000,000 in sugar alone.[15]

It was cotton, however, which was the chief staple and reliance of the South. The greatest power in the world was that of the British Empire, and the greatest industry of England was that in textiles, and nearly five-sixths of all her cotton supply, on which her wealth was largely based, came from the Southern States, the same proportion holding for France. The South, not unnaturally, considered herself as the one producing district without which the modern world could not survive. Prompt recognition and probably assistance, if needed, from Europe seemed without question. English writers for some time had been pointing out the precariousness of the position of that country in its almost entire dependence on the American South for nearly one-half of its manufacturing and export trade.[16] What the South did not realize was that there had not only been vast over-production which in any case would have led in 1861 to a disastrous fall in price but that new sources of supply could be tapped.

Allowing for all the factors in the situation, it is not difficult to understand why it was an enthusiastic and en-

---

[15] *The Richmond Enquirer*, issue, April 16, 1860.
[16] F. L. Owsley, *King Cotton Diplomacy* (Chicago, 1931), pp. 1 *ff.*

tirely hopeful lower South which passed their Ordinances of Secession. Seven States having gone out of the Union, the next step immediately to be taken was to organize the new Confederacy.

For this purpose a convention of delegates assembled at Montgomery, Alabama, February 4, 1861, and four days later adopted a Constitution for the "Confederate States of America," which although intended to be provisional only, was, owing to the exigencies of the war, never altered. If the South had had opportunity to revise and alter it, it would have been exceedingly interesting to be able to note what they might have done. The Southern President, Andrew Jackson, and of course the leading Northern statesmen, had denied the possibility of carrying on government if the doctrines of secession and nullification were admitted. In fact, also, one of the reasons given by South Carolina for breaking up the Union was the nullification by Northern States of the Fugitive Slave Law. The new Constitution had, naturally, to embody the Southern doctrine, and it is noteworthy that a modern scholarly historian, born within the very county in Alabama in which the Convention sat, does not hesitate to assert that, giving due allowance for all other causes of the fatal collapse of the Confederacy, the "lost cause" really "died of States' Rights."[17]

It is unnecessary to go into the details of the Constitution as adopted. In its main lines, it followed that of the United States, though with some interesting exceptions. States' Rights were somewhat emphasized, and the power of the Executive, who could serve only one term of six years, was increased. An attempt was made to graft the English political system onto the American by allowing Cabinet members to sit in Congress. The old "federal ratio" of counting three-fifths of the slaves in apportioning congress-

[17] Frank L. Owsley, *State Rights in the Confederacy* (Chicago, 1925), p. vii.

men was retained, thus increasing the comparative power of the States with most slaves, though the slave trade was declared unlawful. In view of the recent demands of the lower South for its reopening, this may have been to affect public sentiment in England and elsewhere abroad favorably toward the new government. In one respect, that of allowing the President to veto sections of a finance bill without vetoing the whole, the Southern Constitution marked a distinct improvement over the Federal. The exact terms of the document, however, are not important for our purpose. What did prove so was the spirit which came to animate the individual State Governments with respect to the central one they had created, and which will be noted in due course.

The extremists in South Carolina, having declaimed for a generation against the Federal Government, now started at once to criticize that of the Confederacy. *The Charleston Mercury,* owned and edited by Rhett's son, had been preaching the doctrine that the Federal Government had no constitutional right to prohibit the slave trade, a view in which it said "thousands of the most honest and intelligent men in the Southern States" had come to share.[18] Now it began to attack the new Confederate Constitution, and in an editorial said that "we regret that any provisional government was formed at all, and in one or two important particulars confess to disappointment and surprise at the government and laws enacted. . . . We did not suppose that any Southern government, whether for a month or a year, would sanction the policy of protective tariffs. . . . We enter our protests against the scheme and policy. . . . We deem it also unfortunate and *mal à propos* that the stigma of illegitimacy and illegality should be placed upon the institution of slavery by a fundamental law against the slave trade." The Unionist *Daily True Delta* of New Orleans, quoting this article, commented that the people of South Carolina were

[18] Issue February 18, 1860 *inter alia.*

161

beginning to discover that secession was a barren movement, and not "the feast to which Rhett, Keitt, and their associates invited" them.[19]

Having adopted a Constitution, the convention proceeded to elect a President and Vice-President, Jefferson Davis, who had not been present at the proceedings, being chosen as the former, and Alexander H. Stephens as the latter. Mrs. Davis wrote that when her husband received the telegram announcing his election "he looked so grieved that I feared some evil had befallen our family. After a few minutes' painful silence he told me, as a man might speak of a sentence of death." Davis, a son-in-law of old President Zachary Taylor, though he had been a disunionist and strong for slavery, was one of the few Southern leaders who had no illusions about what secession meant. Like many men who were now to become prominent, such as Lee, Grant, Meade, McClellan, Jackson, Sherman, and Joe Johnston in the military field, the new President had been a West Pointer and had served in the Mexican War.

He had become a prosperous planter and a fervent believer in the "good" of slavery. His own plantation, as we have noted, was a model in his management of the slaves, who remained devoted to him. He had been an expansionist and considered one of the ablest Southern men in Congress, though his course in national politics for the preceding dozen years or so reveals a somewhat confused policy. His personal integrity was unquestioned, and it is possible that no man could have been chosen to the difficult office who would not have made enemies and lost the confidence of the people. Unhappily, however, Davis was of a temperament to make them by scores, both among military and civilian leaders. He had a high opinion of his own ability, particularly as a soldier, and his frequent ill-health may have contributed to his irritability. After the war was over,

[19] *Daily True Delta,* issue February 21, 1861.

Senator Chesnut remarked to his wife that "sometimes I think I am the only friend he has in the world." Commenting on the statement his wife noted that "in Washington when we left, Jeff Davis ranked second to none, in intellect, and may be first, from the South, and Mrs. Davis was the friend of Mrs. Emory, Mrs. Joe Johnston, and Mrs. Montgomery Blair, and others of that circle. Now they rave that he is nobody, and never was . . . and you would think to hear them he found her yesterday in a Mississippi swamp."[20]

Davis, however, in the beginning knew something of the North and of the difficult work ahead for the Confederacy. Some months after his elevation to the Presidency he was speaking to the same Mrs. Chesnut in the White House in Richmond. She wrote that "he laughed at our faith in our own power. We are like the British. We think every Southerner equal to three Yankees at least. We will have to be equivalent to a dozen now. After his experience of the fighting qualities of Southerners in Mexico, he believes that we will do all that can be done by pluck and muscle, endurance, and dogged courage, dash and red-hot patriotism. And yet his tone was not sanguine. . . . He thinks it will be a long war. That floored me at once. It has been too long for me already. Then he said, before the end came, we would have many bitter experiences. He said only fools doubted the courage of the Yankees, or their willingness to fight when they saw fit. And now that we have stung their pride, we have roused them till they will fight like devils."[21]

There was plenty of "red-hot patriotism." Indeed, it was said that in Georgia they poured water on recruits to see if they sizzed; if not they were too cool. And there was to be a magnificent show of every quality that makes a man before the South laid down its arms; but at the beginning few believed with the doomed President that the North might

[20] *Diary from Dixie, op. cit.,* p. 360.    [21] *Ibid.,* p. 71.

163

show courage and persistence also. The fire-eating Rhett certainly had not, and had not believed that any war, certainly not one of any importance, would follow the action he had been urging on the South for thirty years and more. The failure of his forecasts was one of the reasons for his loss in popularity, which in turn was a leading reason for his later bitter attacks on the Davis administration.

In the North the cool head of Charles Eliot Norton of Massachusetts was wiser than that of the hot-headed Carolinian. Writing in December, 1860, he said that "I think it most likely we shall come to the rifle and the sword as the arbitrators of the great quarrel—and I have no fear for the result. . . . But I pity the South; and look forward with the deepest sorrow and compassion to the retribution they are preparing for themselves. The harvest they must reap is one of inevitable desolation."[22]

On the 18th of February, so rapidly had events moved since the election of Lincoln, Davis, President of the newly created Confederacy, delivered his Inaugural Address more than two weeks before Lincoln, under the Constitution, could deliver his. Rehearsing the doctrine of States' Rights and claiming that the North had no cause for aggression, it was neither a great nor an inspiring address. To his wife two days later he wrote that beyond the smiles, plaudits, and flowers, "I saw troubles and thorns innumerable. We are without machinery, without means, and are threatened by a powerful opposition, but I do not despond, and will not shrink from the task imposed upon me." With some weaknesses and without being one of the world's great men, Davis was to go through with the task nobly, though irretrievably hampered by attacks from the leaders of his own people. The Southerner had always held high office in the Federal Government, and, like the English but unlike the Northerner, loved a public career, which he adorned.

[22] *Letters, op. cit.*, vol. I, p. 216.

The stage, temporarily at least, was now smaller, and the Southern hostesses, according to the comments of some of them, were to find Richmond a rather small world after Washington. The pressure for office, as for high rank in the army, was to be constant; and Rhett and others never forgave the election of Davis to the office to which they considered themselves entitled.

Moreover, the President was not happy in the choices he made of men for his Cabinet—Toombs of Georgia as Secretary of State, Memminger of South Carolina in the Treasury, L. P. Walker of Alabama, and S. R. Mallory of Florida for War and Navy, J. H. Reagan of Texas for the Post Office, and Judah P. Benjamin of Louisiana as Attorney General. Not a single one of these men was a close friend or follower of Davis, upon whom he could rely, and only two at most could be considered as belonging to the planter aristocracy class, and these soon resigned. The government was thus cut off from the dominant social and political element in the South. Three members of the Cabinet were even foreign-born. It was rather an odd government for a section which had prided itself so greatly on ancestry and social position; and contained the seeds of serious disharmonies and difficulties.

We must now turn to see what had been happening in the North while events had been transpiring so swiftly in the South that a new nation had been formed, a Constitution adopted, a President elected, and a government set up even before Lincoln could assume office after his own election.

As yet that new nation comprised less than half the slave States, and what action the others, including the important pivotal State of Virginia, might take was uncertain. Owing to our unfortunate form of government, four months had to elapse before the new administration could assume power, and meanwhile the offices in Washington were largely filled by Southerners. Buchanan, the President, was weak and vacillating, though it must be admitted that his position was a most difficult one. He has been most heavily blamed by Rhodes in his history of these years, and in truth the President does present rather a pitiable figure. His message to Congress in December, 1860, was, as Rhodes calls it, "an essay on constitutional law," and an extremely poor one, we may add. Speaking strongly in favor of the contentions of the South as to slavery, glossing over the real difficulties, he yet declared that secession was not a constitutional right, that it would make of "the Confederacy a rope of sand, to be penetrated and dissolved by the first adverse wave of public opinion in any of the States." Nevertheless, after attempting to show in many pages that there was no right of secession he proceeded to declare that there was no Federal right of coercion, and that the Federal Government was powerless to protect its own continued existence.

It has been said that there was a difference, which he should have emphasized, between coercing a State and merely maintaining the Federal laws and protecting Federal property within its borders, and that he should have acted as Jackson acted a generation earlier. The situation, however, was far more serious than the one with which the former President had had to cope. Senator Pugh of Ohio was right when he declared that whether you called it "coercion, or collecting the revenue, or defending public property, or enforcing the laws; you know, and I know, that it means war, and that war will follow it."[23] Had Buchanan reinforced the Southern forts, for example, and prevented the Governor of Alabama from seizing the Federal forts at the entrance of Mobile Bay before that State had even seceded; or the Governor of Georgia from seizing the fort

[23] Quoted by D. L. Dumond, *The Secession Movement, 1860–61* (New York, 1931), p. 167.

at the entrance of the Savannah River, the conflict would only have been precipitated by an administration which was to go out of office in a few weeks.

Moreover, as we have said, in the opinion of many, both North and South, the situation was even yet far from hopeless, and there was much talk of compromise at the eleventh hour. A committee for the purpose was appointed in Congress from which evolved the Crittenden plan. In view of the whole relationship in which North and South had now come to find themselves, it is difficult to believe that compromise of any sort was longer feasible, or could have been lasting if made. That, however, was less evident in the closing months of the Buchanan administration than it is now.

From the standpoint of protection of the slave interest, secession was probably a tactical mistake. The Abolitionists in the North had been trying for thirty years without success to secure emancipation or dissolution of the Union. They were a noisy minority and now less influential than they had been in their earlier period. Practically no Northern business men or statesmen dreamed of disturbing slavery in the slave States. The only point on which Northern public opinion had come to take a fairly firm stand was against the further extension of slavery in the Territories. Yet by secession the South gave up all claim to the Territories and so lost by their own action the only thing which the North denied to them, in so far as slavery was concerned.

Whether Northern States by their personal-liberty laws and in other ways had more or less right to nullify a Federal Act than the South had to nullify Tariff Acts may be an open question. This phase of the controversy might have been settled, as suggested, by cash indemnities instead of the return of the slaves. The problem was, in any case, a somewhat over-rated one. According to the Hon. Charles J. Jenkins of Georgia, the entire fifteen slave States lost a total of only 803 slaves in 1860.[24] Most of these probably escaped from the border and not the seceding States, and the number was much less than that of the illegal importation of fresh slaves from Africa. Moreover, the number of escaping slaves would have been much greater if the Confederacy had become an independent power. The North would then have been under no obligation whatever to restore escaped slave property; and the fleeing slave instead of having to reach the far North or even Canada, as many did, to be safe, would have had to cross only the border line dividing the United from the Confederate States. That an immensely larger number, both from the border and Gulf States, would have escaped under such conditions is not open to reasonable doubt. By secession, the South thus gave up the chief bones of contention—slavery in the Territories, and the enforcement of the Fugitive Slave Law. However, it was not slavery alone but a whole nexus of causes, though springing indeed in large part from controversies in the past about slavery, which was making the far South secede. No compromise perhaps could have altered this plain fact and unhappy situation.

Compromise, however, was not to come, whether it would have availed for a short time or not. In the South Alexander Stephens had probably been right when he had declared in November that "all efforts to save the Union will be unavailing. The truth is our leaders and public men, who have taken hold of this question, do not desire to continue it on any terms. They do not wish redress of wrongs; they are disunionists *per se*." In the North, Lincoln took the responsibility. He was willing to accept practically the whole of the Crittenden plan, to leave slavery untouched in the South, to enforce the Fugitive Slave Law with all his

[24] Quoted by Channing, *History of the United States,* vol. VI, p. 264.

power, to do almost anything except to allow the further extension of slavery in fresh territory. This problem was, in fact, an insoluble one. It is true that the South under the Constitution had the right to protection of its property anywhere, and it may have had as much right to the extension of what had become its anachronistic form of civilization in the territories as had the North to the extension of its. But because, as we have pointed out, Northern free labor and institutions would not go where slavery existed, both sections could not have their way in the same territory at the same time. It was like two owners each of whom claims the right to paint a jointly owned wall the color he wishes. One simply cannot paint it white if the other at the same time insists on painting it black. The South constantly demanded its "rights" in the territories, but it could not get them without destroying the rights of the North, equally demanded. Moreover, on this point both majority opinion in the North and the opinion of the world had turned against the South.

In spite of demands for compromise Lincoln realized this, and was adamant on this one single point. In the middle of December when compromise was being talked, Lincoln wrote to several politicians, North and South. To one member of the Compromise Committee, he said "entertain no proposition for the extension of slavery. . . . The tug has to come, and better now than later," though in the same letter he declared for the enforcement of the Fugitive Slave Law. To another member, from Illinois, he wrote that if the Missouri Compromise line were redrawn as suggested in the Crittenden Plan, "immediately filibustering and extending slavery recommences." To John A. Gilmer of North Carolina he wrote the same week that "on the territorial question I am inflexible. On that there is a difference between you and us; and it is the only substantial difference. You think slavery is right and ought to be extended; we think it is wrong and ought to be restricted. For this neither has just occasion to be angry with the other."[25]

Meanwhile in Washington social and political life was carried on at high tension. Although the guests at the White House reception on New Year's Day tried to appear cheerful there was a pall over all. The Cabinet had already been disrupted over the President's wavering policy. On the 21st of the month there was a tragic drama enacted as one Southern senator after another—Yulee, Mallory, Clay, Fitzpatrick, Jefferson Davis—arose to make his speech and resign his seat. An observer writes that "as each senator, speaking for his State, concluded his solemn renunciation of allegiance to the United States, women grew hysterical and waved their handkerchiefs, encouraging them with cries of sympathy and admiration. Men wept and embraced each other mournfully. At times the murmurs of the onlookers grew so deep that the Sergeant-at-Arms was ordered to clear the galleries. . . . Scarcely a member of that senatorial body but was pale with the terrible significance of the hour. There was everywhere a feeling of suspense, as if, visibly, the pillars of the temple were being withdrawn and the great government structure was tottering."[26]

Although Buchanan had wished above all to avoid having to make any decisions he had been forced to take into consideration the situation as to the Federal forts in the South, and as a result of conflicting statements made with regard to them by various members of the administration, then and later, there arose one of the most heated controversies of the whole conflict. To unravel the entire story adequately would take far more space than is permissible here.[27] The

[25] Quotations from Rhodes, *History of the United States,* vol. III, pp. 160 f.
[26] *A Belle of the Fifties* (Mrs. C. C. Clay), ed. by Ada Sterling (New York, 1905), p. 148.
[27] The most complete account is that given in about 500 pages by S. W. Crawford, *The Genesis of the Civil War, The Story of Sumter* (New York, 1887). The reader is referred to this for original documents and an analysis of the controversy.

conditions in Washington were extraordinary. South Carolina had seceded in December, 1860, and other States were evidently preparing to follow and break up the Union. Whether the action was constitutional or whether it was revolution, as some Southerners at that time preferred themselves to call it, was an open question, even though most of the South was convinced that it was the former. The President of the United States himself believed it to be revolution, and he was sworn to uphold the Constitution. Whether secession would be peaceable or followed by war was again an open question, though most believed in peace. The President of the new Confederacy did not. At such a juncture the government of the United States was still largely in the hands of the South, several members of the Cabinet being from that section, including the Secretary of War, John R. Floyd of Virginia. Southerners were also on important committees in both Houses of Congress, and the government service was filled with them.

The Federal property in and around Charleston, which had been secured to the United States Government in the usual way, consisted of the arsenal in the city, with valuable stores, and three forts, two of which, Sumter and Moultrie, had been included for repair and improvement in the general bill passed by Congress in June, 1860. In December, Major Anderson, a Kentuckian with a Georgia wife, was in command of the latter, Sumter being unoccupied. Anderson had asked for reinforcements if the forts were to be held, but had been refused. Though some of the Cabinet were in favor of the action, the Southern members, including particularly Floyd, were much opposed.

The misunderstandings which arose between the authorities of South Carolina and the Federal Government are largely entangled in a mass of documents and verbal reports. On December 11, Major Buell, who had been sent with verbal instructions from Floyd to Anderson, reduced these to writing and handed them to Anderson in Fort Moultrie. They instructed him to avoid any act which might provoke aggression but on the other hand he was to "hold possession of the forts," and if attacked to defend himself to the last extremity. A copy of these instructions was given by Floyd to Buchanan. Nevertheless, the South Carolina authorities were given to understand that there would be no change in the *status quo*.

Fort Moultrie was a thoroughly untenable position, and not only was the excitement in Charleston increasing, with threats of attack, but Anderson found that small steamers were maintaining surveillance over the forts at night. To his requests for orders from Washington, Anderson could get no reply. He was entirely ignorant of the various communications which had passed between the South Carolina and Federal officials, which are not wholly easy to disentangle even now with the documents before us. Apparently both Buchanan and Floyd forgot, or paid no attention to, the orders Anderson had received through Buell, and which Floyd had approved and sent to the President in writing. At any moment, Anderson felt that he might be attacked in Fort Moultrie, whereas Fort Sumter was a far more defensible position and, in his opinion, less likely to be attacked, and thus bring on bloodshed, which was to be avoided if possible. During the night of December 26, with much ability, he therefore transferred his entire force to the latter fort.

Meanwhile three Commissioners had been sent from South Carolina to Washington to negotiate for a settlement of property and accounts as between the seceded State and the Federal Government, in accordance with the theory of peaceful secession. When Anderson's transfer became known, the wrath of South Carolina was unbounded, and it was believed that she had been wilfully deceived by the authorities in Washington. The loyalty of Anderson to his oath as an officer of the United States army, the imbecility of Buchanan, the carelessness or forgetfulness of the Virginian Secretary of War, all played their part. The forts were unquestionably Federal property. The Carolina Commissioners had gone to Washington to negotiate for them as part of the general balancing of accounts. Anderson had been ordered to hold them. The Federal Government could not abandon him. On the day after the transfer to Sumter was accomplished, Floyd had telegraphed Anderson asking an explanation and denying that any orders justified the move. The President was profoundly disturbed because of the psychological effect on the situation.

At a Cabinet meeting, promptly held, when Floyd declared that Anderson had acted against orders, the Secretary of State, Judge Black, produced the Buell orders which Floyd had endorsed and given to the President. Although Floyd had done this on the 11th of December, the President said he never saw them until the 21st. Thus did Fate again step forward. There would seem to be no doubt that the South Carolinians were deceived, yet the deceit was not intentional but due to a series of mischances, blunders, the mixing up of too many persons in the negotiations, the stupidity of Floyd, and a Cabinet split like the country between North and South in its feelings. Perhaps no other President has ever shown himself so weak as Buchanan did in this whole episode.

Floyd had become involved in a financial transaction which reflected so greatly on his fitness for high office, if not his personal honesty, that the President had asked for his resignation from the Cabinet and the War Office. On December 29, the secretary did at last hand in his resignation, as he should have done some time before, but he now based his compliance with the President's wishes on the ground that the government had broken faith with South Carolina, most unjustly placing the blame on Anderson in

spite of his own orders to him.[28] He also demanded that the
Federal Government should withdraw all troops from South
Carolina, though as head of the War Department he had ordered his subordinate, Anderson, to protect the forts to the
last extremity. It is difficult to follow Floyd throughout this
whole matter, in the documents and fully reported conver-
sations, without accusing him either of crass stupidity or of
dishonesty. In a number of other cases it is also difficult to
reconcile the holding on to positions of trust in the Federal Government while working against it. When Floyd's
resignation was promptly accepted, and Postmaster General Holt was appointed in his stead, Senator Wigfall, of
Texas, telegraphed to M. L. Bonham of South Carolina:
"Holt succeeds Floyd. It means war. Cut off supplies from
Anderson and take Sumter as soon as possible."[29] It would
seem as though a senator who was making war on the
Federal Government should have first resigned his seat in
its councils. His advice in any case was extremely bad, as
the side which made the first armed attack, whether justly
or not, would have to bear the onus of having begun the
war.

Anderson had been vainly asking for reinforcements and
supplies if he were expected to hold the fort, and at last, on
January 5, an unarmed vessel with 200 additional soldiers
and a quantity of stores was despatched from New York,
in place of the man-of-war *Brooklyn* which had first been
suggested. Senator Wigfall and Secretary of the Interior
Thompson from North Carolina, who did not resign from
the Cabinet until two days later, sent secret warning to
Charleston, which was thus prepared to receive the *Star
of the West* when she attempted to enter Charleston harbor
three days later, and which, when flying the American flag
and within two miles of Fort Sumter, was fired upon by the
batteries at Fort Moultrie and Morris Island. Anderson had

[28] Documents in Crawford, *op. cit.*, pp. 150 f.    [29] *Ibid.*, p. 150.

no knowledge of the effort being made, and on consultation decided not to reply to the hostile shots of the Carolina batteries, though he later wrote to Governor Pickens that if the attack was authorized by the State he must consider it an act of war. The unarmed *Star of the West* had to retreat, and returned to New York.

Virginia was making every effort possible to bring about a reconciliation between the lower South and the Union, in the original formation of which she had done more and made greater sacrifices than any other State. During January she had laid the foundation for a "Peace Conference" at Washington, and at her invitation the delegates of twenty-one States assembled there on February 4. It was the very day on which the delegates of the six seceded cotton States were meeting at Montgomery to form the Confederacy, and this fact was of sufficiently ominous import. The time for further discussion had indeed passed, and after three weeks it was clear that the Conference would fail completely, one of the rocks on which it split being the old question of slavery in the territories. There was much devotion to the Union in Virginia and the other border States, but Virginia had already made it clear that if secession were not allowed to be peaceably carried out, and if the North attempted to coerce the South, then she would herself have to secede.

It is idle to speculate on what would have happened had the States been allowed to go in peace. Such could not be. Ever since 1787, men, States, and sections had been splitting logic over the meaning of words, without convincing each other and often shifting ground themselves. On the whole, however, with large exceptions on both sides, the South had come to believe in the right of peaceable secession, whereas the North had come to disbelieve in it. The South wanted disunion; the North union. The goddess of wisdom had completely failed. Only the god of war could decide; unless the majority were willing to concede everything to the minority. Precisely as public opinion in the South claimed the right to secede, public opinion in the North was to claim the right to protect and perpetuate the Union.

On March 3, in a letter to Seward, whom the President-elect had asked to be his Secretary of State, old General Winfield Scott, born and educated in Virginia, head of the army and a hero of the Mexican War, suggested four possible courses— first, to accept the Crittenden Compromise, second, to collect Federal duties outside the ports of the seceded States, third, to conquer those States by military force, or fourth, "Say to the Seceded States, 'Wayward Sisters, depart in peace.'"

The following day, Lincoln assumed office and made his Inaugural Address. The tone was calm and conciliatory. He offered the South everything except independence and further extension of slavery in the territories, the latter an advantage of the South against the North which the South, as we have noted, gave up by seceding and abandoning the territories in question. He stated solemnly that there was no intention of disturbing slavery in the slave States, and that the Fugitive Slave Law ought to be obeyed and was constitutional. He added, however, that he did not believe the Union could be broken without the consent of all the States, and that as President it would be his duty to enforce the Federal laws throughout it.

Almost in the words which we have already quoted from one of his letters, he said, "One section of our country thinks slavery is *right* and ought to be extended, while the other believes it is *wrong* and ought not to be extended. This is the only substantial dispute. . . . Physically speaking, we cannot separate. We cannot remove our respective sections from each other, nor build an impassable wall between them." (Jefferson Davis had had a glimpse of this same thought when he discussed with his wife "the cordon of custom-houses which would be needful, if a commercial treaty of free trade could not be made.") In closing, Lincoln made his final appeal to the South. "In *your* hands, my dissatisfied fellow-countrymen, and not in *mine,* is the momentous issue of civil war. The government will not assail *you.* You can have no conflict without yourselves being the aggressors. *You* have no oath registered in heaven to destroy the government, while *I* shall have the most solemn one to 'preserve, protect, and defend' it. . . . Though passion may have strained, it must not break our bonds of affection. The mystic chords of memory, stretching from every battle-field and patriot grave to every living heart and hearthstone all over this broad land, will yet swell the chorus of the Union again when touched, as surely they will be, by the better angels of our nature."

It was, however, too late for words. We have failed of our purpose in our long review of conditions leading to separation if we have not made it clear why the far South preferred to abandon its claims to the Territories, its claims to fugitive slaves, indeed everything on which the successive quarrels had ostensibly been based, rather than remain in a Union with the North. As far as the lower South was concerned, the die had already been irrevocably cast. The only question was as to the border States, and what was to appear to many the somewhat weak and vacillating policy of Lincoln in the next few weeks had to be based on trying to keep as many of those within the Union as possible.

The new President had, of course, arranged for his Cabinet, and the names submitted were promptly confirmed by the Senate. William H. Seward, the choice of the Eastern Republicans for Lincoln's own office, was naturally made Secretary of State. Among the other officials were Salmon P. Chase in the Treasury, Simon Cameron of Pennsylvania as Secretary of War; Gideon Welles as that of the Navy; Edward Bates of Missouri as Attorney General and Montgomery Blair of Maryland as Postmaster General. Cameron, whose appointment was the result of a political bargain of which the President had known nothing, was soon proved most unfit, and replaced by Edwin M. Stanton. In ability and driving power, Seward, Stanton, and Chase were strong men, though the latter two in especial were to give the President no little trouble at times, and Stanton's bigotry and ambition were to do much both during and after the war to embitter situations and the relations between the two sections. Later, in Johnson's Cabinet he was to become even more a centre of intrigue and a traitor against his chief. In spite of his ability and the services he rendered, it is difficult to feel either sympathy or respect for him. He was always a trouble maker for his own gain, and showed himself unfeeling, hard, and even cruel. Seward, after a few months, displayed his real strength and grasp of affairs, following an absurd beginning subsequent to which he remained loyal to the President.

In view of the immortal place which Lincoln has taken among the statesmen of the ages, it is somewhat difficult to realize the attitude of the country toward him in March, 1861. In spite of his own statements he had been painted in the South as an ultra leader of the radical Abolitionists, while even in the North his strength, balanced judgment, and knowledge of the deeper currents of public opinion were little understood. Homely and uncouth—his own Secretary of State could speak of him as "the original gorilla" —and but little known, he was not in general considered a man of strength or one to be relied upon in the great crisis now confronting the nation. Keeping his own counsel and covering the genuine depth of his thought with a fund of stories and anecdotes, often repellent to the pompous senators, pouter-pigeon "statesmen," and reserved gentlemen like Charles Francis Adams, he did not make a good impression in the first few weeks of his term. Seward, indeed, who felt that he himself should have been in the White House, wrote to Lincoln a letter on April 1, thoroughly insulting, though not intended to be, practically offering to take over the policy of the government himself if Lincoln were incapable of doing so. Somewhat has to be allowed for the real growth of the President after he assumed office, but there is no doubt that he was much underrated by intelligent public opinion in the North during the weeks when he was feeling his way, trying to retain the border States, and waiting for a clarification and unification of Northern sentiment. Indeed, throughout the war, apart from political differences, not a little influential opinion, notably among the intellectual classes in Boston, failed wholly to measure the stature of one of the greatest of Americans. In 1863, young A. W. Thayer, then a Secretary in the Legation at Vienna, wrote to H. L. Higginson that in returning to Europe he should "carry back with [him] the heartiest contempt for Abe Lincoln,'" under whom, incidentally, he was occupying a comfortable civilian post in war times.

Lincoln's Constitutional theory was—and if it could have been retained to the very end by all it would have saved the horrors of Reconstruction—that as the Union could not be broken without the consent of all the partners to it, the seceded States were in reality, whatever they might claim, not out of the Union. He intended, as elected Chief Executive, to administer the Federal laws throughout the whole Union, and leave any overt act of war to the South. Davis was as anxious as Lincoln not to bring on a collision, and appointed commissioners, two of whom arrived in Washington early in March, to treat with the Federal Government for the "settlement of all questions of disagreement between the two governments." To have received them on that basis would have been to acknowledge the independence of the Confederate States, and thus accept without a stroke the doctrines of the South. Lincoln not only refused to meet the emissaries, but told Seward not to do so or to receive any official letter from them. Various go-betweens appeared on the scene, however, and Seward, mistrusting Lincoln's ability, exalting his own, and believing that the South could still be won back, allowed himself to be drawn into discussions. He even went so far, though he was neither President nor Secretary of War, to assert that Fort Sumter would be evacuated in three days, a statement which, in either his private or official capacity, he quite obviously had no right to make. Nevertheless, the Southern commissioners, although they had been denied official access to the government, continued to discuss matters with various persons in Washington and probably believed they were getting information and promises that were binding, though it is difficult to understand why they should have thought so.

Meanwhile nothing had been officially decided as to the Southern forts—Pickens in Florida and Sumter at Charleston. General Scott suddenly advised their evacuation, but only two members of the Cabinet, including Seward, were in favor of such a move. Lincoln reserved his own decision. Finally, early in April, Lincoln made up his mind to provision and retain them. It is not necessary here to go into the details of the disarrangement of the original plans due to Seward's unjustified interference with the orders of both the President and the Secretary of the Navy. Seward, who was to be extremely useful and also loyal to the President later, was now in a state of mind which can only be described as infatuated. Lincoln realized that if the United States as a nation was to keep the respect of foreigners, and if the Union was indeed to be preserved, the time had at last come to make some show of authority, and that to abandon the Federal forts and their garrisons would be virtually surrendering to the claims of secession.

Word had reached Charleston of the intended expedition to revictual Fort Sumter, and the question at once arose as to what to do. Although the State was wildly excited, military operations had by then come under the authority of the Confederate Government, and Davis had to consider the matter. Toombs, the Confederate Secretary of State, far more clear-visioned at that moment than Seward, saw the results of an attack, and expressed his opinion with vigor at a Cabinet meeting. "The firing upon that fort," he said to Davis, "will inaugurate a civil war greater than any the world has yet seen," and later in the grave discussion he added, "Mr. President, at this time it is suicide, murder, and will lose us every friend at the North. You will wantonly strike a hornet's nest which extends from ocean to ocean, and legions now quiet will swarm out and sting us to death. It is unnecessary; it puts us in the wrong; it is fatal."[30]

Nevertheless, Davis ordered General Beauregard, who was in command at Charleston, to demand the evacuation of the fort, and if refused to "reduce it." In answer Major Anderson naturally declined, but said verbally to the three aides who had gone to Sumter to make the demand that if he were not disturbed he would be starved out in any case in three days. This being telegraphed to Davis, he replied that he did not wish to bombard the fort needlessly, and if Anderson would state the day and hour on which he would surrender, Beauregard was not to begin firing; but if Anderson would not, then to reduce the fort as soon as his [Beauregard's] judgment decided should be best. In response to Beauregard's next demand Anderson sent word that he would evacuate the fort "by noon of the 15th instant" and that unless attacked he would not use his guns meanwhile unless prior to that time he should receive supplies or con-

[30] Quoted by Rhodes, *op. cit.*, vol. III, pp. 347 f.

trolling orders from his own government. This being considered unsatisfactory, he was informed that the Confederates would open fire within an hour.

As has been pointed out, "the four men who in the last resort made the decision that began the war were ex-Senator Chesnut, Lieutenant Colonel Chisholm, Captain Lee, all three South Carolinians, and Roger A. Pryor, a Virginia secessionist, who two days before in a speech at the Charleston Hotel had said, 'I will tell your governor what will put Virginia in the Southern Confederacy in less than an hour by Shrewsbury clock. Strike a blow!' "[31] Had the aides who had carried Beauregard's demand to Anderson returned with his answer instead of informing the Federal officer that he would be fired upon, it is impossible to say what might have happened. Beauregard would probably have again communicated with Davis. In any case, it was now too late. Both Toombs and Pryor were right. The North was to be aroused in a blaze of fury and of Union sentiment, while Virginia was to be brought into the war on the side of the South.

At half-past four the three Confederate batteries opened fire on the doomed Anderson and his little garrison of sixty-four men. The guns of Fort Sumter replied, while along the water-front excited Charlestonians watched this most dramatic beginning of the blood-stained pages of our tragedy. The following morning the firing was resumed. At half-past one the American flag was cut down by a shot but promptly replaced. The fort was on fire, the magazine in danger, and the ammunition almost exhausted. Meanwhile the supply ships had arrived from New York but remained below the harbor, impotent witnesses to the mutual bombardment of the four forts.

The end is best described in Anderson's own report to the Secretary of War. "Having defended Fort Sumter for

[31] Rhodes, *op. cit.*, vol. III, p. 349.

thirty-four hours, until the quarters were entirely burned, the main gates destroyed by fire, the gorge walls seriously impaired, the magazine surrounded by flames, and its door closed by the effects of the heat, four barrels and three cartridges of powder only being available, I accepted terms of evacuation offered by General Beauregard [being the same offered by him on the 11th instant, prior to the commencement of hostilities], and marched out of the fort on Sunday afternoon, the 14th instant, with colors flying and drums beating, bringing away company and private property, and saluting my flag with fifty guns."[32]

So infatuated with the belief in peaceful secession were Rhett and other of the secessionist leaders that even after the capture of Fort Sumter the Rhett family paper, *The Charleston Mercury,* could say in the leading editorial of April 18, "Our readers know that we have repeatedly declared that we did not believe that a war between the North and the South would be the result of a dissolution of the Union by the Southern States. With the sound of our cannon still ringing in our ears, we are of the same opinion still."

The news of the attempt to revictual the fort, of its bombardment and the events immediately succeeding, precipitated public opinion both North and South. On April 13, *The New York Tribune* carried large headlines declaring "WAR BEGUN, Fire opened on Fort Sumter," and on the 15th Greeley's editorial began "Fort Sumter is lost, but freedom is saved." Although the stock market was swept by panic, with heavy falls in the prices of the bonds of the border States, the Northern people were suddenly lifted high on a wave of patriotic enthusiasm which has seldom been equalled. The question of slavery at this moment played little part. The aroused passion was all for the Union. There were no more fine-spun argu-

[32] Crawford, *Genesis of the Civil War,* p. 449.

183

ments as to the wording of the Constitution. As one young lad who was to volunteer for the army in a few days wrote in the diary he determined to keep, secession meant for him that "if these States are allowed to go, the remainder may be divided and subdivided again, which means an utter disintegration of the Federal Government."

The old Jacksonian view suddenly made its appeal in its simplest form. If secession were allowed to be a right, the government was a mere rope of sand, the great nation which all the people had been building and developing for eighty years was a mere house of cards, to be tumbled down in the slightest gust of anger or disagreement. There were no more arguments ; just one vast resolve that such a breakdown of all the hopes of generations should not be allowed to take place—though there were still dissentient voices here and there. The unanimity of feeling, however, is attested by almost every contemporary comment. The Illinois youth just quoted wrote on the 15th, "What an excitement we have all been in since these people fired on Fort Sumter! Every one is anxious to do his utmost and determined to raise a force strong enough to go down there and thrash the conceit out of the rascals. The feeling runs mountains high, and thousands of men are offering their services."[33]

A few days later, Wilder Dwight wrote from Washington, "Never, in the history of the world, did opinion, or rather sentiment, take such sudden form. It has leaped, full-armed, into life."[34] Old George Ticknor, writing from Boston to an English correspondent, said, "The heather is on fire. I never before knew what a popular excitement can be. Holiday enthusiasm I have seen often enough, and anxious crowds I remember during the war of 1812–15, but never anything like this. Indeed, here at the North, at least, there never was anything like it ; for if the feeling was

[33] J. M. Favill, *The Diary of a Young Army Officer* (Chicago, 1909), p. 13.
[34] *Life and Letters of Wilder Dwight* (Boston, 1891), p. 40.

as deep and stern in 1775, it was by no means so intelligent or unanimous; and then the masses to be moved were as a handful compared to our dense population now. . . . The whole population seem to be in the streets with Union favors and flags."[35]

The day after Sumter fell, Lincoln called for 75,000 militia to suppress obstructions to the execution of the Federal laws in the seceded States. It was not that the President thought the war would last only that length of time but because, under an old law, the militia could not be called on for a longer continuous period of service. The following week was one of the most anxious the nation has ever known. In the first flush of the easy victory in Charleston harbor, the Confederate Secretary of War promised in a speech that the Southern flag would float over Washington before the 1st of May, and there was too much reason to fear the truth of his statement.

Virginia had been so loath to secede that it had incurred no small degree of enmity among the States of the Lower South. In the Old Dominion probably the great majority of people believed in the Southern view of States' Rights but many were also extremely loyal to the Union. Moreover, both business and social ties with the North had been becoming stronger of recent years. The State, after a long period of somnolence, was once again becoming national. Her politicians had formed Northern alliances, and in 1860 two of her sons, Hunter and Wise, had both been mentioned as possible candidates for the Presidency. The chief ties of affection, of course, were with the South, but Virginia, until the fall of Sumter and Lincoln's call for troops, was a battle-field of conflicting emotions, as she was soon unhappily to be that of conflicting armies. As in the other border States, there were two schools of thought on the

---

[35] *Life, Letters, and Journals of George Ticknor* (Boston, 1909), vol. II, p. 434.

subject of secession. Some considered it a Constitutional right, while others, like Buchanan, denied the right to secede yet nevertheless denied equally the right of the Federal Government to coerce a seceded State. Leaving aside the first view, which we have already discussed, we may say that the second, the Buchanan one, had much to back it in American history and political thought.

It is true that the right of secession would make the nation, as was said a few pages back, a house of cards, but what of the right of revolution? Had not the Revolution of 1776 been fought on the principle of the right of a people to determine their own destiny? Without belying all the principles on which the nation had been founded, could it now insist upon a large section remaining under control of another, though larger, section against its own will? The right of revolution had always been recognized by us. In an ordinary government, the right, in fact the duty, to put down revolution might also be recognized, but could that be said of such a government as that of the United States? Here was another insoluble problem, with no Supreme Judge to adjudicate it. As the young Northern soldier recognized, to allow these States to leave the Union peacefully was the beginning of the unravelling of the entire national fabric. If peaceable secession were allowed, then every serious quarrel over agrarian versus industrial interests, over sectional prejudices, over forms of labor, over the tariff, over the income tax, over Prohibition, might have left behind it new breakings off from the once great nation. There might have been three or four or a score of sovereignties now in place of the United States— an American Balkans. Yet, on the other hand, it was asked in 1861, could there ever be harmony and happiness again if the Union were to be cemented by force and not consent?

However they might differ on the subject of the Constitutional right of secession, most Virginians were a unit as to denying the possibility just mentioned. William C. Rives, in the Peace Conference in Washington, had said "I condemn the secession of States, I am not here to defend it. I detest it [but] force will never bring them together." George Baylor, in the Virginia convention to consider the action of the State, said much the same, as did other Virginians. He denied the right of secession but also that of coercion as both unconstitutional and wrong. Ultra-ardent Southerners dislike both the terms Civil War and Rebellion, but the Virginian case was never better put than by one of the greatest of all Southerners of the period and one of the greatest of Americans. "Secession," wrote Robert E. Lee on January 23, "is nothing but revolution. The framers of our Constitution never exhausted so much labor, wisdom, and forbearance in its formation and surrounded it with so many guards and securities if it was intended to be broken by every member of the Confederacy at will. . . . Still a Union that can only be maintained by swords and bayonets and in which strife and civil war are to take the place of brotherly love and kindness, has no charm for me. If the Union is dissolved and the Government disrupted I shall return to my native State and share the miseries of my people—and save in defense will draw my sword on none."[36]

In spite of great pressure from the South and a large part of her own people, Virginia had declined to secede on account of the slavery question. The convention had been sitting so long without taking action that a "spontaneous" convention had been organized alongside of it, demanding immediate secession. The temper of this body probably better represented the sentiment of the eastern part of the State than did the authorized one. In one debate, speaking of secessionists, one of the members shouted "never Seces-

[36] Quotations from Munford, *Virginia's Attitude Toward Slavery and Secession*, pp. 293 f.

sionists. I detest the word. We are revolutionists—rebels as our fathers were."[37]

Curiously enough, a Virginian wrote in his diary that "many are inclined to think the safest plan would be to obliterate State lines, and merge them all into an indivisible nation or empire, else there may be incessant conflicts between the different sovereignties themselves. . . . I doubt our ability to maintain the old cumbrous, complicated, and expensive form of government. . . . It is true, State Rights gave the States the right to secede. But what is in a name? Secession by any other name would smell as sweet. For my part, I like the name of Revolution, or even Rebellion, better, for they are sanctified by the example of Washington and his compeers. And separations of communities are like the separations of bees when they cannot live at peace in the same hive. The time had come apparently for us to set up for ourselves, and we should have done it if there had been no such thing as State sovereignty."[38]

When, however, on April 17, the authorized convention passed the Ordinance of Secession to be submitted to the people, it was because of the avowed policy of Lincoln and the North to coerce the seceded States and form a Union based on force, and not on account of slavery. Who was right? Thinking in terms of centuries would it have been better for the United States to break up into several or many nations, or to have remained one? Opinions may differ, and, again, there is no over-ruling supreme decision to be had, though there is much to be said on both sides.

The vote of Virginia to secede, followed in a few weeks by those of North Carolina and Arkansas, brought the territory of the Confederacy to the very threshold of the national capital. In fact Lee's own home of Arlington looked down upon the White House from its height across

[37] Pryor, *op. cit.*, p. 124.
[38] J. B. Jones, *A Rebel War Clerk's Diary* (Philadelphia, 1866), vol. I, p. 24.

the Potomac. Northern troops were hastening to Washington in answer to Lincoln's call. Although some, unarmed, arrived from Pennsylvania promptly, Massachusetts was more nearly prepared than any other State for the emergency. On April 17, the Sixth Regiment of that State started, but if Washington faced the enemy across the river to the South it was also cut off from the North by the more than half-hostile State of Maryland; and in crossing Baltimore from one depot to another the troops came into collision with a mob. That night some of the railroad bridges were burned, and it was agreed temporarily that troops arriving from the North should if possible be sent around and not through the city. Railroad connection was thus to a considerable extent cut off from the North, and on the 21st the telegraph was also cut. The capital was isolated except for couriers.

Meanwhile President Davis had issued letters of marque against Northern merchant vessels, and Lincoln had retaliated by declaring a blockade of the Southern ports from South Carolina to Texas, adding that privateers acting under Confederate orders would be treated as pirates, a threat never carried into final execution. According to the theory that the seceded States were in reality not out of the Union, a theory which, as we have said, would have made reconstruction far easier when it came, Lincoln could not have recognized the Confederate Government, but the piracy and rebel theory as a corollary was also to make trouble for him.

On the following day, April 20, Colonel Robert E. Lee, who was considered as possibly the ablest officer in the army and who had unofficially been offered command of the Union troops, resigned his commission, thus striking one of the heaviest blows the North sustained. He had had a distinguished career of more than twenty-five years in the service to which he was devoted and which he had adorned by both his character and achievements. Deeply attached to the Union and disbelieving in secession, it was peculiarly hard for him to reach his decision, which he announced to his sister in the North immediately after resigning. "The whole South," he wrote, "is in a state of revolution, into which Virginia, after a long struggle, has been drawn; and though I recognize no necessity for this state of things . . . yet in my own person I had to meet the question whether I should take part against my native State. With all my devotion to the Union and the feeling of loyalty and duty of an American citizen, I have not been able to make up my mind to raise my hand against my relatives, my children, my home."[39]

The army, like public life, had appealed to the best young Southerners, and the break-up of the nation found many of the ablest officers on the side of the new Confederacy. The question of permissible resignation was one of the indications of the confused and anomalous situation in which the country found itself. In some cases officers of Southern sympathies, such as Major Anderson who defended Fort Sumter, felt themselves obliged by their oath to defend the United States. George H. Thomas, a Virginian and later to be a Federal general, also stood by the Union. Admiral Farragut of Tennessee was another. The Virginian, General Winfield Scott, yet another. As Professor Channing points out, what would have happened had resignations been refused is an interesting question. Could the South have stood out long if the resignations of Lee, the two Johnstons, Gorgas, Semmes, and others had been declined? These men would either have served in the Union armies loyally or if caught have been imprisoned. In either case their inestimable services to the South might not have been available. To accept resignations wholesale in the face of the

[39] R. E. Lee (jr.), *Recollections and Letters of General Robert E. Lee* (New York, 1904), p. 26.

enemy and danger was merely admitting that the situation was not an ordinary one, and that however sure each section was of its own interpretation of the Constitution, there was room for honest difference of opinion. That the North should have allowed many of its ablest military officers to pass quietly over to the ranks of its enemy instead of detaining them is one of the notable facts in history.

The truth was, without prejudging the Constitutional question, by using the term "Civil War," that the war now beginning was a war between brethren. At the time, it was constantly so referred to by Southerners as well as Northerners. Not only was the nation divided, and its armed forces, but countless families, my own among them. I had relations in both the Northern and Southern armies and navies, and other more important instances are countless. Mrs. Abraham Lincoln had three half-brothers in the Southern army. General McClellan's cousin was chief of staff to both General Stuart and Wade Hampton. General Meade's two sisters-in-law were the wives of General Wise of Virginia and Lieutenant Huger of the Confederate navy. Admiral Porter had two nephews in the Southern navy; and the one-time commander of the Union fleet in the James River was a cousin of General Lee. The latter's sister was married in the North and her son was not only in the Federal army but on Pope's staff. The notorious General Hunter, whom we shall mention later, had close family connections in Virginia. Mrs. John A. Logan had a brother in the Confederate army while her husband was a general in the Union one. Stonewall Jackson's father-in-law, the president of Washington College, Virginia, was a Union man and went north at the beginning of the war. Colonel Rush of the Union army was first cousin of Captain Mason of the Confederate navy. General Philip St. George Cooke of the Union cavalry was the father of General John R. Cooke and father-in-law of General J. E. B. Stuart of the

Confederate cavalry. Randolph McKim of Maryland was an officer in the Confederate service while both his parents were Unionists. The wife of General G. W. Smith, who commanded a Georgia division, was a Connecticut woman from New London, and the wife of General A. P. Stuart was from Ohio.

Mrs. Clay speaks of a woman she met after war was declared who said, "Think how my heart is riven! I was born in New Orleans and live in New York. One of my sons is in the Seventh New York Regiment, and another in the New Orleans Zouaves." In the battle of Antietam, the bloodiest of the war, a Union colonel was killed while leading a charge against Confederates commanded by his own brother-in-law, a Confederate general. In another battle, in the Southwest, a young man, fighting in the Confederate army, took his father, a Federal soldier, prisoner, not knowing for a moment whom he had captured. On Sherman's march through Georgia he was accompanied by a young Union lieutenant, Snelling, who was a nephew of Howell Cobb and helped himself to one of his uncle's horses when his plantation was looted. When Fort Walker at Port Royal was attacked by a Federal war vessel its captain was Percival Drayton while his brother, General Thomas F. Drayton, was in command of the fort. When the *Merrimac* destroyed the U.S.S. *Congress* the commodore, Buchanan, in command of the Southern ship, knew that his brother was an officer in the Northern one. Two of the lieutenants on the *Merrimac* had brothers in the Northern army. Senator Crittenden, who attempted to compromise between the sections, had two sons, of whom one became a major general in the Union army and the other held the same rank in the Confederate one. A daughter of Mr. Mallory, Secretary of the Confederate Navy, was married to a Northerner, Mr. Bishop, of Connecticut.

The list of divided families, prominent or lowly, could be

continued indefinitely. Mrs. Roger Pryor tells a story of the women of Norfolk making material for cartridges when "a gentle, blue-eyed woman joined us and asked for work. But when it was explained to her, her lips quivered. 'Oh, I can't! I can't!' she begged. 'Let me roll bandages for wounds! I can't help with the cartridges! You see, all my people live in Pennsylvania. My husband is going to fight them, I know; but don't ask me to make the cartridges.'" General Gordon, of the Confederate army, relates that a Kentucky father who had lost his two sons in the war, one in the Confederate and one in the Union forces, erected a joint monument over them both with the inscription "God knows which was right."

No one knows, but we may quote the words of the English Colonel Henderson who wrote the life of General Jackson. "If Stonewall Jackson," says his English biographer, " had been a New Englander, educated in the belief that secession was rebellion, he would assuredly have shed the last drop of his blood in defence of the Union; if Ulysses Grant had been a Virginian, imbibing the doctrine of States' Rights with his mother's milk, it is just as certain that he would have worn the Confederate gray. It is with those Northerners who would have allowed the Union to be broken, and with those Southerners who would have tamely surrendered their hereditary rights, that no Englishman would be willing to claim kinship."

# CHAPTER VI

## CIVILIAN WAR, 1861

WHEN the American nation finally entered upon what was the greatest war of modern times until the recent World War it was, as usual, wholly unprepared for military action on the grand scale. The army consisted of only a few thousand men although there were a number of brilliant officers, some of whom had seen service in the Mexican War a dozen years before. As already noted the Southerners as a rule had cared more for a military career than the young men of the North of the same quality, and a majority of the finest officers of the regular army seceded with their States, giving an inestimable advantage in that respect to the South. But both parties to the conflict had to create, organize, and train their armies, and as it takes time to make a soldier, the first year of the struggle may be considered as merely a preparatory period in which hordes of civilians were led and moulded by officers who, with distinguished exceptions, had themselves to learn the art of war.

Although the tragic event had been coming nearer year by year, it seemed, at the end, to leap upon the country almost unawares. There were few trained and equipped troops on either side. Massachusetts could send one first-class regiment to the defence of Washington in the emergency and the New York 7th was equally good. The condition of the 71st New York, however, which hurried after, was more typical. Starting for the capital on April 21, in response to urgent calls, the men received each a rifle, bayonet, cartridge box, cap pouch, and blanket, but, as one of them wrote in his diary, "our new uniforms were not ready so the greater part of the regiment appeared in every day clothes and hats. . . . The greatest difficulty was an absence of knapsacks, which necessitated carrying valises, a very awkward arrangement, giving us more the appearance of a lot of emigrants than a regiment of soldiers."[1] An army of raw recruits from farms, offices, and every department of civil life travelling in business suits with valises to defend the capital of the nation!

However, even if without training, discipline, experience, and often equipment, the human material of the armies on both sides was excellent, although as always happens in a great war, it was the best in the first year, and was to deteriorate both North and South after 1862. As a rule it is the most ardent, intelligent, patriotic, and finest of the younger generation which volunteers in the first enthusiasm when called upon to defend their country at the beginning of a war. Moreover, its horrors have not as yet been felt, and the contest is almost always expected to be a short one. In June *The New York Tribune* scoffed at the idea that the war could last three years and said that if the rebels were not whipped by spring the North would have been betrayed by its leaders and disunion would then have become a fixed fact. With the omniscience which journalists assume in war, the papers of both sections preached the doctrine of a brief struggle and an easy victory. In the first few months it was with vast enthusiasm that the flower of the youth, as well as older men, answered the calls for troops sent out by both Lincoln and Davis, though then and throughout the terrible years to come the South contributed more generously of its educated and socially prominent classes than did the North. The students and alumni of Harvard who were of military age numbered about seven to four of those at the University of Virginia, yet the Harvard dead numbered only 117 as against 503 from the smaller institution of the

[1] J. M. Favill, *op. cit.,* p. 15.

Old Dominion, while the latter contributed over 2500 men to the service as against Harvard's 938.

On the other hand, there was in the North a far larger class of the soundest sort between the highest and the lowest to be drawn upon than in the South. Edward Dicey, the English observer, could say of the Northern army of the Potomac that "I have seen the armies of most European countries, and I have no hesitation in saying that, as far as the average raw material of the rank and file is concerned, the American army is the finest." Naturally, on both sides, young men of education and position strove for commissions as officers but the private soldier of our Civil War probably represented a far higher level of education and morale than had ever been known before. Turning from North to South we get a glimpse of a group of privates as given by Randolph McKim of Maryland in describing his messmates in the winter of 1861–62. There were, he says, Harry Oliver, a country gentleman of large means; Wilson Carr, a successful lawyer of Baltimore; William D. McKim, a former president of the Hasty Pudding Club at Harvard, and an intimate of Rufus Choate; George Williamson, educated abroad; and two men educating themselves for the Episcopal ministry. Of course this was exceptional even for the first year of the war, but Mrs. Chesnut has an illuminating passage in her journal of May, 1861, as to her husband's young nephew John. "Johnny," she writes, "has gone as a private in Gregg's regiment. He could not stand it home any longer. Mr. Chesnut was willing for him to go, because those sandhill men said 'this was a rich man's war,' and the rich men would be the officers and have an easy time and the poor ones would be privates. So he said: 'Let the gentlemen set the example; let them go in the ranks.' So John Chesnut is a gentleman private. He took his servant with him all the same."[2] Many of the

2 *A Diary from Dixie, op. cit.,* p. 58.

Southern officers kept slaves with them as servants through the war but it is to be presumed that the custom quickly died out in the rank and file. An amusing story has often been told of an officer who before going into battle ordered his negro servant to watch his tent and take care of his property. The skirmish over, the officer was annoyed to find the negro had deserted his post for the woods. On his return later, when the master threatened to chastise him, the slave said, "Massa, you done tol me to take care of your property, and *dis* property," touching his breast, "is wurf fifteen hundred dollars and I done took care of it."

Each side, before the war, had been taught to look down upon the other. The Southerner had been led to consider the Northerner, or Yankee, as a more or less hypocritical, money-grubbing person who would never put up a fight, and five or six of whom could easily be whipped by any one from South of Mason and Dixon's line. On the other hand, the Northerner had come to consider the Southerner as a blusterer and a bully who would back down when he found that bluster would no longer avail. Both North and South were to learn that they were fighting men of the same virile race, and to acquire respect for each other's qualities and courage. As always, journalists, women, and other stay-at-homes were the bitterest decriers of the qualities of the enemy whereas the men who actually faced each other in fierce battle came, in general, to respect and fraternize with one another, of which we shall give some examples later.

Both North and South trusted to volunteering at first, though both had later to come to conscription, with resultant debasement of quality. Lincoln's call for 75,000 men when Fort Sumter fell was followed on May 3 by a call for about 42,000 more volunteers to serve three years if need be; an increase of 22,714 men for service in the regular army; and the enlistment of 18,000 seamen for the navy. Except in the still wavering border States there was no trouble in raising the required numbers. In the South there was equal or even greater enthusiasm to enlist but President Davis soon began to discover the inherent difficulties of the States' Rights doctrine. He had been authorized to call for and accept a hundred thousand volunteers in March, and later Acts of the Confederate Congress in subsequent weeks added to the numbers he could use, though the principles of short enlistments and election of officers by the privates were embodied in the laws, to make constant trouble.

In the South there was no difficulty at all in getting men in 1861 but much in getting arms. There was a large supply in the various seceded States, either recently purchased, taken over from Federal arsenals, or acquired in other ways. For example, it has been estimated that Virginia alone had 100,000 stand of small arms in the fall of 1860, increased by later purchases. But when the Confederate Government tried to obtain these it at once ran into State jealousies or fears. The Governor of Mississippi refused more than a few troops for the general service as he wished them to protect his own State from invasion. By the beginning of 1862 the Governor of North Carolina was even demanding the return of arms sent out of the State, and soon after issued a proclamation against the purchase of arms or any kind of military equipment within the State by the Confederate Government, promising to protect the North Carolinians by force if necessary against the central government. In September, 1861, Governor Pickens of South Carolina wrote that the State could supply no more arms to the Confederacy until it had armed its own 15,000 local troops. Tennessee, Texas, Arkansas refused to supply any at all. Virginia was as reluctant as the others. Georgia not only would not contribute but tried to get more for herself from the Secretary of War. Indeed, Governor Brown of that State even threatened to seize a cargo from abroad bought by the Confederate Congress, which threat called forth the caustic reply from the Secretary of War that "it is scarcely necessary to observe that if the government cannot have its property intended for public defense landed or deposited at any point of the Confederacy without being exposed to having it seized and appropriated to meet supposed local exigencies it would be better to abandon at once all attempts to conduct the defense of the country on an organized system and deliver over the control of the military to the local militia and popular meetings."[3]

In the next year there was to be similar trouble over the supply of men by the individual States but there would seem to be little question, as Professor Owsley has pointed out, that the doctrine of States' Rights reaped its first disastrous harvest in the important early months of the war when the Confederate army might have overwhelmed the North by numbers could the arms which were on hand have been supplied to the volunteers who had to be rejected.

Time, like many other factors, was to be on the side of the North. Dividing the population of the border States between the two sections, the North had approximately a white-man power of 21,000,000 to the South's 6,500,000. The disparity was not as great as the figures would indicate because, although until almost the end of the war it was unthinkable that the Confederacy would put slaves in its army, the 3,500,000 blacks could be used in raising food and "carrying on" in other ways behind the lines. But even so, the proportion was more than two to one against the South. Financially the North was not only immensely stronger than the South in accumulated liquid capital and credit, but it had the advantage that, whether it won or lost, its government obligations would remain those of a young and rich sovereign power, whereas those of the South could retain value only if the South won and would be wholly worthless if it lost. The North if defeated could stagger

[3] Owsley, *State Rights in the Confederacy, op. cit.,* pp. 7 *ff.*

and go on; the South staked all on the chances of war, as it had staked almost all, economically, on the raising of cotton.

The nature, and, to a great extent, the concentration of wealth in the South were shown by the estimate of the total made by the Confederate Secretary of the Treasury and the subsequent assessment for taxation. The latter returned a total of $4,220,755,834, made up of approximately $1,500,-000,000 in slaves, $1,400,000,000 in real estate, $500,000,-000 in money at interest, and $94,000,000 in bank stocks. If we accept the Southern estimate that eighty per cent of the men who fought in the Southern army were not slave-holders, and recall that the great majority of the remaining twenty per cent owned only a few slaves each, we can realize how extraordinarily concentrated the chief item of Southern wealth must have been.

Outside of cotton the Confederacy, although it had enormously rich natural resources, was economically weak. The total bank stock holdings were, as noted, only $94,000,-000, which compared with bank capitalizations in the two cities of Boston and New York alone of over $106,000,000. The plantation system was wholly dependent on credit, yet the Census of 1860 states that there was not a single bank in Mississippi or Arkansas, only two small ones in Florida and one small one in Texas. Although there was a certain amount of manufacturing in the South, the almost complete lack of interest in industrialism as contrasted with the North was shown in the number of patents granted to the citizens of the several States. In 1857, for example, only 12 were granted to South Carolina as against 855 in New York. Alabama led the lower South with 27 contrasted with 421 in Massachusetts. *The Charleston Courier* could say in 1861 that with the opening of the new Confederate Patent Office Southerners could become the "Goodyears, McCormicks, Colts, Singers," of the nation, but the fact remained that they never had been and that they did not wish to be. The plantation ideal of life with its charm and comparative ease had gripped them all, whereas large areas in the North were humming with industrial activity, which told heavily when war material of all sorts had to be produced.

A glance at the railway maps North and South reveals a net-work of easy transportation in the former section as compared with a few main lines in the latter. But more than that disparity, important as it was from the military point of view, the Southern lines were in bad shape. All travellers reported the fact, and in 1862 a Southern naval officer trying to reach Norfolk said that "the trains in the Confederacy were not allowed to run faster than ten miles an hour, and the particular train on which we travelled broke down every few miles, so I doubt if we even averaged that slow speed."[4] When Forts Donelson and Henry were captured, as we shall see later, Colonel Wooley, C.S.A., reported that "the railroad was almost bare of transportation. The locomotives had not been repaired for six months, and many of them lay disabled in the depots. They could not be repaired at Bowling Green, for there is, I am informed, but one place in the South where a driving wheel can be made, and not one where a whole locomotive can be constructed."[5] When the Confederate Government was formed and there was immediate need of issuing both bonds and treasury notes not an engraver on steel or stone could be found in the entire South, and the work had to be done by the American Bank Note Company in New York! Unfortunately for the Confederacy the Federal Government discovered what was going on and confiscated the issues as contraband of war. Later, engravers were imported from Europe.[6]

[4] J. M. Morgan, *Recollections of a Rebel Reefer* (Boston, 1917), p. 78.
[5] W. P. Johnston, *Life of General Albert S. Johnston, op. cit.,* p. 485.
[6] Capers, *Memminger, op. cit.,* p. 316.

On the other hand, the South had certain elements of strength, some fancied and some real. Chief of the former, and one which had had most to do with fostering a spirit of arrogance in the section, was the supposed coercive power exercised over Europe by cotton. A Southern observer at the capital before it was moved from Montgomery says that "two ideas seemed to pervade all classes. One was that keystone dogma of secession, 'Cotton is King,' the other that the war—did one come—could not last over three months. The man who ventured dissent from either idea, back it by what logic he might, was looked upon as an idiot if his disloyalty was not broadly hinted at."[7] Perhaps the two illusions cherished by the South which did most to embitter feeling when they were shattered were, first, that the North would allow peaceful withdrawal, and second, that, if war should come and the South did not win promptly, England and France would be forced to intervene on her behalf and ensure her success. We have already spoken of the effects on the mind of the South resulting from the need for defending her own institution of slavery against the public opinion of the world. It was not one of the least damaging of these effects that the South came not only to over-rate her own importance in world economy but failed to take into consideration intellectual, political, and economic factors in the world outside herself which were to ruin her calculations.

If cotton were to prove a weak reed on which to lean, nevertheless, the South had certain real advantages. As all it asked was to be let alone, it could act on the defensive if it chose, whereas the North was bound to invade her if it insisted upon maintaining the Union by force. Although the lack of railroads and manufacturing was a handicap for the South it also made the task of an invader almost hopelessly difficult. The South had no vital spots at which to

[7] De Leon, *Belles, Beaux and Brains, op. cit.,* p. 50.

strike—great cities which might be centres of production or controlling points for transportation routes. The roads were bad and the distances great. What could happen to even a superbly trained army of veterans led by a military genius when it entered upon the conquest of a vast and unorganized territory had been clearly demonstrated by Napoleon's disastrous campaign against Russia. As one of the best military commentators on our war has written: "A march of eighty or one hundred miles sounds a simple feat, but unless every detail has been most carefully thought out, it will not improbably be more disastrous than a lost battle. A march of two or three hundred miles is a great military operation; a march of six hundred miles an enterprise of which there are few examples. To handle an army in battle is much less difficult than to bring it on to the field in good condition," and he adds that it was not until after the first year of the war, when the auxiliary services had been trained, that generals dared to manœuvre freely.[8]

In addition, as an agricultural country, the South could make itself largely self-sustaining. Its civilians could never be starved into submission by a blockade, though the problems of transport and distribution might offer internal difficulties. Again, the number, homogeneity, and character of its white population appeared to put out of question any permanent holding of her by force even if conquered. Though her armies might be defeated in the field how rule over six million Anglo-Saxons against their wills? To many, both in the North and in Europe, who believed in the Union and who were opposed to the setting up of a new slave empire, this question of permanent control appeared insoluble, and caused the war to appear as a useless shedding of blood with no possible lasting gain. There will probably always be difference of opinion as to the real cause or causes

[8] Colonel G. F. R. Henderson, *Stonewall Jackson and the American Civil War* (London, 1913), vol. I, p. 107.

of the ultimate collapse of the Confederacy but there is
much to be said for the theory increasingly advanced that
the end came not so much from exhaustion of resources as
from the political and psychological factors operating on
the Southern people. Of that we shall speak later, but when
young John Chesnut and thousands like him left their
plantations gaily for the front there was no reason for
them to envisage the grim years and terrible disaster which
were to ensue.

The adherence of Virginia, North Carolina, and Tennessee to the Confederacy had somewhat shifted both the
balance of power and the geography of the new nation.
Many places had been suggested for its capital which had
been temporarily located at Montgomery, and on May 20
Congress decided upon Richmond, the capital of Virginia
and one of the largest and most delightful cities in the
South. Although Congress adjourned to meet there on
July 20, President Davis and the government moved to
the new centre soon after the decision was made. It is not
without interest to note that the charming old house, with
its white columns, in which the President took up his
residence, became known as the "White House" of the
Confederacy. With all the feeling there was against the
North, there was a curious running close in many ways to
old names and symbols. Unless we attribute this to lack of
originality in the Southern mind, which there is no reason
to, it must have stemmed apparently from long habit and
some lingering affection for the old Union. The Constitution, with some exceptions, was taken wholesale from the
Federal one. The residence of the Chief Executive was
given the same name as that in which the then hated Lincoln
was living in Washington. The old flag, the "stars and
stripes," was only slightly modified into the "stars and
bars."

If Virginia had given the capital to the new Confederacy,

one of the very first results of her secession was to be the
permanent loss of a large and rich portion of her territory,
that which now constitutes the State of West Virginia. It
must be recalled that the great State which finally threw in
her lot with the South was at the time of the action more
than a third larger than at present, and extended to the
State of Ohio. The northwestern portion, however, over
the mountains and adjoining Ohio and Pennsylvania, was
neither secessionist nor slave. Its mining, farming, industrial economy allied it to its Northern neighbors rather than
to the plantation economy and society of the South. A
glance at the map on page 53 will show the extreme importance of this section of old Virginia, penetrating northward
as it does almost opposite the very spot at which the Northern
boundary of the United States dips farthest South. There
was approximately only a hundred miles between the north-
ernmost tip of Virginia and the shore of Lake Erie, and this
narrow strip afforded the only connection between the
eastern and western sections of the Union. Had the Virginians in this section of the State, embracing 24,000 square
miles as against the 40,000 of the eastern and present State
of Virginia, not chosen the Union side, the military history
of the war would have been quite different.

Fortunately for the North they did so, although General
Beauregard was at once sent to stop the movement of sectional secession from the seceded State. He was faced by
General McClellan, who, however, did not enter the section
with his troops until after he had heard the result of the
popular vote. He then, May 26, sent a detachment over the
line, and on June 3 defeated the Confederates, after which
the obviously large majority of Union men proceeded to set
up the machinery of separate State government, the senators from the new State being admitted at the next session
of Congress although the State was not formally admitted
to the Union until 1863.

The Federal Congress met on July 4 in special session, and the next day Lincoln asked for 400,000 more men and $400,000,000 to make the contest "short and decisive." Congress not only gave him practically what he asked as to money but also permission to accept 500,000 men. It was becoming evident that Rhett and the other Fire Eaters who had helped to lead the South to secession on the promise of no war had as completely failed to read Northern feeling as had the Abolitionists who for thirty years had been vainly advocating breaking the Union on account of slavery. Both groups of extremists had shown themselves totally incapable of understanding the mass of their fellow countrymen, yet to them were largely due the bitterness and the hatred of the crisis, which were now to be immensely increased by the newspaper press North and South, whether reporting facts or telling lies.

Meanwhile both sides—civilians not realizing the difference between genuine armies and merely large bodies of untrained men—were becoming impatient for action. The newspapers took up the hue and cry and by the end of June *The New York Tribune* was appearing with flaring headlines demanding that Richmond must be taken before the Confederate Congress could sit there. Operations on a large scale were as yet a military absurdity. The South had a group of remarkable officers, such as Lee, J. E. Johnston, A. S. Johnston, Jackson, Beauregard, Bragg, and Longstreet. The North had not as yet. Scott was old and overwhelmed by his duties. Sherman, after having declined the Chief Clerkship of the War Department, had been made a colonel. McDowell had remained in the army since his West Point days, and so also had McClellan until about four years before the war when he had entered business. Grant's application for a commission had been mislaid in the files of the Department. But apart from officers, the troops on both sides were raw and not properly supplied with uniforms or arms. In the first great battle, now about to take place, not only did they wear all conceivable clothing, from civilian dress to the gaudiest of unsuitable militia uniforms, but a number of the Confederate officers still wore their Union blue while the 2d Wisconsin, on the Union side, wore Confederate gray. Neither officers nor men had taken part in large manœuvres. Scott realized all this and stood against the tide for immediate action, but at last had to give way against political pressure and newspaper clamor and operations soon began.

Harpers Ferry had quietly been occupied by the Federal General Patterson with about 20,000 troops, after the withdrawal of the Confederates under Joe Johnston, against Jackson's advice. McDowell had 30,000 or more near Washington.[9] Johnston's troops who had retired southward from Harpers Ferry should have been menaced by Patterson, while the main body of the Confederates, about 22,000 under Beauregard, lay about thirty miles southwest of Washington on the way to Richmond. It was this main body of the enemy which it was determined to attack, McDowell being willing to take the offensive provided Patterson could hold Johnston, and Jackson who was serving under him, and their 11,000 troops from reinforcing Beauregard.

McDowell, who had just been promoted brigadier general from a major, had less than two weeks to organize his army of raw troops into brigades and divisions. When the march toward Richmond began the men had no discipline, and straggled to pick blackberries or otherwise amuse themselves along the road. Johnston, however, had as much reason to complain of his troops as had McDowell. On July 18 there was a slight contact between the two armies which ended badly for the Northerners and helped to shake

[9] It is extremely difficult to arrive at accurate figures for either the total numbers in the two armies throughout the war or for the numbers in any specific engagement. Authorities not seldom differ widely.

their morale. McDowell, having decided, as he should have in the first place, that a frontal attack by raw recruits could end only in failure, now decided to try to turn the Confederate left. The Confederates had the same idea with reference to the Yankees.

Beauregard, who was in command of the Confederate forces until the arrival of Johnston, had withdrawn across the narrow stream of Bull Run which with its steep and slippery banks made a fairly formidable obstacle to inexperienced troops when attacking. Nevertheless the morning operations were in favor of the Federals and as they pressed one portion of the enemy up the slope toward what was known as Henry House Hill the retreat became almost a rout. Unfortunately for McDowell, however, Patterson, far to the westward, had totally failed to hold the forces of Johnston and Jackson, which had completely eluded him owing to his own stupidity, and which had been called to the rescue of Beauregard. After giving the self-confident Patterson the slip, they had marched twenty miles through the Blue Ridge at Ashby's Gap, and were nearing the scene of battle. It is said that when at two o'clock in the morning they reached the village of Paris to halt, the men were so exhausted that they fell to the ground and slept where they were, and that when it was pointed out to Jackson that there were no pickets guarding the encampment, he replied: "Let the poor fellows sleep. I will guard the camp myself."

Jackson reached Manassas early in the morning of the 19th. Johnston did not get there until noon next day, and some of his force did not arrive until the battle was in full swing on the 21st, when their appearance seems to have turned the tide in favor of the Confederates. Meanwhile Jackson had stemmed the rout at Henry House Hill. As the Federals saw Jackson "standing like a stone wall" with his fresh men they wavered in an attack which had become a direct frontal one for them. McDowell appears to have ordered individual regiments to attack in turn instead of a general advance of the brigade which was on hand, and as each failed in its dash against the enemy panic began to spread.

Had McDowell, who like Scott had disapproved of the whole attempt, been able to attack promptly, say on the 19th, it is probable that he would have won a victory, judging by the action of his troops on the morning of the 21st. He would have occupied a more favorable position on the earlier date, and there would have been no time for Johnston and Jackson to reinforce Beauregard and bring the disparity of numbers, which had been heavily in favor of McDowell, to a practical parity. On the other hand, as Colonel Henderson points out, it is only fair to say that McDowell's force of about 28,000 men was a larger one than any American officer had yet commanded. The privates had been only little over a week in their new organizations. The staff officers did not yet know their work. There had been practically no musket practice and some of the troops went into battle without having ever fired a gun in their lives. The folly of undertaking a large offensive under such conditions was evident to any man with military training, and the blame for the utter rout that ensued must be placed on the shoulders of politicians and journalists, as well as the impatient public, led by both, who had insisted upon immediate action.

When the word passed quickly through the Union ranks that Johnston's whole army had arrived to reinforce Beauregard, the ranks wavered and then ignominiously fled. As Captain Hart has written, "if the defeated gradually became, with certain exceptions, a confused mob of stragglers, it was not under shock pressure but under the influence of mass suggestion. Men had had enough, they saw others walking away, and they followed. The battle ended like a bath—draining away through a waste pipe," for, as he also says, "real battles are rarely decided in the manner made familiar by heroically minded artists."[10]

The brigade of Sherman was "the last to feel the suction," and that commander did his best to stem the tide, but it was impossible. Three days later he wrote to his wife that "the battle was nothing to the shameless rout that followed and still exists." The correspondent of *The Tribune* wrote, "the agony of this overwhelming disgrace can never be expressed in words, or understood by those who only hear the tale repeated. I believe there were men upon that field who turned their faces to the enemy, and marched to certain death, lest they should share the infamy which their fellows had invited and embraced. The suffering of a hundred deaths would have been as nothing compared with the torture under which the few brave soldiers writhed who were swept along by that maniac hurricane of terror. . . . A perfect frenzy was upon almost every man. Some cried piteously to be lifted behind those who rode on horses, and others sought to clamber into wagons, the occupants resisting them with bayonets. All sense of manhood seemed to be forgotten. . . . Every impediment to flight was cast aside. . . . All was lost to that American army, even its honor. . . . We passed now and then groups of disabled men, who had forgotten their injuries in their fear, and had striven to drag themselves along by their companions. Some of them still streamed with blood, and yet would wrench themselves forward with all the power they could command. . . . Baggage wagons were overturned, ambulances broken in pieces, weapons of every kind cast off. Horses lay dead and dying. Food was heaped up by the wayside. Bags of corn and oats were trodden into the ground. Piles of clothing were scattered at all sides."[11]

[10] Hart, *Sherman, op. cit.*, p. 89.
[11] *New York Tribune*, issue July 26, 1861.

It may be noted that *The Tribune* itself had been largely responsible for what its correspondent now described.

Henry Villard, then a newspaper correspondent, mounted on the fastest horse he could get to carry the news to the wires, wrote that even so he was passed by Colonel Ambrose Burnside, who shouted as he flew toward safety, "I am hurrying to get rations for my command!" A touch of comedy was given to the ghastly tragedy by the flight of congressmen and other civilians who had come out to see a battle and the first Union victory. Mixed with the fleeing troops, the whole motley crowd fled along the road through Fairfax Court House to the fortifications near Washington, many of the troops not stopping until they even crossed the Potomac into the city itself. Thus ended the first battle of Bull Run, and such was the start the North made in the war.

From what the Southern commanders have written of the lack of discipline on their own side the tale would have been reversed had Patterson's troops appeared upon the scene at the critical hour of the afternoon instead of Johnston's, but the South had reaped the first harvest from its superiority in officers. Patterson, nearly seventy years old, had never had military training, although he had served in the War of 1812 and that with Mexico, was unfit for command and soon removed, whereas both Johnston and Jackson were West Point men and were to prove themselves, as a number of such were not, among the ablest leaders thrown up by the war. Although many circumstances connected with the battle became the subject of not very edifying controversies among the commanders on both sides, the Southern success would seem to be certainly attributable to the reinforcements led by Johnston and Jackson, and they were able to reach the field because both those men were far more competent than Patterson, who had been ordered to hold them in the West.

In spite of the utter rout of the Northern army, the Confederates were also badly shattered, and no effort was made to follow up the victory. This seems to have been due to failure to realize how great the panic was among the Federals and to military reasons, rather than, as has sometimes been claimed, to any interference on the part of President Davis who had appeared upon the field. One of the curses of the South was to be the constant efforts made to exalt one general at the expense of another, and to cause controversy between the Executive and the military. Davis had been a West Pointer and had seen service in the Mexican War, in which he had done well. The temptation to take part in the decision as to what to do that night of the 21st may well have been great but there is no solid evidence that he was in any way responsible for the failure to follow the retreating Federal army and try to capture Washington, even if the latter had been possible. The claim that he had prevented the South from reaping the full fruits of victory appears to have been merely part of the campaign of slander already beginning against him among some of his own people.

On the other hand, though McDowell may have made a mistake in not throwing heavier forces simultaneously against the enemy and in delaying operations, we may recall that the whole expedition was against his advice, and may take the word of Sherman given later in his *Memoirs,* when he could study the whole situation calmly, that "Bull Run was one of the best planned battles of the war, but one of the worst fought."[12] "We had," he adds, "good organization, good men, but no cohesion, no real discipline, no respect for authority, no real knowledge of war. Both armies were fairly defeated, and which ever had stood fast, the other would have run."

[12] *Memoirs of General William T. Sherman* (New York, 1875), vol. I, p. 181.

However, from whatever causes, it had been the North which had finally run, and the South was jubilant, too jubilant, for it assumed the truth had now been shown of its claim that the Yankees could not fight and that the war would soon be over. On the other hand the sarcastic Southern editorials were no more severe than were those of Northern journals, and the North now settled down to its job with a grim earnestness that boded ill for the South. It set to work to make a fighting machine, and McClellan was called from West Virginia to organize it.

With the first great battle of the war came the first group of atrocity stories, and we must pause to speak of one of the darkest corners in the storm-cone in which our tragedy had now centred. For a generation or more the radicals on both sides had been vilifying the people of the other section in speech and public press. In some ways this had been worse in the South than in the North, for whereas *The Liberator,* published by Garrison, was the organ of a comparatively small group of extremists, the Rhett organ in South Carolina, *The Charleston Mercury,* was one of the leading papers of the whole South, as was also *The Richmond Examiner.* Moreover, the Southern monthly magazines contained far more frequent and bitter articles against the character of the North than did any of the Northern magazines against that of the South. Indeed, it is somewhat difficult to reconcile the assumed and to a great extent real Southern chivalry toward woman with articles which Rhett and others allowed to appear in their journals giving not only the most unfair and untrue but insulting picture of Northern womanhood in general.

However, pernicious as such articles on both sides were before the war began, they were expressions of opinion which the people might or might not accept in fairly cool temper. With the beginning of war, as always, there began on both sides the publication of every sort of story as fact, not opinion, which could be calculated to stir the anger of one section against the soldiers or citizens of the other.

The history of propaganda and incitement in war has yet to be written. They are as old as the human race. Even the most warlike races appear to indulge in dances, speeches, and other methods of incitement before they feel fit to start on the war-path, methods which have been superseded among democracies and in the age of print by propaganda. It has now become an art or a science, like advertising, as any one will realize who saw the inside working of the propaganda section of any army of any nation in the recent World War. Books are published on its technique, but the main lines of appeal are simple. Each side must be worked up to believe in its own righteousness and the complete deviltry of the enemy. Passions must be stirred by stories of the cruelty and inhumanity of the enemy and the horrors perpetrated by them. War at best is horrible and there are always sufficient real cases to bring its terrors home to people, but undoubtedly many of the stories told in every war have no specific foundation in fact. There is a curious similarity of type in all war propaganda tales. There was scarcely anything used in the World War, for example, which had not appeared in the War of the Revolution in 1776. The newspapers of that earlier period tell of scalping by the British, of their poisoning supplies of drinking water, of their digging up the dead in the burying ground of Newport and desecrating them, and one story of a rape by Hessians appeared with slightly varied details in half a dozen different colonies. It may or may not have occurred as an isolated incident, but it was that and nothing more if it happened at all. Certainly there was no poisoning of water and no digging up of graveyards, yet these things were believed at the time and played their part long years afterwards in the bitter feeling against the British, just as the nations of Europe will be embittered for years by the belief in the propaganda stories of the late war, some true and many false. There is always, alas, too much that is true, and in many cases it is not easy later to sift all the true from the false. In war-time psychology no one wishes to do so, and any story against the enemy is eagerly seized on and believed.

Thus, within a week after the battle of Bull Run what claimed to be authentic stories, with names and all circumstances given, began to appear in Northern papers as to the atrocities committed by the Confederates on the Union wounded. It was claimed that ambulances had deliberately been fired on, as had surgeons working under their green flags, that wounded men had been bayoneted as they lay on the ground asking quarter, and that groups carrying wounded officers off the field had had whole batteries trained on them.[13]

Most, if not all of it, was probably as false as an item a few days earlier in *The Richmond Enquirer* and other Southern papers which stated that the Yankees at Philippi, "not content with seizing and appropriating to their own use and destroying every kind of private property which may fall in their way, the Monsters have been hunting married females from house to house, for the gratification of their brutal lusts."[14] Shortly after *The Tribune* published an account of how a certain Miss Gierstein, a Maine woman teaching in the South, had been stripped to the waist by a vigilance committee between Memphis and Cairo, and severely beaten because she had expressed Northern sympathies, and two Northern men, trying to escape from the South, had been wholly stripped and beaten until their flesh was in strips.[15]

It is now impossible to disentangle the evidence, even

[13] *Cf., e.g., The Tribune,* July 28, 1861.
[14] Issue, July 17, 1861.
[15] *New York Tribune,* August 7, 1861.

where there is any, for each case. I speak of these, as I
shall have to of other incidents occasionally, as samples of
the poison which throughout the next four years and more
was to be distilled into the minds of each section against the
morality and humanity of the other. Whether true or false,
all such stories, as well as those of the wanton destruction
of property, cruelty to non-combatants and others, were to
have their effect, not only in the heat of conflict but for long
years after. It may be affirmed at the beginning of our
story of these years that the South was to have far more
to complain of in the actual barbarism, cruelty and wanton-
ess of the enemy than the North. For this there were several reasons. In the first place the South, except for the
negro who did not fight, had an almost homogeneous white
population. The North had a mixed one of many races with
multitudes of new immigrants. Again, the men in the Confederate army came practically wholly from a rural life,
whereas, especially after the drafts had to be started, the
Northern army was largely recruited from the lower population of the cities. Such a population is not likely to be-
have as well as a rural one under such conditions. Further,
it most be remembered that none of the large lower class of
the South, about one-third of the whole people, that is the
slaves, entered the army. Both armies deteriorated in quality after conscription in the respective sections, but the
Southern would have done so more had the South dared to
reach down to its lowest class, which until almost the closing
days of the war it did not dare or care to do.

Further, we may note that, for the reasons given earlier,
the South had from the beginning the greater number of
trained officers, and troops take their color largely from
their superiors. For example, Mrs. Chesnut mentions that
in Georgia "Confederate soldiers had committed some outrages on the plantations and officers punished them promptly." Moreover, the South, from the original nature of the

quarrel, was the section which became the invaded one, and except for certain expeditions into Northern territory, the Southern armies for the most part operated within their own country and among their own fellow citizens. We shall speak later of specific incidents, such as the march of Sherman, and others, but even Sherman realized the dangers of invasion by motley volunteers instead of disciplined regulars. At the very beginning of the war he said "the greatest difficulty in the problem now before the country is not to conquer but so to conquer as to impress upon the real men of the South a respect for their conquerors. . . . If Memphis be taken, and the army move on South, the vindictive feeling left behind would again close the river. . . . It is for this reason that I deem Regulars the only species of force that should be used for invasion." And after Bull Run he wrote, "no curse could be greater than invasion by a volunteer army. No Goths or Vandals ever had less respect for the lives and property of friends and foes, and henceforth we ought never to hope for any friends in Virginia."[16] But with the constant recruiting the armies were to be largely civilian throughout the war, and as the years went by and the long arms of both governments had to dip lower and lower in the social strata the quality of the material was also lower. It is well to recall these remarks of Sherman's when he came to consider his "bummers."

What he wrote his wife about the dangers of letting loose untrained troops in an enemy country, and the "Goths and Vandals" of Bull Run, is borne out by the testimony of a young officer of the New York 71st, which stopped at Fairfax Court House on the flight. "Many of our men," he wrote in his diary, "acted like barbarians. We halted, stacked arms, and rested in the main street of the village. As soon as ranks were broken, the men made a dash for the large houses, plundering them right and left; what they could not

16 Hart, *Sherman, op. cit.,* pp. 77, 90.

carry away, in many cases, they destroyed; pianos were demolished, pictures cut from their frames, wardrobes ransacked, and most of the furniture carried out into the street. . . . What was not considered portable or worth keeping, was smashed, destroyed; in this general sack, the deserted houses came in for the most attention, few of those having any one in charge being molested, and I did not hear of any personal indignities."[17] Shortly before the battle a Southern woman wrote to her husband, an officer in the army, begging that there might be no scalping, saying it was too horrible to believe but all sort of stories were afloat. He answered that of course there would be none, though they owed little to those who deliberately invaded the country, and the latter note is constantly sounded. Another Southern woman, later, wrote: "We are harassed to death with their ruinous raids, and why should not the North feel it in their homes? Nothing but personal suffering will shorten the war."

The complete difference in the interpretation of the Constitution in the two sections, and the utter belief each section had in its own rendering of it had disastrous results in the field of emotion. The South, believing implicitly in the right of peaceable secession, regarded the Northerners as wanton invaders of their territory; whereas the Northerners, believing in the inviolability of the Union, looked upon the Southerners as traitors who had plunged the nation into needless suffering and bloodshed, and who deserved to suffer themselves for having brought suffering on others. In the North, at the end of the year, Miss Sedgwick wrote that the Southerners could "only be cured of their frenzy by being made to feel their impotence" but that she could not see how "peace and good neighborhood are ever to follow on this bitter hate."[18] Ticknor wrote in

17 *Diary of a Young Army Officer, op. cit.,* p. 28.
18 *Life and Letters, op. cit.,* p. 392.

despair that "such insane hatreds as are now indulged in by both parties—still more at the South than with us—can, I fear, only end in calamities which none of the present generation will live long enough to survive," and a little later that "we are now separated by hatreds which grow more insane and intense every month, and which generations will hardly extinguish."[19]

The South was completely convinced of the view expressed in *The Mercury* and dozens of other papers. "Since the foundation of the world" reads an editorial in the Rhett organ, "we do not suppose there has been a more wicked and causeless war than that proposed by the Northern upon the Southern States." It then reviewed what it considered the continued series of "aggressions" of the North upon the South since the founding of the Union. Ignoring all economic and social causes which had made the agrarian civilization of the South what it was, partly by Southern preference, *The Mercury* declared that the Northerners had forced the South to become "tributary to them." "Our cities ceased to grow, or lingered in their prosperity, mere suburbs to the cities of the North. . . . Our submission only fostered their impertinence and intermeddling arrogance. . . . We simply separate ourselves from them, and keep our own, and for daring to do this they muster their hosts together to conquer and subdue us."[20]

On the other hand, the North believed quite as firmly that it had been wronged by the South. A lawyer like Hitchcock spoke of secession as an "awful and enormous crime," and endorsed "Dr. Post's solemn denunciation of the rebellion as 'the greatest crime since the crucifixion of our Lord' "! "For fifty years," wrote Stedman, "the character of Southerners has become daily more domineering, insolent, haughty, scornful of justice. They have so long cracked the whip

[19] *Life, Letters, and Journals, op. cit.,* vol. II, pp. 387, 392.
[20] Issue April 25, 1861.

over negroes that they now assume the right to crack them over white men; assume the positive rights of a superior race; and have taken advantage of the North's desire for quiet and peace to impose upon us without stint."[21] Among the many sermons quoted by *The Tribune* on the crisis, we read: "We have been forbearing, patient, slow to anger, most anxious for peace. But we are not men—much less Christians—if we suffer the great fabric of our American civilization, the great inheritance of our Constitution and Union, to lapse into ruin from intestine treachery or local passion without a tremendous effort to save it."[22] All, Secessionists and Unionists alike, felt themselves eternally right, and fighting for a great idea, the Unionists that of preserving the Union which had come down from the fathers, the Secessionists that of saving, by Disunion, those liberties which had likewise come down to them. Convinced of their rightness, there were few on either side who could be sufficiently broadminded and dispassionate to recognize that those who differed from them could be other than traitors or knaves.

Rarely was a voice raised like that of Ticknor in Boston who, writing to a violent young correspondent, said: "I heard with great pain the tone of your remarks about the Southern Secessionists and their leaders. They are in revolt, no doubt, or in a state of revolution, and we must resist them and their doctrines to the death. We can have no government else . . . but, besides this, we should, I think, recollect, in dealing with our present enemies, not only that they are fighting for what they believe to be their rights, in open recognized warfare, but that, whether we are hereafter to be one nation or two, we must always live side by side, and must always have intimate relations with each other, for good or for evil to both; and I therefore deprecate, as for twenty years I have deprecated, all bitterness and violence toward the Southern States, as of

[21] *Life and Letters, op. cit.,* vol. I, p. 243.    [22] Issue April 15, 1861.

the worst augury for ourselves, and for the cause of civilization on this side of the Atlantic."[23] Though the men who risked their lives to fight each other could reach this point of mutual understanding and respect, few civilians could resist the madness of the war passions.

Both sides had learned the need for training, and there was little more serious fighting in the first year, although some clashes in Kentucky and especially in Missouri had important results. In the latter State, the governor was a violent secessionist and tried to carry his commonwealth over to the Confederacy. After a series of minor contests, however, the Confederate forces were driven into Arkansas, and Missouri was saved to the Union. Sherman, who had been sent to the West, realized that the key to the military situation lay in that section. He could not, however, impress McClellan, who had 200,000 men in the East, and the authorities in Washington, though Lincoln, irked by McClellan's inactivity, suggested if that general had no use for his army he would like to borrow it. Bickerings, into which it is not necessary to enter here, also broke out between some of the Northern commanders, and the newspapers started a campaign against Sherman, even declaring that he had gone insane. When one newspaper editor was confronted with the lie by an irate relation of the general's he was met with the journalistic reply that whether true or not it was part of the "news" of the day.

In the South also difficulties had begun, especially in the ill-feeling which started between Davis and General Joseph E. Johnston, one of the best men upon whom the Confederate President had to rely. Moreover, Davis was obsessed, like most Southerners, by the King Cotton theory, and the possibility of forcing European intervention, on which account he mistakenly did not care to force large military operations. To a non-military writer it would seem

[23] *Life, Letters, etc., op. cit.*, vol. II, p. 442.

as though Captain Hart were right in contending that through this policy the South lost its best chance, as during the rest of 1861 its forces were superior in "quality, mobility and command" to those of the North, and should have been used against it before the greater latent resources of that section should come into play as a make-weight.

The South's misunderstanding of the international situation was both economic and psychological. As early as March, Davis had sent three commissioners abroad, W. L. Yancey, P. A. Rost, and A. D. Mann, to seek recognition of the new government and to make treaties. None of them was well qualified for his mission. Neither of the latter two was a man of mark or ability, and although Yancey was, his qualities were unsuited for the purpose. As one Southern woman remarked, "send a man to England who had killed his father-in-law in a street brawl![24] That was not knowing England or Englishmen surely. Who wants eloquence? . . . Yancey will have no mobs to harangue. No stump speeches will be possible." In fact although the Commissioners met Earl Russell, the English Foreign Minister, they accomplished nothing. Such action as England took at the time was entirely independent of their representations, in which according to their instructions they stressed the necessity to Europe of Southern cotton. Moreover, Yancey had been one of the greatest expounders of the theory that slavery was a moral good, a doctrine thoroughly distasteful to both the English and French publics, even though governments might be willing to catch fish in the troubled international waters. However the commissioners might discourse on States' Rights, they emphasized the fact that the new nation claiming recognition had slavery as its corner stone.

[24] This was not true. Yancey had, under provocation and in self-defence, killed his wife's uncle. He had been sentenced to pay $1500 fine and to spend a year in jail. He had been immediately released from confinement and two-thirds of the fine was remitted. The whole incident, however, affords interesting sidelights on some aspects of the Old South.

Both the fact of the war itself and Lincoln's blockade of the South had raised the question of neutrals. Lincoln's theory that the seceded States were not out of the Union might simplify matters even for the South if the Union were eventually preserved, though it involved for him the inconvenient and untenable corollary that Southern men-of-war were pirates. Foreign nations, however, could not take that ground. In consequence England decided to acknowledge the Confederacy as a belligerent, proclaiming the fact on May 14, the morning after the new American Minister, Charles Francis Adams, landed at Liverpool. It was fortunate that he found a *fait accompli* instead of having had to fight against it and meet with a rebuff, but the action was bitterly resented in the North and correspondingly approved in the South.

What the South wanted, however, was recognition of her nationality and not merely of her status as a belligerent, and that recognition she could not obtain. Some months after the status of the South had been acknowledged by England and other European nations, the North had tacitly to do the same. In June the *Savannah,* a Southern schooner, after capturing a Union brig was herself captured, and the question came up as to what disposition to make of her officers and crew. When news reached the Confederate Government that they were to be tried as pirates, a like number of Northern prisoners was set aside with the threat that they should meet the same fate as should be meted out to the men of the *Savannah.* By luck the Northern jury disagreed, and no further effort was made to carry out the impossible, if logical, implications of the theory that the Southern States were still in the Union.

Meanwhile, in spite of the blockade, the South was procuring arms and other supplies in England. There is much disagreement among authorities as to how effectively the Southern ports were closed to commerce but it would seem as though the South were never as completely cut off from the world as was formerly thought, and that consequently the blockade diminishes in importance as a cause of the downfall of the Confederacy. In the fall of 1861 the Southern commissioners tried to use the ineffectiveness of Lincoln's measure as a means of securing its denouncement by England and France and so possibly involve them in war with the North. They claimed that between April 29 and August 20, less than four months, 400 vessels had cleared through Southern ports.[25] In addition, there was a large trade carried on through Mexico, which for a while at least played the part with regard to supplying the South which the Scandinavian countries did for Germany in the World War. Had the Confederacy played its hand well, this back door might have been kept open for many necessary imports, but her representative there, John T. Pickett, was about as unsuitable for his post as could well be, and, until the occupation by the French, the Mexican tricks after the beginning were taken by the superior diplomacy of the North.

The South had not been fortunate in its diplomats, and determined to replace those in Europe, Yancey having gone home. The two new ones chosen were former Senator John Slidell of Louisiana, a man with marked ability for political intrigue and an uncle of August Belmont who was the American representative of the great banking house of Rothschild; and James M. Mason of Virginia. Of the latter, one Southern woman wrote at the time, it "is the maddest thing yet. Worse in some points of view than Yancey, and that was a catastrophe." Over here, as she said, "whatever a Mason does is right in his own eyes. He is above law," but the English did not like his spitting tobacco juice in the visitors' gallery of the House of Commons.[26]

[25] Owsley, *King Cotton, op. cit.,* p. 79.
[26] Chesnut, *A Diary from Dixie, op. cit.,* p. 116.

In addition the South had other agents, such as Captain Bulloch of the Navy, and Caleb Huse, who appear to have been authorized to act independently of Slidell and Mason. Mason and Slidell got to Havana, and there boarded a British mail steamer, the *Trent,* for St. Thomas, where they intended to take another steamer for England. As bad luck would have it, word of this reached a Federal naval officer, Captain Wilkes of the U. S. S. *Jacinto,* then in the West Indies on her way back from Africa. Wilkes, who had more patriotism than knowledge of international law, decided to intercept the *Trent* and take off the two rebel emissaries. A slight show of force against the unarmed vessel enabled him all too easily to effect the transfer of her two passengers, and he then allowed the captain of the *Trent* to proceed on his way. Had Wilkes, instead of acting as he did, taken the English steamer into some port and had the case tried before a prize court she would have been condemned, for, in spite of the Queen's proclamation governing England's duties as a neutral, the ship was not only carrying the Confederate agents but despatches from the Confederate Government. By making himself judge and jury, however, as well as capturer, Wilkes had clearly transgressed both international law and the comity of nations, and as soon as the facts were known public opinion in both America and England was aflame. The United States went wild with joy, and Wilkes became the hero of the hour, Congress at once voting him a gold medal. England went equally mad with rage. Used to dominating the seas, she could not brook the insult and illegality of Wilkes's act. The South was almost as joyous as the North, for it could well spare two representatives temporarily if England would join her in the war against the Union.

Fortunately there was as yet no cable, and as news was slow there was time for tempers and enthusiasms to cool, though England despatched 10,000 troops to Canada in case of possible war. The situation abroad was a less simple one than Southern diplomacy quite realized. Napoleon was in favor of the South, with dreams also of a Mexican empire, but the French people as a whole were in favor of the North, and Napoleon realized that with his own people against him and plenty of enemies on the continent he could take no step without England. In that country upper-class opinion was almost solidly Southern in sympathy, as was most of the press. On the other hand, there was a considerable body of opinion both strongly opposed to slavery and in favor of democracy. Moreover, as we shall note presently, there were important interests which were making money out of the war and even out of the blockade. The British Government itself—a coalition one—though divided somewhat in sympathies, apparently tried to steer a genuinely neutral course throughout our struggle.

On both sides of the water, newspapers which thrive on war and sensation fanned the flames, but fortunately saner counsels prevailed. Lincoln himself had had grave doubts as to the legality of Wilkes's action. Yet it was a delicate task suddenly to set public opinion in reverse, especially when it was wrought up against England, which at that time was our traditional foe. The settlement of the dispute, anticipated by Lee, released him at least from further illusions as to intervention. "You must not build your hopes," he wrote to his wife, "on peace on account of the United States going into a war with England. . . . We must make up our minds to fight our battles and win our independence alone. No one will help us. We require no extraneous aid, if true to ourselves."[27]

We may note that in the same letter Lee recognized what non-combatants rarely did, the essential destructiveness of war. In a letter to his wife, speaking of their beautiful old home at Arlington, looking across the Potomac to Wash-

[27] R. E. Lee (jr.), *Recollections, etc., op. cit.,* p. 59.

ington, he said: "If not destroyed, it will be difficult ever to be recognized. Even if the enemy had wished to preserve it, it would have been almost impossible. With the number of troops encamped around it, the change of officers, etc., the want of fuel, shelter, etc., and all the dire necessities of war, it is vain to think of its being in a habitable condition. I fear, too, books, furniture, and the relics of Mount Vernon will be gone. It is better to make up our minds to a general loss."

Even at the end of the first year there was a certain ominous difference to be discerned in the finances of the two sections. At the beginning of the war, there had naturally been a financial panic in the North, and the losses on money owed Northern banks and merchants by Southern planters had been heavy.[28] As one Northern paper commented, "the breaking out of a civil war, whereby the country was suddenly riven into two hostile sections, with a common frontier some 2000 miles in extent, could not but work fearful disruption and stagnation in business. . . . Trade of course sank for a season to zero. Few bought, or could afford to buy, new dresses or other finery, in view of the sudden curtailment if not destruction of business, the instantaneous collapse of incomes, the blight of nearly every enterprise. Building, improving the construction of railroads, of bridges, etc., etc., came nearly to a dead stand. And the millions thus thrown out of employment were not readily absorbed into new pursuits. They wandered from shop to shop and from city to city in quest of work, producing nothing, running into debt for subsistence, or making acquaintance with famine and rags."[29]

[28] The debts, which have been put by some as high as $400,000,000, were probably not much more than one-tenth that sum as represented by actual losses, the money advanced on cotton being protected by cotton consigned. *Cf.* J. C. Schwab, *The Confederate States of America* (New York, 1901), pp. 111 *ff.*

[29] *New York Tribune,* a review of the year's business, September 18, 1861.

But as the war got under way Northern industrial plants fairly hummed with activity while new demands from abroad for Western wheat, due to other causes, helped to make the agricultural sections prosperous. Moreover, the West was rapidly filling up with new settlers. The Illinois Central Railroad, which had been built only in 1856 through a sparsely settled country, was carrying, at the beginning of 1862, 13,000,000 bushels of grain, besides cattle, hogs, and other farm produce.[30]

Writing to his mother in Italy, the New York banker, Edmund C. Stedman, told her: "You need be in no trouble about your income. The railroads were never making so much money. The North has this year paid the entire expense of the war in decrease of importations and increase of crops for export. We need not borrow one cent abroad. I assure you that we do not expect, unless the war is prolonged beyond 1862, to experience any of the pecuniary hardships of such contests."[31] There is a great difference between manufacturing for reproductive purposes and for the waste of war. The vast destruction of permanent capital in a war is bound to make itself felt some years later in prostration of industry, but for the time being in a country which is supplying its own war material, and especially one which is at the same time feeding itself, there is bound to be a feverish if false prosperity engendered. In the North both taxation and government loans were easily met at this time.

In the South conditions were different, and there also economic and diplomatic policies became interwined. Having preferred both the agrarian type of life and the greater profits which it believed lay in cotton culture, it had become, as Southern journals kept pointing out, almost wholly de-

30 *New York Tribune,* February 19, 1862.
31 L. Stedman and G. M. Gould, *Life and Letters of E. C. Stedman* (New York, 1910), p. 245.

pendent on the North for manufactured goods. When the North was cut off, that dependence was to a large extent temporarily transferred to Europe. But there are only three ways of settling foreign debts—the shipment of gold, the creation of a favorable balance of trade, and floating foreign loans. As the South had depended chiefly on Northern banking facilities, the supply of gold was extremely limited. Although a loan of $15,000,000 was made, only a portion of which was available, the South found it difficult to use this method of financing purchases. Finally, there was no possibility of creating a favorable trade balance, in the face of a hugely increased demand for imports and with virtually nothing to export except cotton.

Around this point there was much contemporary controversy, which is still maintained. As we have seen, the leading cotton planters and secessionists were convinced that the world must have Southern cotton or break down, and consequently that if it did not get cotton it would intervene on the side of the Confederacy. Although sure of this, Southern public opinion was on the side of making doubly sure by not shipping even what cotton might have slipped through the not very effective blockade. Planters and factors held cotton back, and Congress was in favor of placing a complete embargo on it. Davis, however, realized that while a threat of embargo, and certainly lack of actual shipments, might hasten trouble in Europe and therefore intervention, actual passage of an embargo law might so irritate England and France as to make them side with the North, to crush more quickly the power which was deliberately causing them to suffer. Moreover, the North was making the best propaganda possible of the partial fact that Northern wheat was as essential to feed the working population of the two foreign countries as Southern cotton was to keep them employed. The policy of non-shipment, however, meant that the South was creating no credits abroad while it was buying heavily of war supplies, and building ships of war.

In addition, the drain for government and war expenses at home was immensely heavy, while the sources of personal income rapidly dried up. Government loans and taxation require ready money on the part of multitudes of individual citizens. The South, having chiefly depended on cotton and credit, had little or no ready money when sales of cotton stopped. Even for the first loan of $15,000,000, authorized in February, 1861, there was difficulty in obtaining specie, but on the whole it was a success, though it bore eight per cent interest. The second, which is known as the "$100,-000,000 loan," authorized in the summer, was expected to be paid at least half in goods and supplies, and of these, as it turned out, about ninety per cent was in cotton. In fact the loan appears to have been made in part to help the cotton planters, who were rapidly sinking into debt.[32]

Very early, however, it became evident that with the people unwilling, and mostly unable, to pay taxes, and with no specie to be obtained from loans, recourse would have to be had to the printing-press for paper money. Most of the specie raised by the first, and only successful, loan went abroad promptly for war supplies, and in the first year of the war seventy-six per cent of the money raised was from notes, twenty-two per cent from bonds, and the small balance from confiscated Federal property and customs receipts, which last were almost *nil*. As we learned in the American Revolution and as many countries have learned since, there is only one end to a steady increase of paper money. In the course of the next few chapters we shall watch the value of Confederate money fall as prices of goods rise until the former became worthless in purchasing power. The task of the Confederate Secretary of the

[32] Schwab, *op. cit.*, p. 13.

Treasury was, in reality, hopeless from the beginning. Both during the life of the Confederacy and after its collapse, controversy was rife as to the reasons for things not going better, and many complained of the policy of Secretary Memminger, claiming, among other things, that he should have sold all the cotton in the South abroad in anticipation of the blockade and so established a large credit there. His biographer states that the total crop of the year 1860–61 was 3,849,000 bales, of which 3,000,000 bales had been shipped by February when the new government was formed, but Memminger's own letter in 1874 to General J. E. Johnston would seem the answer to the criticism. He claimed that if the approximately 4,000,000 bales had been shipped by the government it would have taken 4000 ships. "Where would these vessels have been procured in the face of the notification of the blockade? and was not as much shipped by private enterprise as could have been shipped by the government?" The government, he explains, could have obtained the cotton only by seizure, purchase, or donation. He points out that it could not have been seized, and if bought the bonds would have been thrown on the market at once, and ruined the credit of the government at the very start. As for donation, so far was this from being possible "that the Treasury actually had to issue a circular in response to applications to the government for aid to the planters in making loans to them, and not a bale of the crop of that year was contributed to the government."[33]

Although *The Richmond Enquirer* could talk in August about an "overflowing treasury" because of the resources of the section in cotton, the North already saw the position more clearly. In an editorial *The Tribune* pointed out that "the entire political economy of the South is embraced in one word, and that word is 'Cotton.' . . . It will probably puzzle our friends across the water how the Confederacy

[33] Capers, *Memminger, op. cit.,* pp. 350 *f.*

can have an overflowing treasury' by exchanging bonds for cotton which is not permitted to reach the consumers. . . . Whatever the present struggle may be, it is evident that the loans of a Government supported by the wealthy States of the North are perfectly secure, and if needed $1,000,000,-000 can be obtained on its simple promise; but when the cotton expedients of the Southern Confederacy fail, where is the money to come from? The Confederate bonds depend upon the issue of the conflict. If the Rebels succeed in establishing an independent Government, they may be paid; if not, they are worthless beyond dispute. . . . The schemes adopted by the Confederate financiers are destined to put into circulation an irredeemable paper currency, which, as the war progresses and the quantity increases, must suffer a ruinous depreciation. . . . In due time, this money question will present itself with great force to the Confederate leaders, and if now, at the very edge of the contest, they are compelled to barter bonds for cotton, how will they meet the immense expenditures required to prosecute a long and exhausting struggle?"[34]

*The New Orleans True Delta* had anticipated the difficulty also and quoted John Quincy Adams as saying of a debased currency that "no expedient ever devised could equal it in efficiency for fertilizing the rich man's field with the sweat of the poor man's brow," a fact which each generation appears to have to learn for itself.[35]

The fact was that the South had made a bad economic and political miscalculation in its theory of King Cotton. Cotton *was* necessary to the world, and there was to be a famine, but that famine could not possibly have occurred in the year in which the South seceded, and by the time it did other factors had come into play to complicate the situation. In June, 1861, there was a stock of cotton in England, thanks in large measure to previous over-production in the

[34] Issue August 4, 1861.       [35] Issue December 11, 1860.

232

South, of 450,000 bales in excess of normal, or of 1,105,-580 as against 636,860 two years earlier. At the end of the year, when the Confederate Congress was futilely talking about bringing on European intervention by an embargo on cotton, England had on hand over 700,000 bales as compared with 400,000 four years earlier. The great prosperity of the South in 1859 and 1860, with the rising prices for lands and slaves, which had been one of the factors giving her an excessive self-confidence, had overstocked the European markets, and destroyed her own hopes of help from over-seas.

# CHAPTER VII

## THE WAR GETS UNDER WAY

AT the beginning of 1862 the South still indulged its delusion as to King Cotton. Jefferson Davis, against military advice, clung to his belief in a purely defensive war because of his firm conviction that France and England must soon intervene on the side of the South and thus end the conflict. Why waste lives and treasure if independence were within sight without doing so? The provisional government came to an end, and Davis and Stephens having been re-elected for the full seven-year term, Davis delivered his inaugural address on February 22, the anniversary of the birth of the man who had done more than any one else to assure the Union. News had just been received of the fall of Fort Donelson, and as the President spoke to the crowd from the steps of the State House, a cold rain fell in torrents. Whispers went round among his listeners of the bad omen, but a few days later, Secretary of War Benjamin, speaking to Congressman Reuben Davis, said: "There is no doubt that the Southern Confederacy will be recognized by England in ninety days, and that ends the war." Congressman Davis added that other members of the Military Committee, on which he was placed, were equally confident, and so opposed to expense and taxation.[1]

With this belief went that of the efficacy of curtailing the new crop of cotton in 1862, which in fact was cut down to only about a million and a half bales as compared with three times that amount in the previous year. As a corollary to this theory of forcing foreign intervention, there began also the burning of cotton, especially of such as might fall into

[1] *Recollections of Mississippi, op. cit.*, pp. 431, 433.

the hands of the advancing Federal armies. At first embargo, then limitation of planting, then burning were tried to force the hands of France and England. By 1863 the delusion had largely disappeared but it was potent in 1862, and in the first two years of the war it undoubtedly hampered effective military operations.

There were other ominous signs for the Confederacy. Both the ideals and the life of the prosperous Southerner had made "team work" difficult for him. The owner of a plantation, although he learned self-reliance and mastery, was a little despot, even if frequently a beneficent one, on his own estate. Mrs. Chesnut, describing her father-in-law, the father of the distinguished United States Senator from South Carolina, spoke of him as "partly patriarch, partly grand seigneur . . . the last of a race of lordly planters who ruled this Southern world. . . . His manners are unequalled still, but underneath this smooth exterior lies the grip of a tyrant whose will has never been crossed. . . . Colonel Chesnut came of a race that would brook no interference with their own sweet will by man, woman, or devil. But then such manners has he, they would clear any man's character, if it needed it."[2] Another Southerner, describing the Virginia gentleman, writes that he was "ever an individualist, a man of will and honor with license to peculiar bents. . . . He took on a certain show of aristocracy which approached reality in paternalistic notions of government; of culture, which manifested itself in the love of books; and of that sort of poise which those surrounded by dependents are apt to develop. . . . In the end a lovable tyrant appeared, with some tradition of leisure and culture amid the pressing realities of acres and slaves and large families and southern weather."[3]

As a result of this inevitable tendency to petty despotism,

[2] *Diary from Dixie, op. cit., p.* 391.
[3] Craven, *Edmund Ruffin, op. cit.,* p. 4.

the impulse to individual power and place was almost as inevitable as the theory of States' Rights. One of the curses of the South was that all wanted high office, and were sensitive as to their own position. Davis had already quarrelled with General Johnston, and relations were becoming strained with Beauregard. It is impossible to recount all the large or small quarrels between generals, statesmen, State governors, and President, and the universal criticism and recrimination which went on in the Confederacy during the years of struggle against a common and outside foe. That all this friction, waste motion, and hard feeling had their effect on the final result would appear to be beyond doubt. The only periods, both North and South, when military affairs went well, were when the politicians kept their own hands off, and concentrated the power in those of the respective generals in the field. At the beginning of 1862, Benjamin, a Jewish lawyer with no military training whatever, interfered so much with the armies that even Stonewall Jackson handed in his resignation, which fortunately he reconsidered when promised a freer hand. The Southern disaster at Roanoke Island, largely the fault of the Secretary, brought forth fierce denunciations of him, but in the general reorganization of his Cabinet in March, Davis raised him to the Secretaryship of State.

Davis himself was under severe fire. Leading papers which had been most conspicuous in bringing about secession roundly denounced him. *The Richmond Whig* was scathing. *The Charleston Mercury* attacked him without mercy and announced that "the people, the press, and Congress must save the country from the impracticable incompetency of the Executive. Our cause must be made triumphant, in spite of his follies."[4] It had been the States' Rights doctrine, with its attendant State jealousies, which had in part led to the ineffective preparation for war, but

4 Issue March 22, 1862.

*The Mercury* continued to preach it. "The States," it said, "must use their resources and wisdom, and energy and enterprise, to work out our redemption. Let them provide for the importation or manufacture of arms, cannon, salt-petre, and gun powder. Let them build gunboats, raise troops, and use all their resources independent of the Confederate Government, although co-operating with it. The Confederate Government will doubtless receive them, assume the debt they may incur [sic], or return the money they may expend in the holy cause of our defence."[5] The absurdity of a dozen or so jealous governments carrying on operations against one common enemy does not seem to have struck the Rhett family. If there could not be united counsels in the Congress of the Confederacy, what hope was there of united action when the decisions would be in the hands of eleven separate legislatures?

As one surveys the internal history of the Confederacy one cannot escape the conclusion that, in spite of courage and enormous sacrifices, the people and more especially the State executives did not give the central government nearly as much support as they could and should. The reason is not far to seek. The whole theory of secession, as well as the whole complex of Southern psychology, was based upon the assumption that the first loyalty of a citizen was due to his own State and not to any combination into which that State might enter. The united Confederacy was built upon the quicksand of shifting local loyalties. Even Lee had said, when he resigned from the Union army, that he would use his sword solely for the defence of his native State. The flame of loyalty and affection for the Confederacy as a whole burned weak and pale as against the hot fire of love each Southerner felt for his own commonwealth. The general government was new, with no past tradition of united effort and sacrifice and happiness. The absence to a large

[5] Issue February 26, 1862.

extent in high positions of the old and well-known families went counter to the strongest social tradition of the section. The constitutional theory of its existence was that of a loose league and not of a nation. Indeed, *The Richmond Whig* said: "We are sorry to see the word 'national' sometimes used with reference to Confederate affairs. We think it should be henceforth a forbidden word. This Confederacy is not a nation, but a league of nations—and we think it would be better . . . to drop the name of Confederate States and substitute for it that of The Allied Nations or The Allied Republics."[6]

This attitude was a heavy handicap for the South. In the North there were "Copperheads," traitors, profiteers, luke-warm patriots, and other poor fry, but the vast majority of Northerners did not question that their first love and loyalty were to the Union. This gave Lincoln a decided advantage over Davis. Both sides made gigantic efforts and sacrifices for the cause for which each felt it was fighting, but al-though the South did so to an even greater degree than the North, its insistence on States' Rights nullified to a large extent the efforts put forth. Moreover, in many cases gov-ernors and other politicians played on popular feeling, fears, and prejudices for their own selfish purposes.

We saw in 1861 that the insistence on separate State action prevented the central government from securing the arms which it otherwise could have had and from placing a much larger army in the field. *The Mercury* insisted that Davis might have had 600,000 men by the end of the first year but it failed to admit that State jealousies would have left most of them unarmed. In 1862 this same doctrine of States' Rights, together with certain politicians' personal ambitions, kept back men from the Confederate forces. Be-ginning with Alabama in January, the States began to build up separate State "armies," not to be confused with the

[6] Quoted with approval by *The Richmond Enquirer*, August 15, 1862.

238

militia. Other States did the same, fear of attack by sea being one of reasons given. In the first six months, Alabama had 2500 men, Mississippi 5000, North Carolina 20,000, Tennessee over 20,000, Virginia 40,000, South Carolina between 15,000 and 20,000, and Georgia probably about the same. In vain did the Secretary of War write that such a policy could result only "in the defeat of each in detail" and that "companies already organized and ready to be mustered into Confederate service for the war marched out of the camps of rendezvous to enlist in the State service for three, four, six months."

Perhaps 100,000 men were thus held out of the Confederate armies, men whom General Brandon bitterly denounced as "skulking from the service . . . going and coming when they please . . . little better than an armed mob . . . with no discipline" because subject to court martial only by their own elected officers.[7] In April the Confederate Congress passed a conscription Act, calling out, with certain exemptions, all able-bodied men between the ages of eighteen and thirty-five, and in September a second one extending the upper limit to forty-five. On the whole, the press and even men like Rhett and Yancey supported the measures, though they were directly aimed at what had been considered the rights of the States. On the other hand, others, like Vice-President Stephens, Toombs, Brown, and Orr, considered both acts unconstitutional. The Governor of Georgia, who did not represent the general opinion of that great State, declared that "I entered this revolution to contribute my humble mite to sustain the rights of the States and prevent the consolidation of government, and I am still a rebel till this object is accomplished, no matter who is in power."[8] He was in fact, to a great extent, a rebel against the Confederate Government

[7] Owsley, *State Rights, op. cit.,* pp. 24 ff.
[8] A. B. Moore, *Conscription and Conflict in the Confederacy* (New York, 1924), p. 24 *et passim.*

throughout the war. Usually the courts sustained the Congress, though the brother of the Vice-President asserted that sovereign States could not be so coerced though "all the judicial tribunals on earth" should affirm the contrary.

There were many exemptions allowed under both acts, the one calling out the loudest criticism being that exempting one white man on each plantation with twenty negroes. In other words if the owner of a plantation with twenty slaves was the only member of his family of military age, he was exempt, which gave a new sting to the taunt that it was a rich man's war and a poor man's fight. If his presence at home were indeed necessary for the sake of safety, it again emphasized the peculiarity of slave as contrasted with any other form of property. There were also acts passed allowing the purchase of substitutes for those called to the colors by conscription, and, on a lesser scale, this gave rise to all the scandals which the same system did in the North, as we shall note in the next chapter. The two Southern historians who have made the most exhaustive studies of these problems both agree that the conscription acts failed to bring out anything like the man power which they should have done. The States continued to try to keep men in their own service and out of the Confederate armies, and by 1863 General Bragg and seventeen other generals in a joint letter to Davis declared that 150,000 possible soldiers had employed substitutes, not more than one in a hundred of whom was actually in the ranks for duty. This figure doubles the usual estimate of the time, but the evil was a serious one and may easily have changed the result of important battles. As the currency fell, the price of substitutes went as high as $500. This took the heart out of many of the poorer classes, who deserted or escaped enlistment by taking to the woods. By the end of 1862 the same causes had worked much the same effects in the North, but leaving the discussion of that until later, we must turn to the military events which succeeded the lull of the early winter of 1861–62.

In a general narrative, which attempts to deal rather with the causes and background of our tragedy than with details of specific events, it is impossible to describe even all the leading battles which took place between the combatants, or the quarrels between generals. Both were too numerous for our purpose.

At this stage of the conflict we have to consider two main theatres of operations, the eastern seaboard and the Mississippi Valley. The former seized the imagination of the people and of the journalists, who were perhaps affected by one another. The capture of either the Confederate or Union capital seemed important, though except psychologically the loss of Richmond would not have worked great havoc to the Southern cause. The loss of Washington, with the then possible adhesion of at least eastern Maryland to the Confederacy, and the capture of east and west lines of communication in the narrowest part of the Union, might have been a different matter. In reality, however, the more important theatre was in the West, as Sherman had realized. If the river systems of the Ohio, Cumberland, Tennessee, and Mississippi could be secured, with their auxiliary railroads, the Confederacy would be bisected and receive a deadly blow.

Although Halleck was in command of the Union forces in the West, Grant had at last had his offer of service accepted and was serving under him, as was also Sherman, with whose views of the importance of the Western theatre Grant entirely agreed. A West Pointer, Grant had served with reasonable distinction as a young officer in the Mexican War, after which he had been rather stranded in army posts on the Pacific coast. Lonely, unable to have his young family with him both for financial reasons and because of the dreariness of the tiny frontier settlement where he was

241

quartered, he began to drink too heavily, and was warned by his superior officer. He then decided to resign and his resignation was accepted by Jefferson Davis, who was at that time Secretary of War. Grant next tried various means in minor positions in the Middle West to support his family, but appeared to have proved a failure when the war came which was to make him at its end the generous conqueror of Lee, a world figure and twice President of the United States.

Short, stocky, silent, careless of his dress, a cigar perpetually in his mouth, this apparent failure was to prove himself one of the world's great generals and one of the determining forces in the national crisis. On November 7, 1861, when descending the Mississippi in a steamboat he had gone into the pilot house and thrown himself on a sofa to rest. As the boat was being fired on by the Confederates, he got up to go out on deck to see what was happening. A moment later a musket ball entered the room he had just left, passed through the head of the sofa, and lodged in its foot. For those who discard the theory of the influence of the individual on history and believe only in "social forces" it may be interesting to speculate on what the military and political history of the United States would have been in the next dozen years had Grant been killed at the beginning of his career; or had Lee and Jackson, like Thomas, decided to stand by the Union instead of their State.

Grant had been operating in the West in the fall of 1861 but Halleck had vetoed his suggestion to capture Forts Henry and Donelson on the Tennessee and Cumberland Rivers. At last receiving permission to make the effort, he advanced against the former, supported by gunboats, and captured it on February 6. He then proceeded against Fort Donelson, defended by Generals Floyd, Pillow, and Buckner. The first, as we have seen, had been Secretary of War under Buchanan, and, whether in the course of routine business or with secession in view, had at that time transferred 115,000 muskets of various sorts from Northern to Southern arsenals. Floyd had been exonerated of any sectional intent by a Committee of the House investigating the case in January, 1861, but gossip had continued and in any case he apparently did not wish to be captured by the Union forces. He had marched out of the fort with his own brigade, escaping and turning command over to Buckner, for which action he was removed without court martial by President Davis. Pillow also escaped, but Buckner had to surrender the fort and about 15,000 troops to Grant. The victory was clearly Grant's but Halleck immediately telegraphed to McClellan in Washington: "Give me the command in the West. I ask this in return for Forts Henry and Donelson." Soon after, he wired that Grant would not answer communications and had resumed his drinking habit, a statement which had no foundation in fact. On the other hand, Sherman, although Grant's superior, had offered to serve under him, and had been most loyal in giving him every help.

As a result of the fall of the two forts, the Confederate General A. S. Johnston retreated to Corinth, an important railway point, while the Union armies overran the western part of Tennessee. Obviously the next move would be to take Corinth. Johnston had 40,000 men, and Grant 45,000, while the Union General Buell was on his way with 35,000 more. Grant was expecting him any day, and unfortunately placed his own force at Pittsburg Landing, twenty-three miles north of Corinth, without entrenching, he himself making his headquarters eight miles farther off. Johnston decided on a quick blow, and attacked Grant's forces although the surprise was not complete. The battle of Shiloh, as it has been called, lasted for two days, Johnston being killed late on the first, with consequent discouragement to his troops. Although the Confederates appeared to have conquered on the first evening, Union reinforcements to the extent of 20,000 fresh troops arrived on the next morning, and Beauregard, then in command, had to retreat to Corinth again, and later farther South. Sherman had taken full share in the fight and in view of the hatred of the South for him due to later events a minor incident may be told. Before the war, he had been superintendent of the Louisiana State Seminary of Learning, a military institute situated near Alexandria on the Red River, and after the battle, recognizing among the prisoners one of his former Southern pupils, he fitted him out with much-needed new clothing.

The campaign down the Mississippi continued to be prosecuted, Halleck, with much criticism of Grant and praise for Sherman, having taken command in person. General Pope pushed down the river and in March captured New Madrid, soon to be followed by Island Number Ten. As indicating the necessities, or supposed necessities, of war, the destruction of the former town by the Confederates themselves is not without interest. J. M. Morgan, of New Orleans, then in the Confederate navy, writes that the houses of New Madrid were in the way of the firing on a Federal gunboat, and that he received orders from his commodore to burn the town. The young Confederate remonstrated that by chance the town was on land which his ancestor had been granted and that it would be terrible for him to have to destroy it, whereupon the commodore replied that it was a singular coincidence but made it the more appropriate that Morgan should be detailed for the work. There being nothing else for it, Morgan went ashore, and starting with a barn full of hay, aided by a high wind, burned the entire town.[9] If such could be done by forces operating within their own country, some allowance can be made for forces operating in the country of a bitterly hated

[9] J. M. Morgan, *Recollections of a Rebel Reefer* (Boston, 1917), p. 67.

enemy. Union advance down the Mississippi continued and Fort Pillow and Memphis fell in June.

Meanwhile, the lower end of the river was also opened. New Orleans, the most important port in the South, was guarded lower downstream by the two forts of Jackson and St. Philip, and recently the Confederates had also placed obstructions in the channel to hinder the threatened advance of Union war vessels. Lieutenant David Porter had suggested the possibility of anchoring a fleet of mortar boats to the banks below the forts which could then be reduced by bombardment and, the obstructions removed if possible, war ships might then proceed upstream, take New Orleans, and eventually co-operate with the forces in the North to clear the river completely. Taking both the military and mere physical features of the proposed expedition into account, there were formidable difficulties in the way, but it was brilliantly carried out, the naval force being under command of Captain David Farragut, and the troops, who were to be landed after the city was captured, under that of General Benjamin Butler. All efforts of the defenders were in vain. The obstructions in the river were broken; the forts reduced, one after a mutiny by the garrison; the Confederate war ships defeated; and the city taken, the last event occurring on April 25.

General Butler became the Military Governor of the conquered city and section, a position which called for delicate feeling and infinite tact and judgment, as well as the strong hand. Unhappily few men were less fitted for the post than Butler, who had none of the qualities requisite except possibly the last. Nowhere in the South was resentment against the North stronger than in New Orleans, and nowhere, owing to the large Latin influence among the population, was that resentment likely to take more difficult forms of handling. Some of these difficulties, particularly as they concerned the women in New Orleans, are unconsciously revealed in the diary of one of them, Miss Le Grand. Speaking of the Confederate forces she wrote: "The wretched generals, left here with our troops, ran away and left them. Lovell knew not what to do; some say he was intoxicated, some say frightened. . . . *The women only* did not seem afraid. They were all in favor of resistance, *no matter how hopeless.* . . . Flag Officer Farragut demanded the unconditional surrender of the town. He was told that as brute force, and brute force only, gave him the power he might come and take it. . . . Four days we waited, expecting to be shelled, but he concluded to waive the point; so he marched in his marines with two cannons and our flag was taken down and the old stars and stripes lifted in a dead silence. We made a great mistake here; we should have shot the man that brought down the flag. . . . The blood boiled in my veins. . . . Mrs. Norton was afraid of me, I believe, for she hurried me off. . . . This is a most cowardly struggle—these people can do nothing without gunboats. . . . It is a dastardly way to fight. . . . We should have had gunboats if the Government had been efficient, wise, and earnest."[10]

The state of mind reflected in these passages—the refusal to admit military results, the passionate hatred, the belief in the dastardliness of the North in using weapons which she claimed the South should have provided for its own use—was all too symptomatic of that of the fairer portion of New Orleans. Presently a man hauled down the flag which the Union forces, having won the city in fair military fight, had run up, and Butler, most unwisely, had him hanged. Although after the first the general maintained order in the city, he was himself a coarse and brutal person, high-handed in action, always in controversy wherever he went in the course of his career, and whether guilty himself or not, there was considerable peculation and scandal among

10 *The Journal of Julia Le Grand,* Richmond, 1911, pp. 40 *ff.*

his command. Some officers of lower rank did not hesitate themselves to loot private houses, and Mrs. Dawson gives a vivid description of the sacking of her house in Baton Rouge—"libraries emptied, china smashed, sideboards split open with axes, portraits slashed, and other deviltries committed."[11] Her brother-in-law arriving when the damage was almost complete appealed to a Union captain in the street who at once entered the house, and finding another Union captain and lieutenant in hiding, took them off to a superior officer. With conspicuous and notorious exceptions, however, most of the officers and the main body of privates do not seem to have acted badly in the difficult task of occupying a hostile city for months, in which hatred of them was daily shown, and the contempt for the ill deeds of some was visited upon all.

On the other hand, the ladies of New Orleans were intolerably bitter against all in the Union uniform, and showed it in ways which would have immediately brought on street fights had the tormentors been men instead of women. Miss Le Grand noted of the Federals that "I think their plan is to conciliate" but "they know they are hated and hang their heads. Shopkeepers refuse to sell to them." Again she remarks that "Mrs. Norton got quite impatient today with Miss Marcella Wilkinson for praising several officers who had been kind to her family, and interested themselves in procuring the release of her brother, who had been arrested by Butler. Mrs. N. thinks no one can be a true Southerner and praise a Yankee. She thought it no honor 'to be treated decently by one of the wretches; she wished the devils were all killed.' "[12]

This feeling was expressed constantly in ways which it

[11] Sarah M. Dawson, *A Confederate Girl's Diary* (London, 1913), p. 191. It may be noted that the preceding pages contain an account of a low-class Confederate officer. Unfortunately there were such in both services.

[12] *Ibid.*, pp. 44, 76.

was impossible to control by ordinary means. There were continual minor incidents, maddening to troops who were behaving themselves and could not fight women who did things which men would not have dared to do, protecting themselves behind their claim of sex. Finally, on May 15, Butler issued his famous order which made his name execrated throughout the world and perhaps did as much as anything to make the Northern name hated in the South. He announced that thereafter any woman insulting or showing contempt for a Union officer or private should be "regarded and held liable to be treated as a woman of the town plying her vocation." Butler's innate coarseness probably prevented him from realizing the storm he would rouse, and he certainly had no intention, as President Davis said in his proclamation, of encouraging the soldiers "to outrage the wives, mothers, and the sisters of Southern citizens," or as *The Saturday Review* said in England that he was protecting himself "by threats of rape." The order was brutal, and naturally the most was made of it to stir anger, but in fact there is no evidence that any soldier offered an insult to a woman in consequence of it, and, on the other hand, the women ceased at once from insulting the soldiers.

Even with the long indictment, much of it true, that Davis in his proclamation, which resembled the Declaration of Independence in its list of crimes against King George, issued against Butler, there was no excuse for his declaring that "all commissioned officers" under Butler's command should "not be entitled to be considered as soldiers engaged in honorable warfare, but as robbers and criminals, deserving death; and that they and each of them be, whenever captured, reserved for execution."[13] Such a proclamation, including many wholly innocent men, marked the increasing bitterness of feeling as the war progressed. There is little

[13] Davis, *Jefferson Davis, op. cit.*, vol. II, p. 256.

in the career of Butler, who was soon transferred by Lincoln, to arouse any sympathy on the part of a gentleman, but we may note the comment the following year of Mrs. Chesnut that "Roony Lee says 'Beast' Butler was very kind to him while he was a prisoner. The 'Beast' has sent back his war-horse. The Lees are men enough to speak the truth of friend or enemy, fearing not the consequences."[14]

We must now leave the West, where, with the exception of a short stretch, the entire Mississippi was in the hands of the Union, and where little more was accomplished until the beginning of the new year, to consider events in the East.

One of the interesting features of the war, from the standpoint of military technique, was the introduction or use on an important scale of new methods, such as the trench warfare before Richmond, to become such a feature of the World War two generations later. This novelty, however, does not apply, although it is generally considered as doing so, to the introduction of iron-clads at sea. France had employed them in the Crimean War some years earlier, and both that country and England had or were building several large iron-clads when our war broke out. Indeed, the Southern agent in England, who managed to buy the vessel later named the *Florida* to prey on Northern commerce, reported that even if he had the money, which he had not, to buy iron-clads for the Confederacy, he could not get them because England and France were both so anxious to add to their own supply. It is impossible to reconcile the facts with the statement often made that the battle between the *Monitor* and the *Merrimac* revolutionized the navies of the world, though the battle certainly did emphasize the belief already held that wooden ships were soon to be obsolete as fighting craft.

Unable to get such vessels abroad, the Confederacy had undertaken to make some itself, although under great

[14] *Diary from Dixie, op. cit.,* p. 300.

handicaps as the only plant for welding and hammering was at Richmond. Stephen R. Mallory, throughout the war a most efficient Secretary of the Confederate Navy Department, though, like most Southerners in high office, he became unpopular for reasons not obvious, considered the building of iron-clads almost at the beginning, realizing that the South could not compete with the North in number of wooden ships, either by building or purchase. Control of Chesapeake Bay and the James River would be of vast importance to the South, and the Department went to work to raise the hull of the U.S.S. steam sloop *Merrimac,* which had been sunk, partly burned, at Norfolk. This was to be transformed into an iron-clad by sheathing her hull, and turning her into a ram by giving her an iron "beak." The work was done quickly under great difficulties in the beginning of 1862, and in March she was ready, with many faults of construction, to move against the wooden vessels of the Union navy in the Bay.

Re-christened the *Virginia,* though she has popularly retained her old name, she moved out of the Navy Yard on the 8th, and succeeded in sinking two fine Union vessels, the *Congress* and the *Cumberland.* Her construction, however, had not been unmarked by the Navy Department in Washington, which had accepted plans drawn by the Swede, John Ericsson, for quite a new type of vessel, the *Monitor.* This flat iron-clad, scarcely rising above the water, had a revolving turret in which two guns were mounted, and offered hardly any target for the enemy's fire. Constructed at Hoboken, and then towed through the open sea to the Chesapeake, it had nearly sunk on the way, but when, on the morning of the 9th, the *Virginia* again steamed out of Norfolk, minus her ram which had been broken off in the first encounter, she was met by this curious new craft. In the battle which ensued, the *Virginia* had to retire, damaged, while the *Monitor* was scarcely touched; and the Southern vessel ceased to be a menace.

As we shall note presently, the land forces in the East did not get into motion until spring, but events had been rather distinctly in favor of the North when, on March 6, Lincoln sent a special message to Congress urging the passage of a Joint Resolution offering financial aid to any State which would adopt gradual emancipation of its slaves, he believing that a gradual was better than a sudden emancipation, and that the Federal Government should bear at least a considerable part of the financial burden "to compensate for the inconveniences, public and private, of such a change of system."

To those who looked ahead with clear vision, it was evident that if the North won, slavery was doomed, and many in the South, like President Davis, ex-Senator Chesnut and others, realized it was equally doomed if the South should win. Many others, like General Lee, hoped it would be in either case. Nevertheless, though Congress passed the Resolution, and the offer was open, none even of the border States accepted it. With the Constitutional basis of the war and with the passions which had been aroused both before and during its progress, it was naturally impossible for any State in the Confederacy to accept, although the offer was made to all. As the conflict was prolonged Lincoln saw that the two wings of his party, the major one which fought for the Union, and the lesser, radical one which favored Abolition, would have to be conciliated. Already many newspapers, notably *The Tribune,* were demanding a clarification of the issues of the war, and European opinion, which was largely pro-Southern but antislavery, also had to be taken into account. Looking into the future, and seeing the action which he would probably have to take later as a military measure, it should be noted that

Lincoln did what he could to avoid the evils of both sudden freedom for all slaves and the loss to innocent slave-holders of the total value of their property.

Meanwhile, affairs were not going well in the Confederacy. Apart from the serious military disasters in the West, internal affairs were causing anxiety. The fifty dollars bounty and other privileges accorded to those who would enlist for two years or more had tided over the threatened break-down of the forces as the time of the twelve-months men had come to an end, but there was still trouble with the individual States, and recrimination was everywhere in the air. Just before his gallant death at Shiloh, General Sidney Johnston was the target for abuse, the newspapers charging him not only with incompetence but, wholly unfairly of course, with corruption, and one said that soldiers when enlisting made it a condition that they should not serve under him. Davis, as we have seen, had quarrelled with Generals Joseph Johnston and Beauregard, but stood by Sidney Johnston, and so was roundly denounced by many. "Shall the cause fail because Mr. Davis is incompetent?" asked one paper. "The people of the Confederacy must answer this plain question at once or they are lost."[15] "There never was on the tide of time such a Cause and such a People so unnecessarily exposed to the imbecility of man," wrote *The Richmond Whig* of the President.[16] The tradition of a thoroughly united people fighting through together is not borne out by the facts of the contemporary scene. Of course there was also much division of opinion in the North, and generals and the President were bitterly assailed, but on the whole Lincoln got more support, especially from the States and Congress, than Davis did, which made the task more difficult for the latter.

Everything which Davis did that might seem to run

---

[15] Johnston, *A. S. Johnston, op. cit.,* p. 511.
[16] Issue March 5, 1862.

counter to the extreme doctrine of States' Rights made him unpopular with a section of the people and the local politicians, though consolidation of power has been proved essential over and over in a national crisis. At this time, another step which he had to take hurt him with many. He had held up Lincoln, as had also the Southern papers, as a monster of tyranny in consequence of his suspension of habeas corpus, the commitment of certain persons to prison, and other war acts, but the conditions in Richmond had become such by March that Davis himself had to declare martial law in the city and a circuit of ten miles round, and real or alleged Unionists began to be arrested and imprisoned in "Castle Godwin" with disturbing frequency. On March 6, *The Richmond Enquirer* noted that Charles Palmer, a shipping merchant, and William Fay, both rich, had been interned, the latter not even being allowed to see his father for consultation. The editor added that there was plenty of room for more of the same sort, though the charges against Palmer were proved false the next day and he was discharged. Two more were imprisoned on the 7th, two on the 8th, two on the 10th, four on the 13th.[17] General Winder was given arbitrary power to govern the city and district, and although he cleared the town of much of the riff-raff which war had brought to it, he appears to have been both tyrannical and vindictive against his own personal enemies, or those whom he considered as such.

Scarcity and high prices were already becoming notable. Various items in the papers are suggestive even before the war had run a year. We read that due to lack of coloring matter the green five-cent stamps will hereafter be blue; that the Ordnance Office of South Carolina is badly in need of lead "and appeals to the patriotic citizen to rid us of the ruthless speculator"; that ladies are sending in their copper kettles to be used for cannon; that *The Mercury*

[17] *Richmond Enquirer,* issues as above.

will hereafter be printed on half a sheet; and so on. The lack of industrial resources was already beginning to tell. *The Mercury* could say that the South should build up a big fleet though "we know that there are portions of an iron-clad steamer which could scarcely be made within the limits of the present Confederacy" but "there is no reason why immense quantities of machinery and iron plating should not be fashioned in the forges of Europe."[18] But where was the money to come from? The wealth of the South had been cotton, and by summer Mrs. Chesnut wrote: "Cotton is five cents a pound and labor of no value at all . . . people gladly hire out their negroes to have them fed and clothed, which latter cannot be done."

In March, Secretary Memminger declared that the currency was already redundant, and owing to this cause, and speculation and extortion (also rife in the North), prices began their upward climb, although low as compared with what they were to become. The papers were filled with complaints of extortion in particular. *The Mercury* complained that drivers were charging three dollars to carry wounded soldiers from the Savannah Railroad to the South Carolina depot, and ten dollars for a dead body.[19] Mrs. Chesnut wrote in her diary that "we, poor fools, who are patriotically ruining ourselves, will see our children in the gutter while treacherous millionaires go rolling by in their coaches." Yet less than a year of the long agony had passed.

As bad news came, however, the papers redoubled their fury against the North. After the fall of Fort Donelson, which cast a gloom over the South, *The Richmond Whig* wrote: "War, interminable and relentless, and submission to any nation rather than to the vulgar, sordid, filthy Yankees. That, the intensest infamy, will be the last alternative. War to the knife—extermination—foreign alliance—any fate

[18] Issue March 17, 1862.    [19] Issue of January 24, 1862.

rather than that. But in sacrificing our property and lives we shall take care to make the sacrifice cost our enemies its full value."[20]

Atrocity stories continued in the papers of both sections, fanning the flames of hatred. During 1862 the quality of the new recruits for both armies declined, as we have said. Even *The Mercury* by fall stated that there should be guards on all trains in the South moving troops as "there are always some turbulent ones who . . . throw aside all rules of decorum . . . frequently intruding their presence into the ladies' car and behaving there in a style scarcely to be tolerated in a bar room." The quality of the Northern troops was worse, for reasons we have noted, but it may be said that during the entire war, although there was colossal destruction of property in the invaded section, there were extraordinarily few crimes against the person. In all my reading of even the bitterest Southern contemporary documents, I have failed to find a single authenticated case of a sexual attack upon a white woman. There was evidently truth in the comment of a young Northern lieutenant who wrote of a pleasant evening spent with the young ladies of a Virginian family in March of this year, "who entertained us with rebel songs." "We stocked their larder," he added, "supplied them with coffee, tea, sugar, placed guards over their barns and stock. . . . Nearly all the inhabitants had fled, those remaining being exclusively women and superannuated men. These Southern men, although heaping most outrageous abuse upon the Northern armies, seem to have no fear for their wives and daughters, whom they leave behind in charge of their property with apparent confidence, which proves that they do not really believe what they say about us."[21] This would appear to have been true of the personal safety of women to a greater degree than in any other war.

[20] Issue February 22, 1862.
[21] *Diary of a Young Army Officer, op. cit.*, p. 72.

Meanwhile, to go back to military operations, Lincoln had issued his "Special War Order Number 1" on January 31, ordering McClellan to begin a forward movement February 22, the day of Davis's inauguration. He was to capture Manassas Junction from Johnston, who was stationed there with an inferior force, and then take the direct road to Richmond. McClellan had a magnificent army, largely created by himself, and was popular with his men, but although he was an able strategist he had the fatal failings of always over-estimating the strength of the enemy and of never feeling that his own force was quite ready to take the offensive. With many excellent military qualities, he was, moreover, utterly incapable of realizing the importance of the political factors in a nation at war, and, as his letters to his wife show, was almost incredibly puffed up with conceit of his own ability and importance.

Although his army outnumbered Johnston's by perhaps two to one, he had fantastic notions as to Johnston's strength, and was even deceived by wooden cannon which the Southern general had displayed. Johnston, with more certain grasp on the realities of the situation and not yet knowing McClellan, withdrew his army across the Rappahannock, and left Manassas to the Federals, an empty victory for them as McClellan did not pursue. His own plan, which may or may not have been superior to Lincoln's under the conditions of February, though it was later adopted under quite different conditions by Grant, was to use the sea and move his army up the Peninsula, attacking Richmond on the flank instead of making a direct approach, which latter was the line of greatest resistance, though it would have kept the Federal army between the Confederates and Washington.

Lincoln finally acceded to the general's wish, but instead of having defeated Johnston in February, April found McClellan only ready to begin his march up the Peninsula. On the 4th, he received word that the President had decided to keep McDowell's corps for the protection of the capital, though McClellan had counted on using it on the north side of the York River to lessen the pressure against his own advance. Even so, he still outnumbered the reinforced Confederates, under both Lee and Johnston. Nevertheless, he wasted another entire month in the siege of Yorktown, giving Johnston ample time to bring his army from Manassas. McDowell was now allowed to co-operate provided he did so without uncovering Washington, and in his slow advance McClellan spread his force northward to make a converging movement with McDowell, which proved temporarily disastrous, due to Stonewall Jackson.

As on June 1, owing to a severe wound to Johnston, Lee was placed in command of the Confederate army, we may pause here to consider two of the most distinguished soldiers whom the Confederacy produced. Lee and Jackson, who were to work together in the most perfect harmony, were as different as two men could well be. Of distinguished lineage, connected with most of the great families of Virginia, brave, handsome, courtly, considerate, Lee was the beau ideal of what the South loved to call the "cavalier." Military opinions differ as to whether he, Grant, or Jackson may have been the greatest general but there is no doubt that he belongs on the roll of the great soldiers of the world. He also belongs among its great characters. It is impossible, as is pointed out by Major General Sir Frederick Maurice, who ranks Lee above Wellington, to assign precise comparative rank to great generals whose problems were different.[22] The latest English military critic is rather severe on Lee as contrasted with Grant, pointing out especially his deference to the civil authority.[23] He does not, however, appear to have given full consideration to the difficulties of dealing

[22] *Robert E. Lee* (London, 1925), pp. 283, 290.
[23] Major General J. F. C. Fuller, *Grant and Lee* (New York, 1933), *passim.*

with Davis; and General Longstreet shed more light on that point than Fuller when he wrote that Lee's "early experience with the Richmond authorities taught him to deal cautiously with them in disclosing his views, and to leave for them the privilege and credit of approving, step by step, his apparently hesitant policy, so that his plans were disclosed little at a time."[24] Had Lee, who knew the men he was dealing with, not have been able to keep Davis's entire confidence and friendship throughout the war, the Confederacy would have crashed long before it did.

That Lee made a number of bad mistakes is unquestioned but all generals have, and Lee's list is comparatively short. He has been accused of weakness as a military commander, and there assuredly was never a gentler or more considerate soul at the head of a great army. But we can judge that criticism by another standard. Colonel Henderson, to cite another and disinterested English military authority, said, quoting Napoleon: "In war men are nothing; it is the man who is everything. . . . It was not the Roman army that conquered Gaul, but Cæsar; it was not the Carthaginian army that made Rome tremble, but Hannibal." Colonel Henderson adds that "the history of famous armies is the history of great generals, for no army has ever achieved great things unless it has been well commanded."[25] In spite of desertion, in spite of a scandalous lack of supplies, in spite of all that General Fuller brings against Lee as a commander, few armies have accomplished greater things than the Army of Northern Virginia for three years, and Lee, and Lee alone, was the idol and the soul of that army.

We have already spoken of the real diversity of the South as contrasted with the popular romantic stereotype of the aristocratic planter. Jackson, as a contrast to Lee, was an example of that South of which the North was large-

[24] James Longstreet, *From Manassas to Appomattox* (Philadelphia, 1896), p. 337.
[25] *Stonewall Jackson, op. cit.*, vol. II, p. 338.

ly ignorant and which ardent Southern writers of both the ante- and post-bellum periods themselves largely ignored. Of humble Scotch-Irish pioneer ancestry, a staunch Presbyterian, this Southern general, who was the chief arm on which Lee leaned, was in some respects more like a New Englander than the popular conception of the Southerner, except for his wide tolerance. A West Pointer, like Lee, he had become professor of artillery at the Virginia Military Institute at Lexington. A strict teetotaller, never smoking or playing cards, giving carefully one-tenth of his small income to charity, teaching a negro Sunday School, never reading or writing a letter on the Sabbath, until the exigencies of war demanded it, shy, with few intimates, he was yet not unsociable and won both the respect and affection of his men. The late Viscount Wolseley said of him that he was "a child in purity; a child in faith; the Almighty always in his thoughts, his stay in trouble, his guide in every difficulty, Jackson's individuality was more striking and more complete than that of all the others who played leading parts in the great tragedy of Secession."[26] Although his soldiers genuinely admired his sincere piety they also came to have unbounded faith in his ability to out-wit the enemy by swift movements. After his death, a story was current that the Lord had sent down angels to find him and lead him to Heaven, but they could not find him until their return, when he was already there. "Old Jack," the soldiers said, "had outflanked the angels and got to Heaven before them."[27]

Perhaps the greatest soldier the South produced with the exception of Lee, it was now Jackson who was to upset the plans of McClellan. Norfolk had been captured by the Federals, the Southerners themselves destroying the *Merrimac* (or *Virginia*) before they evacuated, and the James

[26] Henderson, *Jackson, op. cit.,* vol. I, p. viii.
[27] McKim, *Soldier's Recollections, op. cit.,* p. 95.

River was open to the Union gunboats. If McDowell could unite with McClellan their vastly superior forces threatened Richmond. Jackson was in the Shenandoah Valley, far away, but he was now to show the tremendous influence which could be exerted by an inferior but mobile force led by a great strategist. His object was to force the withdrawal of McDowell and thus relieve the pressure on Johnston and Lee. In pursuance of this plan, he first made a surprise attack on General Milroy, who was also in the Valley, and defeated him. His advance so frightened General Frémont that *he* retreated. Jackson next defeated the force under General Banks, sending them toward the Potomac in a rout from Winchester. The next thing Lincoln knew Jackson and his dreaded forces were at Harpers Ferry, and it was feared he intended to attack Washington. Always sensitive to this possibility, as Jackson realized in his feint, Lincoln ordered McDowell back to unite with other forces to cut off Jackson's retreat and defend the capital, but Jackson was too quick for them, retired to the Valley again, and hastily executing his brilliant moves had joined Lee near Richmond by the end of June.

Meanwhile, the withdrawal which he had forced on McDowell had disarranged McClellan's plans and exposed his Northern flank to attack. On May 31, Johnston drove back the two isolated corps in the battle of Seven Oaks, and when the following day, owing to Johnston's wound, Lee assumed command, he began to entrench. Heavy rains delayed operations for a fortnight, but on June 27, the Confederates attacked the portion of McClellan's army which lay north of the Chickahominy in what is known as the battle of Gaines's Mill. Although the Union lines were shattered and forced to retreat, McClellan rearranged his position, taking the James River as his base instead of straddling the Chickahominy. During this process the Confederates launched a series of attacks known as the "Seven Days" Battle and by July 1, McClellan was at Harrison's Landing, twenty miles from Richmond. On June 25, his outposts had been only four miles from the Confederate capital, and on the day of Gaines's Mill he had 60,000 men south of the river as against only 25,000 Confederates in Richmond.

As usual, however, he had vastly exaggerated the numbers of the enemy and estimated the defenders at 100,000! His position at the beginning of July was a strong one and his army was not discouraged, but all McClellan's weaknesses had asserted themselves. He decided to advance slowly against the city, entrenching as he went, and kept furiously demanding heavy reinforcements from Washington. He had on several occasions since he had been made head of the army treated Lincoln with studied contempt, though the President, with his infinite patience, had remarked to some one on one of these occasions that he would hold the general's bridle if he would only win victories. After Gaines's Mill, although McClellan's forces far outnumbered those of his opponents, he had written to the Secretary of War that the battle had shown what he had been claiming: that his forces were too weak, "a few thousand more men would have changed this battle from a defeat to a victory"; and that "if I save this army now, I tell you plainly that I owe no thanks to you or to any other persons in Washington. You have done your best to sacrifice this army."[28] On July 7, Lincoln visited the general in person at Harrison's Bar, where McClellan handed him a long letter he had composed, laying down the law to the President on the whole civil as well as military policy of the war. One can imagine what would would have happened had any of the Confederate generals treated Davis as McClellan frequently did Lincoln, who, however, read the letter carefully, put it in his pocket with a word of thanks, and never men-

[28] G. B. McClellan, *McClellan's Own Story* (New York, 1887), p. 425.

tioned it again. The episode reminds one of the earlier one of Seward and the President.

The Cabinet, after several consultations, decided that there was nothing to be gained by allowing McClellan to absorb a large part of the military strength of the Union indefinitely, although it was later to take Grant many more months than McClellan had yet been in command before he finally captured the Confederate capital. However, action was demanded, and after his long and quite unnecessary delay before Yorktown, McClellan had now twice retreated from instead of advancing on Richmond, which he should have captured had he had the ability of either Lee or Jackson. On the other hand, it should be noted that he was considered by Lee as the ablest of the Federal generals to whom he found himself opposed during the war. The dispute as to his ability as a great commander still continues, and it would be unwise for a civilian to attempt to decide when military critics disagree, but at the time of which we are writing his four months' effort to take Richmond was considered a failure in Washington, and on August 3 he was ordered to re-embark his troops and return North to join General Pope in a general southward overland thrust toward Richmond.

The relief to the Confederates was great. So uncertain had they been of the fate of their capital that on May 10 the President's family left for Raleigh, and most of those of the Cabinet members had taken refuge in one place and another. About a week later the Confederate archives were sent to Columbia and Lynchburg. During the subsequent battles the city seemed to be on the edge of the field. "All day the wounded were borne past our boarding-house," wrote Jones of the War Department, and again, "There are fifty hospitals in the city, fast filling with the sick and wounded. I have seen men in my office and walking in the streets, whose arms have been amputated within the last three days." "Thousands of fathers, brothers, mothers, and sisters of the wounded are arriving in the city to attend their suffering relations, and to recover the remains of those who were slain." So near was the fighting that he reports even on June 26 the vivid flashes of artillery could be seen from the President's Mansion, and hundreds went to the higher portions of the city to watch the conflict.[29]

It is possible, although allowing for his characteristics open to doubt, that McClellan might have captured the capital had he at no time been interfered with by Lincoln and the War Office. On the other hand, as we have pointed out, the fall of Richmond would have had no such lasting results as the fall of Washington, and one of the leading English military historians upholds Lincoln in his insistence primarily upon the safety of his city, not as an important centre but for the psychological influence its loss would have exerted not only in the North but as leading to possible intervention on the part of England and France.[30] The risk of the situation could not be prolonged indefinitely. On July 11, General Halleck had been called from the West to assume a rather anomalous position as chief military adviser in Washington with the title of general-in-chief, the western successes of his subordinates having given him a reputation which his own abilities did not warrant. One of the first results of the new move was to consolidate the forces of Banks, McDowell, and Frémont under the single command of Pope, whose work in the West had also made him over-estimated.

At the very beginning of his new command Pope alienated his men and made himself ridiculous by a grandiloquent address, said to have been inspired by Stanton, which was summed up, though he had not used the precise words, by the public in the statement, which went through both the

[29] *Rebel War Clerk's Diary, op. cit., passim.*
[30] Henderson, *Jackson, op. cit.,* vol. I, pp. 235 *f.*

Union and the Confederacy, that his headquarters would be in his saddle!

Unhappily he did not make himself merely ridiculous, but by a series of orders applying to civilians as well as troops he caused a natural anger in the South. The celebrated Order Number 11 provided that all disloyal male citizens within the lines of the Union army should be arrested; if they took the oath of allegiance they should be allowed to remain at their homes; if not they should be sent South and if found North again be considered as spies; while those who violated their oath should be shot. The orders, at least in their more rigorous parts, were never put into effect, but they served, like many other incidents, to embitter the conflict, and Davis in retaliation notified Lee that commissioned officers in Pope's army would not be considered as prisoners of war. Halleck himself had considered the orders as "very injudicious" and Pope was forced to alter them by order of Stanton, although Pope later stated that this and other orders had been drafted substantially under the direction of Stanton himself.

A few days after Pope issued his Orders, Lincoln issued a general one which while authorizing Federal commanders to take over private property for purely military purposes insisted that "none shall be destroyed in wantonness or malice." Meanwhile, the editor of *The Richmond Enquirer* was asserting that Lincoln had the spirit of a Nero, and that thereafter if there were no more prisoners to be exchanged it would be his fault, for "the men whom he sends into our midst under existing orders, come as wild beasts; and it is as sacred a duty to slay them in their tracks, as it is to shoot down a tiger or a panther that invades the homestead."[31]

Pope's career in his new command was brief and inglorious. Lee, assured that McClellan's army was leaving the

[31] Issue August 8, 1862.

Peninsula, determined to crush Pope before the whole of Mc-Clellan's forces could be added to his, although the Southern army was heavily outnumbered. He first despatched Jackson with 24,000 troops, who came into collision with Banks in the desperate battle of Cedar Mountain. By August 24 the Confederates had about 55,000 troops opposed to Pope's more than 70,000, and it was clear that Pope would not voluntarily give battle until reinforced by McClellan, who was then rapidly approaching. Lee, who did not fear Pope as a general and who realized that his first thought would be the defence of Washington, decided on one of the most audacious strokes of the whole contest, a move which has been said to be contrary to all the known rules of war. He determined to divide his army in the face of the superior force of the enemy, and send Jackson around by the Bull Run Mountains to fall on Pope's line of communication, which would require the Federal general to fall back to a less strong position than the one held on the Rappahannock, and get him farther away from McClellan, while Lee himself would come up with the other half of his army through the same gap in the mountains and fall on Pope while engaged with Jackson. The plan worked. Pope, hearing that his stores at Manassas had been destroyed, marched there to meet the enemy, but Jackson had disappeared, deceiving Pope as to his destination. The Union general became bewildered as to his opponent's movements, and wearied his men by marching and counter-marching. Jackson had merely gone a short way off, concealing his men in a dense grove of trees, to await the arrival of Longstreet and Lee. On August 28, King's division, on its way along the Warrenton Turnpike to Centreville, passed in front of Jackson, who was in the woods about a mile distant, and Jackson at once attacked. Both sides held their ground in severe fighting, though some hours later King moved to Manassas. Jackson's position having been revealed, Pope the following day attacked in force but was driven by Lee across the stream where the Federals had sustained the first great defeat of the war, and on toward Washington. A second "Bull Run" was more than could be condoned after Pope's boasting, and he applied to be relieved,[32] McClellan meeting him as he fled with orders to assume command.

Both Lee and McClellan were now to make serious blunders, blunders which in McClellan's case derived from his temperament but it is not easy to explain Lee's move. In suggesting it to Davis he said that his army "is not properly equipped for an invasion of an enemy's territory. It lacks much of the material of war, is feeble in transportation, the animals being much reduced, and the men are poorly provided with clothes, and in thousands of instances are destitute of shoes."[33] Yet he planned nothing less than to invade the North with his 60,000 ill-equipped soldiers. He knew he could not take Washington, but hoped that Maryland would rise in favor of the Confederacy, for it had been considered as a loyal Southern State only held in the Union by fear. It was not realized that just as there had been eastern and western sections of Virginia there was the same difference in Maryland. On September 6 Lee reached Frederick and his army passed through the delightful old town, though there is no substantial evidence that Barbara Frietchie, who her nephew later said was bed-ridden at the time, ever waved the Union flag as so graphically pictured by Whittier. Colonel Mosby, who was one of those marching through, said he never heard of any such incident until he read the poem, and it is to be feared that the poet's historical accuracy, in this case at least, was not greater than Longfellow's when he attempted history in verse.

[32] For a military defence of Lee's move *vide* Major General Sir Frederick Maurice, *Robert E. Lee, the Soldier* (London, 1925), pp. 127 ff.
[33] *Ibid.*, p. 145.

Instead of swarming to the Southern cause, the Maryland farmers would not even sell food to the Southern army. Lee decided to open a line of supply from the Shenandoah Valley, but that necessitated ejecting the Federal garrison of over 12,000 men at Harpers Ferry, which was accomplished under Jackson. That in turn, however, meant dividing Lee's army in what had proved to be hostile country. It was the 14th of September that Jackson captured the Ferry, eight days after McClellan had been verbally reappointed to command by Lincoln. The new commander started to move on the 8th but did not reach Frederick until the 12th. The following day he came into possession of a Confederate despatch which showed him that Lee's army was divided, but still he waited until next morning before attempting to take the mountain gaps.

There were further delays after a severe small engagement at South Mountain and it was not until the 17th that the two armies engaged in the bloodiest battle of the war, Jackson having had time to arrive at a critical moment. There has been much dispute as to the numbers engaged on either side. Rhodes states that McClellan had 87,000 to Lee's 55,000, although Livermore, whose estimates in general are considered as accurate as any we have for the war, gives them respectively as 75,316 and 51,844. Carmen's estimate of the numbers actually engaged is 55,956 and 37,351, the latter bearing out Lee's claim that he fought the battle with less than 40,000, although Major General Sir Frederick Maurice in his life of Lee has claimed this is an underestimate. Other figures may be found, and the incident shows the difficulty of arriving at anything like precise figures. In any case all agree that McClellan greatly outnumbered his opponent, and Rhodes claims that the Union loss the first day was only 12,000 to Lee's 11,000, but it would appear to be impossible to make accurate estimates. Although both Livermore and Carmen give the figures for McClellan's losses as 12,410, Livermore estimates Lee's as 13,724, whereas Carmen places them at 10,316, a discrepancy between two careful men of approximately thirty per cent. In any case, the Federal general did not renew the conflict next morning, and allowed Lee to make a successful and leisurely retreat. Lee had been wrong in attempting such an audacious move, but as Lincoln said of Grant's whiskey to some one who complained of his drinking, "a little of that spirit in others might change the war." McClellan had none of Lee's spirit, and in spite of hard prodding by Lincoln he allowed one of the greatest opportunities of his career to go unutilized. It was in vain that Lincoln wrote with unwonted asperity, "Are you not over-cautious when you assume that you cannot do what the enemy is constantly doing?" or when McClellan complained of his weary horses, "Will you pardon me for asking what the horses of your army have done since the battle of Antietam that fatigues anything?" McClellan having allowed Lee, inferior in numbers, ill-supplied, farther from Richmond than he himself was, to escape, Lincoln removed him and appointed Burnside in his place.

It is true that the army when McClellan had again been given command of it had been thoroughly demoralized and needed reorganization. Also there had been another attack of the nerves in Washington, exceptionally severe in the case of Halleck, who feared lest the capital be uncovered and opened to attack. But as we read the correspondence between McClellan and his chiefs in the following few weeks we cannot but feel that he exhibited one of his besetting sins, the constant overrating of the enemy's strength and his own inability to move unless certain of success. He was a great organizer and it is to his credit that he won the confidence of his men. It may be, as the magnanimous Grant said some years later, that had McClellan's rise to high command not been so rapid he might have equalled the best of the Union leaders, but, on the other hand, Lee's rise had been no less rapid, and had the rôles been reversed at this time it is inconceivable that Lee and Jackson would have allowed *their* enemy to escape with so little effort made to catch him.

However, Antietam had been a Northern victory and Lee had been driven south again, a fact that was to be of profound influence in many directions. During the bloody conflict there occurred one of those family tragedies which stamped the war, quite apart from any Constitutional connotation, as a *Civil* War, that is a fight between kinsmen of the same household. General D. R. Jones was commanding the Confederates immediately opposing the 11th Connecticut Regiment, which was led by Jones's brother-in-law, Colonel H. W. Kingsbury, and when the latter was killed, Jones was so affected that he asked for leave of absence not long after and within a few months died.

Before speaking of the great military disaster for the Union forces which closed the year, we must stop to consider some of the events which had been occurring behind the fighting lines in the past few months.

It has been said that one of the reasons for Lee's unfortunate effort to invade the North was its possible effect on Europe, with the hope of forcing intervention if it could be shown that a Confederate army was well inside the lines of the Union and threatening Washington, Baltimore, or Harrisburg at pleasure. It is impossible to recount in detail the many and tortuous diplomatic moves by both American Governments and their representatives in relation to England and France. Mason and Slidell were hopeful, but had accomplished little of real value after being allowed to continue their journey; and both North and South complained of the attitude of England, which perhaps is a fair indication that she was attempting to be neutral, though both belligerents denied it. In 1862, however, the lack of cotton was beginning to make itself keenly felt. The issues of the war were not well understood, and although England preferred the South and its fight for freedom, it was strongly opposed to slavery. On the other hand, the North had not yet officially indicated that it would do anything about slavery even if it won, beyond limiting its further extension. The suffering among the cotton-mill operatives in Europe was about to begin. The loss of life and property in America was obviously colossal. As the war got well into its second year, it was not unnatural that foreign countries should watch the swaying success of one side and the other with a view to intervening to stop the struggle if its continuance should begin to seem hopeless for either belligerent. Lee's failure at Antietam, like the earlier Northern victories in the Mississippi, thus had enormous international value.

The Southern agents laid great stress upon the alleged fact that the blockade was not an effective one, but England would not be moved by this argument, and the Southern policy of withholding and even destroying cotton in its effort to force intervention made Slidell's arguments in France difficult to maintain. "Why," he would be asked, "if the blockade is ineffective do we get no cotton?"

The effectiveness, both from the legal and practical standpoints, of the blockade has long been a matter of controversy. It used to be over-estimated. Now, in the re-writing of all of our history, perhaps the tendency is too great to under-estimate it. Owsley, for example, speaks of the Herculean task of blockading a coast line of "3,549 statute miles." Ocean-going vessels, however, can land only at certain points on any coast. Blockade running in small boats which can deliver cargoes through the surf on a beach is a very different matter from normal commerce, just as is smuggling in ordinary times. That a great many vessels got through the blockade even at some of the larger ports is undoubtedly true, but it would seem as though, at least after the first few months, the closing of Southern ports was fairly effective.

In 1803 James Madison, in defending our rights as a neutral in the Napoleonic struggles, had laid down the rule that a blockade required the presence of a force "rendering access to the prohibited place manifestly difficult and dangerous." That running the Southern blockade had become both seems evident from the description of blockade runners which a young Confederate naval officer gives of those he saw in Bermuda in 1862. "Their business was risky," he writes, "and the penalty of being caught was severe; they were a reckless lot, and believed in eating, drinking, and being merry, for fear that they would die on the morrow and might miss something. Their orgies reminded me of the stories of the way the pirates in the West Indies spent their time when in their secret havens. The men who commanded many of these blockade-runners had probably never before in their lives received more than fifty to seventy-five dollars a month for their services; now they received $10,-000 in gold for a round trip, besides being allowed cargo space to take into the Confederacy, on their own account, goods which could be sold at a fabulous price, and also to bring out a limited number of bales of cotton worth a dollar a pound."[34]

Moreover, although the Confederate policy might account for the limited supply of cotton going out, it could not for the limited supply of goods coming in. On the latter point the evidence from innumerable sources is overwhelming. High prices were in large measure due to depreciation of the Confederate paper money, but in addition there was evidently genuine scarcity of imported articles. Innumerable substitutes had to be developed for coffee, tea, and sugar. Salt was so hard to obtain that even the dirt under smoke-houses was dug up and washed to procure it. The simplest

[34] *Recollections of a Rebel Reefer, op. cit.,* p. 101.

household utensils became unbelievably scarce. One Southern woman hired a skillet from a negress at a dollar a month. Thorns were used instead of pins; persimmon seeds were made into buttons; and we are told that the loss of a sewing needle was a household calamity.[35] Another woman records that they were "precious as heirlooms." Gourds were used as wash-cloths. Ink was made from oak galls or even from soot scraped from chimneys.[36] Leather became so scarce that not only civilians but the armies themselves suffered heavily from lack of shoes. It may be that, as Mason in France claimed, between 500 and 700 vessels (a rather indefinite estimate which reflects on its accuracy) passed through the blockade in 1861, its least effective year, yet we must recall that Memminger said it would take 4000 to move the cotton crop alone, and that the South was dependent on imports for almost everything it used outside of food. It is not strange, therefore, that England considered the blockade sufficiently effective to be lawful.

In other ways, however, she had appeared to favor the South. In the Proclamation of May 13, 1861, proclaiming the Confederate States a belligerent, the Queen had clearly stated strict neutrality should be observed, and that in pursuance of that aim British subjects could not attempt to break any lawful blockade, enter the armed forces of either contestant, fit out, arm, or equip any vessel designed by either party as a ship of war or privateer, nor could English vessels carry military stores, soldiers, or despatches for either belligerent. Yet the *Trent* had carried Confederate despatches, British vessels continually ran the blockade with contraband, and not only was the *Florida* allowed to leave England for the Confederate service but on July 29, 1862, the much larger *Alabama* was permitted, through a com-

[35] M. P. Andrews, *The Women of the South in War Times* (Baltimore, 1920), pp. 21 *ff*.
[36] *A Belle of the Fifties, op. cit.*, p. 227.

bination of circumstances, to escape to sea and was to become, under command of the redoubtable Captain Semmes, the most formidable ship in the Confederate navy. Neither ship had left England armed, and it was claimed, possibly justly, by some of the highest legal authorities, that international law did not prevent the building and selling of unarmed vessels. The American Minister, however, had built up a case which left no doubt of what the intention of the *Alabama* was, and at the last moment, after the papers submitted by the Foreign Minister, Lord Russell, to the Queen's Advocate, who unknown to all but his wife had been insane for five days, reached the Attorney General and Solicitor General, it was too late. Possibly as change of policy in regard to neutral rights, they decided that the ship must be detained, but she had slipped out to sea some hours before. Later efforts of the Confederacy to build ships in England were foiled, and in the following summer, as the easiest way out, after much negotiation between Adams and Russell, two rams which had been built by the Lairds were first detained and then purchased by the British Government.

The critical period of possible intervention, and in so far as affected by that, of the success of the South, was precisely that of Lee's advance into Maryland. The number of cotton operatives out of work in England rose to 550,000 by the end of the year and to 300,000 in France. Napoleon, with his Mexican adventure in mind, had been pressing steadily for action against the North, and in the military situation as it was in America in September the British Cabinet began to waver. Russell suggested to Gladstone on September 26 that possibly soon mediation might be offered, and in case of refusal by the North, that the South should be recognized.

The importance of Lee's move may be seen in a note by Palmerston three days earlier in which he said: "It is evident that a great conflict is now taking place to the northwest of Washington, and its issue must have a great effect on the state of affairs. If the Federalists sustain a great defeat, they may be at once ready for mediation, and the iron should be struck while it is hot. If, on the other hand, they should have the best of it, we may wait awhile and see." Granville pointed out that if the war continued after England recognized the South, it could not be long before she would be drawn into it, but although opposed to intervention he feared it could not be avoided.[37] Had Lee won at Antietam it probably would have meant the eventual independence of the South. But the last chance of intervention passed when Lee, beaten, turned southward.

France, as we have pointed out, could not intervene without England, and various reasons have been given as to why, with the deepening cotton famine, England did not consider it seriously after the fall of 1862. It has been said that, aside from some prominent friends of America, such as John Bright, the cotton operatives themselves were so in favor of democracy and freedom that they preferred suffering to recognizing the South. It has also been said that the demand for Northern wheat was a heavy offset to the need of Southern cotton. Rejecting these explanations, the latest student of the subject looks for the cause in the great increase in the supply of cotton from India, which during the war seemed to offer the possibility of such continued increases as would make England independent of America; and also in the enormous profits which the war was bringing to various classes of business, not least the cotton trade itself. As the war continued and cotton rose in price, the larger mill owners, controlling about two-thirds of the trade, speculated heavily in the raw material and a

[37] E. D. Adams, *Great Britain and the American Civil War* (New York, 1925), vol. II, pp. 40–43.

cessation of hostilities would have meant corresponding losses. He also points to the unexpected and huge profits being made in the woollen and linen trades, in munitions, and, largest of all to England, the destruction of American sea-borne trade, our magnificent clipper fleet giving place forevermore to British shipping.[38]

When a new factor is discovered to account for the historic process, the first tendency is to minimize the old explanations, but history is not simple, and it is probable that in varying degrees all these factors worked through public opinion and parliament against intervention after Lee's defeat. The moment had passed for good.

The South also began to realize that history is complex. King Cotton, which was to win the world for them, had failed. The extremist Southern papers were vitriolic in fury. On December 2, *The Richmond Whig* in two editorials expressed its opinions of both the Yankees and the English. It described the former as "the vilest race on the face of the earth. They are without the one redeeming virtue of which the Roman Historian speaks. . . . Bigoted and intolerant, rapacious and stingy, fraudulent and roguish, boastful and cowardly, ostentatious and vulgar, envious and spiteful . . . an odious race." It then pays its respects to Lord John Russell. "There is not in Massachusetts a more narrow-minded, bigoted and malignant fanatic. . . . Taking him as the exponent of English sentiment, there is not the slightest probability that any action favorable to our cause can ever emanate from Great Britain. . . . It cannot be that England is afraid of the Yankees—those base dastards, who, less than twelve months ago, surrendered Mason and Slidell, under circumstances which forever must attach to their names the stigma of infamous."[39]

[38] Owsley, *King Cotton, op. cit.*, final chapter,
[39] Issue of December 2, 1862.

On the other hand, Northern readers were fed by newspapers like *The Tribune* with diatribes as wild and whirling against the South. "There is one characteristic," reads one article, "which distinguishes this war, on the part of the Northern Free and enlightened States, namely its humanity. There is another characteristic which distinguishes this war, on the part of the Southern and semi-barbaric States, which is its inhumanity." After reciting many alleged incidents, it continues "in coincidence with this Southern ferocity was the crowning wrath of turning human skulls into drinking cups, and bones into souvenirs to be strung like beads. In mean fury the women outdid the men. From the statements of the late Southern refugees at the Cooper Institute, it appears that the murders of Unionists South were as infernal as were those by East Indian Thugs. . . . So butchered were they by crowds, that there was no time to make the rudest coffin or box for the carcasses, which accordingly were, uncased, thrown into the ground. Such terrific butcheries were the law of the guerillas, that a Union general recently was obliged to resort to the act of ten-fold sacrificial vengeance to stop them."[40]

As we contrast these unhappy outpourings of stay-at-home editors, both North and South, who never got to know the enemy by fighting him, with the understanding which grew up between men at the front, we can echo Sherman's description of them as miserable and corrupt. "They are the chief cause of this unhappy war," he wrote to his wife. "They fan the flame of local hatred and keep alive the prejudices which have forced friends into opposing ranks. . . . Each radical class keeps its votaries filled with the most outrageous lies of the other." Speaking of Grant and the Northern press he added, "Grant . . . is not himself a brilliant man . . . but he is a good and brave soldier

[40] *New York Tribune*, November 21, 1862.

. . . sober, very industrious and kind as a child. Yet he has been held up as careless, criminal, a drunkard, tyrant, and everything horrible."[41]

Unfortunately one cannot understand the times nor the hatreds engendered in those who were behind the lines without occasional citations of what editors of leading papers were feeding to them. It is with hesitation and with no wish to stir again old animosities that we quote them from time to time, but perhaps more than any other contributing cause, even the destruction of war itself, they deepened, malignantly and unnecessarily, the blackness of our tragedy. Thinking not of the dead but of the hatreds engendered among the living, we may echo the words of a Union officer "My God, what a terrible thing war is!" For relief, we may insert a little story, one of many such, told by the Confederate General Gordon. In the fighting around Knoxville, the Confederates, unable to take the Union fort and equally unable to retire from a semi-sheltered position during the day, were famishing from thirst in the direct heat of the sun. Finally a young Confederate made a dash across a space exposed to the guns of the Union soldiers to where he could get water. But how to get back with his heavily loaded canteens? As General Gordon recounts the result: "The brave Union soldiers stood upon the parapet with their rifles in hands. As they saw this daring American youth, they stood silently contemplating him for a moment. Then, realizing the situation, they fired at him a tremendous volley —not of deadly bullets from their guns, but of enthusiastic shouts." The general adds "if the annals of war record any incident between hostile armies which embodies a more beautiful and touching tribute by the brave to the brave, I have never seen it." There were, however, many similar kindly incidents between the opposing forces, some of which

[41] Hart, *Sherman, op. cit.,* p. 149.

we shall note; while safe in their offices in the rear editors were spitting venom and building up putrid hatreds in their readers' minds.

The failure at Antietam, which may be considered one of the most decisive battles in our history, had repercussions other than those in Europe.

Lincoln had assumed office with no intention of interfering with slavery within the slave States, which he considered unconstitutional, but only of preventing its further spread, and of maintaining the Union. When in August, 1861, Frémont on his own initiative had declared the slaves of all Missourians in arms against the Federal Government to be free, Lincoln had disapproved the proclamation and removed the general. When in May, 1862, General Hunter declared the slaves in South Carolina, Georgia, and Florida free, Lincoln declared the proclamation void as soon as he heard of it.

The problem, however, was one which the President had increasingly to consider. What he wished for was a gradual and compensated emancipation. In his appeal to the border States when Congress passed the act we have noted, he said: "You cannot, if you would, be blind to the signs of the times. I beg of you a calm and enlarged consideration of them. . . . This proposal . . . acts not the Pharisee. The change it contemplates would come as gently as the dews of heaven, not rending or wrecking anything. Will you not embrace it?" We have seen, however, that they would not. We have also seen the divided sentiment of the North, although the greater part of it went to war for the Union and not for the Abolition cause. As the conflict deepened, and as Northern editors stirred up their readers as Southern editors did, what we may call the Left Wing of the President's party became more insistent upon freedom for the slave as one of the objects of the war. Lincoln's voiding of Hunter's proclamation and his generally conservative atti-

tude toward the slavery question was diminishing his influence in the North as well as making the Northern cause
ambiguous in Europe. In the summer of 1862 the failure
of McClellan's expedition against Richmond deeply depressed the North, and by autumn European intervention
was dangerously near. On July 13 he told two members of
the Cabinet, Seward and Welles, that he had "about come to
the conclusion that it was a military necessity . . . that
we must free the slaves or be ourselves subdued."[42] The
next day he asked Congress to place a sum in his hands—
the bill called for $180,000,000—to be used as compensa-
tion to slave owners in loyal States, but it was too late in
the session to secure its passage.

Meanwhile, Congress had passed the so-called Confiscation Act, which permitted the courts to commute the death
sentence for treason to fine and imprisonment, but confiscated the property of all the civil and military officials of
the Confederacy, and, after sixty days, of any who might
be in its armed forces, and freed their slaves. Lincoln
objected to the Act as going too far, especially as to real
estate, but signed it with explanations. This Act was undoubtedly severe, too severe for Lincoln himself. Yet it
sprang from the different interpretations of the Constitution and the nature of the Union which had developed into
assumed axioms in the North and the South. At the time
of secession, many Southerners, as we have seen, including
Lee, preferred the term rebellion. If so, Northern radicals
cannot be blamed too heavily for adopting the same view,
and treating the Southerners in arms as rebels. It is difficult to draw the line between successful revolution and
thwarted rebellion. As Franklin said, when signing the
Declaration of Independence in 1776, "we must hang together or we shall hang separately."

To have asked the North not to consider the Southerners

[42] *Vide* Rhodes, *History, op. cit.,* vol. IV, pp. 69 *f.*

as rebels was equivalent to asking the majority to acquiesce
in the Constitutional opinion of the minority without hesitation. As Horace Greeley said in answer to O'Sullivan's
demand that the North should have accepted the Crittenden
Compromise, "By what right do you and yours assume to
judge for me and mine in the premises? . . . You are not
a God to forgive—nor even a priest to absolve. How can
you decide that I should assent to that which I feel to be
intensely wrong?"[43] In view of the fact that there was no
supreme power capable of rendering a decision, and also of
the numbers engaged on both sides with perfect honesty of
opinion, it would have been best if each could simply have
agreed to recognize that and fight it out without rancor.
This, however, was asking too much of human nature—and
of editors. The feelings which had been engendered were
too intense. The South, believing absolutely in its own
interpretation of the Constitution, regarded the North as a
brutal invader of its soil and rights; the North, equally confident of its own interpretation, felt that it was trying to
save the nation from an uncalled-for rebellion on the part of
a portion of it, and that those who had brought on the disaster and suffering should be made to pay the penalty.

On July 22 Lincoln stated to his Cabinet that he intended
to ask Congress at its next session to pass an emancipation
and compensation Act. The object of the war, he said, was
solely the restoration of the Union, nevertheless he felt that
it was a necessary measure for that object that he should
declare all slaves held in States which had not returned to
their allegiance by January 1, 1863, to be free. Although
the Cabinet as a whole agreed in principle, Seward pointed
out that the time was inopportune, in view of the reverses
of the Union arms.

A few days later, August 3, the President issued his call
for another 300,000 men, and the gloom of the North and

[43] *New York Tribune,* Aug. 2, 1862.

its distrust of himself increased. On the 20th, Greeley in *The Tribune* published what he called "The Prayer of Twenty Millions," in which he bitterly assailed the President for lukewarmness on the matter of slavery. To this Lincoln replied, as soon as he saw it, "I would save the Union. . . . If I could save the Union without freeing any slave, I would do it; and if I could save it by freeing all the slaves, I would do it; and if I could save it by freeing some and leaving others alone, I would do that also. What I do about slavery and the colored race, I do because I believe it helps to save the Union; and what I forbear, I forbear because I do not believe it would help save the Union." Certainly this does not agree with the Southern view, prior to secession, of Lincoln in 1860 as a rabid Abolitionist.

Lincoln had been thinking the matter over in all its aspects since his first mention of it, and had finally come to the conclusion that it was a necessary military measure which should be announced at an opportune time. He afterwards said that "when the rebel army was at Frederick, I determined as soon as it should be driven out of Maryland to issue a proclamation of emancipation. . . . I said nothing to any one, but I made the promise to myself and my Maker."[44] This was the second and greatest significance of Lee's defeat at Antietam.

On September 22 the President announced to the Cabinet that he had decided to issue the Proclamation, adding: "I do not wish your advice about the main matter; for that I have determined for myself." The following day the Proclamation was given to the public declaring that after January 1, 1863, all slaves in such sections of the United States as should then remain in rebellion "shall be, thenceforward, and forever free." He repeated his wish to work for compensated emancipation in the loyal slave States and

[44] Quoted by Rhodes, *History, op. cit.,* vol. IV, p. 160.

for loyal owners in the States in revolt, and requested measures leading to that end when Congress met in December. Although the legality of Lincoln's proclamation is open to grave doubt, it was subsequently validated beyond question by the XIIIth Amendment to the Constitution adopted in 1865.

The immediate results were also doubtful. The fall elections went rather heavily against him, although the border slave States were notably for him. Mid-term elections, however, are likely to register opposition to any administration, and the lack of victories in recent months was a heavy handicap, and probably counted much more than any opposition to the proclamation. If many Northerners felt that the war had been changed from one to save the Union to one to free the slave, the position was distinctly clarified in Europe. Thereafter if England and France should join the South they would have to fight for slavery against free labor.

From the South, naturally, a howl of rage went up. *The Richmond Whig* called the proclamation the "last effort and the vilest . . . the last resource of the baffled and enraged tyrant"; and declared that Lincoln had endeavored to make the slaves assassins, but "the new phase the war is to assume is not our fault. A seditious negro, no matter in whose company, or under whose protection found, will die the death."[45] *The Richmond Enquirer* declared that the war had now become "an invasion of an organized horde of murderers and plunderers, breathing hatred and revenge for the numerous defeats sustained on legitimate battle fields." It claimed that Lincoln had issued the proclamation solely with a view to bringing on a servile insurrection. President Davis's own comment on the proclamation was that "it has established a state of things which can lead to but one of three consequences [none of which came to pass]—the

[45] Issue of September 30, 1862.

extermination of the slaves, the exile of the whole white
population of the Confederacy, or absolute and total separation of these States from the United States."[46]

The suggestion that negro troops might be used by the
Federals brought threats of most drastic retaliation, including the immediate killing of any negroes caught in the
armed service as well as any white officers who might command them. Few indeed could agree with Mrs. Chesnut
that "if anything can reconcile me to the idea of a horrid
failure after all efforts to make good our independence of
Yankees, it is Lincoln's proclamation freeing the negroes,"
although she quotes Miss Mary Cantey as saying in June:
"I may not have any logic, any sense. I give it up. My
woman's instinct tells me, all the same, that slavery's time
has come. If we don't end it, they will." In July she wrote:
"Uncle William says the men who went into the war to save
their negroes are abjectly wretched. Neither side now cares
a fig for these beloved negroes, and would send them all to
heaven in a hand-basket, as Custis Lee says, to win in the
fight."

The whole issue brought out afresh the peculiar and
anomalous form of property, and the tragedy of the presence of the negro. As we have seen, slaves formed the
largest single item of wealth of the entire South, though it
was highly concentrated in comparatively few hands. In
so far as the property question was concerned, the South
could feel as bitterly as the North might if the South had
confiscated *its* largest single item of wealth. But there could
be no question if railroad bonds or real-estate mortgages
were declared "free" of their engaging in a servile insurrection. Moreover, what was "property" in the South was
a United States citizen in the North. Any citizen of the
South going into the army could not raise an insurrection
in the North, but a Northern citizen, if black, was threat-

[46] Davis, *Davis, op. cit.,* vol. II, p. 217.

ened with death, if he appeared in the South, because of
that fear.

So long as racial feeling exists in the world, and it will
for a long time yet, there will be objections to use of troops
of other races against the white, but we may note that six
months after the Emancipation Proclamation went into
effect on January 1, Mrs. Chesnut wrote in her diary that
"General Lee and Mr. Davis want the negroes put into the
army. Mr. Chesnut and Major Venable discussed the subject one night, but would they fight on our side or desert
to the enemy? They don't [now] go to the enemy, because
they are comfortable as they are, and expect to be free any-
way."[47] As to the mere use of negro troops in the army,
with Lee and Davis both in favor of it, there would seem to
be little question that the South would have used them
in the second year of the war except for fear of their deserting and for the influence on the general body of slaves.
Negroes were used in the Southern army in various capacities, and *The Tribune* declared it could not see why the
South should use them for some military purposes at the
front and deny the North the right to use them for the same
or others.[48] In fact, it had been the South and not the
North which had taken the lead in the use of negro troops
in some of the seceded States. In September, 1861, the
Tennessee legislature had passed an act to utilize the military services of free negroes between the ages of fifteen and
fifty, and the following year Louisiana used a regiment of
free negroes in the defence of New Orleans. As we shall
see later, almost at the end of the struggle, the Confederate
Congress itself authorized the use of slaves as soldiers.
Certainly the negroes who did fight in the Northern ranks
deserve the highest praise for courage, for slavery if not
death frequently awaited them after capture if they escaped
the dangers of the battle-field. After the second battle of

[47] *Diary from Dixie, op. cit.,* p. 224.    [48] June 25, 1863.

Bull Run, a burying squad of negroes, under a flag of truce granted them by the Confederates, were taken into custody, "most of them being claimed as runaway slaves, though the flag should assuredly have protected them."[49] We can only note the intensifying bitterness as the second year of the conflict drew to a close.

It was to end in a great disaster to the North. General Burnside, who gave his name to a type of whiskers but to no great victory, was, as we have seen, placed in command of the Army of the Potomac when McClellan was dismissed. Possibly as a result of the fact that he had been chosen to replace a man whose chief fault was dilatoriness, he felt that action was necessary for his reputation. Lee, in retreating, had crossed the Rappahannock and taken up a strong position on Marye's Heights near Fredericksburg, where he and Longstreet made their headquarters, Jackson being within easy reach. Although Burnside had about 113,000 men to Lee's 78,000, the Southern general had eluded every attempt to surprise him until he was almost impregnably fixed in his position. Below the hill were a stone wall and a ditch which afforded ample protection for the Confederates, and in front of these stretched a meadow down to the river, both of which the Federals would have to cross if they attempted an attack. Against Lincoln's advice, though with Halleck's consent, Burnside determined to make one. It was an almost inconceivably colossal blunder, and the night before the battle Burnside himself seemed uncertain and without a well thought-out plan.

He had divided his army into three divisions under Hooker, Franklin, and Sumner, the Second and Third Divisions crossing the river on December 12, and on the 13th, the assault, chiefly against Longstreet's troops on Marye's Heights, took place. So well defended was the position that Long-

[49] *New York Tribune,* September 11, 1862. *Richmond Examiner,* September 5, 1862.

street's Chief of Artillery had said that "a chicken could not live on that field when we open on it." Nevertheless, Burnside ordered an advance and three divisions of the Federals swept across the meadow, the first led by French, the second by Hancock, and the third by Howard. One of the Confederates describing the scene wrote : "What a magnificent sight it is! We have never witnessed such a battle-array before. . . . It seemed like some huge blue serpent about to encompass and crush us in its folds. . . . Nearer and nearer the enemy's line advances, and now they are within reach of canister, and we give it to them. Now they are near enough to the infantry in the sunken road, the Georgians and the North Carolinians ; and they are unseen by the enemy, for smoke is beginning to cover the field. All at once the gray line below us rises ; one moment to glance along the trusty rifle-barrels, and volley after volley is poured into the enemy's ranks. Great gaps appear; we give them canister again and again ; a few leave ranks—more follow; the lines halt for an instant, and, turning, are seen running in great disorder towards the town. The first assault has been met and repulsed. The field below us is dotted with patches of blue ; they are the dead and wounded of the Federal infantry."[50]

The total Federal loss in the charge was over 6600 in killed and wounded, Hancock losing over 2000, of whom 156 were commissioned officers, out of his 5000. Yet six times did Burnside order his men to the slaughter, division after division, until as one observer said, "it is only murder now." At the end of the day 12,653 Federals were dead, wounded, or missing whereas the Confederates, still in possession of their position, had lost only a little over 5000. That night Burnside was overcome with chagrin and grief, and made wild plans for renewed attempts, but both the weather and the opinion of his officers were against them,

[50] W. M. Owen, *In Camp and Battle* (Boston, 1885), p. 186.

and on the night of the 15th, he withdrew his army across the river, Lee having made no effort to follow up his victory. In fact, strong as Lee's position was it failed in two particulars in that it gave no facility for counter-stroke or pursuit, and the position chosen was in those respects as faulty as was Burnside's attack. The six bridges were in Federal hands, and the fords, which might have been used for cavalry flank attacks, were useless owing to the rapid rising of the river. Moreover, the Army of the Potomac was too close at Aquia Creek, so that Lee, although he had forced the retirement of the enemy, had nothing beyond that to show for a victory which had cost him dear.

It is pleasant to turn, as one so often can, from the ranting of editors and the necessary slaughters of the battlefield, to the interchange of courtesies by the combatants on both sides. A young Confederate artilleryman tells in his reminiscences that both before and after the battle, as the enemies faced each other across the Rappahannock, they rigged up little boats which they sailed from one shore to the other. "The communication was almost constant," he wrote, "and the vessels many of them really beautiful little craft, trim sails, closed decks, and perfect working steering apparatus. The cargoes, besides the newspapers of the two sides, usually consisted on our side of tobacco and on the Federal side of coffee and sugar, yet the trade was by no means confined to these articles, and on a sunny, pleasant day the waters were fairly dotted with the fairy fleet. Many a weary hour of picket duty was thus relieved and lightened, and most of the officers seemed to wink at the infraction of military law, if such it was."[51]

General Gordon, however, states that the commanders of both armies decided the fraternizing was getting too frequent, and that he was ordered by General Lee to stop it.

[51] Robert Stiles, *Four Years Under Marse Robert* (New York, 1903), p. 157.

In pursuit of this duty he rode along the river bank, and found an unusual commotion at a certain point on his approach. It developed that a very scantily clad Yankee was hidden in the weeds on the Confederate side. On stern interrogation he admitted that he belonged on the other side but thought there was no harm in coming over to "see the boys just a little while." "What boys?" said the general. "These Johnnies," was the answer. "Don't you know, sir," said the general, "that there is a war going on in this country?" The frightened Yankee replied that he did "but we are not fighting now." Gordon records that this naive answer was almost too much for him but when he threatened to send the intruder to prison the Confederates in the group all clamored that they had asked him over and it would ruin their honor if he were not allowed to go back. At a word from the general, the Yankee, as he says, "leaped like a bull frog into the river" and swam to the enemy side.[52] If only the non-combatants behind the lines could have felt even a little of the spirit of the actual fighters!

The following month, having lost the confidence of both the army and the country, Burnside offered Lincoln his resignation from the army but it was not accepted. He was, however, relieved of his command and Hooker was appointed to succeed him. It was the saddest Christmas the North was ever to experience.

[52] Gordon, *Reminiscences, op. cit.,* p. III.

# Chapter VIII

## 1863

The new year opened with the formal proclamation on January 1 by Lincoln that the slaves in such States or parts of States as were still in rebellion "are, and henceforward shall be, free," adding that "I hereby enjoin upon the people so declared to be free to abstain from all violence, unless in necessary self-defence; and I recommend to them that, in all cases when allowed, they labor faithfully for wages." Although, as we have noted, the effect was to infuriate the South and was not altogether favorable politically in the North when the first announcement had been made in September, the result of the discussion in England during the following weeks had been to clarify public opinion in that country. Even if we allow that public mass meetings can be engineered and that there were many held in favor of the South as well as of the North, there can be little doubt of the increasing fervor of those in favor of the latter; and Adams, the American Minister, who never took a rosy view of affairs, felt that the tide of English opinion had turned definitely away from the wish for Southern success.

Of course, the upper classes and most of the newspapers which voiced their views were still for the Confederacy, but it is notable that in defending the South such journals as *The London Times* and *The Saturday Review* had now also to come out in plain and unvarnished defence of slavery also. Both papers began to quote the Bible as upholding the institution, but the English people on the whole were in favor of freedom. The Census of 1860 had shown approximately 4,000,000 slaves in the United States, increasing at the rate of about twenty per cent every decade, indicating about 8,000,000 by 1900, unless the natural increase declined. If the North won the war this enormous mass of humanity would be freed, for although the proclamation did not free those in the loyal border States there could be no doubt that slavery as an institution was doomed throughout the entire nation if all the slaves in the Confederacy were freed and the States brought back into the Union. Slavery could have but a short life after that hidden in nooks and corners. That other factors entered into England's refusal to side with the South is quite true, but the stark fact noted above was of powerful influence in a nation which had freed all its own slaves a generation earlier. By the end of the year, the Confederacy had withdrawn its representatives from England, cancelled the exequaturs of British consuls in the South, and made a complete break with that power. King Cotton had crashed from his throne, and the only hope of foreign help lay in Napoleon's Mexican schemes.

At the beginning of 1863, however, although there was intense anxiety over the possible fate of Vicksburg, against which Grant was manœuvring, the South was still hopeful. There was much disaffection in the North where the remnants of the Democratic party, shorn of that important part of its strength which had lain in the Southern States, was politically opposed to Lincoln and all his policies. Moreover, the third year of the war was bringing weariness to many. Those opposed to the administration and in favor of peace—the "Copperheads" and various secret societies—with certain newspapers combating the government of Lincoln bulked much larger in Southern, and even Northern, opinion than they deserved. At the end of January a clerk in the Southern War Office set down in his journal as his honest opinion that "there are indications of a speedy peace, although we are environed by sea and by land as menacingly as ever. . . . All over the North, and especially in the Northwest, the people are clamoring for peace, and denouncing the Lincoln Emancipation Proclamation. I have no doubt, if the war continues throughout the year, we shall have the spectacle of more Northern men fighting against the United States Government than slaves fighting against the South.[1]

Moreover, at the beginning of the year the price of slaves (perhaps since Lincoln's proclamation the most sensitive barometer of Southern belief in success we could have) was holding up fairly well. In Charleston early in February *The Mercury* reports the sale of sixty-three negroes in a lot and also "several single negroes at prices ranging from $1600 to $1880 for prime fellows, and $1200 to $1360 for prime wenches." As gold had by then risen to about three for one in Confederate currency, we have to divide these prices by that figure, but even so, considering the business stagnation and the problem of feeding, confidence in the future of the institution and of the Confederacy would seem to have been rather strong.[2]

The flotation of a foreign loan of $15,000,000 early in the year through the Paris house of Erlanger & Cie., may have helped the hopeful feeling, though it should not have done so. The bonds, which bore interest at seven per cent, were bought by the French firm under secret agreement at seventy-seven to be sold at ninety, and could be exchanged for New Orleans middling cotton at six cents a pound if desired, provided the buyer could get it out of the Confederacy. Cotton was then selling at over forty-two cents a pound in England, but in spite of this the bonds fell in price, and the Confederacy wasted about $6,000,000 in gold trying to support the market. By the end of the year

---

[1] *Rebel War Clerk's Diary, op. cit.,* vol. I, p. 249.
[2] *Charleston Mercury,* Feb. 6, 1863; Schwab, *Confederate States, op. cit.,* p. 167.

the price was as low as thirty-seven, which would indicate an extremely tight blockade, as otherwise the purchaser would be getting cotton at about two cents a pound less freight. Either the blockade was genuinely effective or the shrewdest business men in England and France were losing the opportunity of making fortunes.

All bonds of the Confederacy fell very heavily in the year, which was, in fact, disastrous for Southern finances. Before its end, the Confederacy's European cash resources, which had never been great, were wholly exhausted, although *The London Times* and *The Economist* had claimed that the Erlanger bonds were more valuable than those of the Federal Government. As had been the case in the colonies in the Revolution, taxation bore only a small proportion to the total cost of the Confederate Government, paper money being largely relied upon. In his report on January 10, the Southern Secretary of the Treasury had pointed out the inevitable result of a redundant currency. "By a law as invariable as any law of physical nature," he said, "prices rise or fall with the actual volume of the whole currency. Neither skill nor power can vary the result."

When he wrote, it took three dollars in paper to buy one in gold; by the end of the year it took twenty. The rise in prices and cost of living which ensued was due not only to this factor but to scarcity of foreign articles owing to the blockade and of domestic articles in larger centres owing to the breakdown of transportation and distribution. The disastrous results of all factors were shown by the rise in the expenses of the Confederate Government from seventy millions annually in November, 1861, to fifteen hundred millions estimated for 1864 at its beginning. Of the more than six hundred millions raised for the use of the government in the first nine months of 1863 only five came from taxation.

All contemporary Southern diaries and letters are filled

with the account of prices and domestic suffering, from now until the end of the war. By February 1 white wheat was selling at $4.50 a bushel as compared with $1.50 before the war and flour at $22 a barrel as compared with $7.50, which almost exactly measured the depreciation of Confederate money at three to one for gold at the moment. Many other things, however, had already risen in far higher proportion. Cotton sheeting had gone up at the rate of eight to one; coarse shoes ten to one; sweet potatoes six to one; nails per pound fifteen to one. By November flour was $110 a barrel which was about seventy-five times pre-war prices though at the same time it took only fifteen paper dollars to buy one gold dollar. As in America there has been a demand for inflation and paper money about once in each generation, it is interesting to follow the course of the Confederacy in which, as in the American colonies and recently in Germany, the experiment was carried through until paper became worthless. Secretary Memminger's biographer, writing in 1893, noted that he would suggest to certain political economists who were then "advocating an indefinite expansion of the currency of the United States, that the study of the reports of Mr. Memminger to the Confederate Congress will give them an answer to their theories, not only logical and perfect, but which has been approved by the experience of the ages."

What happened was that the quantitative theory of money worked out, as Memminger feared, to a certain extent. That is to say, the minimum rise in the price of commodities was fully equal to the depreciation of the currency, but most rises went far beyond even that. This was partly due to scarcity and partly to speculation and profiteering. In imported and manufactured goods there was a real scarcity, as we have noted above, and there was also the difficulty of distribution, but as the fall in the value of the paper money became accelerated, people, as always under such conditions, held back the goods they had for sale hoping to get higher prices, while others sought to buy goods, not for use, but to hold for speculation. A false demand was imposed upon a false scarcity, and prices soared.

Wages and salaries, however, cannot keep up with the quick changes in the speculative market for commodities, while incomes derived from bonds and mortgages remain hopelessly rigid. On the farms and plantations, not ravaged by the troops of either side, there was still ample food and comfort of many sorts, but the condition in the cities became deplorable. In April there was a food riot in Richmond, and stores were looted. In July the war clerk we have quoted wrote: "We are in a half starved condition. I have lost twenty pounds, and my wife and children are emaciated to some extent."[3] In January, 1864, *The Whig* gave the figures for a government clerk on a salary of $1500. "This gentleman," it said, "rents an unfurnished room for which he pays $50 a month. There goes $600 of his salary. He cannot afford a fire. Since the first day of May, he has not sat down with [his three small sons] to one meal except when asked to share the hospitable board of a friend. Their only food is dry bread, and this costs $2 a day, and here goes $730 more of his salary. The sum of $170 remains for the tuition and clothing for the boys, and the wardrobe of the gentleman himself. Observe that father and boys must not think of getting sick."[4] As to clothing we may note that in November a suit of clothes had already risen to $700 and a pair of boots to $200. "We are a shabby looking lot now—gaunt and many in rags," wrote Jones. In August he had written, "we are used to wounds and death; but can hardly bear starvation and nakedness." This is what a depreciating currency invariably does to the man of small means and the middle class.

On the other hand, there was much mismanagement in the

[3] *Rebel War Clerk's Diary, op. cit.,* vol. I, p. 381.
[4] *Richmond Whig,* January 9, 1864.

Commissary Department of the army, and many speculators were growing rich fast. Although in November the fields were full of corn, Lee had to warn Davis that for the previous five days he had received only three pounds of corn per horse for his forces and that "at this rate, the horses will die and cannot do hard work." Shopkeepers in Richmond were rapacious and cold-blooded. Jones reports the case of a woman who went into a Carey Street shop to buy a barrel of flour. When told the price, she said, "My God, how can I pay such prices? I have seven children; what shall I do?" The shopkeeper answered, "I don't know, madam, unless you eat your children."[5] The contrast between that and the entry on the next page of the journal as to the gambling establishments is characteristic of war times and a falling currency. The gambling hells, Jones noted, were at last being broken up temporarily by the legislature, "and the furniture of their gorgeous saloons is being sold at auction. Some idea of the number of these establishments may be formed from an estimate (in *The Examiner*) of the cost of the entertainment prepared for visitors being not less than $10,000 daily. Their agents bought the best articles offered for sale in the markets, and never hesitated to pay the most exorbitant prices."

Although some were making fortunes in the South, eventually to be worthless unless transferred into a foreign currency, the difference between an almost wholly agricultural society and one which was also largely commercial and industrial when at war had clearly become manifest by 1863. It is almost cruel to compare the rising economic fortunes of the North with the falling ones of the South, but it was due at this period not to great victories in the field but to the more varied and different type of civilization. Nature was lavish with discoveries of new gold and silver mines and especially of petroleum, but it was in the

[5] *Rebel War Clerk's Diary, op. cit.*, vol. II, pp. 96, 78.

main the training and willingness of the Northern business man to make the most of all natural resources and opportunities which made the difference. It was typical of the Old South that in 1870 the present great steel and iron city of Birmingham was a mere cotton field on which two railroads happened to cross. War makes a varied, rapid, and high-priced demand for many sorts of goods. But partly due to the blockade and partly to the deliberate policy of the Confederate Government, the chief source of revenue of the South—cotton—was wiped out, whereas to a considerable extent its two greatest items of capital, its $1,500,000,-000 invested in slaves and $1,400,000,000 in land, ceased to produce business profits. As for manufacturing, we have already seen how although in the Birmingham district it possessed one of the best and cheapest locations for producing iron in the world, it had to rely upon Europe for the iron for its vessels, and could not produce an entire locomotive. About the 1st of May, 1863, the presidents of the various Southern roads met at Richmond and calculated that it would take 49,500 tons of rails to keep the roads fit merely for military purposes whereas the iron works at Richmond and Atlanta could produce only 20,000 a year. Three months later the president of the Central Railroad asked for protection for the four bridges near Hanover Junction as, if they were destroyed, it would take months to replace them. To a great extent in the South, the war instead of stimulating industries, giving employment at high wages, creating profits and new liquid capital, merely cut off supplies.

In the North the situation was wholly different. No Southern statesman appears to have envisaged the possible and almost certain contrast between the sections before the war. The belief that the North would not fight; or, if it did, that the war would be quickly won by the South; or, failing that, that "King Cotton" would win by forcing the rest of

# 1863

the world to accept intervention or ruin, blinded them to all other factors. But by 1863 the North was fairly humming with business activity. The agricultural West, thanks in part to three successive crop failures in Europe, was extremely prosperous. The extensive building of railroads, which had been one of the causes of the panic of 1857, gave the Western farmers ample facilities for getting their crops to market; and the closing of the Mississippi caused them no loss and consequently exerted no pressure. Immigration from Europe was fast building up new communities, and the rapid development can be discerned in the figures for the chief Northwestern centre, Chicago, which during the war increased in population from 109,000 to 178,000; built 7000 buildings in 1863 and 8000 in 1864; and laid twenty miles of sidewalks in one year.

Not only war supplies but the demands of a rapidly expanding country made manufacturing prosperous. The farmers, hampered for laborers by loss of men in the army, looked with a more favorable eye on farming machinery. The sewing machine came in to stimulate the garment trade on a large scale. The shoe machinery devised in the first year of the war multiplied a hundredfold the output of each operative. More patents were granted in the North alone in 1864 than ever before for the entire Union of earlier days. The railroads, carrying emigrants, machinery, and other goods west, and huge crops east, rose from near bankruptcy to great prosperity; and stimulated the industries which in turn supplied them. Munitions, uniforms, and all war material provided industry with a colossal business and often scandalous profits. Throughout 1863 the North, instead of importing, was manufacturing 3000 rifles a day. "Shoddy" millionaires, with fortunes running to $20,000,-000, were springing up. Young Henry Lee Higginson, speaking of prominent Boston families, whose names are represented only by initials by the socially considerate Bliss

Perry in his biography, says, "the list of incomes for last year [in Boston] over $25,000 has just been published, and gives one a start. These people have been reaping this harvest while we have defended them, but few remember it. Think of $365,000 (A), $188,000 (B), $150,000 (C), ... the heirs of (G) $170,000."[6]

In some cases, labor suffered somewhat from the increased cost of living, as the North had also issued paper money, but the rise in prices was nothing as compared with the South, only one and a half paper dollars being required to buy a gold dollar in the North at the end of 1863 as against twenty in the South. The new banking system devised for the North was also a stabilizing factor for both business and government bonds. The prosperity and confidence were reflected in such facts as that during 1863 Lincoln's government had no difficulty in raising $500,000,-000; that the people willingly bore heavy taxation of many sorts which they had not been used to before; that savings banks showed great increases both in deposits and number of depositors; and that the volume of life insurance doubled during the conflict. Although the apparent prosperity of war times is always largely illusory, owing to the accompanying enormous destruction of capital, on the part of victor as well as vanquished, the Union was adding hugely to its population, its industrial equipment, its liquid capital and future possibilities, whereas the Confederacy, even apart from the final collapse of its currency and the loss of its slave property, was adding but slightly to the variety or strength of its economic life and was actually losing part of its market for its chief product.

All of this was ominous for the South if both contestants could hold out. Nevertheless, the first large military test of strength of the year was a distinct victory for the Confederacy, though it was to be practically the last.

[6] Bliss Perry, *Life and Letters of Henry Lee Higginson* (Boston, 1921), p. 236.

After Burnside had been retired, following the diastrous battle of Fredericksburg, General Joseph Hooker had been put in his place. The Federal administration was still searching for a competent commander. Hooker was a good disciplinarian and organizer but he could not compare with either Lee or Jackson. He had, however, brought up the morale of the army, which had suffered badly. We shall discuss the problem of desertion in the armies of both sections later, but it was typical of each that Hooker found, when he took command, that there were nearly 3000 commissioned officers and almost 82,000 non-commissioned officers and privates absent from his force, mostly without leave.

During the winter the armies confronted one another across the Rappahannock, and as usual fraternizing went on among the men at the front. The pickets were quite near to one another across the narrow stream, and one night the Confederate officer in charge at one point invited the Union lieutenant, who told the story, to come across and attend a dance they had got up with some country girls. After some hesitation, he consented, and at the appointed hour the "Rebel" paddled over in a boat, with a suit of civilian clothes for the Union lieutenant, who spent a very pleasant evening in the company of the men whom he might have to fight at any moment. It was fortunate for both officers that there was no unexpected call to arms that night! On another occasion, a Yankee band came down to the river and played "Dixie," the Confederates across the stream cheering lustily. They then played "Yankee Doodle" and the Yankees cheered. Next they played "Home, Sweet Home," and the voices from both sides joined in.

By spring, Hooker had brought his army up to about 133,000, whereas Lee, still at Fredericksburg, had less than 60,000, his army having been depleted of some 20,000 for an expedition under Longstreet against Lee's advice.

Nevertheless the Confederate position was a strong one, and Hooker decided to divide his army, each part striking at Lee's supplies and communications rather than making a frontal attack. In this way, he hoped to force him to retreat and attack him while in confusion. In spite of greatly inferior forces, Lee and Jackson planned one of the boldest strokes of the war, dividing the Confederate army, so that one part should frighten off Sedgwick, who was making a feint against Lee's rear, another section under Jackson to strike against the Federals near Chancellorsville, and Lee himself to attack and force Hooker back. By May 1, the Union general, having made his dispositions, advanced against Lee whom he had hoped to demoralize. Instead of finding the Confederate general in retreat, he found him advancing against himself, and uncertain of what it meant, Hooker suddenly prepared for defence instead of, as his advisers wished, continuing the offensive he had so elaborately prepared. The following day Jackson fell on the Federal right and threw it into complete confusion. By the next morning "Chancellorsville" (which consisted of one house) was in possession of the Confederates, and Hooker had fallen back. On the 4th, Lee with superior numbers drove Sedgwick across the Rappahannock, and on the 6th, the entire Union army had been forced to retreat, an army of 130,000, had Hooker used all his men, defeated by the superior ability of a man at the head of 60,000.

The victory, however, cost the Confederacy dear. A little before 9 on the evening of the 2d, Stonewall Jackson had ridden with a few officers to reconnoitre ahead of his troops toward the Federal position, which had been abandoned. When only sixty yards or so in front of the 18th North Carolina Regiment, standing in the trees, a few of the Federal infantry, trying to find their way through the woods, got near the Southern lines, and skirmishing began in the dark. After an unexpected shot rang out, Jackson and his group spurred toward their own men, but mistaken for Federals, were met by a fatal volley of rifle bullets. Jackson was struck three times, one bullet severing the main artery in his arm. The error discovered, he was carried to the rear, and the arm amputated, but ten days later he died from pneumonia, and the Confederacy had lost its greatest soldier with the possible exception of Lee. The two men, moreover, had worked together with the perfect harmony of body and mind. We need not enter upon the controversy as to which was greater in planning; but in executing plans Lee had been able to count upon Jackson with absolute certainty, and there was no one to take his place. Lee was soon to undertake another offensive movement against the North and move into Pennsylvania, only to meet disaster, and from that tragic May evening, when Jackson was killed by his own men, there was to be no great victory, except Chickamauga in the West, anywhere for the South. Before following Lee northward, we may emphasize again some aspects of the war, the first of great modern wars in which the whole population was involved.

In 1863, a Richmond man wrote: "How often have I and thousands in our youth expressed the wish . . . to have partaken of the excitements of war! Such is the romance or enchantment which 'distance lends' to the view. Now we see and feel the horrors of war, and we are unanimous in the wish . . . that neither we nor our posterity may ever be spectators or participants in another war."[7] Yet each generation has to learn the lesson over again, and even now a new one is growing up which has not known the horrors of the last Great War and which begins again to dream of romance and glamour.

We have already spoken of the suffering caused in the homes of ordinary people when paper money gets out of control; and have tried to bring out, even at the risk of

[7] *Rebel War Clerk's Diary, op. cit.,* vol. II, p. 88.

stirring the embers of now dying fires, the hatred which editors do their best to spread in such crises of nations. Both in the Spanish War and the World War our own losses were so slight compared with the size of the entire population, that we did not realize what it means, as Europe realized in 1914–18 and our fathers and mothers realized in 1861–65, to receive day after day news of the deaths of those nearest and dearest. In the diary of one Southern woman in May, we read in closely successive entries, "General Paxton, of the Stonewall Brigade, was killed." "Two more of the dear ones over whose youth we so anxiously watched have fallen —Hill Carter of Shirley, and Benjamin White of Charleston." "Major Channing Price and Colonel Thomas Garnett are gone." "Sad, sad tidings were brought to our cottage this morning. Washington, the youngest and darling son of our dear friend, Mrs. Stuart, has fallen."[8] Another woman wrote: "It seems we are never out of the sound of the Dead March in Saul. It comes and it comes, until I feel inclined to close my ears and scream." In the North it was the same. In the next chapter we shall speak of other aspects—of the destruction of homes by invading armies— when we have to describe the desolation wrought by a Sheridan and a Sherman.

But what of the soldier at the front? To those who have never known war it seems a glorious thing—uniforms, banners flying, martial music, battle, and a hero's life or death. A Pickett's charge is magnificent but battles are comparatively rare, while the day-to-day life drags on. But even after a battle there are pictures which most brief histories do not present. Let us look at a few vignettes from this war period of our long national tragedy. In the Seven Days battles were two Yale boys in the Confederate army, Judson and Carey Smith of Mississippi. Carey was killed. "Judson went almost deranged," wrote a friend and ob-

---

[8] *Diary of a Southern Refugee, op. cit.,* pp. 210 f.

server. "Yes, I think altogether deranged. He bore his dead brother out of the woods. . . . He kept the body folded to his bosom, and all through the night his comrades heard Judson kissing Carey and talking to him and petting him, and then sobbing as if his heart would break." Finally he allowed the body to be taken to Richmond, and next day when the terrible charge was made at Malvern Hill, and the troops turned back, Judson did not turn back but walked into the solid shot and shell, and was never heard of more. When his father heard of the death of his two sons, he joined Price's army as a private, and at Iuka did as Judson had done.[9]

"Walking over Malvern Hill the morning after the battle, I saw two young Federal soldiers lying dead, side by side, their heads upon the same knapsack, and their arms about each other. They were evidently brothers and enough alike to be twins. . . . One had first been wounded, perhaps killed, and when the other was struck he managed to get to his dead or dying brother, placed the knapsack under his head, and then lying down by him and resting his head on the same rude pillow, slipped his dying arms around his brother's body and slept in this embrace."[10]

After the battle of Williamsburg, "A number of wounded Federal prisoners were brought up in an ambulance and laid temporarily on the grass. . . . Among them was a poor wretch shot through the bowels, who was rolling on the ground in excruciating agony and beseeching the bystanders to put him out of his misery . . . when a couple of Turcos, or Louisiana Tigers . . . came up and peered over the circle of onlookers. Suddenly one of them pushed through the ring, saying, 'Put you out of your misery? Certainly, sir!' and . . . brained the man with the butt of his musket."[11]

[9] Stiles, *Four Years Under Marse Robert*, op. cit., p. 117.
[10] *Ibid.*                    [11] *Ibid.*, p. 80.

After the battle of Cold Harbor, a boy Union soldier wrote: "The poverty of the South was plainly shown by the clothing and equipment of her dead. These dead men were hardly stiff when we saw them. All of their pockets had been turned inside out. That night, while searching for fresh clean water, I found several dead cavalrymen in the woods, where they had probably crawled after being wounded. I struck a match so as to see one of these men plainly, and was greatly shocked to see large black beetles eating the corpse. I looked at no more dead that night."[12]

Again, "The killed and wounded of the first day's fight lay unburied and uncared for between the lines. The stench of the dead men became unbearable, and finally a flag of truce was sent out. There was a cessation of hostilities to bury the dead and to succour the wounded. I went out to the ground in front of our picket line to talk to the Confederate soldiers and to trade sugar and coffee for tobacco. Every corpse I saw was as black as coal. It was not possible to remove them. The wounded must have suffered horribly before death relieved them, lying there exposed to the southern sun o' days, and being eaten alive by beetles o'night."[13]

One quotation I have as to the ravages of maggots and other vermin in the wounds of those left on the fields is too horrible to quote. What was possible was always done on both sides, but the suffering, even in improvised hospitals, was great. "The sorriest sights upon a battle-field," writes another soldier, "are in those dreadful field hospitals, established in barns, under large tents and in out-houses. The screams and groans of the poor fellows undergoing amputation are sometimes dreadful—and then the sight of arms and legs surrounding these places, as they are thrown

[12] Frank Wilkeson, *Recollections of a Private Soldier* (New York, 1887), p. 125.
[13] *Ibid.*, p. 139.

into great piles, is something one that has seen the results of battle can never forget."[14]

Let us take the fighting in May of '64. "Warm and sultry," notes another soldier. "The stench from the dead between the lines is terrible." The next day: "The stench from the dead is sickening and terrible." On the 13th, after the fight at the "Bloody Angle," he writes "the sight of the enemy's dead is something terrible. There are *three* dead lines of battle a half mile more or less in length—men killed in every conceivable manner. The wounded are fairly bound in by the dead. . . . No wonder from its present appearance this place has been christened the 'Bloody Angle' and the 'Slaughter Pen.' For several hundred yards—fully a half mile or more—in the edge of the heavy oak forest of immense trees skirting an open field, the enemy's works are faultlessly strong of large oak logs and dirt shoulder high with traverses fifty feet back every sixty feet or so. This breastwork is filled with dead and wounded where they fell, several feet deep nearly to the top in front, extending for forty feet more or less back. . . . Think of such a mass of dead! Hundreds and hundreds piled top of each other! . . . Many of the bodies have turned black, the stench is terrible, and the sight shocking beyond description. I saw several wounded men in the breastworks buried under their dead, just move a hand a little as it stuck up through the interstices above the dead bodies that buried the live ones otherwise completely from sight. . . . Could anything in Hades be worse?"[15]

Let us follow the Confederate army on its retreat from Corinth as seen by a young officer. "In this ride of twelve miles alongside the routed army, I saw more of human agony and woe than I trust I will ever again be called on to witness. . . . Here was a long line of wagons loaded with

[14] Owen, *In Camp and Battle, op. cit.,* p. 45.
[15] L. A. Abbott, *Personal Recollections and Civil War Diary* (Burlington, Vt., 1908), p. 58.

wounded, piled in like bags of grain, groaning and cursing, while the mules plunged on in mud and water belly-deep. . . . A cold, drizzling rain commenced about nightfall, and soon came harder and faster, then turned to pitiless, blinding hail. . . . I passed long wagon trains filled with wounded and dying soldiers, without even a blanket to shield them from the driving sleet and hail. . . . Some three hundred men died . . . and their bodies were thrown out to make room for others."[16]

It must be recalled that practically all men in both armies were drawn from civil life and unaccustomed to the sort of existence which they had to lead. Most of them became quickly inured to the ordinary hardships of cold and mud and heat and the physical life in general. "No hardship, or enforced self-denial of food, or rest, or comfort," wrote one, "was as hard to bear" as the lice, or the "cootie" of the World War later. "One of the horrors of this kind of life" wrote another, "is that the men's bodies and clothes are literally alive and nothing can be done to relieve them as they have no change of clothing and seldom any opportunity to bathe. The officers if they exert themselves and change their clothes frequently can escape the affliction, but the poor private drags his tormented carcass in utter helplessness to the end of the campaign."[17] "I'm so tired and lousy," wrote another, "I do wish we could stay somewhere long enough to wash and boil our underclothes. However, the general officers are as lousy as the rest of us. . . . I hope this won't shock any one when they read it. . . . It's part of the history of the civil war, and should be recorded."[18]

Another hardship was the lack or poor quality of the

[16] W. G. Stevenson, *Thirteen Months in the Rebel Army,* quoted by A. B. Hart, *American History Told by Contemporaries* (New York, 1917), vol. IV, p. 281.

[17] Lieutenant Colonel Samuel Merrill, "Letters from a Civil War Officer," *Miss. Valley Hist. Review,* vol. XIV, p. 520.

[18] Abbott, *Personal Recollections, op. cit.,* p. 61.

clothes, the former felt more in the South and the latter in the North. By the end of 1862 Longstreet reported over 6000 of his troops without shoes, and it is no wonder that after battles Northern dead were stripped of shoes and other clothing. Even Lee's army appeared like "tatterdemalions" when they invaded Pennsylvania so that they frightened children.

Owing to better organization of the Commissariat Department, more abundant resources and better transportation, the food was usually more ample in the Northern than the Southern army, but as usual the rascality of contractors and inspectors added frequently to the quite unnecessary misery of the soldier in the form of bad meat, hard tack filled with maggots or weevils, and other inedible stuff for which the government paid high prices. In the Southern armies there was frequent scarcity and, later in the war, even almost starvation. The Confederate soldier like the Northern, and indeed all soldiers everywhere, looked upon "pigs and poultry, fruit and corn, vegetables and fence-rails" as his "lawful perquisites." Looting, of minor and major sorts, naturally increased when operating in enemy country, and also when the quality of the troops declined with the progress of the war. On the whole the Confederate army contained a larger leaven of the social upper class, but in 1863 *The Richmond Whig* was complaining bitterly of the actions of Southern troops even among their own people. In the fighting against Pope, many people declared, it asserted, that "our own men were worse than the troops of McClellan. . . . No amount of devotion to the cause sufficed to protect the Southern citizen from the Southern soldier, and when complaint was made of fences torn down and burnt, of gardens robbed of every vegetable and trampled into mud, of outhouses stripped of doors and planks, the reception too often given to the complainant was a volley of oaths. . . . After Fredericksburg was vacated by the Yankees, the Southern soldiers sent to protect the town stripped the battered houses of what little remained to them . . . and in that vast wilderness which now stretches from the Upper Rappahannock to the Potomac—the same story of pilfering by the Southern soldiery is told."[19]

In any of our wars, from that of Revolution down, it is a mistake to think that every soldier was a noble patriot. In all our wars we have had a large number of them, fortunately, but it is not the mere fact of service but of how a man carried himself in service and what he was as a man which alone can be a matter of pride to his descendants, a point too often lost to sight by patriotic societies. By 1863, owing to conscription, bounties, the hiring of substitutes, war weariness, and other causes the character of the individual soldier had been averaged to a much lower level than at the beginning when patriots on both sides, young and old, had flocked to their respective colors from a sense of duty. In the North a young boy of sixteen, seized with the war fever, gave a vivid picture of what he found when he enlisted. When he joined his "regiment" he found "eight hundred or a thousand ruffians, closely guarded by heavy lines of sentinels . . . to keep them from running away"—all bounty jumpers and scoundrels. A recruit's standing among them was based on the number of times he had got a bounty and escaped. "If there was a man in all that shameless crew who had enlisted from patriotic motives, I did not see him. There was not a man of them who was not eager to run away. . . . Almost to a man they were bullies and cowards, and almost to a man they belong to the criminal classes."[20] This may have been a very exceptional case, but it is war in its later stages.

The Southern army, however, was also declining in quality. Straggling and desertion were becoming extremely se-

[19] Issue of March 30, 1863.
[20] Wilkeson, *Recollections, op. cit.,* pp. 2 f.

rious, although they did not reach the proportions of the next two years. What is more notable is the character of these deserters. *The Richmond Enquirer* stated that although the Southerners were always complaining of the Union army there were numerous ruffians in the Confederate one. From Bladen County, North Carolina, came the complaint that "great difficulty is experienced in a portion of that county from the acts of lawless deserters from the army. . . . There are 17 to 26 desperadoes of this class, armed to the teeth, rambling through the county, putting at defiance the laws of God and man by house-breaking, plundering, killing stock, insulting decent women and contaminating the slaves."[21] Such items came with increasing frequency from various parts of the South.

These desperadoes helped to make prison life a hell for the soldiers of either side who came to be confined in the prison camps as the war went on, and we may here refer to one of the most bitter and lasting controversies of the conflict, that concerning the treatment of prisoners. As we have seen, the Constitutional theory of the North at the very beginning of the war required that those in arms against the United States be considered rebels, which complicated the problem of their exchange or parole as ordinary prisoners of war, although no prisoner ever suffered the extreme penalty under the theory. For long, unwilling to make any agreement for a general exchange which would seem to recognize the independent government of the South, Lincoln's administration declined to do more than make occasional special exchanges of individuals or groups on the score of humanity, to which method the South finally refused to agree. The protracted negotiations wrought feeling on both sides to a high pitch, and ended in practical deadlock. Meanwhile prisoners on both sides accumulated, and suffered much in the concentration camps of each

[21] Issue of April 28, 1863.

section, all of them too frequently over-crowded and supervised by incompetent men.

We have spoken of the "war psychosis," which, as one writer expresses it, seemingly makes it "necessary for the supporters of one cause to identify their entire personality with that cause, to identify their opponents with the opposing cause, and to hate the supporters of the enemy cause with a venom which counterbalances their devotion to their own."[22] Anything which makes the enemy appear devilish makes one's own cause appear more spotless and just. It is the sort of thing which made us believe the Germans were cutting off the hands of the Belgians and which after the Confederate disaster at Gettysburg led *The Richmond Whig* to publish the statement that the Yankees were cutting off the hands of the Southern prisoners.[23]

Conditions in a prison concentration camp are always likely to be difficult. The ennui, the sanitary arrangements where large numbers of men are suddenly herded together, the change of diet from what they are accustomed to have to that of the enemy, the fact that officers of high standing and ability are not likely to be kept from the front for such commands, the sudden access of large numbers after a victory, and other causes frequently conduce to hardship when none is intended by the higher authorities. Moreover, prison conditions lend themselves easily to war propaganda against the enemy. Such opportunities were used to the full both during and after the war. Especially in the North, Libby Prison in Richmond and Andersonville in Georgia became names to conjure horror with. The conditions at the latter were extremely bad, 29,000 prisoners being herded together with insufficient preparations, housing and guarding. A report by Colonel Chandler, C. S. A., who was sent to report when nearly 50 per cent of the prisoners were dead or dying,

[22] W. B. Hesseltine, *Civil War Prisons: A Study of War Psychology* (Ohio State University Press, 1930), p. 172.
[23] Issue of August 12, 1863.

was made too late to reach President Davis until the end of the war. On the other hand, Northern prisons, with less excuse than the Southern, owing to greater resources of all kinds, were also bad. At Camp Douglas it was shown that the inmates had no proper beds, were without change of clothing and covered with vermin, and that if the death rate continued the camp would be empty in less than a year. As one side and the other used conditions, actual or exaggerated, for propaganda, and individuals wrote their stories of treatment, belief of each contestant in the calculated inhumanity of the other grew. Probably the best summing up of the wide literature, filled with hatred and misrepresentations, on the subject is that about 26,000 Southern prisoners died in the North and 24,000 Union soldiers in the South, a proportion with reference to the totals about equal to that of the deaths from disease in the Union army. As Professor Channing has pointed out, "if these figures are anywhere near accurate, it would seem that each government cared for its enemy prisoners about as well as it cared for its own soldiers."[24] Unhappily, several things combined to keep alive the agitation in the North. The large literature of ex-prisoners which continued for a generation or more was due to the desire to recount the story of personal suffering, to need for personal gain, or to secure pensions from the Federal Government. Organizations were formed, such as "The Andersonville Survivors' Association" and the "National Ex-Prisoners of War Association," backing pension legislation, and, as too often happens with our patriotic societies, became more bent on showing the barbarity of the enemy and getting plums for members than on holding up examples of heroism or helping us to understand the past. The North continued bitter in attack, and in turn embittered the South by its accusations. The prison controversy bulked large in our tragedy, not a

[24] *History of the United States, op. cit.,* vol. VI, p. 439.

little of it filled with lies and forgeries with pensions as the goal. It was one of the many unhappy legacies of the war.

We must now return to the two armies facing each other in Virginia. Whether due to intemperance, as charged by several authorities, or from some other cause, "Fighting Joe Hooker" had suddenly become disinclined to fight. It was a surprising psychological change, but Lee had now to decide on his own next move. Beauregard again urged the West as the chief theatre of war but Lee, who always thought largely in terms of Virginia, was not impressed. The "Copperheads" and other defeatists had been showing increasing strength in the North and, as we shall see, there was to be serious resistance to the draft for more men in the summer. It was probably with a view to increasing the disaffection and war weariness in the Union that Lee, whose army since he had been rejoined by Longstreet numbered well on to 80,000, determined on another raid into Pennsylvania, although the military advisers of neither Davis nor Lee appear to have been enthusiastic over it. That Lee could maintain a long campaign in enemy country with numbers so heavily against him was impossible and even a raid, on so large a scale, was dangerous, though he calculated most of the possibilities to a nicety. He had, however, apparently come to underrate the power of the Union army from his experience with Pope, Burnside, and Hooker, and to rely too much on his own superior generalship. Moreover, he no longer had the assistance of his superb *alter ego* Jackson, of whom he had said that he had such implicit confidence in him that "I never troubled myself to give him detailed instructions. The most general suggestions were all that he needed." Of Lee, Jackson himself had said that "he is the only man I would follow blindfold." The particular combination worked admirably, but it may be questioned, when we compare the frequently verbal and general orders of Lee with the invariably written and specific ones of Grant, whether the great and constant reliance on Jackson's quick comprehension may not have been in that respect somewhat harmful to Lee.

Unlike Davis, Lee had long since given up hope of foreign intervention, although he had said on several occasions that without such intervention the South could not win. Writing to Davis on June 10, after he had started his army on its northern march, he said that the Confederacy's resources in men were constantly diminishing, and the disproportion between it and the Union constantly increasing. Apparently the invasion planned by him was a desperate throw, although carefully worked out. His plan was to use the Shenandoah and Cumberland Valleys as sheltered approaches to the heart of Pennsylvania, and then perhaps fight a decisive battle in the North, or at least frighten the public by his bold thrust.

The army was divided into three corps under Longstreet, Ewell, and Hill, and by June 26 all three had crossed the Potomac. The cavalry, under the lead of the brilliant General Stuart, had screened the earlier movements from Hooker, but after the Northern drive had become clear and the Washington authorities had in vain implored Hooker to take action, his request to be removed from his command was granted. His various delinquencies had proved too great and General George G. Meade was appointed in his stead. This had not been counted upon by Lee, who now had to deal with an abler opponent than in the past, and he also issued too vague an order to Stuart, as a result of which that dashing officer, fond of dangerous exploits and one of the conspicuous military figures of the South, actually passed between Meade's army and Washington. It was a daring but disastrous exploit, and in consequence of it Lee was deprived of his cavalry, the "eyes of the army," for ten days, until the very morning of Gettysburg.

It was characteristic of Lee that the first paragraph of this important order was taken up with directions that no private property should be seized, and his general orders for the expedition were to the same effect. In spite of this, Early, when the Confederates reached York, laid the town under contribution, seizing 1000 hats, 1200 pairs of shoes, three days' rations, and other property, including over $28,-000 in United States money.

Ewell had practically reached Harrisburg to attack the State capital when Lee found that Meade was in pursuit, and at once ordered all three of his corps commanders to concentrate at Gettysburg. Meade himself had chosen a position about thirteen miles away, but on July 1 advance troops of both armies came into accidental collision at Gettysburg. Had Hill known, as he would have if Stuart had been with him, that he was far stronger than the Federals at the moment, the whole result of the battle might have been different, and the Confederates might have won in detail, as the Federal army was strung out in lines of march for thirty miles. As it was, both armies had rapidly concentrated on a field which neither had chosen. Lee arrived in the afternoon when fighting had already begun, the Confederates being on the low height of Seminary Ridge and the Federals holding Cemetery Ridge and two small hills. Although, as Lee wrote in his report, he had had no intention of fighting a major battle so far from his base unless attacked, he now had no choice. Owing to the absence of his cavalry, he had come on the whole Union army unawares. In the face of them he could not retreat through the mountain pass into the Valley, and without adequate supplies in an enemy country he could not await attack or choose the place. He had over 76,000 men to feed, and could not forage in the face of a strong enemy ready to attack.

As a result of the first day's fighting the Federals were

overborne and so great was their confusion that it appeared like a disaster. In fact Northern historians admit that at this stage Gettysburg was a Confederate victory. Successive portions of the two armies, however, continued coming up to take part in the unplanned struggle. Meade's was farthest away and on the night of July 1–2 Lee decided on an attack before the full Union strength could arrive. Longstreet, always rather averse to attack, preferred a flank movement, but unquestionably Lee's plan was the only one which could have won victory, and Longstreet was ordered to attack at dawn and seize one of the hills, Little Round Top. Unfortunately he did not get into action until three in the afternoon, by which time the Federals were in sufficient strength not to be dislodged. Every war is followed by re-criminations between generals and their followers, and we need not enter into the controversy carried on with bitterness for years as to who lost the battle of Gettysburg for the South. General Longstreet denied that any order to attack at dawn was given, but perhaps we can say that if either Lee had given as specific orders in writing as did Grant, or had Stonewall Jackson been in Longstreet's place, the attack would inevitably have occurred. The delay, fatal to the South, appears to have derived from a combination of Lee's weakness and Longstreet's stubbornness.

By night no decision had been reached in the fighting, but Lee could not retreat. He had got himself in a trap. The following day it was proposed to break the Union centre, which happened to be on the lowest ground of the ridges, by a direct charge by Pickett's division, which had come up fresh, reinforced to between 12,000 and 13,000 men, and supported by the artillery. It was a desperate move but possibly the most glorious charge in history. Going to meet almost certain death, Pickett advanced with his men down the slope of Seminary Ridge and on to the little mile-wide plain which was defended on the other side by an overwhelmingly superior force of Federal troops on the height of the other slope. With flags flying, and in perfect order, the Confederate troops advanced as though on parade, while the Union artillery mowed them down. Halfway over was a small ravine in which they took shelter for just a moment, and then on again. As they got within musket range the carnage was colossal. A hundred actually got to the top of the ridge and planted the Confederate flag among the Federals, but the opposing numbers were too great, and Pickett ordered a retreat which was no less sanguinary than the attack. Of his own 5000 men, approximately 3400 were dead, wounded, or missing and the Federal General Hancock, who had been badly wounded, wrote in his report that "not a rebel was in sight upright when I left." The battle of Gettysburg was over, and more then 50,000 Americans were dead, wounded, or captured.

Meade made no effort to follow up his victory, and both shattered armies spent the Fourth of July in their own camps. That day Grant received the surrender of Vicksburg, and the tide of war had definitely turned. Unmolested, Lee slowly retreated to Virginia; Meade, who had done well at Gettysburg, letting him slip from his grasp without an effort to finish the work begun. As Lincoln wrote, the golden opportunity was allowed to pass and the war was indefinitely prolonged. Both Lee and Meade offered their resignations to their respective Presidents, but neither was accepted.

The star of a great general, that of Grant, was meanwhile rising in the West. Sherman's idea from the start had been to cut ever deeper at the *roots* of the Confederacy, whereas McClellan and those who believed in the Virginia seat of operations merely tried to lop off the *top*. Largely because of the location of the two capitals, public interest had centred in the East, and the West had had to "forage for itself." Nevertheless, there the two generals who were to give the final blows to the Confederacy had been steadily at work. With that air of profound wisdom which civilian editors assume in war, *The Tribune* had announced in the middle of 1862 that "it seems to us inexplicable that such a general as Mitchell should be in the shade, and such a one as Burnside holding a subordinate position, while such as Buell, Grant, etc., are presiding over important departments."[25]

It may be questioned whether, taking the whole psychological and political situation of the time into account, the West was the better theatre of operations or not. Recent English historians, such as Captain Liddell-Hart and Major General Fuller, would appear to over-stress the purely military aspect of the case. Lee with the strongest Confederate army was in the East. If the Federal Government had drained its resources there in order to attack in the West, it is more likely than otherwise that Lee instead of leaving his beloved Virginia to go West would have threatened Washington, Philadelphia, and possibly New York. The damaging effect, both at home and abroad, of the fall of any of those cities would have been incalculably dangerous to Northern hopes of victory. There would have been panic in the North and intervention from Europe. Grant and Sherman, however, went steadily on, and by the end of the year were to be hammering at the hard nut of Vicksburg.

That city, which stood on high bluffs overlooking the Mississippi, was of the utmost importance. It was the only rail and river junction between Memphis and New Orleans, both in Union hands, and also served as the connecting link between the sections of the Confederacy east and west of the river. The rail line running from Vicksburg eastward intersected the north and south lines of the Confederate system, and if it could be captured that system would begin to unravel and the South would be open to invasion from the

[25] August 15, 1862.

river, and split in two. The city, however, had been strongly fortified, and the marshy ground to the north made it
peculiarly difficult of attack by a large force.

During the late months of 1862 various attempts had
been made against the city without success, when Grant decided to take all the operations into his own hands, and in
March undertook to carry his troops down the river below
Vicksburg and then march on the city from the South instead of the North. By early April he had about 33,000
men at Grand Gulf, about fifty miles below Vicksburg, the
latter place being held by Pemberton with 40,000 men.
General Joseph Johnston, however, had started with about
15,000 more to the relief of the city by way of the railway running through Jackson. By a quick move, and for
the first time leaving his supplies behind and living on
the country, Grant captured the city of Jackson, an important railway junction before Johnston got there. The
Federal army, outnumbering each of the others, was thus
between them, and Johnston, foiled, could only try to march
around farther to the North to join Pemberton, whom he
ordered out of the city, and to make a joint attack on Grant.
After a few days' delay, however, Pemberton, not realizing
that Grant was subsisting on the country and believing that
he must have a line of communication, decided to march
south to cut it, and so force Grant back for its protection.
Realizing too late his mistake, he returned toward Vicksburg but by that time Grant had made it impossible for
Johnston to join him, and thereafter Pemberton had to depend upon himself. Retiring within his fortifications on
May 18, he remained besieged until the final surrender on
July 4.

Two assaults by Grant were easily repulsed, but the
Union siege lines were extended northward to the Yazoo
River until they entirely encircled the city, and as Grant's
reinforcements brought his force up to about 75,000, and

supplies were easily carried down the river, the fate of the besieged became merely a question of time and starvation. Johnston had been able to gather only 30,000 and was held by Sherman when he again attempted to relieve Pemberton at the end of June. Meanwhile the plight of the besieged, both military and civilian, was pitiable. The constant bombardment, the fear of mines and assaults, and the lack of food all combined to wear down the strength of those in the doomed city. The defence was heroic, and a Confederate general records the chivalry shown by both sides, in spite of the fight to the death. The men in the front trenches, both besiegers and besieged, wrote Gordon, would now and then call "to each other to stop firing for a while, that they 'wanted to get out into fresh air!' The call was always heeded, and both sides poured out of their bomb-proofs like rats from their holes when the cats are away. And whenever an order came to open fire, or the time had expired, they would call: 'Hello, there, Johnnie,' or 'Hello, there, Yank,' as the case might be. 'Get into your holes now; we are going to shoot.' "[26] It is of the essence of our tragedy that men of that sort, on both sides, should have had to shoot, and shoot to kill.

Finally the soldiers' rations within the beleaguered city were cut down to one small piece of bacon and one biscuit a day, on which it was impossible to stand the strain and live. Some became so weak they could not even lift their spades to work on the entrenchments. Civilians ate rats, and the army had come to the end by July 2 and was ripe for mutiny. The men had no longer even the mere physical strength to repel an assault or to try to cut their way out. There was nothing to be done but to surrender, and on the 3d, Pemberton asked for an interview with Grant. Commenting in her diary, a bitterly anti-Yankee Southern woman wrote: "The terms of capitulation seem marvellous-

[26] *Reminiscences, op. cit.,* p. 109.

ly generous for such a foe. What can the meaning be?"

It has been estimated that the Confederate loss in the campaign had been about equal to Grant's, that is about 10,000, but the Federal General now took almost 30,000 prisoners, all of whom he released on parole, 170 cannon, and about 50,000 stand of small arms, mostly of an improved make which had not long before been received from Europe. As soon as the news travelled down the river, Port Hudson surrendered, and the entire Mississippi was in the possession of the Union. Sherman at once moved on Johnston who retreated toward the city of Jackson, shooting cattle, hogs, and sheep and leaving their carcasses in the ponds of water, so that the Union troops in pursuit suffered much from thirst in the great heat of the Southern summer. After the city of Jackson had been besieged and shelled for a week, Johnston withdrew farther south, and the pursuit was abandoned. The city, railroads, and much of the countryside destroyed, Sherman rejoined Grant, and there was now a wide band of Union territory stretching up and down the entire length of the Mississippi dividing the Confederacy in twain. For months the Southerners had been watching the fate of Vicksburg and, important as that fate was from a military standpoint, it had also taken on a psychological importance. The defence of Vicksburg, like that of Richmond later, had become a subject of pride, and the grief and disappointment were correspondingly great when it fell, especially as the news was coincident with the defeat of Lee at Gettysburg. The South did not lose courage and struggled on, but it lost, in thousands of hearts, the spring of confident hope after that fateful July 4. On the other hand, the North felt it had at last found a leader in Grant.

It has been claimed by some of the leading generals on each side and the historians that the war should have ended then, but the South was not ready to acknowledge defeat, and Davis issued one of his worst addresses to "the Soldiers of the Confederate States" in August, a few weeks later. The eventual triumph of the South, he said, was inevitable, but nevertheless the Northerners insisted upon continuing the struggle, and "their malignant rage aims at nothing less than the extermination of yourselves, your wives, and children," and that the homes of the Southerners were to "be partitioned among the wretches whose atrocious cruelties have stamped infamy on their government."[27] As we contrast such wild and whirling words with the always measured ones of Lincoln, ever looking forward to the peaceable adjustments of the two peoples after the war should end, we realize the inadequacy of Davis as a statesman.

So far from the triumph of the South being inevitable, her armies had been defeated, her territory reduced and divided, and her resources diminished, whereas those of the North were probably greater than at the beginning of the struggle. Both sides had grown weary, and volunteering had practically ceased. The draft riots which occurred in New York City, however, in July, only ten days after the two great victories, did not represent the spirit which still animated the North. The Ninth District, in which the trouble started, was largely inhabited by foreign laborers, and the "rich man's war and poor man's fight" slogan of the South had found frequent echo in the North, largely due to the permission to escape service by the payment of $300, which at first the equivalent of the cost to the government of a substitute had ceased to be so owing to the rise in prices and wages due to the depreciation of the currency. Moreover, there was much bad feeling in the city between the immigrant Irish laborers and the negroes, who were competitors for work, and the Irish objected to being drafted for an "abolition war," though that does not diminish the excellent record of thousands of Irish who, either as volunteers or drafted men, fought through it. The drawings for

[27] Channing, *History of the United States, op. cit.,* vol. VI, p. 595.

the draft began about half past ten on the morning of the
13th, and the rioting started within an hour, to last until
moderate quiet was restored on the 18th. During the intervening days, largely on account of the supineness of both
the Mayor and Governor Seymour, the city was terrorized,
order being restored only by troops sent from Pennsylvania by Lincoln.

The headings in *The Tribune,* in type as large as for any
battle, give a rough outline of the story on successive days.
Detailing the events of the 13th, the edition next morning
notes: "The Riot in the Ninth Congressional District . . .
Headquarters of the Provost Marshal Burned . . . The
Draft Slips Destroyed . . . Several Other Buildings Fired
. . . Telegraph Wires Cut and Fire Bells Not Allowed to
Ring . . . Pavements and Railroad Tracks Torn Up . . .
Soldiers Mobbed . . . Private Houses Sacked." The next
day we read "The Riot Continued . . . Violence and Pillage
. . . General Rioting About the City . . . Labor Suspended
in Factories . . . Citizens Stoned and Beaten . . . A Num-
ber of the Rioters Supposed to Be Killed . . . Col. O'Brien
Nearly Beaten to Death . . . Railroad Travel Suspended."
On the 16th the headlines were: "The Mob Fully Organized
. . . Notification to Suspend Business . . . The Rebels
Slaughtered by the Military . . . Two Colored Men Beaten
to Death and Then Hung . . . No Cars or Stages Running
. . . The Murder of Col. O'Brien . . . Pillaging of Stores
. . . A Lumber Yard Burned . . . The Gas Houses in Jeop-
ardy . . . Storehouses of the Atlantic Dock on Fire . . .
Great Fire in Jersey City." On the 17th the fighting be-
came more severe but order was beginning to be restored.
"Fighting in the 18th, 20th, and 21st Wards . . . The Rioters Again Mowed Down . . . Thirty Shot and Bayonetted
in One Attack . . . The Garrotters' Watchword . . . Attacks
on Negroes . . . The Ferocities of the Mob . . . Return of
Our Militia Regiments . . . They Are Anxious to Sweep

the Streets . . . Cars and Stages Running . . . Business Partially Resumed." The following day it was reported that quiet had been restored, but in the meantime it was estimated that 8000 persons had been killed or wounded and $1,500,000 of private property stolen or destroyed.

There had been certain injustices in the allotments under the draft, and Governor Seymour tried to induce Lincoln to suspend it, but it was clearly impossible to suspend recruiting at the dictation of a mob, and the draft went on, for the most part quietly, throughout the rest of the country, and in New York after troops had restored order.

While Lee and Meade continued to watch each other without moving in the East, and Grant had been busy with Vicksburg, Rosecrans, with 70,000 Federals, had been waiting for a decision on the Mississippi before moving against Bragg whose business was to defend Chattanooga and Tennessee. Burnside had also been sent to succor the strong Unionist element in the eastern part of that State, while Longstreet had also been detached with troops from Lee's army to act with Bragg. The centre of the war storm was thus drifting westward. By unskilful manœuvring, Rosecrans, although he gained Chattanooga, allowed himself to be bottled up in it with no way of getting supplies except over sixty miles of bad wagon roads. The battle of September 19–20, in which General Thomas for his determined stand when Rosecrans was driven into Chattanooga won for himself the sobriquet of "the Rock of Chickamauga," thus resulted in worse than a stale-mate, as the Union army could neither escape from, nor remain indefinitely in, the city. Bragg had so fortified himself on the heights overlooking the town, known as Missionary Ridge and Lookout Mountain, that Rosecrans could not avail himself of the railroads and was in danger of being starved out.

Grant was now made commander of all the forces between the Alleghanies and the Mississippi, and his first task in the widest field he had yet had was to save Rosecrans and the State of Tennessee. On October 23, he reached Chattanooga, and after waiting for the arrival of Sherman and his troops, he attacked Bragg, who was driven back and whose army, after he had been deprived of his command by Davis, settled into winter quarters in Georgia. In the eastern part of Tennessee, partly owing to Burnside, who did better here than in the East, and partly to the loyalty of the inhabitants of the Union, Longstreet accomplished nothing, and also withdrew, rejoining Lee in Virginia. The entire State was thus in the hands of the Federals, and the Confederacy had again shrunk in territory and resources.

In the fall elections, Rhett, "the father of secession," was defeated for Congress in South Carolina by a huge majority, and he was not alone. Others who had been among the first to preach secession shared Rhett's fate, until *The Charleston Mercury* said bitterly that "those who made this revolution do not direct it."[28]

If the previous Christmas had been gloomy for the North, this one of 1863 was for the South. Various diaries of the day in Richmond show the contrasts and feverishness of war. Jones, the clerk in the War Department in Richmond, writes: "A few pistols and crackers are fired by the boys in the streets—and only a few. I am alone; all the rest being at church. It would not be safe to leave the house unoccupied. Robberies and murders are daily perpetrated. I shall have no turkey to-day, and do not covet one. It is no time for feasting."[29] On the other hand, Mrs. Chesnut wrote: "Others dropped in after dinner; some without arms, some without legs; von Borcke, who cannot speak because of a wound in his throat. Isabella said: 'We have all kinds now, but a blind one.' Poor fellows, they laugh at wounds. . . .

[28] Cited by White, *Rhett, op. cit.,* p. 235.
[29] *Rebel War Clerk's Diary, op. cit.,* vol. II, p. 120.

## 1863

We had for dinner oyster soup, besides roast mutton, ham, boned turkey, wild duck, partridge, plum pudding, sauterne, burgundy, sherry, and Madeira. There is life in the old land yet!"[30]

[30] *Diary from Dixie, op. cit.,* p. 268.

# Chapter IX

# THE FALL OF THE CONFEDERACY

WE ended the preceding chapter with a Christmas dinner, and perhaps we cannot indicate the sad months in store for the South from now until the end better than by quoting the successive prices of a barrel of flour. Beginning the New Year, 1864, at $200, it was $500 in June, dropping then temporarily to $300 only to rise to $700 by Christmas, $1000 a few weeks later, and $1500 by March 20, 1865, after which it practically could not be bought at any price in Confederate money. These simple figures, like a graph, show the decline and end of the Confederacy.

Many reasons have been given for the final collapse of the South, and there were doubtless several causes at work, which we shall discuss later, but from the military standpoint the most important was the revival by the Federal Congress at the end of February of the army rank of Lieutenant General and Lincoln's prompt appointment of Grant to that office on March 1. Not only had the man for whom Lincoln had been searching been found, but the way was also at last opened to utilizing the entire military strength of the North under a unity of command, and with a minimum of interference from Washington. Before the incalculably important step was taken of placing Grant in supreme charge of all the forces, there had been seventeen independent commanders and the same number of armies which, as Grant said, had for the most part "acted separately and independently of one another." There was to be henceforth only one army with one head, Grant. The effective simplicity which replaced the confusion and inherent weakness of the system which had been employed for three years is best expressed by the new leader himself. Speaking of the former dispersion of strength and effort Grant wrote later: "I determined to stop this. To this end I regarded the Army of the Potomac as the centre, and all West to Memphis along the line described as our position at that time, and North of it, as the right wing; the Army of the James, under General Butler, as the left wing; and all the troops south as a force in the rear of the enemy."[1]

Moreover, Lincoln, in an interview with him, informed Grant that he himself knew nothing of military matters and had never wished to interfere but various reasons had forced him to do so in the case of many of the preceding generals. He further stated that he now wished Grant to assume the supreme responsibility, not even telling the President of his plans, merely calling on him for any assistance which he could give and to which he pledged himself to the utmost. It is impossible to over-estimate the increase in strength due to this unified command and release from civilian interference in the North during the rest of the war as contrasted with the divided commands, and frequent meddling by President Davis, in the South.

Moreover, Lee had suffered an irreparable loss when deprived of his "right arm," Stonewall Jackson, whereas Grant was now provided with such an arm to rest upon in the person of Sherman, whom he advanced to his own previous position of command of the Military Division of the Mississippi. The letters which the two exchanged when Grant's name had been sent to the Senate are so characteristic of the relationship between them we may quote a few sentences. "While I have been eminently successful in this war, in at least gaining the confidence of the public," wrote Grant to Sherman, "no one feels more than I how much of this success is due to the energy, skill and the harmonious putting forth of that energy and skill, of those

[1] *Personal Memoirs* (London, 1895), vol. II, p. 56.

whom it has been my good fortune to have occupying subordinate positions under me . . . what I want is to express
to you and McPherson, as *the men* to whom I feel above all
others indebted for whatever I have had of success. How
far your advice and suggestions have been of assistance,
you know. How far your execution of whatever has been
given you to do entitles you to the reward I am receiving,
you cannot know as well as I do."

In reply, Sherman wrote that "you do yourself an in-
justice and us too much honor in assigning to us so large
a share of the merits which have led to your high advance-
ment. . . . You are now Washington's legitimate suc-
cessor, and occupy a position of almost dangerous elevation;
but if you can continue as heretofore to be yourself, simple,
honest, and unpretending, you will enjoy through life the
respect and love of friends, and the homage of millions of
human beings. . . . I believe you are as brave, patriotic,
and just, as the great prototype Washington; as unselfish,
kindhearted, and honest, as a man should be; but the chief
characteristic in your nature is the simple faith in success
you have always manifested, which I can liken to nothing
else than the faith a Christian has in his Saviour. . . .
When you have completed your best preparations, you go
into battle without hesitation, as at Chattanooga—no
doubts, no reserve; and I tell you that it was this that made
us act with confidence. I knew wherever I was that you
thought of me, and if I got in a tight place you would come
—if alive."[2]

These were the two men who were now to work together
in closest harmony and confidence to crush the Confederacy,
in so far as military operations could do so. We have already spoken of the contrast between Lee and Grant but
there was in many ways a similarity between Jackson and
Sherman. Both were of pioneering stock, both were West

[2] Sherman, *Memoirs, op. cit.,* vol. I, pp. 399–400.

Pointers, and each had given up an army career to teach, both being attached to Southern military institutes when the war broke out. Although both were deeply attached to family life, and kind in their more intimate social relations, neither cared for society and were bored by many of the lighter sides of life. Both were independent thinkers in military matters, and although Sherman did not have Jackson's deep and unaffected piety, he shared with him a ruthless logic concerning the necessary operations of war. Sherman was to carry his logical conclusions much farther than Jackson but in his clear realistic view of war and its requirements, Jackson was much nearer to Sherman than to Lee. There was much of the Old Testament in each, in Jackson, the Scotch-Irish Presbyterian and in Sherman, descendant of English Puritans and three generations of judges. Neither cared for applause or public opinion, and each could be counted on to carry through to the end any course of action on which he had decided. Jackson was the greater and nobler character of the two but Sherman was to plan and carry out one of the greatest military feats of modern times.

In 1864 the war was entering upon a more terrible phase than before, as propaganda and atrocities were answered by counter strokes. Nothing could change the essential, in truth the too great, gentleness of Lee, but the altered phase was felt by others, and as Sherman's biographer, Captain Hart, points out the hardening process was noticeable in him after 1863. In the Vicksburg campaign there had been much plundering by some of the Union army, and Sherman had then written to a divisional commander, "War at best is barbarism, but to involve all—children, women, old and helpless—is more than can be justified. Our men will become absolutely lawless unless this can be checked."[3]

He was to retain much of his personal kindness, and even

[3] Hart, *Sherman, op. cit.,* p. 183.

on his march to the sea was to perform many kind acts to individuals, but as he worked out the problem of war in his cold logic, he came to the conclusions that a government which could be broken up was no government; that if the rule of the majority could not peacefully prevail, then there must be the appeal to might; and that there could be no permanent settlement of the question until the resisting minority should not only be defeated in the field but should also, in their own hearts and homes, become so sick of war as to prevent any early reopening of the question and a new struggle. Once that was accomplished he would end all ill-feeling and do everything he could to help the enemy. When he had captured the town of Jackson in the Vicksburg campaign, and had found that the will to resist was really finished, he had gone so far in supplying the people with provisions as to call forth a rebuke from even Grant. The march to the sea of 1864–65 and the terms arranged at the end of the war with General Johnston carried out in both respects the same relentless logic. During the Vicksburg campaign he had written to Grant that "the amount of burning, stealing, and plundering done by our army makes me ashamed of it. I would quit the service if I could, because I fear we are drifting into the worst sort of vandalism." Nevertheless, he expressed himself as "amazed" at the completely subjugating effect, not of battles won, but of the continued advance of a hostile army and the loss of property. Experience and logic combined to raise in his mind the conception of how to end the war in not only the quickest way but the most final.

When Grant assumed supreme command, the Federal troops guarded the Arkansas River and the entire Mississippi from St. Louis to its mouth; in Texas they held the mouth of the Rio Grande; east of the Mississippi they were in control of Tennessee, West Virginia, all Virginia north of the Rapidan and east of the Blue Ridge; of Fortress

Monroe and Norfolk; of three ports in North Carolina; of several points on the coasts of South Carolina and Georgia; and of Fernandina, St. Augustine, Key West, and Pensacola in Florida. The remainder of the Confederacy was held by its various armies confronting the Union troops, the most important being Lee's in front of Grant, who had decided to remain personally in the East, Johnston's faced by Sherman's, and the opposing forces in the Shenandoah Valley, on which section Lee now largely relied for supplies. Grant's plan, when the Federal army was unified, was to concentrate all possible troops against the several Confederate armies and defeat or wear them out by attrition. At the end of April, he ordered for this purpose a general advance along the entire line—Sherman to push back Johnston and seize the important railway centre of Atlanta; Sigel to invade the Valley; and Butler to advance by the James River against Lee, while he himself, with the Army of the Potomac, should join in the latter movement.

Meanwhile the growing bitterness of the war was evident. Early in March *The Richmond Whig* urged that on the basis of reprisal (an excuse always advanced in war) the South although unable to send a military expedition to Philadelphia or New York should spend a million dollars which would "lay in ashes New York, Boston, Philadelphia, Chicago, Pittsburgh, Washington and all their principal cities, and the men to do the business could be picked up by the hundreds in the streets of those very cities. . . . We will add that we know and talked with a man—a well-known officer of the army—and every way competent and fit—who is ready and anxious at once to proceed to Canada on this business."[4] Of course, the Confederate authorities did not give the slightest countenance to the plan which probably had existence only in the mind of the editor of *The Whig,* but the editorial was reprinted in Northern papers with

[4] Issue of March 9, 1864.

comment which naturally stirred up greater hatred of the South.

About this same time false orders were placed by some one on the body of a Union cavalry colonel killed in a raid on Richmond which indicated a plot to burn the city and assassinate Davis and the Cabinet. The orders had been forged and were utterly repudiated by the Union authorities. On the other hand, *The Tribune* and other Northern papers published despatches and letters indicating a plot either to kidnap or to assassinate Lincoln, which had no more backing by the Confederate Government than the forged orders found in the dead Dahlgren had had from the Federal one. Thus the editors made their diabolical contributions to our tragedy.

> "As quiet fiends would lead past our crazed eyes
> Our children to an unseen sacrifice."

On April 12, however, there occurred a dark deed which marked the changing temper of the struggle and is the darkest blot on the armies of the Confederacy, which in general fought the entire war with conspicuous chivalry. General N. B. Forrest, a somewhat crude Southerner, the son of a blacksmith and who had himself been a slave dealer, had shown a marked ability for leading, far within the Union lines, cavalry raids which were notable for their daring though frequently rather inconsequential in important effect. He determined to attack a small Union force of 557, composed of 295 whites and 262 colored troops, behind the earthworks known as Fort Pillow on the Mississippi, and suddenly appeared with 1500 men, demanding unconditional surrender. It was his general custom to try to frighten the attacked by threats of "no quarter" though he had hitherto not carried that horror into execution. The little fort was easily carried by assault, the Confederates shouting "Forrest's Orders!" as they entered. Of the subsequent massacre there is no doubt, and whites and blacks were indiscriminately slaughtered. Only fourteen Confederates were killed whereas the Union dead numbered several hundred. In his first despatch, toned down in his official report, Forrest wrote that "the river was dyed with blood for two hundred yards. The approximate loss was upwards of 500 killed, but few of the officers escaping. My loss was about twenty killed. It is hoped that these facts will demonstrate to the Northern people that negro soldiers cannot cope with Southerners."[5] Although there is no evidence that Forrest gave the order for the massacre, he was on the ground, the engagement was a small one, his troops outnumbered the enemy three to one, and the responsibility must be placed upon him and the other Southern officers. The episode, with harrowing embellishments, appeared in the Northern papers and did much to inflame opinion and increase the demand for reprisals.[6] Forrest, who in the course of his war experience is said to have had twenty-one horses shot under him, is described by his latest biographer as habitually mild, quiet, and kindly but when in anger or excitement "transformed into a seeming maniac, terrifying to look upon, savage and profane."

Before considering Grant's own campaign directed against Lee and Richmond we may turn to consider the terrible havoc wrought in the Shenandoah Valley. One of the richest and most beautiful valleys in our country, it was of extreme military importance to both armies, as it had become both the chief source of supplies for Lee and a covered route by which the Confederates could pass northward into Pennsylvania or threaten Washington itself by way of Harpers Ferry. When Grant assumed command, the German General Sigel was in charge of the army operat-

[5] Grant, *Memoirs, op. cit.*, vol. II, p. 64; Rhodes, *op. cit.*, pp. 510 *ff.*; article on Forrest, *Dictionary of American Biography* (New York, 1931), vol. VI, p. 532.
[6] *Cf., e.g., New York Tribune*, April 16, 23, May 6, 1864.

ing in the Valley but proved so incompetent that he was succeeded toward the end of May by General David Hunter, a man who justifiably bears one of the most hated names in the South, and who was then in the Valley. One of his officers describes him as subject to frequent fits of anger and dominated by intense prejudices and antipathies.[7]

Even so it is difficult to understand the sheer brutality of his acts among a people with some of whom he was closely connected by blood. The appointment was made at the intimation of Stanton, to whom Hunter had suggested in the summer of 1863 that the house of every slave-holder ought to be burned. Grant, who knew nothing of this, when asked if he would accept the replacing of Sigel by Hunter, had unfortunately agreed to the appointment of Hunter "or anybody else." Hunter had been in hot water with Lincoln almost from the start, and it is possible that his venom against all Southerners had been increased when President Lincoln had repudiated his general order in 1862 declaring the slaves in South Carolina free, and when President Davis had declared him to be a felon not entitled to the rights of a prisoner of war if captured. At any rate he entered upon a career of wanton destruction which greatly distressed most of his own officers and for which he had no authority. Grant was anxious to destroy completely the military utility of the Valley but his orders to both Hunter and Sheridan, severe as they were, read that you may "take all provisions, forage and stock wanted for the use of your command; such as cannot be consumed, destroy. It is not desirable that the buildings should be destroyed—they should rather be protected; but the people should be informed that, so long as an army can subsist among them, recurrences of these raids must be expected, and we are determined to stop them at all hazards."[8]

[7] H. A. Du Pont, *The Campaign of 1864 in the Valley of Virginia* (New York, 1925), p. 37.
[8] *Memoirs, op. cit.*, vol. II, p. 418.

One of the most picturesque figures on the Southern side was Colonel Mosby whose small force of cavalry assembled and dispersed, appeared and disappeared in the Valley, unattached to any larger body of troops, and was chiefly occupied in raiding. It is unfair to call them guerillas but in the heat of war they were so considered, and it must be admitted that they were not always careful in their methods. At the time of the investment of Fredericksburg a Southern woman had complained bitterly of the Federals that "the Vandals threw a shell at a train of cars filled with women and children." In the autumn of 1864 Mosby gleefully tells of how he derailed a Northern train and then set fire to it. One of his men told him, he says in his *Memoirs,* that one of the cars "was filled with Germans, [who] would not get out. I told him 'Set fire to the car and burn the Dutch, if they won't come out.' They were immigrants going West to locate homesteads, and did not understand a word of English, or what all this meant." His men went into the car and set fire to it. "Suddenly," he continues, "there was a grand illumination. The Germans now took in the situation and came tumbling, all in a pile, out of the flames. I hope they all lived to be naturalized and get homes. They ought not to blame me, but Sheridan; it was his business, not mine, to protect them. . . . Whether my men got anything in the shape of pocketbooks, watches, or other valuable articles, I never enquired. . . . We left the civilians, including the ladies, to keep warm by the burning cars."[9] One is reminded of Sherman's words later that his destruction was the fault of Jefferson Davis and not his own.

Hunter got the fixed idea that Mosby's men came from the towns of the Valley, though this was not true, and he determined that if an attack was made on any Federal army wagon train near a village or town he would burn it. Soon after he took command, such an incident occurred near

[9] *Memoirs of Colonel John S. Mosby* (Boston, 1917), pp. 314 ff.

Newtown and he at once gave orders for its destruction. The officers in charge protested, and also even the private soldiers became so restive that the order was rescinded. Hunter did, however, destroy all the buildings, with the exception of one, of the Military Institute at Lexington, though his Chief of Artillery states that all his officers were opposed to burning more than the barracks of the cadets, which was legitimate warfare. His destruction of many private homes in the Valley was utterly without orders or justification. He even burned the house of Edmund J. Lee, which called forth from Mrs. Lee a letter which has become a classic in the South. Writing on July 20, to Hunter, she said that his orders had been carried out, "the dwelling and every outbuilding, seven in number, with their contents, being burned. . . . My husband was absent—an exile. He has never been a politician or in any way engaged in the struggle now going on. . . . It was my house and my home, and there has your niece, Miss Griffith, who lived among us all this horrid war up to the present moment, met with all kindness and hospitality at my hands. Was it for this that you turned me, my young daughter, and little son out upon the world without shelter? . . . A colonel of the Federal Army has stated that you deprived forty of your officers of their commands because they refused to carry out your malignant mischief. All honor to their names for this, at least!"[10]

Meantime, while these and other atrocities were being perpetrated by Hunter, Lee had sent General Early into the Valley, and he had succeeded in getting through to the North, levying a tribute of $20,000 on Hagerstown and $200,000 on Frederick City. Had he been quicker he might have taken Washington, but that place was reinforced by Grant, and Early turned back, sending McCausland on a

[10] Mathew P. Andrews, *The Women of the South in War Times* (Baltimore, 1920), pp. 196 *ff*.

raid into Pennsylvania where he occupied Chambersburg
and demanded $100,000 in gold or $500,000 in greenbacks.
The inhabitants being unable to pay, he reduced practically
the entire town to ashes.

In August, Grant placed Sheridan in charge of the Valley
campaign and the orders became more stringent. On the
16th Grant sent instructions that the crops in Loudoun County should be destroyed, and animals, negroes, and men under
fifty should be carried off. "If not already soldiers, they
will be made so the moment the rebel army gets hold of
them." If there was no justification for the order there
was a basis for the last statement. A few weeks later the
war clerk in Richmond was writing in his *Diary* that "the
despotic [Confederate] order, arresting every man in the
streets, and hurrying them to 'the front' without delay and
regardless of the condition of their families . . . is still
the theme of execration, even among men who have been
the most ultra and uncompromising secessionists. . . .
They say now such a despotism is quite as bad as a Stanton
despotism, and there is not a toss-up between the rule of the
United States and the Confederate States." And again,
some days later, he wrote, "the 'dog-catchers,' as the guards
are called, are out again, arresting able-bodied men (and
sometimes others) in the streets, and locking them up until
they can be sent to the front."[11]

On the 26th Grant sent another order confirming the
earlier one and adding "if the war is to last another year
we want the Shenandoah Valley to remain a barren waste."[12]
Sheridan was an able and dashing cavalry officer of the
regular army but with no sensitiveness of nature, and was
likely to exploit such orders to the full. That generous
Southern officer, General Gordon, wrote of him that "his
style of conversation and general bearing, while never dis-

[11] *Rebel War Clerk's Diary, op. cit.,* vol. II, pp. 304, 317.
[12] *Personal Memoirs of P. H. Sheridan* (New York, 1888), vol. I,
p. 486.

courteous, were far less agreeable and pleasing than those of any other officer of the Union army whom it was my fortune to meet . . . there was an absence of that delicacy and consideration which was exhibited by other Union officers."[13] The responsibility for the *carte blanche* order, however, must be ascribed to Grant, though Sheridan's own comment is illuminating. He adopted the program, he said, "for I do not hold war to mean simply that lines of men shall engage each other in battle. . . . This is but a duel, in which one combatant seeks the other's life; war means much more, and is far worse than this. Those who rest at home in peace and plenty see but little of the horrors attending such a duel, and even grow indifferent to them. . . . It is another matter, however, when deprivation and suffering are brought to their own doors . . . reduction to poverty brings prayers for peace more surely and quickly than does the destruction of human life."[14]

The Civil War, as we have said, was the first great war fought under modern conditions. It was not simply that the rapid-fire rifle first appears with its counterfoil of trench warfare, or that other new inventions affected the technique of the soldier's trade. What was of more sinister significance was that for the first time war meant practically a *levée en masse* of whole populations instead of being fought by professional standing armies. Before the advent of democracy, war had been a sort of game of chess in which those professional armies were moved over the board. It is true that where these armies marched, the wake of ruin was wide and deep, and accompanied by rape and other crimes of violence from which, on the whole, our war was singularly free. Indeed, considering the enormous numbers of men engaged and the long period involved, it is remarkable, in spite of vast damage to property and consequent

[13] *Reminiscences, op. cit.*, p. 441.
[14] *Personal Memoirs, op. cit.*, vol. I, p. 488.

suffering of those in invaded areas, how few authenticated crimes against the person have been recorded, even though the prisons of both sections were occasionally tapped for recruits. On the other hand, as we learned again in the World War, the change in warfare from the professional soldier and army to the *levée en masse* of a great democracy has, in a protracted struggle, led to the effort to break down the morale of the civilian population as even more effective than defeating an army in the field. Now recognized, this was first seen to be the case in our war, and practised by the North rather than the South. The latter section, steeped in the Walter Scott version of mediæval chivalry and with the tradition of the personal duel, clung naturally to the old idea of war, and on the whole unquestionably conducted its operations more "chivalrously" than the North.

On the other hand, Sheridan had grasped the fact that a war in which the entire activities and resources of a whole people were actively engaged instead of the old-fashioned wars of professional armies could no longer be considered as a mere duel between selected men at the front. That sort of war, to the great increase of suffering for humanity, had passed as completely as had the mediæval trial by single combat between chosen leaders from each opposed army. Grant and Sherman, both of them in their private lives humane men, had also reached the same conclusion, namely, that under modern conditions when an entire people as well as an army are engaged, each must be reached. Indeed, under modern conditions the distinction between soldier and civilian has become hard to draw for even the most tender-hearted, if he is logical. For example, in all the wars until after the Napoleonic period there was no such thing as a railroad; but why now is the teamster who drives the horses of a battery into action, or the driver of a motor lorry toward the front, a soldier while the locomotive engineer who runs the train which brings the ammunition from the factories or troops from the rear is a civilian? If a battery can be bombed from the air, why not the munitions factory which alone makes the battery effective? And how about the banker, whose placing of a war loan may be the sole means of making the munitions factory function?

The old professional armies of history before recent generations had few such problems. In the early days there were no munitions, there was no transport except the army's own, the troops lived mostly on the country, and the civilian population could be distinguished from the combatants. The former, indeed, were subject to massacre, rape and every form of suffering. Gradually the treatment of civilians became more humane, and war might have continued to become increasingly so had it not been for modern conditions which have almost completely merged the civilians of both sexes into the great war machinery of our times, due to inventions and democracy. The shift occurred in the middle of the nineteenth century, and if it has become difficult to draw a logical line indicating where military service ends and pure civilian life begins, it has also become evident that one of the chief aims of modern warfare must be not merely to defeat armies at the front but to affect the will to war of the peoples themselves behind the lines. The first efforts of this sort were made in our Civil War, and were harsh and brutal.

Grant and Sherman at least had to harden their hearts to carry out the program, but they were the first of the moderns to realize the change in conditions of warfare, which democracy had altered as it has altered all else. What the horrors of the next war are to be, no one dares envisage. The knight had passed with all the rest of the environment of the feudal age. Even the South, though the diaries of the women are full of references to him, had been cured of its Walter Scott. When a romantic young lady said to General Johnson that General Jeb Stuart reminded her of "the knights of olden time," Johnson replied that "the mediæval knight, my dear young lady, would be of little use in this war. He would have stood no chance with one of Stuart's men."[15] The "gentleman," as understood by those of us who are still old-fashioned, derived from the knight to meet altered conditions. Whether in the modern world he can survive any more than the knight survived the change of his period remains to be seen. In America, the Civil War, as we have said, marked the change from the old world to the modern. The North, as we pointed out earlier, was far more in the full current of world change than the South. That some of the Northern generals perceived the shift in the type of war and crudely attempted to reach results which all nations strove for in the World War is the key to the military events of 1864 and 1865.

It is not unlikely that the Germans developed their own theory of war and "frightfulness" from a study of the policy of some of the Northerners in the Civil War. In 1870, when Germany was fighting France, Sheridan had gone over as a private observer but was received by Bismarck and other high officials, both civil and military. Doctor Busch, the biographer of Bismarck, notes that at a dinner given by the Chancellor the discussion turned to the recent conduct of some of the German forces, and Councillor Abeken thought that war should be conducted in a more humane fashion. Sheridan denied this, says Busch, and expressed himself roughly as follows: "The proper strategy consists in the first place in inflicting as telling blows as possible upon the enemy's army, and then in causing the inhabitants so much suffering that they must long for peace, and force their government to demand it. The people must be left nothing but their eyes to weep with over the war." The German noted in his journal: "Somewhat heartless it seems to me, but perhaps worthy of consideration."[16] Dur-

[15] Pryor, *Reminiscences, op. cit.*, p. 205.
[16] Moritz Busch, *Bismarck* (New York, 1898), vol. I, p. 128.

ing the World War the Bishop of London, in an address, quoted the words of the American general but attributed them to the Kaiser!

To return to the Valley of the Shenandoah, we may say briefly that Sheridan in September defeated Early and drove him southward, so devastating the farms and towns of the Valley that Grant could write to Halleck "crows flying over it for the balance of this season will have to carry their provender with them." Lee having sent reinforcements to Early, the latter again attacked the Union forces at Cedar Creek, while Sheridan was at Winchester, twenty miles away. Hastening to rally his retreating army, he snatched victory from defeat, and the chief purpose of the Federal campaign having been attained there was no further conflict of importance in the Valley during the remainder of the war.

Meanwhile, Grant had begun to hammer away at Lee, planning, with double the enemy's forces, to drive his way by sheer overwhelming by numbers. On May 3, he crossed the Rapidan and entered the tangled wooded district called the "Wilderness." The fighting in the next three weeks was intensely severe, Grant trying both frontal attacks and flanking operations in most difficult country which Lee knew by heart. By the 21st, the Federal losses had mounted to about 31,000 but from Spotsylvania the Union general wrote his famous despatch that "I propose to fight it out on this line, if it takes all summer." Lee, however, manœuvred with remarkable skill and gave Grant no chance. On June 2, the Federals had reached Cold Harbor, only six miles from the beginning of the fortifications of Richmond and Grant unwisely, as he himself admitted, decided on an attack all along the line against the strong position occupied by his adversary. The following day the attack was launched with disastrous results, over 7000 Union troops being killed and wounded in twenty minutes. In all the fighting of the campaign thus far Lee had lost about 17,000 men as compared with Grant's loss of nearly 55,000. If the Confederates retired within the entrenchments of Richmond it was evident that the city could not be taken by assault.

In June of the following year, a Union soldier passing through the district described the sights around Spotsylvania and the Wilderness. "Everywhere," he wrote, "were visible the terrible signs of the struggle. Trees mowed down by the artillery. . . . Bones lay by the roadside, and in a yard . . . lay two skulls. In the thicket near by, where the appalling stillness seems never to have been broken by owl or bat or raven lie hundreds of skeletons. . . . An old gray-haired man, trying to quiet his trembling head, said, 'Ah, sir, there are thousands of both sides lying unburied in the wilderness.' "[17]

In the meantime, Butler had done little or nothing of what had been expected of him on the Peninsula. Instead of taking Petersburg, which would have cut off Richmond from the South, he had allowed himself to be driven off and "bottled up" by Beauregard. Grant now determined to transfer his army to the south of the James River, and, joining Butler's forces, approach the Confederate capital from that direction. On June 14, he effected the crossing and on the same day ordered Butler to send Smith with the 18th corps and to attack Petersburg. As Smith was unavoidably delayed, the movement did not take place until the morning of the next day, after Lee had had an opportunity to send up reinforcements. Grant now set himself down to besiege the place and there confronted Lee for eight months. He made one attempt at assault, which cost him about 10,000 men; and another at entering after the explosion of a huge mine, "the Crater," which cost him nearly another 4000, mostly in captured. Due, as Grant said, to the inefficiency of a corps and division commander,

[17] *Letters from a Civil War Officer, op. cit.,* p. 529.

the latter effort was "a stupendous failure." Nevertheless, when the armies settled down for the winter, Lee was suffering heavily from desertions, and owing to Sheridan's campaign his supplies had been cut off from the Shenandoah. There was less of a will to fight and conquer on the part of the South, and that was due in large part to the third movement which Grant inaugurated and Sherman expanded, which we must now consider.

As we have noted, it was an essential part of Grant's plans, treating all the Federal forces as one army, that Sherman in the West should push back Johnston and take Atlanta, which was not only important as a strategic railway centre in the heart of the lower South but also because its factories provided much of the material of war. In May Sherman started against his adversary. He was not to capture Atlanta until September 2, but it is probable that it was his success in those months that saved the Union; and that the loss of independence to the Confederacy was due to the action of Jefferson Davis, backed by a considerable part of Southern opinion. It has been claimed by some military writers that Johnston was in reality the ablest commander on the Confederate side. Certainly, in spite of some personal idiosyncrasies, he was one of the ablest. He was forced to fall back slowly before Sherman, as Lee was before Grant, but in opposing Sherman in occasional battle and in flanking movements he displayed consummate skill. Sherman, more cautious than Grant and with less men to spare, was more hesitant about the frontal attack, but the game of flanking was a slow one, although his engineers displayed remarkable ability in repairing the railroad which Johnston destroyed as he retreated. Time was passing, and time was of the essence of the problem for the South in the summer of 1864.

The Shenandoah Valley was important but in public opinion it was somewhat of a side issue. Grant was blocked by Lee and the public always wants action. If the South was growing more and more war weary, so was the North, and a Presidential election was due in November. The end of August the Democratic National Convention not only secured the consent of General McClellan to run as candidate but adopted as part of its platform the words "after four years of failure to restore the Union . . . humanity, liberty, and the public welfare demand that immediate efforts be made for a cessation of hostilities." McClellan repudiated the plank but nevertheless accepted the rather anomalous position of standard-bearer for the party which had adopted it. Less than a week earlier Lincoln had written a sealed letter in which he said: "It seems exceedingly probable that this administration will not be re-elected. Then it will be my duty to so co-operate with the President-elect as to save the Union between the election and the inauguration, as he will have secured his election on such ground that he cannot possibly save it afterward."

Time was what the Confederacy needed above all else, and Johnston by his slow retreat, adopting precisely the tactics of Lee before Grant, was providing time. Grant's mature comment in 1885 was that "for my own part, I think Johnston's tactics were right. Anything that could have prolonged the war a year beyond the time that it did finally close would probably have exhausted the North to such an extent that they might then have abandoned the contest and agreed to a separation."[18]

The advance of Sherman, however, slow as it was, alarmed the planters of the lower South, and a clamor was raised against Johnston. Moreover, Davis had greatly disliked Johnston from early in the war, refusing to see his ability, and the general had not been tactful in concealing his own dislike of the Confederate President. At the very crisis of the South, when all depended on the Confederacy's

[18] *Memoirs, op. cit.,* vol. II, p. 88.

retaining Johnston and on Johnston's maintaining his tactics, Davis replaced him by the much inferior Hood, who it was hoped would "fight." Sherman was delighted, and perhaps it is not too much to say that the Union was saved and the Confederacy doomed by that one act of Jefferson Davis.

Hood did fight—to lose—and on September 2 evacuated Atlanta, enabling Sherman to telegraph North next day that "Atlanta is ours and fairly won." The effect in the North was electrical, and coming a few weeks before election did much to assure the heavy defeat of McClellan and the return of Lincoln by a larger majority than he had received in 1860.

Meanwhile, on August 5, Farragut with eighteen ships had defeated the Confederates in the battle of Mobile Bay and captured the two forts on shore, though the city itself was not taken until the following spring. Nevertheless the South had lost another of its most important ports and its isolation from the outside world was increasing.

Although Sherman had captured Atlanta after besieging it, both his position there and his future movements were by no means safe. His sole line of communication with his Northern base was over a single railroad a hundred and thirty miles long. As he penetrated farther into the South there was continual need for leaving more and more men behind to protect the lengthening line and to garrison captured towns. Planning a farther advance into the enemy country, he determined to avoid the necessity of leaving a considerable garrison in Atlanta by deporting all the inhabitants, whom otherwise he might have to feed as well as guard. In the course of the correspondence which followed with General Hood, Sherman pointed out, in reply to Hood's accusation that in the fighting for the town he had shelled it without notice, that Atlanta was "a fortified town, with magazines, arsenals, foundries and public stores," and that according to all the laws of war there was no obligation to give notice, but that on the other hand it had been Hood's duty to warn the people in the city which he was defending.

On September 7, he wrote his first letter to Hood, stating that all the inhabitants would have to leave, either to the South or North as individual preference might dictate, offering transport to those who chose the latter alternative to any points they might choose, and to provide transportation for those going South as far as the little place Rough and Ready, where the railroad was broken, Hood having to care for them beyond that. All were to be allowed to carry with them clothing, trunks, a reasonable amount of furniture, and their slaves, if willing, whichever direction they took. Atlanta, he wrote, "is no place for families or noncombatants, and I have no desire to send them north if you will assist in conveying them south."

Hood, either with a complete disregard of truth or with gross lack of historical knowledge, replied vehemently that "the unprecedented measure you now propose transcends, in studied and ingenious cruelty, all acts ever before brought to my attention in the dark history of war."[19] I may again emphasize that in reading history we must always try to think in terms of conditions at the time and not those of the present. When a reader sees the word "Atlanta," for example, he is likely to picture the beautiful, progressive, populous city of over 270,000 people of today. But when the war began in 1860 Atlanta was scarcely larger than a good-sized village, the census for that year giving its population as 9554. A large proportion of these were slaves, and of the whites a very considerable number must have been men absent in the Confederate armies. Under the laws of war, recognized by both contestants, a large part of the town was clearly doomed to destruction—the public stores,

[19] Sherman, *Memoirs, op. cit.,* vol. II, p. 119.

arsenals, foundries, and so on. The place was fortified, an important railway and strategic military centre, and at the time promised also to be the scene of more fighting. The deportation, carried out by Sherman in spite of protests and as humanely as possible, undoubtedly caused an immense amount of sorrow and suffering, but when one thinks over the treatment of conquered cities in the long history of European war, Hood's characterization of the act becomes absurd. It would seem, indeed, to have had far more justification than Hood's own demand for the surrender of the Federal forces holding Resaca in October, when Hood wrote: "I demand the immediate and unconditional surrender of the post. . . . If the place is carried by assault, no prisoners will be taken." To this the Union commanding officer, Weaver, replied that he was surprised by Hood's threat but that "in my opinion I can hold this post. If you want it, come and take it."[20] Hood did not even try, and the idle threat is a blot on his name. At least at Fort Pillow, Forrest did not order the massacre, and the soldiers were infuriated by the presence of negro troops, but Sherman had insisted, against all political pressure, on having no negro soldiers in his expedition into the South.

In reply to a protest from the Mayor of Atlanta, Sherman wrote: "You cannot qualify war in harsher terms than I will. War is cruelty and you cannot refine it. . . . I know I had no hand in making this war, and I know I will make more sacrifices today than any of you to secure peace. But you cannot have peace and a division too. If the United States submits to a division now it will not stop, but will go on until we reap the fate of Mexico, which is eternal war. . . . If [the United States] relaxes one bit to pressure, it is gone, and I believe that is the national feeling. This feeling assumes various shapes, but always comes back to that of Union. . . . You might as well appeal

[20] *Ibid.*, p. 155.

against the thunder storm as against these terrible hardships of war. . . . I myself have seen in Missouri, Kentucky, Tennessee, and Mississippi, hundreds and thousands
of women and children fleeing from your armies and desperadoes, hungry and with bleeding feet. In Memphis,
Vicksburg, and Mississippi, we fed thousands upon thousands of the families of rebel soldiers left on our hands,
and whom we could not see starve. Now that war comes
home to you, you feel very different. I want peace, and
believe it can only be reached through union and war, and
I will ever conduct war with a view to perfect and early
success. But, my dear sirs, when peace does come, you may
call on me for anything. Then I will share with you the
last cracker, and watch with you to shield your homes and
families against danger from every quarter."[21]

Sherman remained in Atlanta until November 15, matur-
ing his plans, but the mere fact of his presence, far behind
the outer lines of defence, in the heart of the lower South,
combined with other causes was resulting in a decreasing
will to fight on the part of the Confederates. The weariness
of war and its conditions were more or less affecting both
sections, as we have said. Jones, in the Richmond War Office, noted in his *Diary* in September, that "many are re-
flecting on the repose and abundance they enjoyed once in
the Union," and many in the North felt the same way. The
South, however, was suffering materially as the North was
not. At the beginning of this chapter we gave the story of
a barrel of flour and what was true of that was true of
almost all else. Scarcity and impossible prices were wear-
ing down not the courage but the will to war of the South.
Moreover, as prices had risen the government had found it
necessary, even in the preceding year, to pass laws impress-
ing property from farmers and others, setting the government's own price on what it took. This had aroused a storm

[21] *Memoirs, op. cit.,* vol. II, p. 127.

of opposition and created a new host of enemies and of disaffection on the score of States' Rights. In the last months of the war, however, prices became so high and the government so impoverished that it could not even give Confederate money for the lower prices at which it impressed goods but merely receipts and promises to pay, until at the end it owed those from whom it had taken property $500,000,000. While Sherman was on his later march to the sea, a Georgian, P. A. Lawson, wrote to Jefferson Davis that the Confederate cavalry under Wheeler, preceding the Federals, were seizing hogs and stock for miles on each side of their route, and confiscating corn. He added that as the government would not take its own notes in payment of taxes but insisted on payment in kind, the people of Georgia were beginning not to care which army won, as Sherman was making life no harder for them than were their own troops.

Among another class, the impressment of slaves became a grievance. These had come under the general law but as conditions became more difficult this question became acute. Two days after Sherman took Atlanta Lee impressed 2000 to work on the fortifications of Petersburg, and a fortnight later advised Davis that a certain percentage of the army should be made up of slaves as teamsters, laborers, etc. Early in November, Davis asked Congress for 40,000 slaves for the army, to be used as soldiers only in an extremity, suggesting their emancipation after the war. To anticipate slightly, we may say that in the following February a bill was introduced into the Confederate Senate to enlist 200,-000 negroes in the army and was passed by the Congress with some amendments and in a modified form. We have already spoken of a certain confusion in the Southern mind as to why the South went to war in the first place, whether it was for States' Rights, personal liberty, hatred of the Northern connection, slavery, or what-not, a confusion reflected in the various reasons assigned by both contemporary and later Southern writers. When Davis suggested using and then emancipating slaves, after Lincoln's re-election had shown the unyielding temper of the North, R. M. T. Hunter of Virginia asked in the Confederate Senate why the South had gone to war if it was not to protect its slave property. Rhett in South Carolina wrote that "we want no Confederate Government without our institutions," and enquired, if the government was to destroy States' Rights and slavery, what was there left to fight for?

Even in the middle of 1862 Mrs. Chesnut, reporting a conversation, wrote in her journal, "Hampton estate has fifteen hundred negroes on Lake Washington, Mississippi. Hampton girls talking in the language of James's novels: 'Neither Wade nor Preston—that splendid boy!—would lay a lance in rest—or couch it, which is the right phrase for fighting—to preserve slavery. They hate it as we do.' 'What are they fighting for?' 'Southern rights—whatever that is. And they do not want to be understrappers forever to the Yankees. They talk well enough about it, but I forget what they say.' Johnny Chesnut says: 'No use to give a reason—a fellow could not stay away from the fight—not well.' " Mrs. Chesnut added with her usual caustic humor that "it takes four negroes to wait on Johnny satisfactorily."[22]

In the beginning, when both hope and excitement ran high, this confusion of aim had less effect, but after some years of terrible suffering it was a source of weakness. Those who, like Hunter, Rhett, and others, thought the war was for slavery, became disaffected when Davis talked of colored soldiers and emancipation. Those who claimed the struggle was for States' Rights, like the governors of a number of the important States, became more and more disaffected as the central government had to strengthen

[22] *Diary from Dixie, op. cit.,* p. 163.

itself at the expense of the States if the war were to be carried on at all.

Moreover, the feeling, whether just or not, that the rich were not doing their share was as strong in the South as in the North toward the end. "Over 100,000 landed proprietors, and most of the slave-owners, are now out of the ranks, and soon, I fear, we shall have an army that will not fight, having nothing to fight for," wrote Jones in the War Office in September; and again the next day he added that General Lee "writes urgently for more men . . . and he complains that rich young men are elected magistrates, etc., just to avoid service in the field."[23] It is extremely difficult to arrive at accurate figures for desertion but apparently in 1864 the number of absentees in the Confederate army had risen to about 120,000, a number only slightly larger than in the Federal army but more important in proportion to the total and the reserve of man-power.

Although it was not, perhaps, until 1865 that the Confederate Secretary of State, Benjamin, gave up all hope of intervention by Napoleon, that hope had been so long deferred that the people at large no longer looked for any help save from themselves. Breaking the pledges which France had given to the United States Government, Napoleon had set up the Emperor Maximilian as ruler of Mexico with the obvious intention of extending the French Empire, but he had attempted to maintain the quite transparent fiction that Maximilian had been the free choice of the Mexican people in an open and uncontrolled election. Occupied with the war, the Federal Government had had for the moment to close its eyes partially to the obvious deception, which had also in a way tied Napoleon's hands. Aside from European dangers and complications, he could not well go to the aid of the South against the North unless he showed that he did intend to take Mexico and to

[23] *Rebel War Clerk's Diary, op. cit.,* p. 281.

stultify all that he had been telling Seward for many months through the French Minister.

Thus while Sherman was deliberating on his plans in Atlanta, the Confederacy, in spite of its armed forces, was beginning to crumble. Slowly Sherman matured his bold idea. The Confederacy had been cut in two by the loss of the whole Mississippi. Its ports were gradually passing back into Federal possession. It had lost Kentucky, Tennessee, and the Shenandoah Valley as well as West Virginia, but the agricultural resources of the lower South for supporting the armies were still untouched. Now that Lee could no longer count on supplies from the rich Shenandoah, the chief reliance was on the beautiful and fertile State of Georgia. Sherman was at the chief rail centre of that State. To retreat and follow Hood's army toward Tennessee would be to appear to give up the territory conquered. On the other hand it was impossible to advance with an ever lengthening line of communication. For some months he had apparently been turning over in his mind a possible march to the sea but in September and October he worked out the details, writing to Grant and Halleck, though the plan and decision were his own. What he decided to undertake was nothing less than cutting himself loose entirely from any communication with the North and subsisting his troops on the country.

Hood with his army was to the northwest of him and other leaders were gathering, which induced Davis to assure the people of Georgia that Sherman would be forced out and that "the fate that befell the Army of the French Empire in its retreat from Moscow will be re-acted." Thomas, however, and the Federal forces in Tennessee could be left to take care of Hood. On October 9, Sherman wired to Grant that the roads could not be protected to the rear but that "I propose we break up the railroad from Chattanooga, and strike out with wagons to Milledgeville,

Millen, and Savannah. . . . The utter destruction of [Georgia's] roads, houses and people will cripple their military resources. By attempting to hold the roads we will lose 1000 men monthly, and will gain no result. I can make the march, and make Georgia howl."[24]

At first Sherman got little encouragement from headquarters, and the correspondence went on for some weeks. Lincoln, Grant, and Halleck were all timorous as to the possible consequences. On November 6, setting forth his plan again, Sherman wrote: "I propose to act in such a manner against the material resources of the South as utterly to negative Davis's boasted threat and promises of protection. If we can march a well-appointed army right through his territory, it is a demonstration to the world, foreign and domestic, that we have a power which Davis cannot resist. This may not be war, but rather statesmanship," and then mentioned several alternative routes. Finally he received permission, though rather grudging, and on November 15, he left Atlanta, striking to the southeast with about 60,000 men, against all the rules of war dividing his army, leaving the enemy in his rear, cutting loose from all communications, and trusting to subsist a large army without supplies in the heart of a hostile territory.

Before leaving, Sherman burned all the machine-shops, mills, warehouses and stores in the now forsaken city but carried out the unhappy work with perfect order, protecting such buildings as were not of military use to the enemy. That was permissible under the laws of war but unfortunately on the march he was to a considerable extent to lose control of both his men and himself. In the Special Field Orders which he issued before the start, he declared that "the army will forage liberally on the country," but the foraging parties were to be organized only by the

[24] Sherman, *Memoirs, op. cit.*, vol. II, p. 152.

brigade commanders. To corps commanders alone was entrusted "the power to destroy mills, houses, cotton-gins, etc.," and the rule was laid down that where the army was unmolested there should be no destruction of such property, but "should guerillas or bushwhackers molest our march, or should the inhabitants burn bridges, obstruct roads, or otherwise manifest local hostility" then the commanders were to order devastations in accordance with the degree of hostility shown. Except while in a camp, when soldiers could gather provisions in sight of it, all foraging was to be done by special parties detailed for the purpose, and soldiers were ordered not to enter dwellings or commit any trespass unless belonging to such parties.

On frequent occasions, on the march through Georgia, both Sherman and many of the officers tried to stop the worst of excesses, but even if they had been most anxious to preserve all private property other than that tinged with a military use—which some of them were not—it would have been impossible. As a broad consideration we must recall again the different views of the war taken by South and North. The former believing as axiomatic its theory of the Constitution with the corollary of the right of peaceable secession, regarded all Northern troops as wantonly invading its territory. On the other hand, the North, believing in *its* interpretation, regarded the Southerners as rebels who had just as wantonly plunged the nation into the woes and misery and suffering of a protracted civil war. The end of the war did not prove which side had been right—only which was the stronger—but each side believed itself fervently to be in the right. As we have seen, Sherman himself had been changing. This man, who for several years had denounced loot and pillage, and who had been kind and considerate as an individual, now began to conceive of himself, as Captain Hart says, "as the angel of wrath, armed with a flaming sword, to punish a people guilty of a mortal sin—that of bringing division into the Union and hence of bringing war into the land."[25]

When the end came, and he received Johnston's surrender, he was to prove so generous that his terms were disallowed, but he had thoroughly convinced himself that the quickest way to peace was to ruin the morale of the civilian population, according to the theory of the new warfare which we elaborated earlier in this chapter. At times, certainly until Savannah was reached, Sherman felt the same repugnance which he had in the earlier years of the war to what his troops were doing. "I'll have to harden my heart to these things," he said one evening by his fire. "That poor woman today . . . the soldiers will take all she has"; but then added with the same self-justification as Mosby did, only reversing the sides, "Jeff Davis is responsible for all this."

The army moved in several lines, cutting a swath sixty miles wide through the State, and in spite of Sherman's general orders the conduct of the soldiers would depend much on the discipline and principles of their officers. Some of these were gentlemen, good officers and dispassionate, but many were not. Some hated the South for the war and were also constitutionally incapable of understanding the Southern people. Perhaps one of the most illuminating documents is the diary of Henry Hitchcock, one of Sherman's staff, a Northerner, but born in the South of New England ancestors. The volume, with naive unconsciousness on Hitchcock's part, is a damning indictment of himself, of Sherman, and of the inability of the New Englander to understand the Southern gentleman and his attitude toward life.[26]

From scattered bits given by Hitchcock and others it would appear that Sherman rather encouraged the burning of private houses and the general destruction of the coun-

[25] Hart, *Sherman, op. cit.*, p. 334.
[26] Henry Hitchcock, *Marching with Sherman,* edited by M. A. De Wolfe Howe (New Haven, 1927), *passim.*

tryside. He had a loose tongue when a strong hand was needed, and even though few officers were as bad as Kilpatrick of the cavalry, the laxity disseminated itself down from Sherman through the officers to the men, who considered the whole expedition, in the glorious autumn weather, as a lark. There were actual criminals in both the Northern and Southern armies, men released from prison on condition of fighting the enemy, such as those at Milledgeville, Ga., and from both armies there were many stragglers. Considering, however, that there were 60,000 men marching through enemy country, we may again note how few crimes were committed against persons.

The army left behind it, however, a wide wake of ruin. "Everywhere," wrote one officer, "the houses of the wealthy were pillaged, clothes torn up, beds torn to pieces, barns and gins and their contents given over to the flames. . . . It was a melancholy sight to see the books disappear from the shelves of the State Library recalling the vandalism of the Arabs in Egypt. . . . In many of the houses the ladies sat among the ruins of their furniture and tattered contents of drawers and trunks, smiling as if they took all things joyfully. . . . Vast amounts of silverware, hid away in the ground, through information derived from the negroes fell into the hands of the men. Now and then stragglers were guilty of outrages such as hanging a citizen until he would confess where his silver was, or rifling trunks in the presence of the dying, but such disgraceful acts were of rare occurrence and I gave orders to our foragers, and doubtless other regimental commanders did the same, to shoot down anything in the form of a man engaged in unsoldierlike deeds." Hitchcock noted that among other officers: "Howard has issued very severe orders against pillaging, denouncing the punishment of it by death. . . . Also, it is in fact next to impossible—obviously so—to catch, or when caught to identify or convict the guilty parties. The mischief is not done under the eye of officers, and five or ten minutes is long enough to do irreparable harm."[27]

There was no organized opposition to the march. Wheeler's Confederate cavalry, who were almost as bad as Kilpatrick's, raided from time to time, and much property was destroyed in advance of the Federal army. In one case, bombs were placed just under the surface of the road to blow up the Federals as they advanced, but this ended when Confederate prisoners were made to take the lead. Early in December, Sherman had reached the environs of Savannah and the first part of the great march was over. He calculated that he had destroyed $100,000,000 worth of property, and had swept clean of horses, mules, and other supplies a band 60 miles wide and 360 miles long across one of the richest Southern States, besides destroying 265 miles of railway. Sherman had said that if the shell of the Confederacy could be pierced, the inside would be found to be hollow, and there is no doubt of the effect on the morale of the South of the destruction of one of its wealthiest parts, supposedly sheltered far behind the outer defences. The Confederate General Alexander admitted that the effect was far deeper than would have been the loss of a great battle. On December 22, Sherman and the Federals entered the conquered city of Savannah, and meanwhile Thomas in the West had defeated Hood, dispelling all danger to Tennessee and leaving Sherman free for another movement.

Savannah was spared any destruction and excellent order was maintained there. A sinister feature of Sherman's stay, however, was the arrival of Secretary of War Stanton from Washington, and his relations with the negroes. The general had already been warned by Halleck that while every one was praising his great march "there is a certain class having now great influence with the President, and very probably anticipating still more on a change of cabinet, who are de-

[27] *Marching with Sherman, op. cit.,* p. 134.

cidedly disposed to make a point against you. I mean in regard to the 'inevitable Sambo.' " They were complaining that instead of having brought out 50,000 slaves or more from Georgia, Sherman had repulsed them when they wanted to join his ranks. When Stanton arrived he asked Sherman to arrange a meeting with some of the more intelligent negroes in Savannah, which Sherman did, calling together about twenty negro ministers and others. Incredible as it may seem, after asking them various questions, Stanton asked Sherman to leave the room and then asked the negroes what they thought of the general. The plain and unhappy fact already beginning to loom up in view of the possible end of the war was that, apart from professional negrophile sympathy on the part of Abolitionists and others, the politicians were beginning to wake up to the possible potential value of negro votes. As happened in the Mexican War, it was also considered desirable by politicians to gather as much political ammunition as possible against successful generals who might be aspirants for the Presidency.

General Hardee, who had evacuated Savannah when threatened by Sherman, had moved his forces to Charleston but although Halleck hoped that the place might be taken and destroyed, Sherman determined on renewing his march and proceeding North overland. We have already spoken of the especially bitter hatred in the South against Massachusetts, and in the North against South Carolina. To some extent there was also local dislike of these two States among the people of their own respective sections. Sherman relates that many people in Georgia asked him why he did not go to South Carolina, and when told he intended to do so, remarked that they could forgive what he did to Georgia if he would make the Carolinians feel the full weight of war. There was no question that Sherman intended that they should. There had been immense property damage done in Georgia, Sherman estimating $80,000,000 of it to have been sheer wantonness resulting in no direct military benefit; but though the army regarded the Georgians as rebels and plundered them wholesale, the feeling against them and their State was nothing like that felt against South Carolina, which was regarded as the very home of secession and the chief cause of the war. Writing to Grant just before taking Savannah, Sherman suggested that with the city in his possession he could then "punish South Carolina as she deserves, and as thousands of the people in Georgia hoped we would do. I do sincerely believe that the whole United States, North and South, would rejoice to have this army turned loose on South Carolina, to devastate that State in the manner we have done in Georgia, and it would have a direct and immediate bearing on your campaign in Virginia."[28] He fully realized that operating hundreds of miles away he was working as closely with Grant as if he had been in the trenches with him. "Every step I take from this point northward," he wrote to Halleck, "is as much a direct attack upon Lee's army as though we were operating within sound of his artillery."[29]

He added in the same letter that "the whole army is burning with an insatiable desire to wreak vengeance upon South Carolina. I almost tremble at her fate, but feel that she deserves all that seems to be in store for her." He was then thinking of taking Charleston first but wrote: "I look upon Columbia as quite as bad as Charleston, and I doubt if we shall spare the public buildings there as we did at Milledgeville." There would seem to be no doubt—indeed Sherman in his own words has left none—that he deliberately intended to a large extent to let his army have its own way. The wanton destruction of dwelling houses and personal property through Georgia is a blot on his reputation which he cannot avoid, and when planning the new march through

[28] *Memoirs, op. cit.*, vol. II, p. 213.          [29] *Ibid.*, p. 227.

South Carolina, he wrote that "I would not restrain the army lest its vigor and energy should be impaired,"[30] a remark which shows that he had passed, as Captain Hart says, from "the logical to the diabolical."

Briefly, he now planned to keep the enemy still uncertain as to his real route, but to march northward by way of Columbia, then into North Carolina, eventually threatening Lee so in the rear as to force him to retreat from Richmond with Grant on his heels.

On February 1, Sherman with his 60,000 men started on the second part of his march, which, in importance, he himself later rated as ten to one compared with the first. By the 16th they were near Columbia, and the next day, after it had been evacuated by General Wade Hampton and his troops, they took possession of the little capital which in 1860 had boasted only 8000 inhabitants, but which, as a safe place of refuge, had grown somewhat during the war. That night two-thirds of the town was burned to the ground, it being said that over 1400 buildings covering forty-eight blocks were in ashes by the morning. Ever since that catastrophe, one of the most heated controversies in American history has raged round the question as to who was responsible for the conflagration.

As is common in history, the testimony of eyewitnesses and also of those who wrote from memory show irreconcilable differences. Evidence given by prominent men before the British and American Commission on claims in 1872 muddles the problem even more. It was the custom for Confederate forces in evacuating a town to burn the cotton before leaving, but Wade Hampton denied that this had been done. As his word may be considered absolutely good we may accept as a fact that any burning of cotton was not done by his orders and that he saw none burning when he left. That does not preclude the possibility, however, that

[30] *Ibid.*, p. 254.

cotton was burning when the Federal troops entered, as some eyewitnesses claim, and that efforts were made to put the fire out. The general conflagration did not begin until the Federals had been in possession for eight hours or more. A high wind rose, and if cotton had been burning the wind may have started the fire again and carried burning pieces of cotton so as to extend the fire. On the other hand, the evidence is ample that many of the troops were drunk and wild, and that some of these set fire to houses while others were engaged in trying to stop the spread of disaster. After reading all the testimony available and the various summings up by both Northern and Southern advocates, I confess that it seems to me impossible to give a legally unassailable opinion as to the successive steps in the disaster.

Sherman's own testimony is ruled out, for he wrote that "in my official report of this conflagration I distinctly charged it to General Wade Hampton, and confess I did so pointedly, to shake the faith of his people in him, for he was in my opinion boastful and professed to be the special champion of South Carolina."[31] In other words, Sherman lied, though Rhodes incredibly calls his statement "a delicious bit of historical naïveté." There is nothing further to be said about a man who lies in an official report deliberately, and the historian and the general have both written themselves down as not realizing what honor means to a gentleman.

On the other hand, I do not believe Sherman gave orders to burn the town. As Hart points out, if he had done so, he would not have taken up his own headquarters for the night in the centre of it. But he had been careless in expressing himself to others as to his general attitude, and in the months of the march his laxity with regard to private property had seeped down through officers to the men. His own statements as to what might happen in South Carolina are damn-

[31] *Memoirs, op. cit.*, vol. II, p. 287.

ing, and if he is entitled to the glory of the march from the military point of view, he must bear the burden of the un-military aspect of it. Whether there was cotton burning or not when the Federals entered the capital, the extent of the disaster the following night must be attributed to a portion of the soldiery, drunk or sober, acting without orders but fairly certain of escaping punishment. We may dismiss the story that the inhabitants plied the Union soldiers with liquor. That peaceful citizens should make enemies, whom they not only hated but feared, drunk in order to "propitiate them," is too obviously absurd to be entertained. That the soldiers obtained liquor and became drunk is attested by Union officers, and discipline appears to have been ex-tremely lax. Apart from his acknowledged lie as to Hampton, Sherman was curiously reticent on the subject, and al-though in his *Memoirs* he denies on one page that his army had anything to do with the burning, on the next page he says that "having utterly ruined Columbia, the right wing began its march northward."

That statement at any rate was true, and by March 23, after having twice defeated Johnston, who had been called to try to oppose him, Sherman had reached Goldsboro, about 160 miles south of Richmond, where he remained a fortnight and was joined by General Schofield with an addi-tional 26,000 men who had come by way of Wilmington which had been captured by the Federals. Lee's position had now become so precarious that Grant no longer needed Sherman's direct help and the latter was able to turn and force Johnston back to Greensboro.

Meanwhile, Sherman went to City Point, Va., to have an interview with Grant, and the 28th met the prin-cipal officers of the Northern army and also Lincoln him-self, who had come from Washington. He reports that al-though both he and Grant felt that one more great battle would have to be fought, Lincoln asked several times if it could not be avoided, as more than enough blood had already been shed. It was evident that the end was fast approaching. Charleston had fallen and practically every Southern port was in Union hands. With the Shenandoah Valley gone, with a Federal army of 85,000 in North Carolina, cutting Lee off from the South, his army, even though heavily depleted, was beginning to suffer severely from want of supplies. Desertion had become colossal. Men can put up with almost any hardship at the front if they feel that their families are safe at home, but now between the occupation of almost all the seacoast and Sherman's wide sweep of desolation through the heart of the Confederacy, no home seemed safe, and poverty and suffering were intense. The Northerner might place loyalty to the Union above that to his State, whereas the Southerner might reverse the position, but at all times practically every man places loyalty to his own family—parents, wife, and children—above all others. The Southern woman, if she had been extremely bitter toward the enemy, had been a marvel of courage, and there is no more glorious page in our history than the one telling how she bore all the anxiety, suffering, loss, and deprivation of more than four years of war with a smile as sweet and a dignity as unruffled as her spirit was lofty. But the pressure was becoming unbearable, and the armies at the front were melting.

A little more than three weeks before, on March 4, Lincoln had delivered his second inaugural address, in which he had said: "Neither party expected for the war the magnitude or the duration which it has already attained. . . . Both read the same Bible, and pray to the same God; and each invokes His aid against the other . . . let us judge not, that we be not judged. The prayers of both could not be answered—that of neither has been answered fully. . . . With malice toward none; with charity for all; with firmness in the right, as God gives us to see the right, let us strive to finish the work we are in; to bind up the nation's wounds; to care for him who shall have borne the battle, and for his widow and orphan—to do all which may achieve a just and lasting peace among ourselves, and with all nations."

By the time Sherman and Lincoln met, the end, as we have said, was evidently in sight; and Sherman asked if Lincoln was prepared for it. The substance of the talk may be given in the general's own words. "What," he wrote in his *Memoirs,* he asked Lincoln, "was to be done with the rebel armies when defeated? And what should be done with the political leaders, such as Jeff. Davis, etc.? Should we allow them to escape, etc.? He [Lincoln] said he was all ready; all he wanted of us was to defeat the opposing armies, and to get the men composing the Confederate armies back to their homes, at work on their farms and in their shops. As to Jeff. Davis, he was hardly at liberty to speak his mind fully, but intimated that he ought to clear out, 'escape the country,' only it would not do for him to say so openly. As usual, he illustrated his meaning by a story: 'A man once had taken a total abstinence pledge. When visiting a friend, he was invited to take a drink, but declined, on the score of his pledge; when his friend suggested lemonade, which was accepted. In preparing the lemonade, the friend pointed to the brandy-bottle, and said the lemonade would be more palatable if he were to pour in a little brandy; when his guest said, if he could do so unbeknown to him, he would not object.' " From which illustration, Sherman added, "I inferred that Mr. Lincoln wanted Davis to escape, 'unbeknown' to him." In commenting on the interview, Sherman added, "I know, when I left him, that I was more than ever impressed by his kindly nature, his deep and earnest sympathy with the afflictions of the whole people resulting from the war, and by the march of hostile armies through the South; and that his earnest desire seemed to be to end the war speedily, without more bloodshed or devastation, and to restore all men of both sections to their homes."[32] Sherman then returned to his army and left Grant facing Lee.

An attempt at peace, in February, had failed because Davis would not accept anything less than the acknowledged independence of the South and Lincoln could not accept anything but Union and emancipation. There was nothing to do but to continue to fight it out, though it was clearly hopeless for the South. The Confederate Congress adjourned *sine die* on March 19, passing none of the measures recommended by Davis. The next day flour was $1500 a barrel, bacon and butter each $20 a pound, and the government was hastily sending away the archives. Confederate negro troops paraded in Capitol Square in Richmond and it was reported that only 180 out of 5000 Texas cavalry remained in Virginia. Gold was selling at 100 to 1 in paper money.

On April 1, Sheridan won the battle of Five Forks, and Lee was obliged to evacuate first Petersburg and then Richmond, starting southward to try to unite with Johnston at Greensboro. When the Confederate troops left the capital all was in confusion. Davis and other members of the government had already fled southward to escape capture. The magazines, public stores, cotton, and tobacco were ordered to be burned to prevent them from falling into the hands of the Federals. During the night of April 2–3, the inhabitants were wakened by the loud explosions and soon after fires started in various parts of the city. The civic authorities were busy having all the liquor which could be found poured into the gutters but the mob, as far as they could, filled pitchers and pails from the flowing streams. By morning the city was ablaze and the poor were looting

[32] *Memoirs, op. cit.,* vol. II, pp. 326 *f.*

stores and private houses, even that of Lee himself being sacked.

"Who shall tell the horror of the past night!" wrote Mrs. McGuire next day. "Hope seemed to fade . . . but I do not think that any of us felt keenly, or have yet realized our overwhelming calamity. The suddenness and extent of it is too great for us to feel its poignancy at once. About two o'clock in the morning we were startled by a loud sound like thunder. . . . It was soon understood to be the blowing up of a magazine below the city. In a few hours another exploded on the outskirts. . . . It was then daylight. . . . Many ladies were now upon the streets . . . the pavements were covered with broken glass . . . women, both white and coloured, were walking in multitudes from the Commissary offices and burning stores with bags of flour, meal, coffee, sugar, rolls of cotton cloth, etc.; coloured men were rolling wheelbarrows filled in the same way. I went on and on toward the depot, and as I proceeded shouts and screams became louder."[33]

Early in the morning, after the Confederate troops left, the mayor had ridden out to the Federal lines to surrender the city and to request that Union troops be sent in at once, "to preserve order and protect women and children and property." They entered and did so, but the fire kindled by the Confederates themselves continued to burn out the heart of the city before it could be brought under control. Later in the day, Mrs. McGuire wrote that "the fire was progressing rapidly, and the crashing sound of falling timbers was distinctly heard. Dr. Read's church was blazing. Yankees, citizens, and negroes were attempting to arrest the flames. The War Department was falling in; burning papers were being wafted about the streets. The Commissary Department, with our desks and papers, was

[33] *Diary of a Southern Refugee, op. cit.*, p. 345.

consumed already. Warwick & Barksdale's mill was sending its flames to the sky. Cary and Main Streets seemed doomed throughout; Bank Street was beginning to burn, and now it had reached Franklin. At any other moment it would have distracted me, but I had ceased to feel anything." The following day she wrote grudgingly that "I feel as if we were groping in the dark; no one knows what to do. The Yankees, so far, have behaved humanely. As usual, they begin with professions of kindness to those whom they have ruined without justifiable cause, without reasonable motive, without right to be here, or anywhere else within the Southern boundary. General Ord is said to be polite and gentlemanly, and seems to do everything in his power to lessen the horrors of this dire calamity."[34] It is, perhaps, not necessary to point out again that the Northerner was just as honestly and sincerely convinced that it was his duty to maintain the Union, and that Richmond and the rest of the South were a part of it, as Mrs. McGuire was that he had no right to cross the boundary which the Confederacy had set up.

Meanwhile, Lee's shrunken and almost starving army was on its way toward Danville by several roads, Grant in pursuit. On the 4th, Lee reached Amelia Court House, but was disappointed to find none of the supplies he had expected there. A day was lost collecting food, and the next Sheridan cut the railway to Danville, and Lee had to turn toward Lynchburg. By desertions his army was melting rapidly whereas, by the 8th, he found General Ord and a large Federal force in front of him at Appomattox Court House. The day before, Grant had sent him a note saying it was obvious that further resistance was useless and asking for the surrender of the Army of Northern Virginia to avoid further bloodshed. An exchange of letters followed

[34] *Ibid.,* pp. 348 *f.*

and as a result, on the 9th, Generals Grant and Lee, accompanied by members of their staffs, met at the house of Mr. McLean at Appomattox to discuss terms of surrender.

The story has often been told. Grant, who had been ill and had not expected the meeting quite so soon, had hurried to the appointed rendezvous in the usual somewhat rough garb he wore in the field. Exhilarated at first by the news that the enemy was about to surrender, he wrote later that as he rode to the place of meeting his feelings became "sad and depressed." "I felt like anything rather than rejoicing," he says in his *Memoirs,* "at the downfall of a foe who had fought so long and so valiantly, and had suffered so much for a cause," though he himself did not believe in that cause. Lee, handsome, over six feet tall, dressed in a new uniform and with a handsome sword, made a striking contrast to Grant, in the uniform of a private with only the shoulder straps of a lieutenant general to show his rank. "But this," wrote the Federal commander, "was not a matter I thought of until later."

When the two leaders, who had contended so long, met they "soon fell into a conversation about old army times," Grant recorded. Lee "remarked that he remembered me very well in the old army; and I told him that as a matter of course I remembered him perfectly, but from the difference in our rank and years (there being about sixteen years' difference in our ages), I had thought it likely that I had not attracted his attention sufficiently to be remembered by him after such a long interval. Our conversation grew so pleasant that I almost forgot the object of our meeting. After the conversation had run on in this style for some time, General Lee called my attention to the object of our meeting," and asked for the terms on which surrender might be made. To this, Grant replied that he meant merely that Lee's army should lay down their arms and not take them up again during the continuance of the war, to which Lee agreed, and then the conversation again went off to more pleasant topics.

After a while, Lee came back again to the object of the meeting and suggested that Grant put the terms in writing. Grant says that when he started to write he had only the general idea of surrender already suggested in his mind but that when he put his pen to the paper the thought occurred to him that the Southern officers owned their own horses and should be allowed to keep them; also that it would "be an unnecessary humiliation to call upon them to deliver their side-arms." He therefore covered these two points in the paper he drew up, and when Lee read them he said "with some feeling" that this "would have a very happy effect on his army." He then suggested that the Southern army was somewhat different in its make-up from the Northern and that many of the privates, as well as the officers, owned their horses. Grant thought for a moment, and said that the agreement as drawn up would not permit them to retain them but as, in his opinion, the recent fighting would probably be the last battle of the war, and as the devastation had been so great, he would change the terms so as to permit any soldier giving his parole and who claimed a horse or mule to take it to his home. Lee again remarked that this would have a happy effect, and then signed the letter of surrender.

This done, he said that his army was in want of food and had been living solely on parched corn for several days, to which Grant at once responded with the promise of all the food which the 25,000 troops, named by Lee as the number yet remaining in his army, would require. The next day, Lee and Grant had a purely informal social visit, and later some of the Union officers went inside the Confederate lines to see old friends and some of the Confederates came over to the McLean house. "Here," wrote Grant, "the officers of both armies came in great numbers, and seemed to enjoy the meeting as much as though they had been friends separated for a long time while fighting battles under the same flag. For the time being it looked very much as if all thought of the war had escaped their minds."[35]

The news of Lee's surrender was, of course, received with jubilation in the North, as it was considered to mark the practical ending of the long war. Not only in the North but in those parts of the South in Federal hands, the occasion was marked by rejoicing and formal celebrations, the most significant of which was held in Charleston when General Anderson raised the identical Union flag over the ruins of Fort Sumter which he had been forced to lower four years before to the day, April 14, 1861.

On the same date, Lincoln, who had visited Richmond, held what was unhappily to be his last Cabinet meeting, and Grant was present. Speaking of Sherman still facing Johnston, the President said: "I have no doubt that favorable news will soon come for I had last night my usual dream which has preceded nearly every important event of the war. I seemed to be in a singular and indescribable vessel, but always the same and to be moving with great rapidity toward a dark and indefinite shore." He considered it "providential" that the end of the war was coming while Congress was not in session, and made clear his own pacific views as to the reconstruction of the South. "If we are wise and discreet," he is reported as saying, "we shall reanimate the States and get their governments in successful operation, with order prevailing and the Union re-established before Congress comes together in December . . . I hope there will be no persecution, no bloody work after the war is over. No one need expect me to take any part in hanging or killing those men, even the worst of them. Frighten them out of the country, open the gates, let down

[35] *Memoirs, op. cit.*, vol. II, pp. 337 *ff.*

the bars, scare them off. Enough lives have been sacrificed. We must extinguish our resentments if we expect harmony and union. There is too much of a desire on the part of some of our very good friends to be masters, to interfere and dictate to those States, to treat the people not as fellow citizens; there is too little respect for their rights. I do not sympathize in those feelings."[36]

Grant left in the afternoon to rejoin the army, and in the evening Lincoln, who had been very happy all day at the prospect of a nation reunited in friendliness, went to Ford's theatre. His box was utterly unguarded, and in the course of the performance the most tragic blow which the South could suffer at the moment fell upon it. John Wilkes Booth, one of a small band of conspirators, Southern in sympathy but not representing the South, entered the unguarded door and shot Lincoln in the head. Shouting *"sic semper tyrannis,"* he leaped to the stage and escaped. As in the case of the later assassination of McKinley, it is probable that the wild denunciations of newspapers had worked on a weak and partially disordered mind. So far from being a "tyrant" Lincoln was at that moment the best friend the fallen South had in all the North and on him alone depended the possible restoration of fraternal relations in the Union which was then assured. Another member of the conspiracy entered the house where the Secretary of State, Seward, lay ill, and attacked him savagely though without mortal wound. Lincoln, carried across the street to a private house, never regained consciousness, the bullet having entered the brain, and he died early in the morning. Like blasts from Hell all the wild winds of fanaticism and hatred were then let loose in the North, and the fate of the South for a decade was sealed.

Johnston had already suggested surrender to Sherman, and the latter was on his way to meet the Southern gen-

36 Rhodes, *History of the United States, op. cit.,* vol V, p. 137.

eral when he was handed a telegram from Stanton stating that the President had been assassinated and that the plot apparently was to include the deaths of Grant and of all the high officials of the government. As soon as Sherman met Johnston in the privacy of a small farm house, he showed him the telegram. "The perspiration," wrote Sherman, "came out in large drops on his forehead, and he did not attempt to conceal his distress. He denounced the act as a disgrace to the age, and hoped I did not charge it to the Confederate Government." Sherman replied that he could not believe for a moment that Lee or any officer in the army could have been privy to it, but he would not trust Davis and some of the politicians, adding that he greatly feared the effect on his army at Raleigh when the news became known lest some foolish woman or man might "say something or do something that would madden our men and that a fate worse than that of Columbia might befall the place." The South, however, as a whole, execrated the deed, and although wholly innocent of any complicity in the machinations of a madman instantly realized the terrible implications.

Sherman, however, did not comprehend the full strength of the Furies which had been loosed now that the gentle but firm hand of Lincoln had been rendered powerless in death. He himself felt that the war was practically at an end, and wrote, soon after, "I confess, without shame, I am sick and tired of fighting—its glory is all moonshine; even success, the most brilliant, is over dead and mangled bodies, with the anguish and lamentations of distant families, appealing to me for sons, husbands and fathers . . . I *know* the rebels are whipped to death, and I declare before God, as a man and a soldier, I will not strike a foe who stands unarmed and submissive."[37]

His fear was that possible guerilla bands might continue the conflict, and indeed at that moment Jefferson Davis was

[37] Hart, *Sherman, op. cit.*, p. 402.

flying southwestward with the avowed object, in his own words, of continuing fighting, if not east of the Mississippi then west of it. Johnston admitted that further fighting would not be war but "murder," and suggested that a general arrangement might be reached providing for the surrender of all the Confederate armies and the settlement of peace terms. Sherman, thinking of his talk with Lincoln and of the re-establishment of a genuine and healing peace, unfortunately went beyond his powers as a mere military commander and drew up an agreement which involved many civil questions, although he made it subject to the action of the Federal authorities. The terms, including an armistice terminable at forty-eight hours' notice, were extremely generous and could they have been put into operation, would have saved the nation much of the tragedy it still had to face.

When, however, they reached Washington, all was in confusion. Andrew Johnson, a poor Southern white, inexperienced and at first thirsting for vengeance against the aristocratic planter class, was President instead of Lincoln. Stanton, always hard and narrow-minded, and now rendered more bitter by what he believed to be the diabolical plot against himself and other members of the Cabinet by the South, was furious at both Sherman's leniency and what he considered to be his encroachment on the civil power. Those of us who took part in the World War well recall the frenzy in which it ended—the calls to "hang the Kaiser," the appeals to vengeance by the popular press, the demands of politicians like Lloyd George that Germany "pay every shilling" of the cost of the struggle. If we should unhappily have had to add to all that the assassination of the King of England or the President of the United States by a German sympathizer and what was believed to be a German plot, we can understand the feeling in Washington and the North when Sherman's terms were read.

He was immediately accused of treachery and of having been bribed by Davis. Stanton behaved outrageously. Disregarding Sherman's plighted word and the armistice, he ordered other generals to advance against Johnston's army and to take no orders from Sherman.

Fortunately the situation was saved, in so far as it could be, by Grant, who went to Raleigh and informed Sherman that the terms were disallowed and that Johnston would have to surrender on the same mere military basis that Lee had accepted. Sherman at once gave the requisite forty-eight hours' notice of renewal of hostilities to Johnston but the latter, refusing to shed more blood needlessly and hopelessly, surrendered his army still numbering 37,000, after having lost several thousand by desertion in the preceding five days. When, later, Sherman found out the treachery of both Stanton and Halleck, he stated in his official report that he "would have protected Johnston's army and defended his own pledge of faith, even at the cost of many lives." So highly did Johnston appreciate Sherman that years later, in 1891, he went North to serve as pallbearer at the funeral of his former foe.

About this same time Sherman wrote that "we cannot kill disarmed men. All this clamor after Jeff Davis . . . and others is bosh. Any young man with a musket is now a more dangerous object than Jeff Davis. He is old, infirm, a fugitive hunted by his own people, and none so poor as to do him reverence."[38] Halleck, however, had written to Stanton that orders be sent to all commanders to take measures to capture the ex-Confederate President, who he claimed was fleeing with a treasure of "from six to thirteen million dollars," when in fact he had practically nothing. On May 10 Davis was captured by a small troop of Federal cavalry near Irwinsville, Ga., and with former Senator Clay was sent to Fortress Monroe to become a

[38] Hart, *Sherman, op. cit.,* p. 399.

prisoner of state and by order of the now implacable and powerful Stanton to undergo the utterly unjustified indignity of being manacled in his cell. Vice-President Stephens was confined in Fort Warren, Boston. The horrors of war were over and those of "peace" were to begin. The curtain had been rung down on the central and bloody act of our tragedy, but it was not to rise for the next one on a united nation. The soldiers who had fought each other to the death on a hundred battle-fields could fraternize after each; Lee and Grant could almost forget the object of their meeting at Appomattox in talk about old times; but the days of the soldier had passed, and that of the fanatic and the politician had come.

CHAPTER X

## THE AFTERMATH

THE three groups, Northern, Southern, and foreign, which have discussed the war, whether they have been composed of historians, military officers, politicians, or mere recorders and commentators, have all differed among themselves as to the cause of the final collapse of the Confederacy. By one or another it has been claimed that it was due to lack of man power in the South; to inadequacy of resources; to bad financing; to the blockade; to cotton policy; to foreign policy; to generalship; to the hampering of the central government by pushing States' Rights to the extreme; to confusion as to the real objective of the war; to the quarrels between Davis and his generals; to quarrels between politicians, such as led to the estrangement between the President and Vice-President for more than two years; to psychological reasons; to the final pressure on troops at the front from their families suffering at home; or to other causes, all cited by one and another writer in each and every group.

No human being is simple, and history, which is the story of the interaction upon each other of huge masses of individuals, can never be so. In modern history the number of recorded "facts," important or unimportant, is colossal, and the writing of a historical narrative inevitably calls for selection. Otherwise history would be a huge collection of unrelated and chaotic entries in an annual chronicle. The historian has first to delimit his field, and then, within it, to try to create some order out of chaos, to attempt to bring his chosen facts into comprehensible relation to one another in some sort of causal sequence. History is not a science, and has never had its Galileo, its Newton or Einstein. There are no great simple laws; and the tendency of historians, giving their views of the causal sequences in any period, has been to over-simplify, to stress one factor, economic or otherwise.

It is likely that each and every one of the reasons given by one writer and another played its part in the defeat of the South. In any case, the North had won the war, though that fact had not settled the issue, other than practically. The questions of abstract right or abstruse logic remained undeterminate. Nevertheless, however opinions might yet honestly differ, slavery had been abolished; the power of a State to secede had been denied; the Union had been shown to be lasting. Both South and North had been sincere in their views. As neither would yield to those of the other without a struggle, there had been nothing to do except to allow brute force to determine the issue. That had now been done, but at enormous cost to both sides, material and spiritual. It is impossible to arrive at accurate figures either for men in service or for deaths, but it would appear that over 300,000 Union soldiers had been killed in action or died during their time in the army, and the casualties for the Confederates were probably heavier in proportion to the population.

The immediate property loss to the South was incomparably greater than that to the North, although by 1864 the war was costing the Union the then unprecedented sum of $1,000,000 a day. However hectic a seeming prosperity may be produced by war during its continuance and in the few years following peace, war always has to be paid for. We have been learning this anew, as each generation appears to be obliged to, since 1929, and our fathers learned it in the long-drawn-out economic misery in the North between 1873 and 1879. At first, however, there was a wild boom in that section for a few years whereas the South was prostrate from Appomattox.

Some of its fairest cities and towns were largely in ruins—Richmond, Charleston, Mobile, Atlanta, Columbia, and others. Much of the countryside, especially in Georgia, Alabama, and South Carolina, was a half wilderness where burned chimney stacks marked the former presence of homes. Approximately $2,000,000,000 worth of property in slaves had been wiped out at a stroke of the pen. When the Confederate currency sank to zero in value, government bonds, securities of banks, railroads, and other corporations, savings-bank deposits, bank balances, and life-insurance policies all became worthless. Many could say with one rich Southern lady that there "is nothing left to us now but the bare land, and the debts contracted for the support of hundreds of negroes during the war." The railroad system, such as it had been, was disrupted and largely ruined. Eight hundred miles in Alabama were useless. Sherman had destroyed some hundreds of miles in Georgia and South Carolina. There was almost nothing left—not merely of rails, depots, and rolling stock, but even of roadbed—of the best line in Mississippi. Cotton had been mostly destroyed. There was only land, some proportion of the houses, ruin, and 4,000,000 of blacks almost wholly unaccustomed to freedom, unused to any wage system of labor, and among the whites, little or no liquid capital with which to pay wages. A whole new form of civilization had to be built up under most difficult conditions.

But the losses on both sides were not merely material. As we pointed out in an earlier chapter, the North for a generation or so had been more open to new ideas and the many movements of the age than the South, owing largely to the latter's having had to concentrate on the defence of slavery and the anachronistic economic form of its society. On the other hand, in spite of this degree of open-minded-ness as to life, the North did not know how to live. Outside of certain Northern groups which worshipped European "culture," and "book learning," the North was a welter of materialism and a chaos of values. There were the riches of a virgin continent to be exploited. Most of the white immigrants who came to America in floods in the nineteenth century, bent on rising in the economic scale, had come to the North. Largely according to race, they either had remained in the cities to form a labor supply for business and manufacturing or had gone on the land, steadily farther westward, to take up homesteads and start as small farmers. In the eighteenth century, after the first hard work and culturally demoralizing experiences of the seaboard frontier were passed, both North and South had begun to build up a cultured, wealthy, and partially leisured class. Whatever may be said both for and against such a class, it must be admitted that in the past, its members have been largely the patrons of the arts and not least of the art of living, their manners and outlook seeping down through the various strata of society. In the war of the American Revolution, a considerable part of this class in the North had become Tories, and had emigrated to Canada and England to a far greater extent than from the South. It has been said that no other country has ever suffered from such an important emigration except France when the Huguenots fled, and that the names of those who left Boston reads "like a bead roll" of its famous families.

Between the departure of a large number of the cultured, wealthy, and conservative families from the North in 1776 and later; the flood of new immigrants bent on gaining economic advantage as quickly as possible; the lack of agricultural labor; the incentive to a business career; and the immense resources to be exploited, the stage was set for the rise of an essentially material civilization in the North before the war, and this was intensified during the struggle by the feverish activity in an industrial community. There was no established society, in the best sense, to give tone and to inculcate a set of values in life to the masses. There was little to balance, on the one hand, the increasing social insolence of the millionaires and multi-millionaires, and, on the other, the impractical and wild doctrines of the radical reformers.

Northerners, depending on their ideas and tastes, might look up to a Charles Sumner, a Vanderbilt, a Wendell Phillips, an Astor, and others in the 1840's, '50's or '60's, as great men but there were few or none to lead in a humane and sane outlook on life, and whose philosophy and manners would help the crowd to humane living. There was money-making on the grand scale; there were innumerable "reforms," wild or sound; there was steady extension of "book learning," quite different from increase in wisdom; but there was no philosophy or way of life. Because there was none, the war and the post-war era greatly intensified the materialistic civilization of the North, and brought on a complete moral debacle and many of those evils against which we are still fighting. In the absence of other standards, wealth and power, however acquired, became the goals of success. Labor, the farmer, art, the contemplative life, became of no importance contrasted with the dazzling fortunes and the political and business control over the lives of tens of thousands resulting from the often unscrupulous pursuit of industrial profits. As the greatest fortunes, quickest made, were usually acquired by men otherwise negligible or harmful, the spiritual effect on the life of the masses was wholly baneful.

The philosophy of mere getting and doing took possession of the North. The North, for decades before and after the war, was in flux, and although such a state brings excitement it does not bring lasting satisfaction. Few men who devote themselves to rapid money-making in a society in which wealth spells prestige ever reach the point where they are satisfied, but people whose views of life are looked down upon by others set up defence mechanisms for themselves, not least the discontented. The South, as we shall presently note, had a philosophy of life, based on quite different values from those of the North, and the North was irritated by it.

Henry Hitchcock was an eminent Northern lawyer, a useful citizen, and considered a gentleman, but his diary unconsciously reveals much of the Northern attitude of his day. Speaking of the wife of a Judge Worden, who as United States tax collector had installed himself in the Rhett house in Charleston, he says: "She is not exactly the oracle I would consult—a plain, rather elderly, rather hard-featured woman, dare say a good woman in her way, though—but a contrast to the 'Southern ladies' who used to rule here. Yet she is a type of a better because more useful and more truly respectable class"! And again the Northern dislike of carefully cultivated manners comes out in his comment on that great Southern gentleman and leader, Wade Hampton, who first devoted himself to the Confederate cause, later rescued his State from the misrule of the carpet-baggers, and eventually became United States Senator after his State was restored to the Union. Writing of his meeting with Hampton during the war, Hitchcock says his "whole demeanor was marked with the easy 'well-bred' essentially vulgar insolence which is characteristic of *that* type of 'gentleman'; a man of polished manners, scarcely veiling the arrogance and utter selfishness which marks his class, and which I hate with a perfect hatred. There is nothing of the true *man* in such 'gentlemen'; their external polish and tact, their knowledge of the world, their easy self-possession . . . count for just as much as the glitter of paste diamonds and no more."[1]

[1] *Marching with Sherman, op. cit.*, p. 310.

Considering Hitchcock's position and attainments, these two paragraphs not only fairly reek with the effects of an inferiority complex, but bring out the instinctive dislike of the man who has to make his own position in a fluid and chaotic society for the man who has an assured position in a stable one; and also the dislike of those who·make a gospel of work and success for those who try to make living an art. In the nineteenth century the ante-bellum South had been the only section of our country which had had a stable, established society and a philosophy of life.

It was not simply that the South was agrarian and the North industrial. The West was also intensely agrarian, but, though its economic interests might clash with the industrial and banking East, it was at one with the East in the formlessness of its social life, in its worship of work and success, in its wish to "get ahead," and in its ignoring of the question of what success was for, what life itself was for.

The difference was that in the South a form of society which we have already partially described had slowly evolved which gave to its leaders a certain security of social position and prestige. The West was still too new, too raw and hustling, to have developed a settled social form, and in the North the elements of stability, that is of family and land, were small and local in the country while in the fast growing cities they were largely overwhelmed by the power of money. It is only in an old, stable, and organized society that an art and philosophy of living come into existence. The South, as we pointed out in an earlier chapter, was far from being a unit, and with the rise of the "Cotton Kingdom" it had its own ample supply of new rich, the "Cotton Snobs," and others. Nevertheless, the old planter aristocracy had an assured position and influence such as no other class in America had. One generation of a family might differ much from another in wealth, and at times there might be very little, but the mere fact that a man was living on a large estate which had been in possession of a line of ancestors, and all of them gentlemen, for a hundred and fifty or two hundred years, and that the name of the estate was linked with that of the family throughout not merely the county and State, but perhaps the whole South, gave to him an assurance, an influence, and a freedom from any necessity of competing with others that was unknown elsewhere in America.

With the formation of this stable society had come the formulation, conscious or unconscious, of the Southern philosophy of life which led directly to an art of life. It was only in the South that the belief in the fully rounded life took root and flourished. Perhaps no people have cared less for mere worldly success than the leaders of the old plantation South. The owner of a big plantation, as also its mistress, in spite of Hitchcock, had ample responsibility, but there was also leisure; and leisure and what to do with it were as important as work, because the Southerner's main preoccupation was how to live a full life. He found this in his plantation responsibilities, in public office, in sport, in reading, in a social life which he made an art. Manners and breeding were worth more than money, and social hours were as important as business hours.

The outlook of the planter class had permeated the whole South, and that section alone of the three into which the country had become divided had found a satisfying way of life. It was, as I have just said, not agrarianism versus industrialism, for a farmer may be just as keen on making money as an industrialist, and have practically the same philosophy or lack of it. One recalls, even in England, Tennyson's "Northern Farmer—New Style," who as he listened to his horse's hoofs ahead of him said:

"Dosn't thou 'ear my 'erse's legs, as they canters away?
Proputty, proputty, proputty—that's what I 'ears 'em say."

The chief distinguishing characteristic of the Southern way of life was that it was primarily based on human rather than material values. Implicit in it was a criticism of the North, in spite of the reforming and humanitarian zeal of that section, and of the West in spite of its being agrarian. Deep below the expressed motives in the long controversy had lain the Northerner's resentment and the Southerner's fear. The Northerner may have hated slavery but he hated quite as much the aristocratic slave owner who would have nothing of the Northern doctrine of getting and doing. The Southerner may have dreaded losing his slaves but he had dreaded even more the overwhelming of his way of life.

The war, however, and almost as much the harrowing period of Reconstruction to follow, did largely overwhelm it. The war completely disrupted its economic base, which would, in any case, have had to be altered peaceably or otherwise, in time. The Confederate soldier, from general to private, went home to start again on the land with what resources he might possess. The slaves, most of whom had been remarkably loyal during the war, were now free. Many stayed on "the old place," many took to wandering. In any case methods of paying and employing had gradually to assume shape. Even nature seemed to take a hand in the general ruin, and droughts and insects played havoc with the crops for a year or two, and want and hunger stalked the land. In the four years after peace the Freedmen's Bureau alone distributed over 21,000,000 rations, of which about three-quarters went to negroes.

The slavery problem had been replaced by the race problem, still with us, and its difficulties were immensely increased by the impractical zeal of Northern reformers and the greed of Northern politicians. We have seen that Lincoln had tried to maintain the theory that the Southern States had never been out of the Union, and that he hoped to get them back into some regular connection with it before Congress could meet. What he could have done had he lived is an unanswerable question but the problem presented difficulties that even he might not have been able to resolve. The North regarded the secessionists, as many of them had designated themselves, as rebels, and it seemed impossible that rebels should be at once asked to take part in the government of the country, to make its laws or to sit as the advisers of the President. It was too much like expecting England, had the American Revolution failed, to have elevated Washington, Hancock, Patrick Henry, or Sam Adams to high office. Public opinion in the North was bitterly opposed to any such action. Pestiferous agitators like Wendell Phillips fanned the flames of hatred and insisted on immediate negro suffrage. Professional negrophiles like Charles Sumner and Thaddeus Stevens seemed to care only to raise the blacks and ruin the whites of the Confederacy. Indeed, Stevens, who was said to have a black mistress and was one of the most powerful Republican figures in Congress, was almost incredibly malevolent in his speeches and efforts. An old man of great ability, soured and embittered in his feelings, one of the wittiest men who has ever sat in the House, now nearing the end of his life, he gave up his last months to an almost Satanic hatred.

Political motives were also leading the Republicans to ruin the South. We have already seen that their party had been from the first made up of incongruous elements, notably the section which wanted a protective tariff without caring about the negro, and the smaller one which was made up of the fanatical Abolitionists who cared about abolishing slavery and enfranchising the negro, and nothing about the tariff. If the negroes were enfranchised, the Republicans counted on being able to get practically all their votes, and so riveting their party rule on the country, ensuring the maintenance of the high tariffs which the war had brought.

The alliance between these sections of the party was thus obviously predestined. Even before his assassination, Lincoln was finding difficulty in keeping the leadership, and the wave of anger which swept over the North when Booth fired his revolver made the success of the radicals certain.

It is impossible to tell in detail here either the political or social story of the dozen years or so of the dark Reconstruction period. Andrew Johnson, who succeeded Lincoln, found a Cabinet divided between the radical and liberal Republicans, with Stanton at the head of the former. Johnson himself was a Southerner, who had been a Democrat before the war but had been the loyal governor of Tennessee and had joined the Republican ranks from his love of the Union. Like Lincoln, he was of very humble origin and for a while had been a tailor, imbibing in his early days a strong resentment against the aristocratic class of the South. The Presidential office unhappily always makes its holder the target of abuse and slander, but Johnson was to suffer more in this respect than any other who has held it, even to the point of being the only President in our history against whom proceedings of impeachment have been brought. In recent years several new biographies and histories of his period have cleared away the calumnies. He was at times vulgar, and hurt himself by some of his public speeches, but he never was a drunkard, as pictured, and although wholly self-educated, he had a powerful mind. The virulence of the abuse and slander poured out against him during his term was due to his opposition to the policies of the radical Republicans, who failed completely in their scandalous attempt to impeach him. He was not tactful and not always a good politician in securing his ends, but so far from being weak his strength impressed, in personal interviews, such diverse judges as Henry Adams and Charles Dickens. The former, indeed, after having known a dozen or so of the residents of the White House, noted that Johnson was the strongest he was ever likely to see.

His sudden accession to an office which he had never expected to hold made a trying position for him, and as Seward was confined to his home for some weeks by his wound, it was hoped by the radicals that the new and inexperienced President could be brought over wholly to their side by the forceful and vindictive Stanton. Wavering at first, it was not many weeks before he began to oppose them and to adopt the policies of Lincoln as to amnesty and reconstruction for the South. In his amnesty proclamation of May 29, 1865, he restored to United States citizenship all Confederates, with prominent exceptions, who would take the oath of allegiance, and in subsequent proclamations, setting up new State governments and ordering constitutional conventions, he excluded negro suffrage; negroes having the vote, in fact, in only six of even the Northern States.

Before the next meeting of Congress, six of the Southern States had accepted the situation, and the North as a whole was satisfied, but when Congress met in December Stevens opposed Johnson's plans for reconstruction, secured a vote excluding the representatives of the reconstructed States from taking their seats, and Congress took the problem of reorganization into its own hands. From that time on, both public opinion and Congress became more bitterly hostile to Johnson and the South. By March, 1867, the point had been reached where the South was divided into five military districts, under army rule, no State to escape until it had accepted the Fourteenth Amendment and negro suffrage. By 1870 all the Southern States had adopted new constitutions as required and had been received back into the Union, but meanwhile they had suffered incredibly under carpet-bag rule which was still to continue.

Innumerable Northerners had flocked South to exploit

either the economic or the political situation. Owing to poverty, debt, and the difficulty of the labor supply, land could be bought for a fraction of its pre-war and real value. Moreover there was the new negro vote to be organized in the interest of the Republican Party, and rich pickings for those who secured public office. That party in the Southern States was now made up of the white "carpet-baggers" from the North, the "scalawags," who were mostly the scum of the white South, and the newly enfranchised negroes. As the negroes in all the States bore a large proportion to the whites even when they did not actually outnumber them, and as considerable numbers of the better-class whites, including nearly all the natural leaders, were still disfranchised, the carpet-baggers, scalawags, and inexperienced negroes, under the protection of United States troops, were in control and free to plunder.

The results were appalling. In 1871, for example, the Republican Governor of South Carolina was Robert K. Scott, who had issued some hundreds of thousands of fraudulent bonds in New York under the influence of a notorious woman who had agreed to seduce him for a percentage of the profits. The Treasurer of the State was Niles G. Parker, under indictment for crime in Massachusetts. The Speaker of the House was a frequenter of negro brothels who had been expelled from his college fraternity. Another important member of the legislature was John Patterson, who was later to remark that "there are five years more of good stealing in South Carolina." In the first legislature under the new government there were eighty-eight negroes, mostly former slaves, and sixty-seven whites, most of them worse than the negroes. Later, the 85,000 negroes in the State, of whom 82 per cent were illiterate, had ninety-four representatives to only thirty for the 62,000 whites. The corruption, to say nothing of the manners, was incredible. Champagne and the finest cigars were served to members free. Two hundred thousand dollars' worth of furniture turned out to be $18,000, the rest being stolen. Pay certificates were issued to 350 attachés in the Senate though there were only 35. The debt and taxes of the State rose by leaps.

Similar conditions obtained in other States. In Louisiana the Governor out of a salary of $8000 accumulated $1,000,-000 in four years. A session of the legislature which before the war had cost $100,000 rose to ten times that amount. The bonded debt increased, as in all the States, by millions (twenty-seven in North Carolina), and taxes became insupportable. In Mississippi they rose 1400 per cent in four years. So it went.

It was an era of colossal scandals in the North also, of the Tweed Ring in New York and similar stealings on a gigantic scale in other cities, but at least in the North the voters could "turn the rascals out" if they chose. After the adoption of the Fourteenth Amendment by the reconstructed States, the South was helpless so long as the alliance between criminal and corrupt whites and ignorant negroes continued, unless the latter could be largely prevented from voting by either fraud, intimidation, or force. The situation was intolerable, and as honest Southerners watched such of their property as was yet left them being literally stolen by taxation, and the credit of their States being ruined by bond issues to cover graft, it is no wonder that there were clashes between the races. These were greatly exaggerated in the Northern press and by interested Northern politicians, and, together with the codes to govern the blacks passed by some of the States, and the obvious efforts of the Southerners not to be ruled and despoiled by the ex-slaves, were all used to make it appear that the South was still in rebellion and must be controlled.

The condition was not the fault of the negro, and the Southerner knew it. There were large numbers of intelligent and honest negroes among both the former free and slave classes, but the great mass was illiterate, without knowledge or experience of the world outside the routine of their plantation work, and utterly unfit in every way suddenly to become a ruling class and to legislate for great commonwealths. We all know the effect of too quickly acquired riches even upon an intelligent and steady-going person, and the sudden acquisition of personal freedom after generations of slavery had much the same effect upon the negroes. Moreover, they were made tools and dupes by both the doctrinaire and impractical reformers in the North, such as Sumner, Garrison, Phillips, and others, and by the corrupt politicians whose only use for their votes was to line their own pockets. It is no wonder that ignorant field hands or even well-trained, loyal, and intelligent house servants became bewildered when they found themselves cajoled and flattered, and the world turned upside down with themselves proclaimed to be on top. The social, political, economic, and psychological revolution wrought in the lives of the Southern negro slaves was probably the greatest and most sudden which any people has had to experience, and on the whole they came through it well.

Nevertheless, the question of white or negro rule, and of home or carpet-bag control of legislatures, had to be solved; and the South solved it in general during these early Reconstruction years by the practical elimination of the negro at the polls. By intimidation by the Ku-Klux Klan and other means, the Southern whites regained control of their own State governments during the early 1870's for the most part, but as a result the "solid South" of the Democratic Party arose and the Republican Party in that section became a skeleton of office holders and local wire-pullers, supported by such negroes as were later allowed to vote. Because it had been the party which in the opinion of the South had caused the war, because it was responsible for

the terrible Reconstruction years following, and because of
its corruption during that period, practically all Southerners
of the better sort, and the leaders as they gradually returned to public life, became Democrats. But as, nationally, that party was to be in power for only eight years between 1860 and 1912, this meant that even the ablest
Southerners were to be excluded for the most part from
participation in the public life of the nation for nearly two
generations.

Just as for thirty years or so before the war, that section
had been largely thrown back on itself and to a great extent
its intellectual life absorbed in a defence, direct or indirect,
of slavery, so now for another thirty years the collapse in
its civilization and its relation to the nation was again to
keep it out of the main currents of modern thought and to
make it ingrowing. The fundamentally important fact as
to our Civil War was that it was waged between the peoples
of distinct geographical sections. Had one part of the population, scattered throughout the whole country, disagreed
with another part similarly scattered, and fought out the
issue, the defeated party would at once have been reab-
sorbed into the general life of the nation. But in the case
of the Civil War, it was not a party which was defeated but
a geographical section. Its peculiar civilization had been
different and it now lay in ruins.

The section, as a section, was faced by problems which
did not exist in other sections. The rest of the country, in
good times and bad as they were to come, had been brought
close together and an enormous impetus had been given to
nationalism—in politics, in business, in ways of thought.
On the other hand, the South, largely excluded from the
national life, had to concern itself with its local problems,
which were of extreme difficulty. It had to rise from the
ashes of stark economic ruin. Its citizens, the former rich
as well as poor, and the new freedmen, had to concern them-

selves for some years with the fundamental difficulties of mere existence, of clothing, food, and shelter. Their educational institutions had been largely destroyed and in some cases those which the war had left were damaged by Reconstruction and the carpet-bag governments. In any case multitudes of young men who would normally have gone to school and college had more pressing tasks in the new struggle for existence.

A revolution was going on in the life of 9,000,000 people. A labor system had to be devised to meet the new exigencies, and the old fear of slave insurrection was replaced by the new fear of the now uncontrolled negro, free to wander and even armed. The slave problem was replaced by the even more difficult race problem. No race ever fully understands another. An Englishman, used to international conferences, once said to me that though he might differ from the conclusions of an American he could understand the mental process by which they had been reached, but though he might agree with those of a Frenchman or Italian, he could not tell how they had been reached. The Southerner, from long contact, certainly understood the negroes better than the Northerner, but even Mrs. Chesnut admitted that they were inscrutable. After the end of the war she wrote of those on her own place: "The shining black mask they wear does not show a ripple of change; they are sphinxes." Disguise it as some may, the race problem in the world at large is becoming more, rather than less, acute; and the problem of 4,000,000 blacks in a total population of 9,000,000 kept the Southern mind concentrated on a question, possibly of life and death, which did not exist in the rest of the country.

The Southern revolution was proceeding in the opposite direction from the Northern, if we may consider one as taking place in that other section. In the generation following the war, in the North wealth was rapidly concentrating;

393

in the South it was being distributed. The great plantations were breaking up. Poverty, outrageous taxes, labor troubles, debts kept throwing land on the market at ridiculous prices. Good land in the lower South could be bought for from three to five dollars an acre, and one Mississippi plantation was sold for thirty-five cents an acre. Southern poor whites and mountain whites, the more thrifty negroes and Northern speculators, descended on them and bought them up in sections. In the absence of slavery, the South was gradually becoming a land of small owners, as it would always have been had it not been for slavery. According to the 1930 Census almost one-third of all the farms in the South are worked by negro farmers, who own about a quarter of these. In the far South one-third of the land is said to be owned by negroes.

Toward 1880 the South began to emerge from the ruins. Better crops, better prices, a wider distribution of land and a greater diversity of occupation were making themselves felt. But it was a new and different South. It was no longer a South in which a great planter class ruled and to which it gave the tone. Many of the planters of old family, from one reason and another, had gone North or into Southern cities to renew fortune as professional or business men, and with this change they to some extent altered the outlook of the section, as did the growth of railroads and industry. There were notable exceptions and General Lee, whose fortune had been swept away by the war, declined the lucrative business positions offered to him and finally became president of Washington College, a small institution in the Valley which had survived the struggle with only four professors and forty students. It had never been notable, and Lee took the position chiefly to give an example to his countrymen. He had pleaded on several occasions for the healing of all dissensions and for loyal efforts to restore as far as possible the old harmony. He knew that education was one of the needs of the new South and also the trial of spirit of the former prominent and wealthy in starting again amid the ruins. No example of resignation and patriotism could have been greater than that afforded by the former head of the Confederate army now quietly taking up the task of leading an obscure institution with forty pupils.

Many, however, passed from the army and plantation to business, and although there had been a complete distinction between the old Southern planter and the landless Northern business man, there came to be less between the landless Southern railway or life insurance or bank president of however old family in the new and rapidly growing Southern cities and his fellow official in a Northern city. With the entrance of Northern capital came also Northern business men, and today a certain element in the South has the same "Chamber of Commerce" complex as North or West. I do not mean that the old South has wholly gone, but, as we shall note later, it is confused.

During the war, the horrible period of Reconstruction which followed, and the gradual change since, it was natural that those whom the war had ruined should have looked backward rather than forward, and that the legend of the Old South as a golden age without its dark shadows should have become stereotyped, as we said in an earlier chapter. Moreover, unhappily, the sectional nature of the struggle; the practical destruction of the two-party system which ensued as a result; activities of "patriotic" societies; the long dominance of the Republican Party, which waved the "bloody shirt" in campaigns for nearly thirty years; the pressure for pensions by Northern ex-soldiers with the putrid scandals involved, all helped to keep alive the hostility between the two sections. Twenty years after the war ended, the sections were drawing together but editors, politicians, and pension grabbers were still doing what they could to stir hatred.

Innumerable incidents in public life as well as private could be given to mark the gradual coming together again of the two peoples. One of the earliest, oddly enough, was a gesture from Charles Sumner, who almost at the close of his life had come to a more understanding sympathy with the South. In 1873 he was censured by the Massachusetts legislature for having introduced into Congress during the previous session a bill to remove from the regimental colors of the United States army the names of the battles won during the war between brethren. Two years later he was dead.

In his impractical reforming zeal he had done much to bring on the war against the South and to intensify her sufferings under Reconstruction, but in the Senate the customary eulogy of the dead statesman was pronounced not by a Northerner, but by one of the most brilliant men of the South, L. Q. C. Lamar, Senator from Mississippi and the original drafter of the Ordinance of Secession of that State. Speaking of Sumner, the orator said: "It has been the kindness of the sympathy which in these later days he has displayed toward the impoverished and suffering people of the Southern States that has unveiled to me the generous, tender heart which beat beneath the bosom of a zealot, and has forced me to yield to him the tribute of respect. . . . The South, prostrated, exhausted, drained of her life blood, as well as of her material resources, yet still honorable and true, accepts the bitter award of the bloody arbitrament without reservation, resolutely determined to abide the result with chivalrous fidelity. . . . The North, exultant in her triumph, and elevated by success, still cherishes, we are assured, a heart full of magnanimous emotions toward her disarmed and discomfited antagonist," yet he noted the acts and words which spread suspicion and distrust. "Would," he added, "that the spirit of the illustrious dead whom we lament today could speak from the grave to both parties to this lamentable discord in tones which would reach each and every heart throughout this broad territory: 'My countrymen, know one another and you will love one another.' "[2]

Fortunately, in spite of the insistence of Stanton and a few of his mind, there were no trials for treason of the Confederate President and others, and after varying periods, of months in length and considerable unneccessary hardship, such officials of the late Confederate Government as had been captured and placed in confinement were released. No blood was shed when the war was over. The North in 1865 considered Davis as a traitor and demanded a scape-goat for the four years of suffering and what it considered an unwarranted attack on the life of the nation, but even so it is probable that Davis would never have been placed in a cell had Lincoln not been assassinated with the double effect of removing a restraining and kindly force in the treatment of the South and of arousing popular fury. In spite of his sufferings, it is possible, however, that Davis fared better than if Lincoln had lived, for, sensing the danger for the Confederate leader, Lincoln had obviously been anxious for his escape from the country, whereas after his imprisonment the ex-President, who had been unpopular in the South at the end of the struggle, returned to his beloved land a hero, and could end his days there in peace instead of in exile.

Various incidents now began to occur from time to time to indicate that the nation was again united. The distinguished Confederate General Gordon sat on the platform of a mass meeting in Cooper Institute, New York, arranged to raise funds, to which General Grant had contributed

[2] *Congressional Record,* 43 Cong., 1 Sess., pp. 3410-11.

liberally, for the erection of a home for Confederate soldiers at Richmond, and one of the most impassioned speakers for the cause was the well-known Union Corporal Tanner, who had lost both legs in fighting near Richmond against the men he was now trying to aid. There were various reunions of the troops of both sides, and when the monument to the gallant Pickett, who died in 1875, was dedicated at Richmond, the remnants of the Philadelphia brigade which had opposed him at Gettysburg journeyed to the South to pay their respects to their heroic foe. When Grant died in 1885 and was accorded a military funeral in New York, the officer who rode at the right of General Hancock, in command, was the Confederate General Gordon, with General Fitzhugh Lee near at the head in a position of honor. Two years later the survivors of Pickett's men went to Gettysburg to view once more the ridge which they had so nobly stormed in one of the most heroic charges in history, and there again the remnants of their opponents, the Philadelphia brigade, came again to stand on the ridge, this time without weapons, to hold out their hands in friendship to their ancient enemies.

The gradual growth of sympathy and understanding, however, had to be slow and spontaneous. It could not be hurried, and there were sinister forces at work to prevent the healing process. In the same year as the reunion at Gettysburg, it having been reported to President Cleveland that many old battle flags, both Union and Confederate, had been found stored in the War Department, Cleveland at once endorsed the suggestion that they be returned to their respective States, South and North. Technically the President had no right to give the order and unfortunately the mercenary portion of the Grand Army of the Republic, stung by the President's recent veto of a new pension grab, was lying in wait to make trouble for him, as were also the Republican newspapers, anxious to create all possible ill-will against the Democrats. Both disappointed pensioners and partisan editors were at once on the war-path, and Cleveland was disgracefully assailed. With thought only of money and politics, the Grand Army so threatened the President if he attended its meeting, to which he had accepted an invitation, that for the sake of the dignity of his office and not from fear of personal violence he withdrew his acceptance; while *The Tribune* began to talk of the flags as "mementoes of as foul a crime as any in human history." Southern editors took up the hue and cry, but calming words came from the oldest State in the Union, and Governor Fitzhugh Lee of Virginia wrote that "the country should not again be agitated by pieces of bunting that mean nothing now. The South is part and parcel of the Union to-day, and means to do her part toward increasing the prosperity and maintaining the peace of the republic, whether the flags rot in Washington or are restored to their former custodians. If any man hauls down the American flag, shoot him on the spot, but don't let us get into trouble because another flag changed its resting place. It will not get into the hands of a standard bearer."[3]

The unhappy and sordid episode had not had its origin in the hearts and genuine feelings of the people of either side, and was the last of its kind. In the campaign of 1888 the Republicans made one final effort to "wave the bloody shirt" and assert that the Democrats were the party of treason and crime, but the people were outliving the rancors of the war and could no longer be stirred to hatred by issues settled nearly a quarter of a century earlier. The South had long been playing her part with honesty and nobility, and the entire people were tired of the self-interested lies and propaganda of the Republican politicians.

[3] Quoted by Allan Nevins, *Grover Cleveland* (New York, 1932), p. 334.

The abler and more honorable members of the party recognized that, and the war had at last passed from the emotional stage of political campaigns.

In 1898 came the Spanish War, and men of both sections fought a common enemy under the same flag. During that brief conflict, when the widow of General Pickett was the guest of his men at Atlanta, her son was at the same moment serving as an officer under the Stars and Stripes; and when a few weeks later the body of the daughter of Jefferson Davis was carried southward from Rhode Island it was accompanied by a guard of honor of veterans from the Grand Army of the Republic. A few years later, in 1905, a Republican President, Roosevelt, could return the battle flags of the South without criticism and with the benediction of the nation. However, even with the common efforts put forth by both sections in the World War it would be false to reality to claim that the old wounds are wholly healed and forgotten. The fire has died down to ashes but there are embers which can be stirred to flame. Yet the South, which had by far the hardest rôle to play, has taken its place with complete loyalty in the reunited life of the nation.

Moreover, in spite of the changes which have been occurring in the South, so that certain elements in it are now scarcely to be distinguished from the "go-getters" of the North or West, the section still retains much of the best which made not only its charm but its spiritual importance in the ante-bellum period. It would be a national catastrophe if prosperity, commercialization, industrialization, and Chambers of Commerce should break down its tradition that what a man is counts for more than what he has, and that life is more than labor.

Indeed, the essence of our national tragedy has been that the section of our new country in which the humane view and way of life developed first should, largely from the accidental nature of its labor economy, have been forced for two or three generations to expend its intellectual energies against the trend of the age, to lose its wealth, and to be left in ruin and without its proper and essential influence on the rest of the nation, which sorely needed, as it needs today, what the South had to give. The Puritanism of New England, with its off-shoots throughout the land, bred in the best instances strong characters, and the "New England conscience" placed duty above gain, but there has ever been an essential narrowness about Puritanism which has in general militated against the creation of a broad, sympathetic, and humane culture. It has tended to emphasize a narrow intellectualism at the expense of the rest of our nature, and so to emphasize the sense of duty as to end, over and over again, in a bigoted and egoistic insistence upon conformity to its own often provincial and limited outlook on life. On the other hand, the unexampled great and rapid development of wealth and power in the North and West tended to make it difficult to keep a sane outlook on life and what makes it worth living. Means too often became ends, and the real end of life has been lost to sight. Speaking broadly of sections and not of individuals, it appears that only in the South was it generally accepted that life did not consist only of doing one's duty or of achieving "success" but, embracing both of these if possible, it was something much deeper, broader, and richer, something good in and for itself.

Whether or not the South would have attained to its philosophy of life and its sense of values as other than material without the basis of slavery for large-scale plantation life is at least debatable. The tragedy has been that that sense of values developed in a type of civilization which, as to its base, could not be preserved in the modern world, and the struggle over which brought hatred, controversy, war, misery, and resentments for a period which has covered nearly a century, or about two-thirds of our national life.

Looking forward, one can only hope most fervently for two things, one that the period of separation in hearts and sympathies is really at last drawing to a close, and, second, that in readjusting itself to the life of the nation as a whole the South may never lose that sense of values which has been its most precious possession, worth infinitely more than slaves or lands or modern mills. It seems to me to be not only, as I have said, the most precious possession, of the new as of the old South, but the greatest possible contribution in the years to come to the cultural welfare and happiness of the nation. The path of the South as of the nation will be difficult.

There have been, of late, evidences of a revolt among the younger and often gifted Southern writers against the possible loss of the special quality of Southern life by industrialization and business. In the Civil War and the long tragedy we have rehearsed, the South was not fighting from 1820 onward merely against the North but against the time spirit, the course of modern life and thought. Much as many of us, myself included, may dislike the present stage reached in industrial development and a machine age, it is impossible to turn the hands of the clock of history backward. We cannot, if we would, physically cross the range into *Erewhon* and find a land where all machines have been destroyed. To insist today upon an agrarian civilization as our sole salvation is to attempt to lead not only an impossible but a parasitic life. Indeed, there would have been no "Old South" of great plantations had it not been for the machines. Cotton would have remained a very minor crop had Whitney or some one else not invented the cotton gin and Arkwright and others the spinning jennies which built up Lancashire and made the Southern Cotton Kingdom of 1860 believe it could rule the world by cutting off the supply of raw material.

What the future of agrarian life may be no one can say. Social prestige and influence are not likely soon again to inhere in ownership of land. If not from the standpoint of mere wealth, then from that of ability it will more probably go to those who manage great industries on which the destiny of thousands if not of hundreds of thousands depends. The president of a great modern corporation, providing possibly for the needs of a large part of the population and controlling the lives of a hundred or a hundred and fifty thousand employees, has a more difficult as well as a more important social task than the farmer or planter. The day of the great land-owner is passing everywhere, even in England. Moreover, the vast populations of today could not be sustained by agrarian pursuits alone, even were they willing to give up the products of invention. Nor can we stay the hands and brains of chemists in research laboratories, of whom one of high eminence recently told me that it would be only a few years before synthetic cotton would be manufactured more easily than artificial silk. To accept what benefits and markets a machine age brings and yet isolate one's self from an industrial life is to try again what the South tried to do before the war— to cut itself off from a hostile world opinion and live its own life within its own borders. It was impossible then, and will be again.

What those of us who are born into this confused age of machines, advertising, new wants, and universal suffrage have to do is to try to bring some order out of the chaos of moral values, and in an irretrievably altered world to reassert the philosophy of the Old South, to bring the new democracies to see that the values of the good life are other than material. That may be the end of the tragedy, and the peculiar and happy function of a yet newer South in a united nation.

One lesson the long struggle should have taught us. In spite of frequent amendment and constant and more subtle change, it is somewhat the fashion now to decry our Constitution as rigid because it is written. This, it is claimed, is particularly the case when the rights of property are supposed to be concerned. Yet the war between the North and the South proved, if it proved anything, that the Constitution must be altered when the opinion of a sufficiently large part of the people determines that a certain form of property is immoral or out-worn.

We have watched the so-called fundamental law constantly altering by interpretation, by custom, by formal change. The slavery question was in itself a property question. Property in human beings was recognized and protected by the original Constitution. The split finally came on the right of the Southerner to take his legal form of property into new territory precisely as the Northerner could take his forms. As we have seen, that had become impossible. Two types of civilization, two social ideals, could not both occupy the same territory at the same time. Not only would free labor not go where it had to compete with slave, but opinion as to the right to hold a certain *kind* of property had become bitter. With the one exception of the long dispute over this one kind of property, the Constitution has been peaceably altered, even though slowly, to meet the other changing needs of the people.

It is probable that the same situation will not again arise. In the case of the Civil War, the majority of the people of the nation was opposed to those who held the special form of property in dispute, but the minority was so strong, the difficulties of getting rid of the form of property appeared so insuperable, and the issues involved such a complete civilization, that there was no possibility of peacefully altering the Constitution by interpretation or amendment. No type of property now owned in the United States is sectional, as slavery property was, or is exclusively owned by one class, but it is clear that if at some future time a majority of the people should come fervently to believe that in some respects the Constitution must be altered so as to guard the rights of persons rather than property, and if a sufficiently powerful minority should play the die-hard and resist, we might have revolution and civil war again, though not sectional. The South, as we have tried to show, had been placed in a most difficult and cruel position, an impossible position. Its civilization as well as a large part of its property appeared to be at stake, and no one could suggest a solution. In the future, we may well have to alter our notions of property but the issues should not be as great. Unless, however, those involved in the sacrifice to the ideas of a new age can bring themselves to acquiesce in a peaceful solution, and agree to allow the rights of man to take precedence over those of some particular form of property, the story we have recounted points to the ultimate and bloody solution of any Constitutional deadlock. History is dynamic not static, and there is always a point beyond which no written document can save what has become obsolete or unjust in public opinion.

Meanwhile as we ponder the long and central tragedy of our national life—the generations of estrangement, the hatreds, the suffering, the loss, as well as the noble deeds of heroic men in both armies, now treasured in memory by each side, and our present problems, not least the presence in our midst of twelve millions of an alien race—we cannot but think to what small beginnings we may trace

some of the vastest streams of history, and our minds go
back to that simple and unforeseeing statement by Rolfe
in 1619: "Came in a Dutch man of warre that sold us
twenty Negars."

# INDEX

Abolitionists, 64, 94, 98, 102, 103, 109, 117, 127, 128, 138, 146, 153, 154, 167, 178; attacks of the, 93; characteristics of, 116 f.; some of the results, 117 f.; fanatical, 386

Adams, Charles Francis, 178, 223

Adams, Henry, 387

Adams, John, 26, 42, 44; not against slavery, 18; term of, 53

Adams, John Quincy, quoted, 54, 127

Adams, Samuel, ablest of agitators, 20, 102, 104, 386

Agrarian life, its future, 403

Agriculturists, number of, 83

Alabama, 25, 76, 82; withdraws from convention, 142; secedes, 149

*Alabama*, case of the, 272 f.

Alien and Sedition Laws, 42

Amendments, formal, to Constitution, 39

Anderson, Major, in command of Fort Sumter, 171 f.; declines to surrender, 181; report of, 182

Andersonville prison, 310

Angela, first negro woman in Jamestown colony, 2

Antietam, battle of, 192, 267 f.

Appalachian Mountains, 6

Appomattox, surrender of Lee at, 369 f.

Apthorp, Charles, wealthy Bostonian, 13

Arbiter on Constitutional questions, 43

Arkansas, withdraws from Convention, 142 f.; votes to secede, 188 f.

Arkwright, inventor, 403

Arlington, home of Lee, 188, 226

Arms, difficulty for South to get, 198

Articles of Confederation, signed, 20, 21

Ashby's Gap, 208

Astor, 59, 381

Atlanta, is taken, 346

*Atlantic Monthly, The*, 149

Atrocity, stories of, in Civil War, 213 f., 255

*Autobiography* of Jefferson, 19

Back country, 11

Baltimore, port of, 22; convention at, 142; troops clash with mob, 189

Bancroft, American historian, 63

Baptists, persecution of, 10

Barbadoes, settlers in South Carolina, 8

"Baronies" of South Carolina, 3

Bassett, J. S., American historian, 66

Bates, Edward, Attorney-General, in Lincoln's Cabinet, 177

Baylor, George, views of, on secession, 187

Beauregard, General, 205, 206, 207, 208, *passim.;* his terms accepted at Fort Sumter, 183

Beecher, Henry Ward, influence of, 148

Bell, John, nominated for President, 142

Benjamin, Judah P., Attorney-General in Confederacy, 165; quoted, 234

"Big house," the, 74, 80

*Biglow Papers*, by Lowell, 123

Bill of Rights, the, 18

Black, Judge, Secretary of State, 173

Black Belt, the, 84

Blair, Montgomery, Postmaster-General, 178

Blockade, effectiveness of, 270

Bonham, M. L., of South Carolina, 174

Boston, 13, 15

Bourne, Rev. George, perhaps the first "immediatist," 116

Bragg, General, 206, 323

Braxtons, famous Southern family, 86

Breckenridge, John C., nominated for President, 142

Bright, John, friend of America, 274

Bristol, wealth in, 13

Brook Farm, experimental community, 62

*Brooklyn*, man-of-war, 174

Brooks, Preston, attack on Sumner, 133

Brown, John, 132, 239; character of, 139; at Harpers Ferry, 139

Brown, W. G., Southern historian, 66

Bryce, Lord, quoted, 45

Buchanan, James, 147, 186; quoted, 166; elected President, 133; his position difficult, 165; on the forts, 170

Buell, Major, instructions from, 171

Bulkeley, quoted, 10

Bull Run, battle of, 208, 210

Bulloch, Captain, Southern agent, 225

Burnside, Ambrose E., 211; General, in command of Army of Potomac, 285; resigns, 288

Burwells, famous Southern family, 86

Business man, type of, in North, 59

Butler, General, military governor of New Orleans, 245 f.; issues famous order, 248

Butler, Samuel, quoted, 106

Butler, Senator, 133

Byrd, William, quoted, 16, 86; library of, 5

Cabot, George, quoted, 49

Calhoun, John C., 63, 85, 91, 99, 108, 110, 111, 112, 119, 123; quoted, 100,

# INDEX

106; doctrine of States' Rights, 104 f.; "Exposition" of 1828, 105
California, to be admitted as a free State, 124
Cameron, Simon, Secretary of War, 177
Cape Cod Bay, 2
"Carpet-baggers," 389
Carr, Wilson, 196
Carroll, Daniel, 29
Carter, Robert, emancipates slaves, 35
Carters, well-known Southern family, 86
Cedar Mountain, battle of, 265
Cemetery Ridge, 314
Census, first Federal, 19
Chancellorsville, battle of, 300
Channing, Professor Edward, quoted, 47, 190, 311
Charleston, 15, 84, 181; important centre, 9; Democratic Convention at, 142; federal property in, 171; the fall of, 364
*Charleston Courier, The*, 200
*Charleston Mercury, The*, quoted, 103, 150, 161, 183, 213, 219, 236, 254, 255, 324
Chase, Salmon P., Secretary of the Treasury, 177
Chesapeake Bay, 1, 22
Chesnut, Mrs. James, quoted, 148, 157, 163, 196, 216, 235, 249, 283, 284, 324, 351
Chesnut, Senator, of South Carolina, quoted, 155
Cheves, Langdon, leader of Union party, 112
Chicago, Republican Convention at, 143
Chickamauga, battle of, 323
Child labor, 61 f.
Chisholm, Colonel, 182
Civil War (*see* War), first great war fought under modern conditions, 338 f.; some of its results, 378
Civilians, treatment of, 340
Clay, Henry, 85, 99, 108, 123, 170; proposes "American System," 102
Clay, Mrs. Senator, attitude of, 138; quoted, 192
Cleveland, President, orders return of flags, 398
Climate, influence of, 5
Cobb, Thomas R. R., important Georgia leader, 125, 150
Cold Harbor, battle of, 342
Colonies, similarities in the, 3, 9
Columbia, S. C., burning of, 361 f.
*Columbian Centinel*, quoted, 50
"Compromise of 1850," 124
Confederacy, recognized by England as belligerent, 223; ominous signs for, 235 f.; lack of support for, 237; disasters for, 252; finances of, 291 f.; prices in, 293 f.; loss of hope and courage, 349; crumbling of, 353; causes for its collapse, 377

Confiscation Act, passed by Congress, 279
Congress of 1858, 137
*Congress*, United States vessel, 250
Connecticut, 2, 3, 9, 12, 13, 20, 21, 32, *et seq.;* blue laws of, 5; number of slaves in, 24
Conscription Act, passed by Confederate Congress, 239 f.
*Constant*, one of our noted ships, 1
Constitution, the, 42, 99, 100, 105, 106, 111, 155, 171, 184, 191, 218; disputable points of, 36 f.; a living thing, 39; change in, 40; question of Louisiana purchase, 47; interpretation colored by sectional prejudices, 50; questions of change, 404 f.
Constitution for the "Confederate States of America," adopted, 160, 161 f.
Continental Congress, 11, 20
*Continental Journal, The*, quoted, 18
Cooke, Philip St. George, 191
Cooper, James F., American writer, 63, 91
Cooper, Thomas, South Carolina agitator, 104, 118
"Copperheads," 290, 312
Cornwallis, surrender of, 20
Coromantees, negro tribe, 72
Cotton, 6, 10, 52, 202, 229, 232; staple crop of South, 63; need for, 229 f.; supply of, 231 f., 274
Cotton, King, 159, 234, 275
Cotton Belt, 114
Cotton Kingdom, 84, 92
Craven, Avery, American historian, 66
Crittenden Compromise, 167, 176, 280
*Cumberland*, United States vessel, 250

*Daily True Delta, The*, quoted, 141, 161
Davis, Jefferson, 56, 85, 91, 119, 127, 149, 157, 170, 179, 195, 204, 212, 221; quoted, 155, 158, 176, 282, 321; born, 51; plantation of, 77; at Portland, Maine, 145; influence of, 152; elected President of Confederacy, 162; character of, 162 f.; orders to General Beauregard, 181; issues letters of marque, 189; some of his difficulties, 198; inaugural address, 234; quarrels with General Johnston, 236; under severe criticism, 236; accepts Grant's resignation, 242; proclamation of, regarding General Butler, 248; abused, 252 f.; dislike of Johnston, 345; replaces Johnston, 346; asks Congress for slaves, 350; peace plans fail, 366; flees from Richmond, 366, 373 f.; capture of, 375; considered as traitor, 397
Davis, Reuben, 150
*De Bow's Review*, quoted, 129
Declaration of Independence, 20, 58; scrapped by supporters of slavery, 119

408

# INDEX

Delaware, 3, 25, 32, 43; population of, 21
Democracy, disbelieved, 10
Dew, Thomas R., one of the Southern prophets, 118
Dicey, Edward, quoted, 196
Dickens, Charles, opinion of Andrew Johnson, 387
Dickinson, demands exclusion of slaves, 32
*Discovery*, one of the noted ships in our history, 1
District of Columbia, 124
Doctrine, Socialist, 62
Dodd, W. E., Southern historian, 66
Douglas, Senator Stephen A., 131; debates with Lincoln, 136 f.; nominated, 142
Drayton, Thomas F., commander of fort, 192
Drayton, William, a leader of Union party, 112
Dred Scott decision, 135
Dwight, Wilder, quoted, 184

Early, General, raids of, 336 f.
Eboes, negro tribe, 72
Economic conditions, shifts in, 76
Education, in North and South, 5; in North, 63
Edwards, Jonathan, a slave owner, 18
Ellsworth, Oliver, 29, 33; quoted, 102
Emancipation Proclamation, 156; issued by Lincoln, 281
Emerson, Ralph Waldo, 63, 140; the prophet, 63
Endicott, John, 63, 117
England, 1, 2; attitude of, in Civil War, 269; effect upon, by proclamation, 289 f.
*Enquirer, The* (Richmond), quoted, 98
Ericsson, John, builder of *Monitor*, 250
Ewell, Confederate leader, 313

Fairfax Court House, 211
Farragut, David, 190; takes New Orleans, 245 f.; defeat of Confederates in battle of Mobile Bay, 346
Federal troops, control of, 330 f.
Federal Government, 161; weakness of, 22 f.; power of, first question of, 42; conflict with Pennsylvania, 49
"Fire Eaters," 115, 125, 206
Fitzhughs, famous Southern family, 86
Five Forks, battle of, 366
Florida, withdraws from convention, 142; secedes, 149
*Florida*, Southern vessel, 249, 272
Floyd, John R., Secretary of War, 171; resignation from Cabinet, 173
Force and Compromise Tariff Bills (1833), 115
Forrest, N. B., cavalry raids of, 332
Fort Donelson, taken by Grant, 201
Fort Henry, taken by Grant, 201

Fort Sumter, 157, 180; fired upon, 182
Foster, S. S., abolitionist agitator, 117
Foulahs, negro tribe, 72
Fourier, French communistic thinker, 62
Franklin, Benjamin, quoted, 279
Fredericksburg, battle of, 285 f.
"Free Soil" party, appearance of, 123
Frémont, General, 133; removed as general, 278
French and Indian War, 11
Frontier, the, 11, 57
Fruitlands, communistic settlement, 62
Fugitive Slave Act, 131, 141; trouble over, 129 f.
Fugitive Slave Clause, 121
Fugitive Slave Law, 131, 141, 150, 152, 154, 168, 176; enacted, 124

Gaboons, negro tribe, 72
Gadsden, Christopher, quoted, 11
Gadsden Purchase, 123
Gaines's Mill, battle of, 260, 261
Galveston, port of, 107
Garrison, William Lloyd, 102, 116, 213, 391; quoted, 117; reward for his arrest, 120
Genealogy, popular in America, 85 f.
Georgia, 25, 32, 43, 56, 76, 82, 120, 163, 198; supports slavery, 33; secedes, 149; the fight for secession, 152 f.
Gerry, Elbridge, member of Constitutional Convention, 29
Gettysburg, battle of, 314 f.
Gilmer, John A., of North Carolina, 169
Gladstone, quoted, 30
*Goodspeed*, one of the noted vessels in our history, 1
Gordon, General, of Confederacy, 193, 287; on same platform with Grant, 397
Grand Army of Republic, 399
Grant, Ulysses, 162, 193, 206, 262; quoted, 327 f., 345; owner of slaves, 156; character of, 241 f.; takes Fort Henry, 242; captures Fort Donelson, 243; receives surrender of Vicksburg, 316; a real leader found, 320 f.; made commander of all forces, 323; tribute to Sherman, 328; plan of, 331; places Sheridan in charge of Shenandoah, 337; moves against Lee, 342; his famous despatch, 342; meets Sherman, 363; at Appomattox, 369 f.; on same platform with General Gordon, 397; death of, 398
Grayson, William, work for freedom, 25
"Great compromise," the, 31
Greeley, Horace, quoted, 147, 280; "The Prayer of Twenty Millions," 281
Griswold, Roger, report on Northern finances, 48
Grow, from Pennsylvania, quoted, 138

Halleck, General, 241, 244; called from West, 263

409

# INDEX

# INDEX

quoted, 187, 190, 226, 266; command at Harpers Ferry, 139; resigns Northern commission, 189 f.; placed in command of the Confederate army, 257; considered as distinguished soldier, 257 f.; movements against Pope, 265; mistakes of, 266 f.; advance of, into Maryland, 273; importance of his move, 273; decides on raid into Pennsylvania, 312; plans of, 312 f.; at Gettysburg, 314 f.; loss of Jackson, 327; in retreat, 368; at Appomattox, 368 f.; news of surrender received in North, 371 f.; becomes president of Washington College, 394

Lee, Mrs., letter a classic, 336

Libby Prison, 310

*Liberator, The,* founded by Garrison, 116, 213

Libraries, public, 5

Life in South, charm of, 66

Lincoln, Abraham, 56, 85, 114, 121, 146, 151, 164, 165, 168, 195, 197, 204, 221, 226, 238, 261, 263, 264, 278, 279; quoted, 96, 136, 139, 169, 176 f., 278, 281, 364, 371; born, 51; debates with Douglas, 136; nominated for President, 143; elected President, 143; inaugural address, 176; attitude of country towards him, 1861, 178; constitutional theory of, 179 f.; decides on forts, 180; call for troops, 185; asks for 400,000 men, 206; sends special message to Congress, 251; issues *Special War Order Number 1,* 256; visits McClellan, 261; questions addressed to McClellan, 268; announces intention to issue Emancipation Proclamation, 280; issues call for another 300,000 men, 280; results of Proclamation, 282; issues Proclamation, 289; measured words of, 321; gives Grant full responsibility, 327; doubts of his re-election, 345; at City Point, Va., 363; second inaugural address, 364; plans for reconstruction, 365; his last Cabinet meeting, 371; assassination of, 372; theory of Union, 385; anxious for Davis to escape, 397

Literature, in North, 63

Living, scale of, 4

*London Times, The,* 289

Longfellow, Henry Wadsworth, American poet, 63; attitude toward South, 128

Longstreet, J. B., Confederate general, 206; at Gettysburg, 315 f.; accomplishes nothing, 324

Louisiana, 76, 82; created in 1812, 52; Creole, 84; secedes, 149

Lovejoy, murder of, 118

Lovell, Mrs., quoted, 72

Lowell, James Russell, 63; quoted, 60, 122, 130, 149; attitude toward South, 128

Madison, James, 28, 42, 69, 90, 118; quoted, 30, 38; becomes leader of Convention, 29; statement on blockade, 271

Maine, 2, 9; desire of, to become a separate State, 53

Mallory, S. R., Secretary of Navy of Confederacy, 165, 170

Mandingoes, negro tribe, 72

Mann, A. D., Southern commissioner, sent abroad, 222

Manufacturing in South, 109

*Marbury vs. Madison,* celebrated case of, 45

Marshall, John, made Chief Justice, 44 f.

Martin, Luther, quoted, 32

Martineau, Miss Harriet, 64, 78

Maryland, 2, 21, 32, 36; number of slaves in, 19

Mason, George, opposed to slavery, 29, 32

Mason, James M., 224

Mason and Dixon, 60, 197

Mason and Slidell, 269

Massachusetts, 2, 6, 16, 18, 20, 25, 28, 32, 43, 56, 101; slavery legal in, 4; oligarchy of, 9; isolation of, 10; character of, 11; population of, 21; sentiment regarding slavery, 24; sends early troops, 189

Mathers, library of, 5

*Mayflower,* the, 2, 86

McClellan, George B., 162, 191, 205, 206, 268; quoted, 261; called to organize army, 213; inactivity of, 221; movements of, 256 f.; mistakes of, 266 f.; candidate for President, 345

McDowell, General Irwin, 206, 207, 209, 212, 260

McDuffie, George, 85, 104

McGuire, Mrs., quoted, 367

McKim, Randolph, Confederate officer, 192, 196

McKim, William D., 196

Meade, George G., 162; succeeds Hooker, 313; in command at Gettysburg, 314

Melville, Herman, American writer, 63

Memminger, Secretary of Treasury of Confederacy, 165; difficulties of, 231; declares currency redundant, 254

Mennonites, 4

*Mercury, The (see Charleston Mercury)*

*Merrimac,* the, Confederate ship, 192; fight with *Monitor,* 249 f.

Michigan, 21

Middleton, Mrs. Williams, at Newport, 145

Middletons, Richard, at Bristol, 145

Migration, family, 57

Miles, W. P., of South Carolina, quoted, 140 f.

Mississippi, 25, 56, 76, 82, 198; with-

411

# INDEX

# INDEX

quoted, 341; at Winchester, 342; wins battle of Five Forks, 366

Sherman, Roger, 29

Sherman, William Tecumseh, 162, 206; quoted, 210, 212, 217, 328, 330; sent to the West, 221; realizes importance of West, 241; character of, 244; great aid to Grant, 327; tribute to Grant, 328; character of, 329; march to Atlanta, 344; answers protest of Mayor of Atlanta, 348; his description of war, 348 f.; his final plans, 353; sets out on crushing march, 354 f.; real character shown, 356; some results of his march, 358; plans regarding South Carolina, 360; meets Grant, 363; questions put to Lincoln, 365; accepts Johnston's surrender, 373; tired of war, 373

Shiloh, battle of, 243

Simms, William Gilmore, Southern writer, 91

Slave trade, control of, 32; some of the horrors, 71

Slavery, increase in trade, 16; emerges as political issue, 23 f.; importance of one vote, 25; earliest views on, 69; the favorable side of, 74; in Virginia, 77; sexual relations, 78 f.; the chief indictment against, 80; change of world opinion regarding, 92 f.; doomed whatever result of war, 251 f.; problem after Civil War, 385

Slaves, South more favorable for, 17; as property, 31; price of, 291; impressment of, 350

Slidell, John, 224

Smith, General G. W., 192

Smith, Judge William, 104

Soil, influence of, 6

Soldiers, number engaged at Antietam, 267 f.; friendly relations of, 287 f., 299 f.

"Solid South," product of historical conditions, 67

Solution, was there a possible one?, 167

South, and North, contrasted, 13 f., 65 f.; growing cleavage between, 51 f.; social differences, 88 f.

South, overwhelmingly agricultural, 67; tradition in the, 86 f.; ideal of English country life, 88; type of culture, 90 f.; intellectual changes, 91 f.; favoring an institution that was doomed, 94 f.; cruel position of, 96; reaction to Abolitionists, 118 f.; realization of secession as possible, 126; hatred of North fanned, 128 f.; affected by John Brown raid, 140; why did it secede? 150; unity in the, 154; civilization different from that of North, 156; failure to realize certain facts, 159 f.; right of revolution, 186; men from, in Northern army, 190; unfavorable regard for North, 197; man-power in,

199; wealth in, 200 f.; certain advantages over North, 202 f.; effect of Bull Run victory, 212; complete difference of interpretation of Constitution from North, 218; sends commissioners to England, 222 f.; questions of blockade, 223 f.; finances of, 227 f.; some disadvantages of States' Rights, 238; limited supply of goods, 271; seemed favored by England, 272; decline in quality of army, 308 f.; desperate condition of, 321 f.; gloomy Christmas of 1863, 324; prices in 1864, 326; some reasons for collapse, 326 f.; prices in, 350; hope for European intervention, 352; the ruins of, 379 f.; its philosophy of life, 382; form of society developed, 383 f.; influence of politics in the, 386 f.; colossal scandals after the war, 389; geographical section affected by war, 392 f.; new and different in the '80's, 394; evidences of sympathy with North, 396 f.; philosophy of life in, 401

South Carolina, 6, 11, 25, 32, 43, 57, 82, 101, 112, 113, 114, 131, 138, 174, 198; differences of, 8; character of, 10; "city-state" of, 14; number of slaves in, 19; denies rights, 107; withdraws from convention, 142; takes steps to secede, 146; and the Federal Government, 171

South Mountain, engagement at, 267

*Southern Literary Messenger, The,* 78, 91, 93, 128, 137

Southern planter, 16

Spanish War, sections united for, 400

"Squatter sovereignty," 131

Stanton, Edwin M., 263, 388; Secretary of War, 178; relation to negroes, 359; bitter toward South, 374; at head of one Cabinet faction, 387; the insistence of, 397

*Star of the West,* merchant vessel, 174

States, some of the early problems of, 21

States' Rights, 22, 44, 57, 107, 141, 155, 160, 164, 185, 188, 193, 198, 222, 236, 253, 350, 351

Stedman, Edmund C., quoted, 219, 228

Stephens, Alexander H., 150, 239; quoted, 132, 168; important Georgia leader, 125; elected Vice-President of Confederacy, 162; put in prison, 376

Stevens, Thaddeus, Northern agitator, 386

Stowe, Harriet Beecher, author of *Uncle Tom's Cabin,* 127

Stuart, General J. E. B., Confederate cavalry leader, 191

Sumner, Charles, 381, 386, 391; attacked by Brooks, 133; change in, 396

*Sumter Whig, The,* 113

Supreme Court, 43, 44, 45, 50, 122, 131; development of, 39

414

# INDEX

415